A Level
Information Technology

P.M.Heathcote, B.Sc.(Hons), M.Sc.

*P.. Heathcote is a Senior Lecturer at University College Suffolk, Ipswich where she has taught since
1... on a range of courses including A Level Information Technology, A Level Computing, BTEC, ACCA
a... A4T courses. Prior to coming to Ipswich she was for several years a programmer at McGill
U... y, Montreal, Canada, and also held posts as a Systems Analyst with a large hospital and
su... ly with a firm of computer consultants. She has been an Assistant Examiner for A Level
C... th the Associated Examining Board and is a member of the Subject Committee for
C...*

Pub lished by
Payne-Gallway Publishers
76-78 Christchurch Street
Ipswich IP4 2DE
Tel 01473 251097
Fax 01473 232758
E-mail payne_gallway@compuserve.com

1998

Acknowledgements

I would like to thank my husband Oliver for his invaluable help, and the many colleagues and friends who have contributed to this book. I am grateful to the following Examination Boards for permission to use questions from past examination papers:

The Associated Examining Board (AEB), London Examinations, a division of Edexcel Foundation (London), Northern Examinations and Assessment Board (NEAB), Northern Ireland Council for the Curriculum, Examinations and Assessment (NICCEA), Scottish Qualifications Authority (SEB).

The answers in the teacher's supplement are the sole responsibility of the author and have neither been provided nor approved by the examination boards.

I would also like to thank the following organisations for permission to reproduce copyright material in the form of articles, photographs and artwork:

Armstrong Healthcare (Figure 4.1)

Bradford & Bingley Building Society (Fig 50.2)

British Telecom (Figures 5.1, 6.4)

British Software Alliance (Figs 11.3,54.1,54.3)

Cambs & Hunts Health Authority (Figure 8.2)

Canon (Figure 32.3)

Ford Motor Company Limited (Figure 68.1)

Herts & Essex Hospital (Figure 8.3)

Formic Limited

Hewlett Packard Company (Figure 32.4)

Kye Systems UK Limited (Figures 26.5,26.6)

Machinery

Network Associates (Figures 8.1, 55.1)

Polartechnics Limited

Sagesoft Limited (Figure 60.1)

Scanner Technologies Limited (Figure 50.1)

The Economist, London

The Guardian

The Guide Association

Times Newspapers Limited

Graphics editor and designer: Flora Heathcote
Cover picture © "The North Unfolds" reproduced with kind permission from Neil Canning
Cover photography © Mike Kwasniak, 160 Sidegate Lane, Ipswich
Cover design by Edward Morgan
Figures 68.2, 68.3 © reproduced with kind permission from Simon Game
Figures 66.5, 66.7 © reproduced with kind permission from Bernard Reader

First edition 1998. Reprinted 1998

A catalogue entry for this book is available from the British Library.

ISBN 0 9532490 0 X

Copyright © P.M.Heathcote 1998

Printed in Great Britain by

W M Print Ltd, Walsall, West Midlands

Preface

The aim of this book is to provide a comprehensive yet concise textbook covering all the topics studied for an 'A' Level course in Information Technology.

The book is divided into 5 sections covering all the material for each paper in a modular scheme such as that offered by the Northern Examinations and Assessment Board (NEAB). Within a section, each chapter covers material that can comfortably be taught in one or two lessons, and the chapters are sequenced in such a way that practical sessions can be based around the theory covered in the classroom.

Section 3 contains topics that need to be covered in order for the student to tackle project work. Sections 1 to 3 cover all the requirements of a typical AS syllabus, with the remaining sections being studied in the second year.

Throughout the book, case studies are used to illustrate the points made. Each chapter contains exercises and questions from past examination papers, so that the student can gain plenty of experience in 'exam technique'. Answers to all the questions are available to teachers in a separate Teacher's Supplement which is available on our Web site http://www.payne-gallway.co.uk which also supplies overhead projection masters.

Contents

Section 1
Data Management   1

Section 2
Information: Management and Manipulation   69

Section 3
Developing I.T. Solutions   171

Section 4
Information Systems in Organisations   193

Section 5
Information: Policy, Strategy and Systems   273

Appendix A
Information Technology   339

Appendix B
NEAB Project Mark Schemes   355

Appendix C
Book List   363

Table of Contents

SECTION 1	**1**

Chapter 1 – The Role of I.T.   2
Computing – a look backwards	2
Computers and employment	2
The changing nature of employment	2
Teleworking	3
Benefits of teleworking	3
The problems of teleworking	4
Case study: Socket to 'em now	4
Changing locations of work	4
Case study: Remote working	5
Consequences of computer failure	5
The millennium bug	6

Chapter 2 – I.T. in Business and Commerce   7
New products and services	7
Changing shape of organisations	7
Case study: Britain's fastest growing companies	7
Using I.T. to set up a small business	8
I.T. in banking	9
Shopping on the Internet	9
Case study: Off your trolley	10
The drawbacks	10
The dangers	10
Case study: Charity database corrupted	11

Chapter 3 – I.T. in Manufacturing   12
Introduction	12
Case study: The sweet smell of success	12
Computer-aided design (CAD)	12
Computer-aided Manufacturing (CAM)	13
Case study: Subcontracting sector uses I.T.	13
Robots	14
Why use robots?	14

Chapter 4 – I.T. in a Caring Society   16
Introduction	16
Computers in medicine	16
Case study: Robot surgeon operates	16
Case study: Deeper Blue checks cancer drugs	17
Expert systems used in medical diagnosis	17
Computers and the disabled	19
Case study: Eyes in the sky	19

Chapter 5 – I.T. in Education   21
Computers in schools	21
Case study: John Cabot City Technology College	21
Will computers replace teachers?	22
Multimedia in schools	22
Authoring software	23
Internet-based services	23

Chapter 6 – Role of Communication Systems   24
Introduction	24
The Internet	24
The World Wide Web	25
On-line information services	25
Electronic bulletin boards	25
Intranets	25
Electronic mail (E-mail)	25
Case study: Monitoring employee e-mail	26
Telephones	26
Facsimile transmission (Fax)	27
Voice mail	27
Teleconferencing	27

Chapter 7 – The Internet in Business   29
Doing business on the Web	29
Advantages to business	30
Advantages to the customers	30
The drawbacks	30
Case study: British Petroleum	31
Business-to-Business	31
Finding new suppliers	32
Setting up a Web site	32

Chapter 8 – Knowledge, Information and Data   33
Input-process-output	33
Data and information	33
Knowledge	33
Access to knowledge	34
Case study: Collecting information	35
Sources of data	35
Encoding information as data	35
Case study: 'Nightmare' scheme to track every pupil	36
Quality of data	36

Chapter 9 – Information as a Commodity   39
The importance of information	39
Case study	39
Collecting and analysing data	39
Information as a commodity	40
Usefulness of data	40
Coding value judgements	40

The benefits of I.T. 40
Drawbacks of information technology 41

Chapter 10 – The Professional in I.T. **42**
Careers in I.T. 42
Personal qualities for I.T. professionals 42
Case study: How to succeed in business 43
The role of professional bodies 43
The Industry Structure Model 44

Chapter 11 – Codes of Practice **45**
Ethics and computing 45
Factors in ethical decision-making 45
Formal guidelines in the computing
   industry 45
Codes of practice 47
Using informal guidelines to make ethical
   decisions 47
Case study 1 47
Case study 2 48
Case study 3 48

Chapter 12 – Computer Crime and the Law **49**
Computer crime and abuse 49
Hacking 49
Theft of money 49
Theft of data 50
Fraud on the Internet 50
Viruses 50
'Logic bombs' 51
Electronic emanations ('Tempest') 51
Digital crime and the law 51
The Computer Misuse Act of 1990 52
Case study 1 52
Software copyright laws 52
Case study 2 54
Using computers to combat crime 54

Chapter 13 – Protecting Data **55**
Issues of privacy 55
Case study: TRW Information Service 55
Threats to information systems 55
Data integrity 55
Standard clerical procedures 56
Write-protecting disks 56
User IDs and passwords 56
Access rights 57
Securing against fraudulent use or
malicious damage 57
Protection against viruses 58
Biometric security measures 58
Case study: Iris recognition technology 58
Communications security 58
Disaster planning 58

Periodic backups 59
Recovery procedures 59

Chapter 14 – Data Protection Legislation **60**
Personal privacy 60
Case study: James Wiggins – a true story 60
The Data Protection Act 60
The Data Protection Registrar 61
Exemptions from the Act 61
The rights of data subjects 61
Implications of the Data Protection
   Legislation 62

Chapter 15 – Health and Safety **63**
Computers and health 63
Stress 63
Case study: Information overload 64
Repetitive strain injury (RSI) 64
Case study: Bank staff 'driven to injury' 65
Eyestrain 65
Extremely low frequency (ELF) radiation 66
Case study: Handsets may be bad for your
   health 66
Computers, Health and the law 66
Classrooom menace: ignore it and you may
   end up in court 67
The ergonomic environment 67

SECTION 2 **69**

Chapter 16 – Introduction to Computer Systems **70**
The components of a computer 70
Types of computer 70
Processing power 71
Main memory 72
RAM and ROM 72
Cache memory 72
Disk storage 72

Chapter 17 – Internal Storage of Data **75**
Digital and analogue computers 75
The ASCII code 75
Parity 76
Representing numbers 77
Binary arithmetic 77
Boolean values 78
Digitised sound 78
Bitmapped graphics 79

Chapter 18 – Operating Systems **80**
What is an operating system? 80
Functions of an operating system 80

Utility programs	81
The DOS operating system	81
The command-driven interface	81
The Apple Macintosh graphical user interface (GUI)	82
DOS with Windows	83
Windows 95 – a full operating system	84
UNIX	85

Chapter 19 – Categories of Software — 86

Categorising software	86
Systems software	86
Applications software	87
General purpose software	87
Who uses application packages?	88
Integrated packages and software suites	88
Generic and specific software	88
Bespoke or off-the-shelf?	88

Chapter 20 – Software Productivity Tools — 90

Types of productivity tools	90
Word processing	90
Spreadsheets	92
Spreadsheet features	93
Databases and Electronic Mail	93

Chapter 21 – Capabilities of Software — 95

Object Linking and Embedding (OLE)	95
About linked and embedded objects	96
The need for portability of data	96
Problems with portability	97
Upgradability	97
Criteria for selecting a software package	98
Evaluating software	98
Software reliability	98
The development of de facto standards	99
Case study: Microsoft's MS-DOS	99
Common operating systems	100

Chapter 22 – Records, Files and Databases — 101

Hierarchy of data	101
Database Management Systems (DBMS)	101
Flat file and file management systems	102
Creating a database file	102
The significance of field types	102
Primary key	103
Validation of input data	104

Chapter 23 – Data Modelling — 105

Traditional file approach	105
The database approach	106
The Database Management System	
(DBMS)	106
The conceptual data model	107
Types of relationship	107
Entity-relationship diagrams	107

Chapter 24 – Relational Database Design — 109

What is a relational database?	109
Linking database tables	109
Normalisation	110
First normal form	110
Second normal form	112
Partial key dependence test	112
Dealing with a Many-to-Many relationship	112
Third normal form	113
Comparing a flat file system with a relational database	113

Chapter 25 – Database Management — 115

Database Administration (DBA)	115
The data dictionary	115
The Database Management System (DBMS)	116
Querying the database	116
Using SQL	117
Using indexes	117
Why index?	118
Sorting	118
Database security	118

Chapter 26 – Input Devices — 120

Keyboard data entry	120
Voice data entry	120
Scanners and OCR	120
Case study: Automating college enrolment	121
Key-to-disk systems	121
Mouse, joystick, light pen, touch screen	122
Magnetic Ink Character Recognition (MICR)	122
Magnetic stripe	122
Smart cards	122
Optical Mark Recognition (OMR)	123
Bar code reader or scanner	123
Hand-held input devices	124
Digitiser (Graphics tablet)	124

Chapter 27 – Data Gathering and Sampling — 127

Data capture	127
Types of error	127
Batch processing	128
Validation checks	129
Check digits	129
Verification	130
Detecting transmission errors	130

Accuracy and validity 130
Case study: Market research survey 131

Chapter 28 – Modes of Processing 133
Processing methods 133
Transactions 133
Master files and transaction files 133
Batch processing 134
Stages in batch processing 134
Interactive processing 135
Pseudo real-time processing 135
Criteria for choice of processing mode 135

Chapter 29 – Storage Devices 137
Primary and secondary storage 137
File processing concepts 137
Floppy disks 138
How data is stored 138
Hard disks for microcomputers 138
Hard disks for minis and mainframes 139
Magnetic tape 139
Uses of magnetic tape 140
CD-ROM 140
WORM disks 140
Magneto-optical disks 140
Microfiche 141

Chapter 30 – Dissemination of Information 142
Characteristics of good information 142
Presenting management information 143
The intended audience 143
Graphs and charts 143
Guidelines for presentations 144

Chapter 31 – Security of Data 145
Privacy and security 145
Keeping data secure 145
Disaster planning 145
Case study: Safe as Houses 145
Backup strategies 146
Keeping backups safe 146
Backup hardware 146
Backing up on-line databases 146

Chapter 32 – Output Devices 148
Printers 148
Dot matrix printer 148
Ink jet printers 149
Laser printers 149
Plotters 150
Visual display unit (VDU) 150

Chapter 33 – Configuring Hardware and Software 152
Communicating with the CPU 152

Parallel and serial data transmission 152
Buffering 152
Spooling 153
Installing hardware devices 153
TrueType fonts 153

Chapter 34 – Network Environments 155
Communications networks 155
Advantages and disadvantages of networks 155
Network topologies 155
Star network 156
Bus network 156
Ring network 157
Server-based vs. peer-to-peer networks 157

Chapter 35 – Wide Area Networks 159
Principle of electronic data communication 159
Wide area networks 159
Communications links 159
Communications media 160
ISDN lines 160
Bridges and gateways 160
Modems 161
Synchronous & asynchronous transmission 161
Data compression 161
Protocol 161
Factors affecting rate of data transmission 162

Chapter 36 – User Interfaces 163
Introduction 163
The importance of good interface design 163
Designing usable systems 163
Interface styles 164
Command-line interface 164
Menus 164
Natural language 165
Advantages and disadvantages of
    natural language dialogue 165
Forms and dialogue boxes 166
The WIMP interface 167
Advantages of a common user interface 167
Speech input (voice recognition) 167
Speech/sound output 168
Case Study: Putting patients in the picture 168

SECTION 3 171

Chapter 37 – Tackling a Minor Project 172
Planning the time schedule 175
The project requirements 176

Chapter 38 – Specification and Analysis — 177
Selecting a project — 177
Investigating the user's requirements — 177
Establishing the objectives — 177
Documenting data flows — 178
Writing up the analysis — 179

Chapter 39 – Design — 180
Design tasks — 180
Justification of chosen solution — 180
Database design (for a database project) — 180
Data descriptions — 180
Input — 181
Output — 181
Menu design — 181
Identifying subtasks — 182
Test plan — 182
Plan of action — 183
Writing up the design — 183

Chapter 40 – Implementation and Testing — 184
Organisation is the key — 184
The implementation — 185
Testing objectives — 185
Steps in software testing — 185
Drawing up a test plan — 186
Selecting tests for the test plan — 186
Presenting the test results — 186

Chapter 41 – Documentation — 188
Introduction — 188
Should the documentation be word-processed? — 188
Word processing skills — 188
Putting it all together — 189
The title page — 189
Table of contents — 189
Analysis — 189
Design — 189
Testing — 189
Documenting the implementation — 190
Technical documentation — 190
User manual — 191
Evaluation — 191

SECTION 4 — 193

Chapter 42 – Organisational Structure — 194
How organisations work — 194
Ingredients for success — 194
Focus on people — 195
Focus on organisation — 195

External pressures on an organisation — 197
Case Study: Preservation vs. the people — 197
Focus on technology — 197
Organisations and information systems — 198
Data processing systems — 198
Knowledge work systems — 199
Management information systems — 199

Chapter 43 – Management Information Systems — 200
Introduction — 200
Information systems vs. data processing systems — 200
Internal and external information — 200
The role of a management information system — 201
What managers do — 201
Types of decision — 202
Stages of decision-making — 203
Case study: Buying a new car — 204
Desirable characteristics of a MIS — 204

Chapter 44 – The Information Systems Life Cycle — 206
Overview of the systems life cycle — 206
The waterfall model — 207
What prompts a new system? — 208
Feasibility study — 208
Requirements analysis — 209
Case study: Computer-dating the customer — 209
System design — 210
Implementation — 210
Methods of conversion — 210
Post-implementation review — 211
System maintenance — 211
Prototyping — 212
Benefits of prototyping — 212

Chapter 45 – Implementation of Information Systems — 214
What is implementation? — 214
Successful implementation — 214
Why do information systems fail? — 215
Case study: Tiptree Book Distributors — 216
Factors in successful implementation — 217

Chapter 46 – Information Systems Strategy — 219
Introduction — 219
Formulating an information system strategy — 220
End-user computing — 221
I.T. for competitive advantage — 221
Case study: Just-in-time at Wal-Mart's — 222

Chapter 47 – Executive and Decision Support Systems 224
Categories of business information system 224
Turning data into information 224
Decision support systems 225
Executive information systems 226
Information flow 226

Chapter 48 – Expert Systems 228
Definition 228
Programming the knowledge base 228
Case study: ELSIE the expert system 229
Expert system shells 230
Uses of expert systems 230
Benefits of expert systems in organisations 230
Limitations of expert systems 231
Comparison of expert systems and decision support systems 231
Case study: Protecting endangered species 232

Chapter 49 – Information 233
Sources of information 233
Levels of information 233
Quality of information 233
Case study: Mortgages - a changing market 234
Channels of communication 234
Case study: Guides need information 235
Keeping everyone informed 235
Marketing information 236

Chapter 50 – Data Collection 237
Using bar codes 237
Other uses of bar codes 237
Magnetic stripe cards 238
Linking customers and suppliers through EDI 238
Smart cards 239
Case study: A smarter way to pay 239
Keying in data 239
Case Study: Bradford & Bingley 239

Chapter 51 – The Management of Change 242
Outcomes from I.T. investments 242
Valuing the workforce 242
Reasons why I.T. systems fail 242
Case study: London Ambulance Service 243
Managing change successfully 244
Case study: Pindar 245
Implications of change 246

Chapter 52 – Security Policies 247
Threats to security and integrity 247
Risk analysis 247
Layers of control 248
Building and equipment security 248

Authorisation software 249
Communications security 249
Operational security 249
Audit trail 250
Personnel safeguards 250
Corporate I.T. security policy 250

Chapter 53 – Disaster Recovery 252
Effects of negligence 252
Stages in disaster planning 252
Contents of a security plan 253
Disaster recovery plan 253
Case study: Trust in the Virtual World 253
Criteria used to select a contingency plan 254

Chapter 54 – Implementation of Legislation 255
Laws relating to I.T. 255
The Data Protection Act 255
A data protection policy 255
Software copyright 256
Health and Safety 258
Encouraging 'ownership' of workspace 258
Taking regular breaks 259
Providing the right equipment 259
The employer's responsibility 259

Chapter 55 – User Support 260
The need for support 260
The help desk 260
Technical support 260
Help desk software 261
Case study: Call centres 262
Bulletin boards 262
User booklets 263
Newsletters and support articles 263
On-line help 263
Documentation 264

Chapter 56 – Training 265
The need for training 265
Training in the use of information technology 265
Training for senior managers 265
Training for middle managers 265
Training for users 266
Methods of training 266
Computer-based training 266
Instructor-led courses 267
Skills updating 267
Corporate training strategy 267

Chapter 57 – Project Management 269
Introduction 269
Selection of a project manager 269

The tasks of a project manager 269
The project team 269
Project planning and scheduling 270
Project reviews 271
Facilities management 271
Advantages of FM 271
Disadvantages of FM 272
Outsourcing 272

SECTION 5 **273**

Chapter 58 – Policy and Strategy **274**
The challenge of information management 274
Consistency with business priorities 274
Centralisation vs. decentralisation 274
Different user needs 275
Hardware and software choices 276
Upgrading hardware and software 276
Future proofing 277
Offers from TIME computer systems:
    Future proof? 277
Emulation 277

Chapter 59 – Security and Backup Policies **279**
Introduction 279
Backup strategies 279
Hardware for backups 280
Case study: Back up that data 280
Grandfather-father-son backups 281
Personnel policy 282
Employee code of conduct 282

Chapter 60 – Software Evaluation **283**
Introduction 283
Choosing software 283
Tailoring the software 284
Upgradability 284
Other evaluation criteria 284
Benchmark tests 285
Checking out the manufacturer 285
Evaluation report 285

Chapter 61 – Communication and Information Systems **287**
Centralised processing systems 287
Dispersed systems 287
Local area networks (LANs) 288
Wide area networks (WANs) 288
Distributed processing 289
Case study: Pubs get a new round of
    touch tills 289
Distributed databases 290
Advantages and limitations of distributed
    databases 291

Using telecommunications for competitive
    advantage 291
Public networks 291
Case study: United Parcel Service (UPS) 292

Chapter 62 – Types of Network **294**
Network topologies 294
Star network 294
Bus network 294
Ring network 295
Connecting LANs on a single site 296
Client-server and peer-to-peer networks 297

Chapter 63 – Network Security and Accounting **298**
Introduction 298
Training users about security 298
Access privileges 298
Access control 298
Firewalls 299
Audit controls 299
Performance management 299
Data encryption 300

Chapter 64 – Data Communications and Standards **302**
Communications software 302
Speed of transmission 302
Modems 302
Direction of transmission 303
Serial and parallel transmission 303
Telecommunications standards and
    protocols 303

Chapter 65 – Human-Computer Interaction **306**
Computers in the workplace 306
Psychological factors 306
Short-term memory 307
Long-term memory 307
Designing good software 308
Text versus graphics 308

Chapter 66 – Music Software **310**
Introduction 310
Music on the micro 310
Sound card 310
MIDI (Musical Instrument Digital
    Interface) 311
Software for creating music 311
Composing music 312
Using technical knowledge 312
Editing music 313
Tidying up the score 313
Editing sound waves 314

Chapter 67 – Geographical Information Systems   315
An overview of GIS   315
Using a GIS in the utilities industry   315
GIS in business   316
Environmental applications of GIS   316
Data capture   317
Case study: GIS to the rescue   317

Chapter 68 – CAD/CAM Systems   319
CAD systems   319
Specialised hardware for CAD systems   319
CAD software   320
Advantages of CAD   321
Disadvantages of CAD   321
Bitmapped versus vector-based graphics   322
CAM (Computer-aided manufacturing)   323
Case study: Rearranging the office
    furniture   323

Chapter 69 – Mathematical and Statistical Software   325
Spreadsheets   325
Sales forecasting tools   325
Statistical functions   326
Graphing tools   326
Specialised statistical packages   327
Case study: Using statistics to stop
    drink drivers   327
Mathematical software   327
Simulation software   328

Chapter 70 – Project Management Software   329
Problems with software projects   329
Planning a project   329
Planning a sample project   329
Critical path analysis   331
Gantt charts   331
Using software tools   332

Chapter 71 – Software Acquisition and Testing   334
Make or buy?   334
End-user-written software   334
Writing software in-house   334
External consultants   335
Buying a package   335
Leasing software   335
Modifying existing packages   335
Software testing   336
Alpha testing   336
Beta testing   336
Software maintenance   337
Maintenance releases   337

APPENDIX A   339
NEAB Syllabus Summary   339

APPENDIX B   355
Criteria for the assessment of the
    minor projects   356
Criteria for the assessment of the
    major project   358

APPENDIX C   363
Book List   364

INDEX   365

Section 1

Information: Nature, Role and Context

In this section:

Chapter 1 – The Role of I.T.

Chapter 2 – I.T. in Business and Commerce

Chapter 3 – I.T. in Manufacturing

Chapter 4 – I.T. in a Caring Society

Chapter 5 – I.T. in Education

Chapter 6 – Role of Communication Systems

Chapter 7 – The Internet in Business

Chapter 8 – Knowledge, Information and Data

Chapter 9 – Information as a Commodity

Chapter 10 – The Professional in I.T.

Chapter 11 – Codes of Practice

Chapter 12 – Computer Crime and the Law

Chapter 13 – Protecting Data

Chapter 14 – Data Protection Legislation

Chapter 15 – Health and Safety

Chapter 1 – The Role of I.T.

Computing – a look backwards

Within half a century, computers and information technology have changed the world and affected millions of lives in ways that no one could have foreseen. Here are some of the things that people have said about computers:

"I think there's a world market for maybe five computers." *(Thomas Watson, the chairman of IBM, in 1940)*

"I have travelled the length and breadth of this country and talked with the best people, and I can assure you that data processing is a fad that won't last out the year." *(The editor in charge of business books for Prentice Hall, in 1957)*

"There is no reason why anyone would want to have a computer in their home." *(President of Digital Equipment Corporation, in 1977)*

Contrary to these predictions, computers are transforming the ways in which we learn, communicate, do business, enjoy our leisure and live our everyday lives. Whatever career you pursue in the future, a knowledge of computer skills and concepts is likely to be beneficial or even essential. This course aims to make you competent and confident in the use of computers and to give you an understanding of the uses and impact of computers in society today.

In this chapter we'll look at some of the ways that information technology has changed patterns of work. We'll also examine how dependent we have become on computer systems, and what the consequences might be when these systems fail.

Computers and employment

Ever since the industrial revolution, people have feared that machinery will displace workers, and information technology is no exception.

In spite of dire predictions, however, there is no evidence that the introduction of computers has led to mass unemployment – in fact, overall more jobs have been created by computers than have been displaced by them. Nevertheless, in some areas computers have substantially replaced the workforce. In the 1980s, thousands of factory workers were made redundant by the introduction of robots on the factory floor making everything from biscuits to cars. In the 1990s, thousands of clerical and white-collar workers have seen their jobs disappear with the introduction of company databases, desktop publishing, computerised accounting systems and increased automation in banks, building societies and organisations of all kinds, large and small.

The changing nature of employment

Today, most people no longer work in farms or factories but are found instead in sales, education, health care, banks, insurance firms and law firms. They provide services such as catering, writing computer software, or advertising and delivering goods. These jobs primarily involve working with, creating or distributing new knowledge or information. Knowledge and information work account for about 70% of the labour force in Britain and the U.S.

Computers have taken over many of the tedious tasks that humans once performed. Consider that only a generation or so ago:

- Taking cash out from your bank account involved queuing at the bank's counter, having the cashier give you the money and manually note the transaction in a book;
- Putting a newspaper together involved picking up individual letters made out of lead and placing them manually in position, with correct spacing achieved by placing a strip of lead ('leading') between lines;
- All long distance calls had to go through an operator who manually made the connection.

The introduction of computers has in many instances led to a change in the types of job available. Many publishing firms feared that desktop publishing would result in fewer jobs in the publishing and printing industries. In fact thousands of new publishing and printing companies have been created in the last decade – a quick flip through the yellow pages under 'Printing' will verify this!

In many cases, workers displaced by computers are retrained to perform computer-related jobs that may be more satisfying than their original jobs.

- A secretary may find it more satisfying to use a word processor to produce high quality output which can be saved and amended, rather than having to retype whole pages because a minor error was made;
- An engineer or draughtsman may find it more satisfying to create designs using a computer-aided design system with complete accuracy, than drawing by hand;
- An accounts clerk may prefer to use an Accounts software package rather than to do the accounts manually.

> ➤ **Discussion: Computerisation often leads to a change in the tasks that a worker has to perform. In some cases the new tasks may be more satisfying, and in other cases, less satisfying. Think of some examples where computerisation has one of these two outcomes.**

Teleworking

Teleworking involves carrying out work away from the office and communicating with the employer through the use of computer and telecommunications equipment. Often teleworkers are based at home, but they can also work from telecentres, satellite offices or even on the move. Although a study done in 1995 at Newcastle University found that less than 1 worker in 100 was a teleworker (spending at least half of their working week at home using a computer), organisations are becoming increasingly interested in various forms of teleworking, which has benefits both for the employer and the employee. According to research done by Henley Business School in 1997, there are already 4 million teleworkers in the U.K.

Benefits of teleworking

- It may be easier to concentrate on work in a quiet environment at home than in a noisy office;
- Workers save on commuting time and costs, with the associated environmental benefits of keeping cars off the roads;
- Workers enjoy greater flexibility, and can arrange their working hours around other commitments such as picking children up from school;
- Employers save on the costs of office space and overheads such as heat and light;
- People in different locations can work in a team;
- People can be recruited from a much wider geographical area;

- People who are not able to take employment in standard office hours can be recruited.

The problems of teleworking

- Management may fear difficulties in controlling a workforce that is not in the office;
- There is a problem in ensuring that remote staff understand corporate goals and retain a sense of loyalty to the organisation;
- Employees may feel isolated and miss the social environment of an office full of colleagues;
- Employees may find it difficult to work in teams, or to get help when they need it;
- Some teleworkers may find it difficult to separate home from work, and find work encroaching on their leisure or family time. Conversely, it may be difficult to concentrate on work with children making demands on a parent's time.

Case study: Socket to 'em now

A survey of 200 companies published last summer by consultant Small World Connections suggests as many as three-quarters of employers have some form of teleworking, and 85% say they expect to be using teleworkers at some point in the future.

The advantages to employees of being able to work from home are obvious, but there is a business case for their employers, too. Employers can reduce their office costs, enabling them to replace permanent workstations with a smaller number of 'hot' desks.

It means they can increase their employees' productivity – one hour less commuting means one hour more work, theoretically. Supporters of teleworking say companies who use homeworkers also find it easier to recruit and retain staff, and it opens the door for companies to attract other sources of labour such as the disabled or women returners.

BT has more than 1,500 staff who telework on a full-time basis and another 15,000 who work from home occasionally. Teleworking has also been embraced by companies in sectors such as retailing, banking and the legal profession. Davis & Co, a firm of City solicitors, allows 30 of its lawyers to enjoy the benefits of teleworking. The firm offers clients 24-hour, seven-day-a-week access to home-working solicitors who use a combination of e-mail, audio-conferencing, faxes and voice mail to keep in touch.

On the down side, teleworking could deal a body blow to the unions, which find it easier to recruit and organise members who are clustered together, not scattered throughout the country. Without effective union representation, teleworkers could be open to exploitation. Research is needed on how well workers are able to cope with long periods of isolation from the office and how this impacts on their motivation, job satisfaction or promotion prospects.

Source: Ian Wylie, The Guardian 1 November 1997

Changing locations of work

Not only are the type of jobs we do changing, the location of work is changing too. When Britain changed in the 19th century from an agricultural to an industrial society, more and more workers were forced to move from farm work into towns and large industrial centres. The advent of communications technology is now starting to reverse this trend. There is no need for much of the work of an organisation to be done at a Head Office in a city; it is often more economical for it to be done in a more remote area where office rates and housing are cheaper, and employees can be paid less. Results of data processing can be transferred to wherever they are needed via a telecommunications line.

In fact, many large companies such as some airlines and the London Underground have their daily data processing carried out in countries like India where labour is cheap and plentiful.

Case study: Remote working

Injured Americans who wind up in emergency rooms at hospitals in Dallas, Denver and Seattle may owe their lives to a group of clerical workers on a farm in Northern Ireland. Emergency room doctors dictate diagnoses and other relevant information for clerks to type into the hospital computer's system. But clerical cover is limited at night, so the voice recording is digitised and transferred by ISDN line to the KITE (Kinawley Integrated Teleworking Enterprise) centre in the village of Kinawley, Co Fermanagh. Here it is typed and instantly transmitted back to the hospital, so that within minutes the patient's records are up-to-date.

KITE also works for Silicon Valley recruitment firms, taking CVs by e-mail and editing them into standard format. Kinawley's working day corresponds to California's night shift, so the finished CVs can be on the consultants' PCs by the time they come into work. "They can double their working day at minimal cost," says Sheila McCaffrey, KITE's director.

Because of its rural location, KITE can undercut the cost of American firms by up to a third. "Office space in the heart of Silicon Valley is £100 a square foot, compared with £3 or £4 per square foot here", says McCaffrey.

Kite is one of about 150 teleworking centres or 'telecottages' around Britain, many of them in disadvantaged rural areas.

Source: Paul Bray, The Sunday Times 27 April 1997

Consequences of computer failure

Individuals, organisations and society in general are totally dependent on computer systems for everything from withdrawing £10 at the local cashpoint to transferring millions of pounds' worth of shares every day of the week on the Stock Exchange. Computers play a crucial role in thousands of everyday tasks such as figuring out how many pineapples need to be imported from Kenya to meet demand in Sainsbury's next week, or recording £10 million worth of lottery ticket sales every week. But what are the consequences of computer failure?

Consider some of the following incidents which have occurred in the last few years.

1. In June 1996, more than 100 women called Fiona who worked for a bank had their mortgage and loan payments wiped out. No one knows why.

2. Pepsi blamed a computer error for a promotion in 1992 in which half a million Filipinos claimed first prize. Riots and deaths followed.

3. Faulty software was said to be responsible for the destruction of the Ariane 5 space rocket in June 1996.

4. In 1995, air traffic control equipment operated by the American Federal Aviation Administration crashed 21 'significant' times.

5. When the Bank of Scotland's system failed in 1996, customers could not withdraw money with cash card machines.

6. A Patriot missile failed to detect an incoming Scud missile that killed 28 American soldiers during the Gulf war. The cause: a software bug.

7. Failures in the London Ambulance Service's 999 Computer system were blamed for staffing and operational weaknesses in 1992.

8. In June 1995, hundreds of flights were delayed by computer problems at Prestwick airport. Air traffic controllers used little pieces of paper to direct flights instead.

Source: The Guardian 9 June 1996

> ➤ **Discussion: Some computer failures result in inconvenience to individuals or organisations, and some are catastrophic. Give examples of each.**

The millennium bug

The millennium crisis threatens almost every company in the world, with the potential for disruption being almost beyond the bounds of comprehension; an American study suggests that preventing a global millennium meltdown may cost £400 billion. All of this is because of a flaw of fundamental simplicity: many computers can tell the date only in terms of two digits. The year 1999 is 99, which is fine, but the year 2000 will be 00, and countless computers will interpret this as the year 1900.

The effects of the millennium bug are already being felt.

- At Marks & Spencer, the company's computers rejected all tins of corned beef stamped with a use-by date in the next century, calculating that the food must be 100 years old.

- A subscriber to a major national weekly magazine renewed her 3-year subscription in January 1997. When the magazine failed to arrive, she was told there was no record of her in the computer, even though she had been a subscriber for more than 30 years. The computer figured that her subscription ran out in January 1900 and wiped her record off automatically.

- British tourists have had trouble hiring cars in America from firms whose computers thought their driving licences had expired in the early 1900s.

B.T. reckons that solving the problem will be a challenge of greater complexity than changing every telephone code in Britain.

Exercises

1. Individuals and organisations have become so dependent upon I.T. systems that the consequences of their failure could be catastrophic to the individual or the organisation.

    Give **two** different examples of types of I.T. system for which failure would be catastrophic. In each case explain why the failure could prove to be catastrophic. (4)

    NEAB IT01 Qu 1 1997

2. The use of computers has transformed the work of office staff. Briefly describe **three** tasks for which computers are now widely used in the offices of business and commercial users. (3)

    AEB AS Computing Paper 1 Qu 1 1997

3. Through the 1990s an increasing number of people have become teleworkers. These are people who work from home using a personal computer linked to a Wide Area Network via a modem and the telephone system. Discuss, with the aid of specific examples, the advantages and disadvantages to individuals, organisations and society of this type of employment. (13)

    New question

Chapter 2 – I.T. in Business and Commerce

New products and services

No matter what career you decide to take up, you will almost inevitably need to be able to understand and use information technology. Information technologies are used to create and keep track of documents in offices, seek out and exploit new ways of marketing, control factory production, design and create new products and enable service industries to function on a global scale.

Information technologies have changed the way that business is done. The explosion of knowledge and information has resulted in a mind-boggling range of products and services that were undreamt of two decades ago. Automated teller machines (ATMs), fax machines, mobile telephones, CD players, video recorders and computer games are some of the new products. New services include a range of telephone services such as caller ID and ring back, shopping and banking via the Internet, e-mail, barcode scanning at supermarket checkouts and libraries.

> ➤ **Discussion: Describe some other new products and services that have appeared in the last decade.**

Changing shape of organisations

Without information technology, businesses large or small cannot remain competitive. As the range of goods and services continues to increase, and markets expand world-wide, some trends can be noted:

- More and more people are going into business for themselves, or working for small businesses.
- Large organisations are becoming 'flatter' and less hierarchical. People work together in groups rather than individually. Information workers need far less supervision than factory workers because they have knowledge – they know what to do and when and how to do it. They need information, not supervision.
- More and more workers are recruited because of their knowledge and skills in problem-solving, communications, their ability to use their initiative and make appropriate use of new technology.

Case study: Britain's fastest growing companies

Fast Track 100 is a league table that ranks the fastest-growing unquoted companies between 1993 and 1996. It shows these firms are creating jobs and pioneering technological innovation. Half of the firms in the top 100 are technology-related industries.

But the record of the Fast Track 100 companies cannot disguise the fact that Britain needs to develop many more growth firms. When compared with the huge loss of jobs that big businesses in manufacturing and banking suffered during the early 1990s, the employment creation is small: the 12,500 jobs created in the sector could be offset by just one redundancy programme at a big group.

Six different types of company were identified in the top ranking small companies:

- Those with a star product such as Eyretel. In 1990, Roger Keenan decided to develop and market his own digital voice recorder. His first big order, worth £80,000 came from an emergency-service base in Virginia, USA, and from then on sales quickly began to grow in America, Britain and Asia.

- Those that identified customer service as the key to growth, such as Simply Computers and Software Warehouse.

- Companies that excel in marketing their goods, such as Vivid Imaginations and Roldec.

- Management leaders such as Wolfe, a building contractor.

- 'People champions' such as Lexis Public Relations.

- Acquirers, who take over other companies to achieve growth.

The successful entrepreneurs cited the key factor in their success as customer service, ahead of marketing and the product itself.

(Source: The Sunday Times 7 December 1997)

➢ **Discussion: In what ways do you think information technology helps these companies to be successful? Consider the three areas of customer service, marketing and the manufacture of the product.**

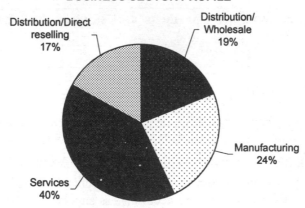

BUSINESS SECTOR PROFILE

Figure 2.1: Types of company in the Top 100 small companies (Source: Fast Track 100)

Using I.T. to set up a small business

Information technology can play a crucial part in the success or failure of a new enterprise. For example:

- A **spreadsheet** can be used to draw up a business plan and to calculate expected income and expenses. It can also be used to perform 'What-if' calculations to test out the effects of raising the price but lowering sales, using less expensive components, subcontracting the distribution of goods, and so on.

- A **graphics package** can be used to design the company logo, headed stationery and business cards.

- A **word processing package** can be used to design invoice stationery and send mailshots.

- A **desktop-publishing package** can be used to design advertising or promotional material.

- A **database package** can be used to keep a mailing list of customers.

- An **accounts package** can be used to set up the company accounts.

- A **PC** with associated peripherals such as a laser printer is needed to run the software.

- A **fax machine** can be used to communicate with potential suppliers, wholesalers, distributors, printers etc.

- The **Internet** can be used to sell products to new and existing customers, and as a valuable research tool.

- **E-mail** can be used to correspond with customers or suppliers.

- **On-line banking** can enable you to keep tabs on your cash flow.

- The **telephone** and **answering machine** are essential to every small business.

I.T. in banking

The banking industry makes extensive use of I.T. in all its operations.

- Using telephone banking, a customer can ring in to check a balance or pay a bill, 24 hours a day, 365 days a year. One major bank has 750 phone banking staff taking up to 50,000 calls a day from 600,000 customers. As soon as the call is answered, the operator asks what service the customer requires, and selects one of 40 items on screen. The customer is then asked for their name and postcode, which enables their details to be retrieved in less than 2 seconds from the mainframe computer in Andover, Hants. As well as handling account queries and transactions, operators can access the bank's central credit-scoring system, empowering them to agree loans and overdrafts on the spot in many cases. If further discussion is needed, the system can arrange for the customer to visit their branch, by automatically booking a slot in the branch's electronic diary.

- Using ATMs, cash can be withdrawn at thousands of cashpoint machines all over the country.

- Using a debit card, purchases can be made at petrol stations, supermarkets, department stores, etc and the customer's account balance checked. If sufficient funds are available, the amount of the purchase is automatically debited to the account.

- Credit cards can be used to make purchases over the phone or via the Internet.

- Millions of cheques are processed each day using MICR (Magnetic Ink Character Recognition).

- Salaries and bills can be paid automatically by Direct Debit.

- Electronic smartcards such as Mondex store money on a microchip which can be topped up just like cash. Goods can be paid for by inserting the card into a reader and typing in the amount to be deducted. Such a card could eventually replace cash.

Shopping on the Internet

On-line shopping is just beginning to attract the attention of all kinds of retailers. In the early days of the Net, small specialist traders found it a useful way of reaching a new, wider market, but today the big retailers are beginning to explore the potential of the 'virtual store'. A Web site can be used as a 'shop-front' and customers can browse 24 hours a day from anywhere in the world. It can be used to build up a database of customers by asking customers to 'register' when they first visit the Web site, giving their name and address and sometimes other information about products they are most interested in. (See Chapter 7.)

Thousands of companies do business on the Internet, including:

- On-line Waterstone's, where a 'Bookseeker' mechanism can be used to search for titles by publisher, keyword and title (www.waterstones.co.uk);

- AutoHunter, the car site, has more than half a million private and trade advertisements, uploaded daily from 700 newspapers. These can be searched by location, make, model, year, price and even colour – to the relief of one young man who crashed his mother's estate car one Saturday night and was able to find an exact replica by the following Tuesday (www.adhunter.co.uk);

- Dell, the computer manufacturer, sells £3 million worth of computers a day at its sites (www.dell.com).

Case study: Off your trolley

Tesco, Britain's biggest supermarket, is running trials that put an attractive combination of on-line shopping and bespoke delivery on the screens of customers in London and Leeds.

Shoppers browse the virtual shelves, fill their baskets and check out when they have everything they need. Then they book a two-hour delivery 'slot' the next day, during which their items will be delivered for a fixed fee of £5. Vans will turn up outside your house at any time between 8.30am and 9.30pm, Monday to Saturday, and are starting to make Sunday deliveries, too.

No one in the retail industry is in any doubt that a major shift in the way we shop is underway. Most analysts believe that the market for on-line retailing will grow to around £4 billion worldwide within the next couple of years. This is still only a fraction of the amount we spend through more conventional means, but on-line shopping may well offer much greater margins for companies since it will enable them to sell direct, without expensive middlemen, and to tailor stock levels to demand more accurately than is possible through a normal supply chain.

Source: David Hewson, The Sunday Times 23 November 1997 and 27 April 1997

➢ **Discussion: Identify some of the ways in which supermarkets are using I.T. to gain competitive advantage.**

The drawbacks

What are the drawbacks in this scramble to jump on the technology bandwagon in which the microchip is a key component to practically everything we do? This new information revolution is comparable to the industrial revolution, only far more wide-ranging in its effects. Information replaces raw materials as the driving force of successful world economics. In future, individuals and countries will only be as good as the marketable skills and knowledge they have accumulated. You are what you know.

But at the other end of the scale, a new underclass is being created in Britain. A survey published in November 1996 reported that 40% of the population did not regularly use any of the weapons of the information revolution such as computers or mobile phones. 80% did not know how to get connected to the Internet, and of those on-line, only 9% used it regularly.

Worse still is the social profile: only 9% of working people (the C2/E/Ds of the socio-economic grading) have ever used the Internet, compared with 25% of the middle and upper classes. This paints a depressing picture of a new two-nation Britain even more polarised in terms of access to the advantages of the information age than the monetary gulf between the rich and the poor that so shamed the eighties. The dream of a new age of equal opportunities for all once again appears to be foundering.

Just as in mediaeval times when many of the great cathedrals were built, the Freemasons represented an elite body of people with specialist skills in stonemasonry which they jealously guarded, so today those with I.T. skills are the indispensible builders of the information age.

The dangers

A reliance on technology brings with it unavoidable dangers. Faulty hospital equipment that delivers the wrong dose of radiation, 'fly-by-wire' aircraft that develop hardware or software faults and fall out of the sky, software bugs that corrupt data held in massive databases, are just some of the catastrophes that can result from our dependence on technological wonders.

Case study: Charity database corrupted

George is a computer consultant who recently travelled to London to arrange some consultancy work with a large national charity, with annual donations of £2.5 million, and a donor database of nearly half a million people worldwide. George was asked to investigate methods of speeding up data entry but, when he examined the application, he discovered that the software had been written some 7 years previously and added to by well-meaning volunteers at different times to cope with each new need. They were using Version 1 of the database software, since superseded by versions 2.0, 2.1 and 3.1...6. He took the details of what was required, and went home to prepare a quote. One problem was that this version of the software was no longer available and he only had a much more up-to-version. This meant the work would have to be done on-site, which would mean travelling up to London every day instead of making the changes on his home PC and going up once to install them. Also, knowing that the early software had suffered from many bugs, he asked whether they had ever experienced problems with data corruption. The boss was not sure.

A week later he received a panic call from the charity. They had just sent out a major mailshot, and now discovered that thousands of people on the database had somehow been given identical 'unique reference numbers'. Their backup copies all showed the same problem. It would now be impossible to update the correct donor's record when a donation was received.

➢ **Discussion: Could this problem have been foreseen or averted? What course of action will George recommend now?**

Exercises

1. 'The development of Information Technology has had significant effects on society, individuals and organisations.'
    With the aid of specific examples discuss this statement. Include in your discussion:
    * the effects of Information Technology on society at large;
    * the effects of Information Technology on employment and work methods;
    * the effect of Information Technology on individuals. (20)
    NEAB IT01 Qu 8 1996

2. Discuss in an essay the concept of a cashless society and the assertion that we will become one. You should refer to steps taken by banks and other financial institutions to move us towards a cashless society and explain why some people feel that it may never be possible to achieve such a goal. (15)
    London Computing Paper 1 Qu 11 1996

3. List **four** different software packages that a small business would find useful, explaining in each case why they would be useful. (8)
    New question

4. Replacing a manual system by a computerised system can have certain unwelcome consequences. Suggest **three** different examples of these unwelcome consequences at least **one** of which should be social and at least **one** economic. (3)
    AEB Computing Paper 1 Qu 3 1997

Chapter 3 – I.T. in Manufacturing

Introduction

In the face of ever-increasing competition from international markets, many labour-intensive manufacturing companies face a stark choice: *automate*, or *evaporate*. Here are some of the many ways in which computers are used in the manufacturing world.

- Order entry and processing systems accept and process customer orders. A fully integrated system will also calculate the quantity and cost of materials needed to make the items ordered, produce reports on any shortages of materials in stock that need to be ordered and raise the purchase order. It will then track the progress of the order through the manufacturing process so that customer queries can be answered.

- Project management software provides management with the information necessary to keep projects within budget and on time. Reports can be produced showing actual costs versus projected costs, and the number of days ahead or behind schedule.

- Expert systems can be used in a multitude of ways from calculating the cost of a new multi-storey office block to detecting when a batch of beer is ready for the next stage of the brewing process.

- Computer-aided design systems are used in thousands of different applications from designing a new jumbo jet to the design of the most aerodynamic material for a ski racer's suit.

- Computer-aided manufacture enables components to be manufactured with the utmost precision.

- Robots are used in every kind of industry from car manufacture to sorting items on an assembly line.

Case study: The sweet smell of success

Bass the brewers has built a machine that can perform the daunting task of smelling beer and deciding if it's up to snuff. The technology that makes this possible is neural computing, the revolutionary process that mimics the way the human brain works. The artificial nose makes a complex series of judgements based on the electrochemical stimuli received by its gas sensors, and could save the brewers a fortune.

"By detecting an over-active yeast or a weak crop of hops at an early stage in the fermentation process, the nose could save us having to throw away a whole batch – 345,600 pints of beer", explained Ian Morris of Bass.

It is not just brewers who are interested in the artificial nose. Manufacturers of instant coffee, perfume and other aromatic products are spending huge sums, in co-operation with researchers at several universities, to build a better-than-human olfactory sensor.

Source: Garth Alexander, The Sunday Times 19 September 1993

Computer-aided design (CAD)

CAD systems allow designers and engineers to create designs on screen for thousands of products ranging from the tiniest computer chip to bridges, buildings and aeroplanes. The software allows users to create 3-dimensional 'solid' models with physical characteristics like volume, weight and centre of gravity. The models can be rotated and viewed from any angle, edited and stored. The computer can perform calculations to evaluate its performance under different stresses, or crash-test a new design of car before it is even manufactured.

Animation software can be used to enable a viewer to 'walk through' a 3-D model of say, a building, that exists only in the computer's memory.

CAD systems ('vector-based' graphics packages) store data in a different way from Paint ('bitmapped') packages. Paint packages store a picture as a two dimensional array, with each element of the array representing one pixel (dot) on the screen. A CAD package stores drawings as a collection of objects such as lines and circles, each represented by specifying coordinates, thickness and so on. This has many advantages, including the following:

- Drawings can be scaled or resized without distortion;

- Drawings are device independent; a drawing created using one type of VDU can be transferred to a screen of a different resolution without distortion;

- The files created tend to be smaller than for equivalent bitmapped images;

- Drawings can be made with a very high degree of accuracy by specifying coordinates.

Figure 3.1: A simple drawing being made in AutoCAD

Computer-aided Manufacturing (CAM)

Computer-aided design is often linked to *computer-aided manufacturing* (CAM). CAD/CAM systems are used in the design and manufacture of thousands of applications from aeroplane and car parts to office furnishings and sports equipment. When the design of the product is completed, the specifications are input directly into a program that controls the manufacturing of parts.

A great advantage of these systems is their flexibility: individual items can be manufactured to a customer's exact specifications.

Case study: Subcontracting sector uses I.T.

Precimax was founded in 1988 and has grown to a 30-employee company with an anticipated turnover in 1997 of £1.4 million. It offers a full manufacturing service from initial design through to supply of fully-finished components and assemblies. Production is predominantly on CNC (computer numeric control) turning and machining centres, and programs can be created from customer drawings or directly from CAD via modem or disk. Batches range from one-off up to 5000, but are more typically in the 50 to 500 bracket. In size, turned components measure up to 250mm diameter.

Precimax is a major supplier of components for train braking and door systems and is currently producing parts for use in the platform edge doors for London Underground's new Jubilee Line extension. It also has a contract with a postal equipment manufacturer for monthly deliveries of rollers and other parts for letter-sorting machines.

Precimax uses Datatrack for Windows for keeping track of its annual 3000 orders. The system includes estimating and quoting, sales order processing, purchasing, job costing and delivery. The commercial director commented "A computerised system to handle this level of business is absolutely essential. Without it, we would be lost. It enables us to control cost and better understand our trading and manufacture. It gives us accurate information, so we can communicate with our customers on costs and deliveries quickly and with confidence."

Source: Machinery 5/19 December 1997

➢ **Discussion: In what major ways are computers being used at Precimax?**

Robots

The word 'robot' comes from the Czech word 'robotnik', meaning slave. Robots come in many different forms and shapes, but they all have the same basic components:

- Sensors, which capture information from the environment;
- A microprocessor to process the information;
- Actuators to produce movement or alter the environment in some way, for example by turning an electronic switch on or off.

Robots may be used for spray painting, spot welding and car assembly. They are also used as security devices inside homes and office buildings, as vehicles in space exploration, as intelligent wheelchairs for disabled people, and as underwater maintenance workers for oil rigs. Hundreds of applications use robots in one form or another.

Why use robots?

- Robots can tirelessly perform repetitive and monotonous tasks, lift heavy loads and reach long distances. They are used, for example, by the U.S. Navy to scrape and repaint ships.
- Labour costs can be substantially reduced. Robots are widely used in car manufacturing as well as in many other industries including printing and publishing. Robots can carry tons of paper coming off presses, bind and trim books and apply book covers. It has been estimated that each industrial robot will replace an average of six workers.
- Quality of work is consistent. A robot is never tired or bored or having an off day.
- Robots can work 24 hours a day, do not need breaks and do not go on strike.
- They can work in total darkness, at low temperatures, thus saving on electricity bills.
- They can be used in hazardous areas, such as fume-filled rooms or radioactive environments. Tests are currently being carried out to set robots to work on clearing mine fields.

➢ **Discussion: Robots are immensely expensive to buy and install, and need to be used for a high proportion of each day in order to recoup the cost. What happens when demand for a product slumps? Would a manufacturer be better advised to stick with manual workers, who can be laid off and rehired when times improve?**

Exercises

1. Computers and information technology are widely used in manufacturing industries. Give **three** different examples of their use in manufacturing, and in each case discuss

    (a) The benefits to the company, the customers and the employees

    (b) The possible drawbacks to the company, the customers and the employees.   (12)

    New question

2. Research an application of computers and I.T. in manufacturing. Describe briefly the end product, the reasons for using I.T. and the software and hardware used.   (8)

    What group of people benefits most from the use of I.T. in the application you have described? Is any other group of people disadvantaged? Briefly explain your answers.   (4)

    New question

3. Describe briefly **one** application for robots in industry.   (2)

    Explain **two** advantages of using robots in the application you describe.   (2)

    New question

4. Some manufacturers are deciding to re-employ people on the shop floor and retire their robots. Give **one** argument to support this action and **one** argument against it.   (2)

    AEB Computing Paper 1 Qu 3 1996

5. The use of computer-controlled machinery in manufacturing and product assembly has become widespread. Give **two** benefits for the manufacturer, other than financial, and **two** implications for the employees of such automation.   (4)

    NEAB AS Computing Qu 3 1995

Chapter 4 – I.T. in a Caring Society

Introduction

In this chapter we'll take a look at some of the ways in which information technology is used in medicine, and the benefits that it has brought to people with disabilities.

Computers in medicine

Computers have had a very significant impact on the quality of medical services. For example:

- Medical records stored in hospital information systems improve the quality of patient care. They are more accurate, they can keep track of prescriptions and tests administered, hospital admissions, dietary requirements and so on. Records are less likely to go astray than manual records and they can be made available to authorised people at any location.

- Databases of organ donors and patients needing transplants mean that when an organ becomes available, a match can quickly be found.

- Computerised devices such as pacemakers, artificial organs and prostheses (artificial limbs) have enabled tens of thousands of people to live longer and have a fuller life.

- Computerised monitoring devices can keep a 24-hour watch on critically ill patients and sound the alarm if vital signs change for the worse.

- Expert medical systems can help to diagnose diseases often at remote locations far from the care of a specialist. Vast amounts of data on symptoms and illnesses are stored in a 'knowledge base' which can help a doctor to arrive at a preliminary diagnosis.

- Surgeons can perform operations at remote locations using a remotely controlled robot arm. (See case study below.)

- Computers can model new drugs and test their effects, significantly reducing the time taken for new drugs to come onto the market.

Case study: Robot surgeon operates

A British robot will next week carry out a biopsy on a live patient in what is believed to be the world's first international robotic operation. A £100,000 robotic arm designed and manufactured by Armstrong Healthcare in High Wycombe, Bucks, will perform the operation on a patient in Lisbon, but the surgeon controlling it will be in Italy.

The robotic arm, called Pathfinder, is similar in shape and function to a human arm. It will seek out a vital organ in the patient, probably the liver, and then extract a piece of tissue. The surgeon in Italy will be guided by ultrasound images taken simultaneously by the arm. He will be able to see live video and ultrasound pictures from the robot, sent down a special high-speed telephone line. To control the robot, the surgeon will hold a 3D computer mouse that can operate both the arm and the needle.

Once the needle is in place over the patient, the surgeon can use the mouse to insert it and remove a biopsy sample for examination. According to Patrick Finlay, the managing director of Armstrong Healthcare, the Pathfinder is actually more accurate than a surgeon's hand, with no risk of shaking or wavering.

Source: Roger Dobson, The Guardian 7 December 1997.

Figure 4.1: The robot surgeon operates (Photograph by permission of Armstrong Healthcare Ltd)

Case study: Deeper Blue checks cancer drugs

The supercomputer technology giving world champion Gary Kasporov a run for his money is to help halve the time it takes to bring new drugs to market.

According to IBM, which developed the Deeper Blue chess-playing computer, the ability to compute millions of calculations a second will be used within two years to enable scientists to model new drugs and test their effects. They claim this could reduce the average 12-year development period for a drug to about 6 years.

A supercomputer the company is building will be able to model within a day the effect of 1m atoms on each other during a split second. Instead of using valuable laboratory time and space, scientists can model a variety of chemicals on the computer and mimic the condition they are designed to combat. The supercomputer can then calculate the reaction of the drug, showing scientists whether they are on the right track within a day, rather than months.

Source: Sean Hargrave, The Sunday Times, 11 May 1997.

Expert systems used in medical diagnosis

Expert systems are computer programs that attempt to replicate the performance of a human expert on some specialised reasoning task. Also called **knowledge-based systems**, they are able to store and manipulate knowledge so that they can help a user to solve a problem or make a decision.

An expert system of this type is being developed in Australia to assist doctors in the diagnosis of melanoma, one of the most common types of cancer which manifests itself as dark patches similar to moles on the skin. In order to build the expert system, 45 different cancerous melanomas and 176 similar but benign non-melanomas were photographed and the images processed to remove hair, oil bubbles, etc. to extract the essential features. From these pictures and the known correct diagnoses, a set of 'rules' can be programmed into the expert system so that when presented with a photograph of a new skin lesion, the computer can make a diagnosis with a high degree of accuracy. The next step is to develop a real-time device.

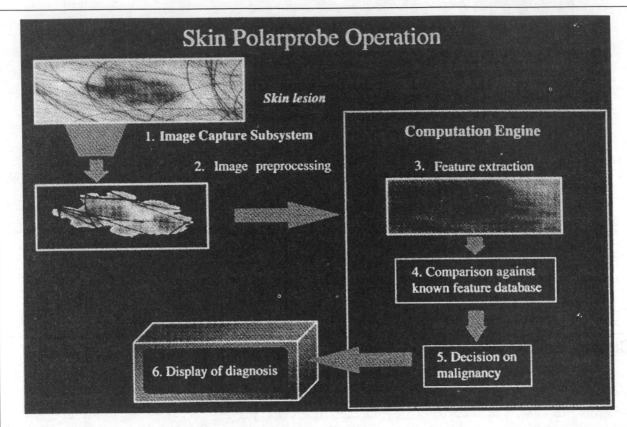

1. An image of the lesion is captured by the Polarprobe® camera system and downloaded onto the Polarprobe® computer system.

2. Calibration is performed. Image preprocessing follows to mask out hairs and oil bubbles and to identify the boundaries of the lesion.

3. The image is analysed by the Skin Polarprobe® software algorithms to extract diagnostic features of the lesion that facilitate the identification of melanoma using multiple discriminants such as colour segmentation, lesion patterns and geometry.

4. The computer algorithms, developed in collaboration with CSIRO, compare the values with stored values inside the computer database. The stored values are based on a large amount of empirical data which has been collected in a data library by Polartechnics and the Sydney Melanoma Unit, Royal Prince Alfred Hospital.

5. The Skin Polarprobe® computes the data using the detection algorithms and a decision is made as to whether the lesion is a melanoma or not.

6. The physician is informed of the computer's diagnosis immediately.

(Reproduced with permission from Polartechnics Ltd, Sydney, Australia)

> ➤ **Discussion: What are the benefits and drawbacks of using such a system for the diagnosis of melanomas?**

Computers and the disabled

About ten percent of people in Britain have some kind of disability. For many of them, new computer technology can dramatically improve their quality of life, their ability to communicate and their opportunities for independence and employment.

Case study: Eyes in the sky

A satellite navigation system for the blind is expected to transform the way visually handicapped people get around towns and cities, and will make travelling to unfamiliar places overseas less of an ordeal and more of a pleasure. It is to be tested by several visually handicapped people in Birmingham.

The system hinges on the Global Positioning System (GPS) of satellites encircling the earth. Receivers picking up the signals from the satellites can calculate precisely where they are on earth. People from yachtsmen to motorists using in-car navigation devices now use the system.

The blind person's version is essentially a portable computer plus a satellite receiver. The computer, fitted with a speech synthesiser so that it can 'talk' to the user, contains electronic Ordnance Survey maps of an area or city. A blind person trained on a keyboard taps into the system his or her location and where they want to go, and it automatically plots the route.

Once this has been done, the user is ready to go and steps out of the house. The computer will then say things like "Walk 100 yards, turn left and then right". It will also inform you of landmarks on the way, such as a fire station, and mention the numbers of houses or buildings on a street.

Source: Nick Nuttall, The Sunday Times, 27 March 1996.

Today there are systems based on personal computers that can talk, listen, teach, communicate and translate. People with control over just an eyelid or a toe, for example, can communicate by means of the proper equipment attached to a P.C.

For example:

- Scanners can convert printed text to verbal output for the visually impaired;

- Voice recognition equipment converts speech to printed or displayed output for the hearing impaired;

- People with physical disabilities can use special pointing devices, pens or touch screens instead of keying devices for interacting with a computer;

- Vision systems have sensors built into special glasses;

- Implanted computerised devices can help physically impaired people to become more mobile.

Exercises

1. Computers and microprocessors are being used to help the physically disabled in many different ways. For each of **two** different types of handicap, briefly describe a way in which patients can be helped by this new technology. (4)

   AEB Computing Paper 1 Qu 1 1995

2. Briefly describe **two** examples of how computers could aid surgeons performing operations. You must show clearly the role of the computer in your answer. (4)

   AEB Computing Paper 1 Qu 6 1997

3. Research an application of information technology in one of the following areas: medicine, the home, education, helping people to overcome disabilities, environmental work. Prepare and deliver a short presentation. Your sources could include magazines and newspapers, TV programs such as Tomorrow's World, the Internet and library textbooks. (10)

   New question

Chapter 5 – I.T. in Education

Computers in schools

In the 1980s money was found to put at least one microcomputer in every school in Britain. Since then, microcomputers have had a mediocre track record in the classroom, with many computers being left unused in a corner. Many of these computers are old, not sufficiently powerful to run modern software, and incompatible with more modern machines. Schools which made a one-time investment in computer technology may not have sufficient funds to train teachers how to use them effectively, to buy the latest software and to upgrade hardware as needed.

Yet in spite of these problems, there is general agreement that computer technology is a crucial resource in education today. Computers and I.T. can bring benefits such as:

- The use of productivity tools like word processors, desktop publishing and spreadsheet software for use in projects and other school activities;

- The use of interactive teaching packages available on CD for many different subjects;

- Access to the Internet and thousands of on-line databases;

- Distance learning facilities for those who are unable to attend school or college, or for minority subjects (such as Russian or Japanese) which do not justify a full-time teacher in a single school;

- Links with other schools or colleges, or with industrial or business organisations;

- Special facilities available for students with disabilities – for example partially-sighted students may be able to change text size and background colour, blind people can use text-to-speech conversion packages, people with arthritis or cerebral palsy may control the computer by speaking to it instead of using the keyboard or mouse.

Case study: John Cabot City Technology College

If the network goes down at John Cabot City Technology College in Bristol, it is the pupils who complain the loudest. "The network has become an essential crutch for them", says Keith McCorkindale, the school's principal. "It's not so much an add-on as a way of life."

The school has several overlapping networks, including one for its 600 students. They can store their work on-line, e-mail each other and publish minutes of student council meetings. They automatically receive copies of school announcements and they can e-mail their teachers, even at the weekend if they have a computer at home.

And there is always the Internet. Learning to use the Net effectively can be an education in itself. "Meandering from hot link to hot link is a superb way of wasting time" says McCorkindale. "Pupils – and teachers – need training on how to use it effectively, just as they would with a big library. And it becomes frustratingly slow after 11am when all the Americans go on-line."

So the staff at John Cabot prefer to download Web pages onto the schools own Intranet. Then access times can be guaranteed, as can the quality of information and its freedom from pornography and other unsuitable material.

Students are encouraged to establish two-way links. When a group of year 10 students were doing a project on under-carriage control systems for their GCSE in Design and Technology, they probed engineers at British Aerospace for advice.

Source: Paul Bray, The Sunday Times 27 April 1997

Will computers replace teachers?

The fear is sometimes expressed that technology will make teachers redundant, and that pupils will lose the skills of social interaction as they become more and more isolated in their own little 'cyber-world'. Computer-aided learning packages have many advantages:

- Students can work at their own pace, repeating sections they don't understand;
- Computers are endlessly patient;
- The material is presented in a consistent way – you are not dependent on the skills of a particular teacher;
- Once the package is paid for, it can be cost-effective as fewer teachers are required.

At the same time, there are disadvantages in this method of learning. It can be very boring sitting in front of a computer screen, and a computer may not motivate students in the same way as a good teacher.

> ➤ **Discussion: Do you think that computers could replace teachers for at least part of the timetable? Would this be desirable from the point of view of the school administration, the teachers, and the pupils?**

Multimedia in schools

Multimedia is the combination of several elements such as text, graphics, animation, video and sound using a computer. To create or run multimedia software, a fairly powerful computer with a large memory, hard disk and a CD ROM drive is desirable. There are hundreds of CD ROMs available for every level of the National Curriculum, on virtually any topic from 'talking stories' for 6-year-olds, to The Complete Physics from BTC, which shows quality animations of solar eclipses and 'Algorithms and Data Structures' from Payne-Gallway Publishers for A Level Computing students. (Figure 5.1.)

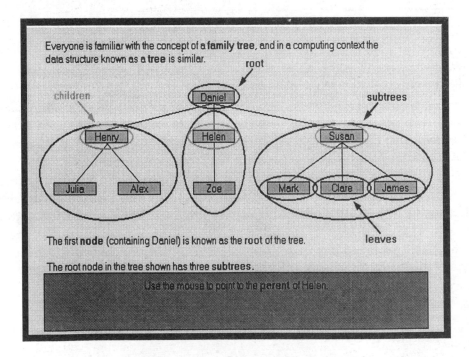

Figure 5.1: Interactive multimedia tutorial

Authoring software

To allow authors from school children to professionals to create multimedia software, *authoring software* is needed which allows text to be entered, graphics to be added and animated, photographs, video and sound files to be imported.

Internet-based services

The Internet provides many sites specifically for education, as well as being a source of more general information. Below is an advertisement for a BT home-learning service.

Figure 5.2: BT HomeCampus service

Exercises

1. The *Internet*, initially set up by the US Defence Department, now has many millions of users around the world. In the UK many schools and colleges have access to this web of computer networks.

   Describe **one** advantage and **one** disadvantage of allowing young people unrestricted access to the Internet. (2)

   AEB AS Computing Paper 1 Qu 8 1997

2. Describe briefly **five** ways in which information technology can aid pupils studying subjects **other** than computing or information technology. (5)

   New question

3. Give **three** advantages and **three** disadvantages of computer-aided learning packages compared with conventional classroom teaching. (6)

   New question

Chapter 6 – Role of Communication Systems

Introduction

The late 20th century has become known as the 'information age'. It would be impossible to conduct modern day businesses without the use of communication technologies such as the telephone, fax machine and computer communications networks. Communications and computer technology have become inextricably linked, resulting in *telecommunications*, the transmission of data of all kinds (text, graphics, sound and video) over a variety of different communication channels such as public telephone lines, private cables, microwave and satellite. In this chapter we'll look at some of the important developments in communications.

The Internet

The Internet is the largest wide area network in the world. In fact it is not a single network, but a collection of thousands of computer networks throughout the world. These linked networks are of two types:

- LAN (Local Area Network), covering an office block or University campus, for example;
- WAN (Wide Area Network) connecting computers over a wide geographical area, even over several countries.

All LANs and some WANs are owned by individual organisations. Some WANs act as **service providers**, and members of the public or businesses can join these networks for a monthly charge.

There is no central authority or governing body running the Internet; it started with an initial 4 computers in 1969 and grew over the next ten years to connect 200 computers in military and research establishments in the U.S. Today there are more than 4 million host computers, any of which could be holding the information you are looking for, and as many as 50 million people connected, any of whom could be future customers, friends or problem-solvers.

Figure 6.1: The opening screen of CompuServe, an Internet service provider

The World Wide Web

The Web is a collection of pages stored on computers throughout the world, and joined by *hypertext* links. A hypertext link enables you to click on a word or graphic, and be taken automatically to the related Web page. It is the fastest-growing part of the Internet, owing much of its popularity to Web-browsing software such as Netscape, which enables you to quickly find references to any particular topic.

On-line information services

Hundreds of companies such as CompuServe and BT now provide on-line information services, enabling subscribers to gain access to the latest news, share prices, weather and sport as well as providing services such as home banking or shopping, education and entertainment and access to thousands of on-line databases all over the world.

Electronic bulletin boards

Electronic bulletin boards are Internet sites for groups of people with similar interests to exchange information and discuss issues. Bulletin boards are used by thousands of different user groups from University 'Open Learning' providers and software manufacturers user groups to less savoury groups interested in terrorist activities or paedophilia.

Intranets

An Intranet is a company-wide network run along the lines of the World Wide Web, making it possible to share documents, databases and applications. Intranets have the potential to revolutionise the way that organisations share information internally, just as the Internet will revolutionise the way that businesses communicate with external suppliers, customers and consultants.

The software to implement Intranets is already available. The latest Microsoft Office suite will let you surf Word and Excel documents, reading them in a local Web site just as if they had been produced by a Web page designer.

Electronic mail (E-mail)

E-mail systems allow you to send memos, letters and files containing data of all types from your computer to any other computer with an e-mail address and a modem, simply by typing the recipient's name and pressing the 'Send' button.

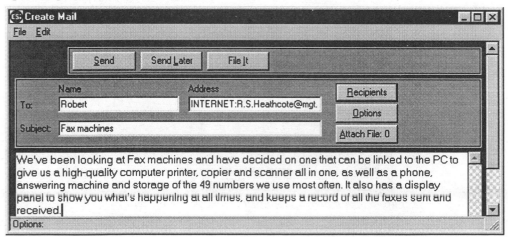

Figure 6.2: Creating an e-mail letter

E-mail has many advantages over both ordinary mail and the telephone. For example:

- A message can be sent anywhere in the world at the price of a local call, without having to leave your desk;
- The same message can be sent simultaneously to a group of people;
- The message will arrive in at most a few hours, and can be picked up the next time the recipient looks at their e-mail;
- It is very easy to send a reply to an e-mail as soon as it is received, using a 'Reply' button;
- Long files including video, sound and graphics can be sent automatically when the cheap rate starts after 6pm;
- Graphics and text can be electronically transmitted and placed in a document by the recipient. The BSA advertisement in Chapter 12, for example, was transmitted by the advertising agency via e-mail and imported straight into this manuscript using MS Word.

Case study: Monitoring employee e-mail

Monitoring employees e-mail is considered by many to be unethical and an invasion of privacy, but is considered legitimate by many companies who claim they need to know that their facilities are being used to further business goals. Some also argue that they need to be able to search electronic mail messages for evidence of illegal activities, racial discrimination or sexual harassment. Others argue that the company needs access to business information stored in e-mails, just as if it were stored in filing cabinets.

➢ **Discussion: Many companies have stated policies regarding e-mail. Do you think employees should be granted privacy, or should companies have the right to monitor e-mail?**

Telephones

It seems incredible that only a decade or so ago, mobile phones were almost unknown. Today they are invaluable for business people and anyone else who needs to send and receive phone calls from anywhere both in the UK and abroad.

Telephones and computers have begun to combine to produce sophisticated call handling and call management systems which can provide facilities such as those offered by BT's Callscape 100 phone:

- As each call comes in, information pops up on your PC screen – including the caller's number and name, for example.

Figure 6.3: A caller is identified before taking the call

- Automatic call logging provides a complete record of all incoming and outgoing calls, their date, time and duration.

- BT's Select Services such as Call Waiting or Three-way calling are easily accessed at a click of the mouse.

Facsimile transmission (Fax)

The popularity of fax machines has exploded over the past decade. They are now regarded as indispensable by even the smallest business and have played a large part in speeding up business transactions. A fax machine scans and digitises images (text or graphics) on a page and transmits them in analogue form over a telephone line to another fax machine, which then reproduces a copy of the image on a piece of paper.

Photo courtesy of BT (BT Products and Services Catalogue Summer 1997)

Figure 6.4: Fax machine from BT

Voice mail

Voice mail is a more sophisticated version of the telephone answering machine. A voice mail system can act as an automated switchboard so that when you dial a company number, you may hear a message along the lines of 'Hello – this is the Customer Service Department of XYZ. If you would like information on new services, press 1. If you have a query about your bill, press 2. For other information, press 3.'

A voice mail system also allows you to leave a recorded message for someone who is absent from the office. The recipient can then save it, delete it or forward it to someone else on another extension.

Teleconferencing

Teleconferencing allows people in different physical locations to exchange ideas and information interactively using either the telephone or e-mail. A more advanced form of teleconferencing is videoconferencing, which allows participants to see and hear one another. A videoconferencing system includes video cameras, special microphones, large television monitors and a computer with a special device called a *codec* that can convert analogue video images and sound waves into digital signals and compress them for transfer over digital telephone lines. (An ISDN – Integrated Services Digital Network – line with a high bandwidth is required to transmit video.) At the other end, another computer reconverts the digital signals to analogue for displaying on the receiving monitor. Such systems are familiar from television programmes in which people on the other side of the Atlantic are interviewed from a studio in London, for example.

Microcomputer-based desktop videoconferencing systems are also available, where users can see each other and simultaneously work on the same document.

Exercises

1. A multi-national company is considering the use of 'teleconferencing'.
    (a) What is meant by the term 'teleconferencing'. (3)
    (b) List the minimum facilities required to enable 'teleconferencing' to take place. (4)
    (c) Discuss **two** advantages and **two** disadvantages to the firm of using 'teleconferencing' as compared to traditional methods. (4)
    NEAB IT01 Qu 5 1997

2. A large company has introduced a communication system which includes electronic mail. This system will be used for both internal use within the company and for external links to other organisations.
    (a) Describe **two** features of an electronic mail system which may encourage its use for internal communication between colleagues. (2)
    (b) Contrast the use of an electronic mail system with each of fax and the telephone. (6)
    (c) Describe **two** functions the communication system might have, other than the creation and reception of messages. (4)
    NEAB IT01 Qu 7 1996

3. A computer manufacturing company has sales offices in a large number of cities. The management has decided to implement an in-house electronic mail system for the staff.
    (a) Identify **five** features which would be desirable for the users of the electronic mail system. (5)
    (b) Describe **three** tasks which would have to be performed by the manager of the electronic mail system. (6)
    (c) State **three** benefits of electronic mail and **one** drawback. (4)
    London Computing Paper 1 Qu 11 1997

4. The Internet is a vast international network of networks. A school library has a dedicated personal computer and communications link to allow students to access the Internet. Describe, in an essay, some of the information which students may wish to access on the Internet to help them with their studies. Explain advantages and disadvantages of students using the Internet compared with using CD-ROMs and books on the library shelves. (15)
    London Computing Paper 1 Qu 12 1997

Chapter 7 – The Internet in Business

Doing business on the Web

Almost no business can afford to ignore the Internet. It is fast becoming an essential business tool for everyday correspondence, marketing, customer feedback and customer support. For businesses from a small country hotel to the world's largest airline, the Web can act as a shop front where customers can browse 24 hours a day, 365 days a year.

The Internet Music and Video shop is one example of a company that does all its business over the Internet. Log on by typing in the address http://www/musicshop.co.uk and you will see the following screen:

Figure 7.1: The Internet Music and Video Shop opening screen

You can then click on **First Time Visitor's Guide** to register and leave your credit card details, or if you are a regular customer, browse through new releases or search for a particular title. Choose, for example, **New Releases** to bring up the next screen (Figure 7.2), click **Order** and your order details will be displayed on the screen. You'll receive an e-mail confirming your order the next day, and your CD should arrive within a few days.

Couldn't be simpler!

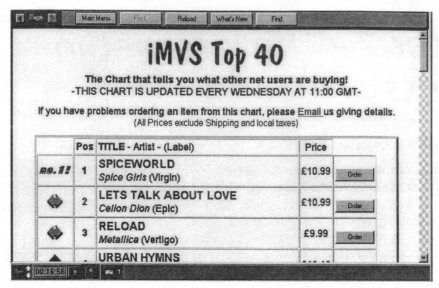

Figure 7.2: Ordering a CD

Advantages to business

For a business such as iMVS, this way of doing business has numerous advantages.

- There is a huge saving on overheads: no costly warehouse space, rent, heating or employee facilities;
- The 'virtual shop' can stock every one of the 16,000 or so CDs produced in the last year whereas a conventional store would stock only between 5-10,000;
- The Internet shop has arrangements for 'Just In Time' delivery from its suppliers, so does not get left with CDs which it cannot sell;
- It is a valuable market research tool – a list of customers' names and addresses, purchases, likes, dislikes and suggestions can be built up at absolutely no cost and used to improve the service provided.

Advantages to the customers

There are advantages to the customers, too. They can:

- Visit the music shop without having to leave home, at any hour of the day;
- Hear snatches of the song before deciding to buy;
- Shop without being jostled by crowds, having to listen to music that is not to their taste.

iMVS estimate that 6% of visitors to their site make a purchase, as opposed to only 1% who respond to a direct mail shot. 40% of their customers return to make further purchases.

The drawbacks

Inevitably, there are drawbacks to this new way of doing business. For one thing, there are worries about the security of giving a credit card number over the Internet. It is possible that hackers could retrieve thousands of credit card numbers and use them to order goods. Secondly, when companies post up information about new products and services, it is not only their customers who will visit the site – competitors will also be regular visitors, indulging in a little industrial espionage to make sure they don't get left behind.

Thirdly, because Internet sites can be accessed from all over the world, companies have to be aware of the laws regarding data protection in every country. Different countries have different laws regarding the holding and passing on of personal information about individuals.

Several companies have experienced problems with people who have set up web sites using their own company's trademark. They then demand large sums of money for the Web address.

Case study: British Petroleum

British Petroleum is taking legal action over a bogus Web site created by a motorist, John Bunt, who claims his vehicle was destroyed in a car wash at a BP service station in Exeter. The site (www.britishpetroleum.co.uk), with a home page identical to that on BP's own site (www.bp.com), offers links to a range of information detailing the vehicle damage and the action since taken, or not, by BP and the service station manager. While the manager says "Talk to BP" and BP says the matter is in the hands of its insurer, Commercial Union, Bunt has put the bogus site's domain name up for sale at £7,000 – and turned a drama into a crisis at one stroke. An expert on the registration of domain names is really put out by Bunt's action, and urges BP to sort out the renegade. "The site causes confusion and could be libellous." It might also win Bunt some attention for his claim.

Source: The Guardian 28 January 1998

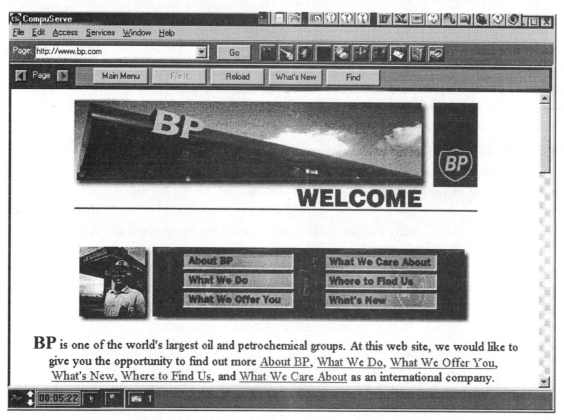

Figure 7.3: BP's Home Page – genuine or an impostor?

Business-to-Business

One of the major growth areas on the Internet is trading between businesses – for example distribution and delivery of manufactured goods. International carriers can make huge savings by taking orders over the Internet, and customers can not only make savings but also get on-line information about exactly where their goods are, and when they are delivered.

Finding new suppliers

The Internet is increasingly being used by businesses to find new suppliers of goods and services. Japan Airlines, for example, has used the Internet to post orders for in-flight materials such as plastic cups. On its Web site it advertises drawings and specifications (such as JAL's logo, which the cups must carry) in order to solicit business from any firm that comes across its site, rather than the usual Japanese suppliers.

Setting up a Web site

It doesn't take much to set up a Web site – a PC and a modem, and a subscription to a Service Provider of about £10 per month will typically include space of between 5-10Mb to use for your own personal site. Huge, complex sites on the other hand can cost up to £500 per month – but savings can be impressive. BA estimates that if they can sell just 1% of tickets over the Internet, it will save them around £6m a year.

> ➢ **Discussion: Imagine you have been asked to set up a Web site for a small publisher specialising in A Level textbooks. What features would you include on the Web site? Who would benefit from the Web site, and what would the benefits be?**

Exercises

1. 'Networked computer systems (e.g. Internet) will revolutionise the way we shop.' With the aid of specific examples, discuss this statement. Include in your discussion:

   - The types of organisation likely to advertise on such systems.
   - The capabilities and limitations of such systems for this activity.
   - The potential security risks for the customers in using such systems.
   - The organisational impact of such systems.
   - The social impact of such systems.

   (20)
   NEAB IT01 Qu 9 1997

2. Over the past few years, many companies have tried to sell their products over the Internet, but have failed. Give **three** possible reasons.
   (3)
   New question

3. A major bookshop uses the Internet for an on-line bookshop. Give **three** advantages to customers of using the Internet to shop for books, and **three** advantages to the bookshop.
   (6)
   New question

Chapter 8 – Knowledge, Information and Data

Input-process-output

The main purpose of using computers is to process data as quickly and efficiently as possible to produce useful information.

Computers read incoming data called **input**, process or operate on it and display or print information called **output**.

Examples of **input data** include:

- The mark achieved by candidate 1342 in A-level Information Technology Paper 1;
- The time at which Jane Rowe clocked in for work at McDonald's on Monday morning;
- The sale of a can of baked beans in a supermarket.

Examples of **information** that might be obtained from processing many items of similar data include:

- The percentage of candidates gaining 'A' grades in Information Technology in a particular year;
- The total number of hours worked last week by Jane Rowe;
- The total weekly cost of paying all employees;
- The total weekly value of goods sold in a supermarket;
- A list of items that need to be reordered.

Data and information

Data can be defined as the stream of raw facts representing events occurring in organisations before they have been organised and arranged into a form that people can understand and use.

Information is data that has been processed into a form that is useful. Information is needed in organisations for the day-to-day running of a business ("How many cans of baked beans do we need to order today?") and to support decision-making and control. Information systems may also help managers to analyse problems, create new products, and find the best solutions to questions such as whether or in which direction to expand.

Knowledge

Data and information are generally concerned with facts and figures. We all carry round a huge number of facts that enable us to function in our daily lives, but we also have a different kind of knowledge in the form of **rules**, or the likely effects of certain courses of action. For example:

- Students are likely to get a good grade in this course IF they attend regularly and IF they do all the homework set;

- A new restaurant is likely to succeed IF the food is good, the location is good and the price is reasonable;

- Double-clicking an icon in Windows will open an application.

'Knowledge workers' are generally people in professions such as engineering, medicine, management or teaching. Their specialised knowledge makes them experts in their field, able to create new products, provide services and make decisions, based on formal and informal facts and rules that they have learned through training or experience.

Many of these rules are based on probabilities, not certainties. Computers can be programmed with a 'knowledge' on particular subjects, consisting of facts, rules and probabilities, and then deliver advice to someone. These so-called 'expert systems' or 'knowledge-based systems', which store the knowledge of a human expert, are used in many areas such as medical diagnosis, oil exploration, the stock market and fault diagnosis of all kinds.

> ➤ **Discussion: A doctor could order various tests for a patient such as blood tests, X-rays and so on. From the results of the tests she would have *information* about the condition of the patient. What *knowledge* would she need to be able to make a diagnosis?**

Access to knowledge

An example of a 'knowledge base' is the McAfee HelpDesk Suite. This software uses an expert system with a knowledge base containing instant answers to over 25,000 questions commonly asked by users having trouble with their hardware or software. The user simply loads the software and uses the 'Knowledge Wizard' to type in the problem. The software may then ask a series of questions before coming up with a diagnosis of the problem. (Figure 8.1.)

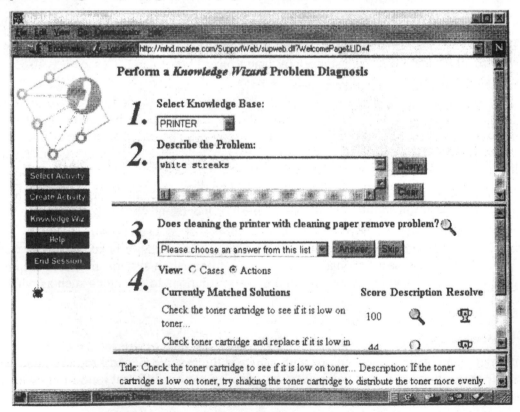

Figure 8.1: McAfee HelpDesk Suite 'Knowledge Wizard'

Case study: Collecting information

Will Havercroft spends his days touring Britain looking for attractive towns for new Waterstones bookshops.

In an age of sprawling out-of-town shopping centres and vast indoor malls, finding new retail space is not a problem but Waterstones does not want anonymous sites in Arndale Centres. Mr Haverstock scours the country looking for unusual locations, such as an old church in Reading and a former cinema in Swansea.

In the last six months he has visited 70 towns from Dunfermline to Torquay. "I have been to many lovely towns I had not been to before, like Kings Lynn, Rugby and Bury St Edmunds. I think about whether it is an attractive place to shop which people who live nearby will travel to. I look at what sort of food is on sale and whether there are nice markets and restaurants. I look out for nice jewellery shops, as they are often a good indicator of the type of town it is, and I size up the competition.

I'm looking, wherever possible, for architecturally interesting buildings, but they must be adaptable for retail use."

Source: The Guardian 2 January 1998

➢ **Discussion: Mr Haverstock is visiting towns and gathering data to help aid management decisions. What other ways could he get data? What *knowledge* does he have which makes his visits a worthwhile exercise? Could this knowledge be coded and entered into a computer? If no decision is made for a year, is the information he collected still useful?**

Sources of data

Data can be collected from many sources, either directly or indirectly. Data which is collected for a specific purpose is said to be collected **directly**. For example, the times at which an employee clocks in and out may be collected by punching a time card, and this data is used in the calculation of the weekly pay packet. Similarly, when a library book is borrowed, data about the book and the borrower is collected by scanning the bar codes of the book and the borrower's library card. This data is used directly to produce information on where a particular book is.

On the other hand, information can be derived from data which was originally collected for a completely different purpose – in other words, collected **indirectly**. For example a credit card company collects data about each transaction or purchase made so that the customer can be billed at the end of the month. This is the **direct** collection of data. At a later date, the data may be used to build a profile of the customer – perhaps they often use their credit cards for holiday travel, for example. The company could sell a list of all such customers to a travel company who would use it in a direct mail advertising campaign. This is the **indirect** collection of data – use of the data for a purpose other than the one for which it was originally collected.

➢ **Discussion: Think of several examples of data which is originally collected for one purpose, and then used for additional purposes.**

Encoding information as data

Precision may be lost when attempts are made to encode information as data. Although it seems desirable in some ways to hold as much information about people or things as possible there are problems in doing so, not only because it is difficult to maintain accuracy but for other reasons, as the following case study illustrates.

Case study: 'Nightmare' scheme to track every pupil

Government proposals are afoot for a national computer record of the educational attainment of every child. Ministers plan to provide every child with a 13-digit identity number which would be used to track progress from the start of primary school through to University.

The Department for Education and Employment would control a central database with information on every pupil's social, economic and ethnic background as well as academic results and special educational needs.

A child's records would start with the score achieved in the proposed 'baseline' test at age 5, measuring elementary verbal and social skills. It would take in results of national assessment tests at 7, 11 and 14, GCSEs, A levels and vocational qualifications.

The file would also include more personal information such as a behaviour record, eligibility for free school meals and whether English was the child's native language.

But the Office of the Data Protection Registrar said the creation of a central databank about individual pupils raised 'nightmare' possibilities of abuse if it was not accompanied by adequate controls on access.

"There would have to be clear rules on access because this would set up a source of information that would be very attractive to somebody who might wish to find a particular child – for example a parent denied access because of violence."

The database on the other hand could reduce form-filling in schools by stopping repeated collection of the same data, and would provide the basis for much useful analysis.

Source: The Guardian 1 January 1998

➢ **Discussion: How could data about a pupil's behaviour be recorded? Who would decide what to encode? Would it be on a scale of 1 to 10?**

➢ **Are there any difficulties in recording a pupil's eligibility for free school meals?**

➢ **What are the benefits and dangers of this proposal to (a) the individual (b) society as a whole?**

Quality of data

To be useful, data must be:

- Accurate;
- Up-to-date;
- Complete.

This is often hard to achieve. Encoding the information from a doctor's notes, for example, could lead to the coarsening of the precision and context of the data, just as the encoding of a pupil's behaviour in the case study above is not likely to give a complete or accurate picture in all cases.

There may be huge costs involved in keeping data up-to-date. Here are a couple of examples:

- An insurance agent may compile a list of which particular insurance company is most competitive for each of hundreds of different types of policy. But insurance companies change their rates all the time; in a few weeks, the research may have to be repeated.

- A company which markets the names and addresses of particular types of organisation, such as educational establishments or firms making agricultural equipment, may spend months gathering the information. But how can they be sure it is up-to-date? Colleges change their names, firms move or go bust and new ones start up. It is useful to **'date stamp'** each item of information, by recording the date that the information was last updated. Then at least someone can check each entry over a certain age.

Exercises

1. Travelling sales representatives working in the U.K. can make extensive use of company credit cards to pay for goods and services. A company credit card is one that is issued by a company to its representative. All charges and information relating to each transaction are sent directly to the company

   (a) List **four** items of data which are captured each time the card is used. (4)

   (b) Other than payment information, suggest **one** other potential use for information which can be derived from this data. (2)

   NEAB IT01 Qu 2 1997

2. (a) Describe briefly what is meant by *data*, *information* and *knowledge*, giving examples of each. (6)

   (b) Describe briefly **three** ways in which data can be or become of 'poor quality'. (3)

   New question

3. What is meant by *direct* and *indirect* sources of data? Give an example of each, and describe the purposes for which the data is used in each case. (4)

   New question

4. Look at Figures 8.2 and 8.3 below. The first is an advertisement for a 'Chief Knowledge Officer' and the second is for an 'Information Analyst'.

   (a) Describe the differences between these two jobs. (4)

   (b) What are the similarities and differences in the desired qualities and abilities of prospective candidates? (4)

   New question

Public Health Genetics Unit

The Public Health Genetics Unit was newly established in 1997 to provide an NHS lead in the policy implications of development in molecular and clinical genetics and in their ethical, legal, social and public health implications. The Unit provides a link between academic research, clinical practice and the development of policy within the NHS for genetics and genetic services. We are now looking to establish a post for a:

Chief Knowledge Officer

Fixed term contract for 4 years

£23,000 - £28,000 per annum,
depending on qualifications and experience

and wish to appoint an enthusiastic and motivated graduate, whose key task will be to keep abreast of issues in genetics and to disseminate matters of interest and importance to policy makers. You will also play a key role in the development of educational materials and will take the lead in the establishment and maintenance of an electronic communications network.

You will naturally be an effective communicator, both orally and in writing, and will have proven skills in the critical appraisal of published literature. In this respect, you are most likely to have expertise in journalism, communications or editorial work. A degree in genetics, molecular or cell biology or a related subject is essential as are skills in computing and the use of the Internet. You will also have the ability to work independently and as part of a team. Formal training in writing or journalism is desirable as is a knowledge of social and ethical issues.

To apply for an information pack, please contact D...
CHHA Personnel Department, Hillview, Fulbourn Hospital, Cambridge

The closing date for receipt of applications is 16 February 1998.

AS AN EMPLOYER COMMITTED TO EQUAL OPPORTUNITIES WE WELCOME JOB SHARERS

Cambridge & Huntingdon
HEALTH AUTHORITY

Figure 8.2: Knowledge in demand

Information Management and Technology

Information Analyst

A&C Grade 5/6
£13,580 - £19,328 plus £194 Fringe London Weighting Allowance p.a.
37 hours per week

The Princess Alexandra Hospital is a progressive NHS Trust. The hospital is situated centrally in Harlow Town. The town offers a wealth of leisure facilities and is surrounded by beautiful Essex countryside. Cambridge, London and Stansted Airport are easily accessed via the M11.

We are currently seeking an Information Analyst to join our friendly team.

Duties will include:

♦ provide information for monitoring, planning and management
♦ support Theatre and A&E Systems and develop systems for monitoring the data contained.
♦ carry out statistical analyses and provide statistical support to managers and clinicians.
♦ work with managers to determine their information needs.

The successful candidate will:

♦ be a graduate in a numerate discipline.
♦ have knowledge of Microsoft applications.
♦ have a high level of numeracy, analytical and problem solving skills.
♦ have good interpersonal and organisational skills.
♦ have an interest in measuring effectiveness of healthcare.

For an application form and job description, please contact Recruitment Services, York House, Herts & Essex Hospital, Haymeads Lane, Bishop's Stortford, Herts CM23 5JH.

Please quote ref: AC-40-203.

Closing date for receipt of completed applications: 4 February 1998.

Interviews will take place 17 February 1998.

Working Towards Equal Opportunities

We operate a No smoking policy.

Figure 8.3:Advertisement for an information analyst

Chapter 9 – Information as a Commodity

The importance of information

Almost overnight, it seems, success in almost any field has become impossible without information technology. In manufacturing, health care, education, policing, retailing, banking, farming and thousands of other fields, information is as valuable a resource as capital or people. Information is gathered about market trends, buying preferences, customer profiles; computers analyse, summarise and present this data to managers who use it as the basis for decision-making.

Accessible, accurate and up-to-date information can help to ensure that decisions of all kinds are likely to be correct, from how many thousands of a particular toy to manufacture in time for Christmas, to whether or not to open a new factory.

Case study

A million Teletubby toys were manufactured for Christmas in 1997. The manufacturers got it wrong; a million would have been enough if only children wanted them, but adults (including large numbers of students, and people buying them as collectors' items) bought them as well, and three million toys were needed to satisfy demand.

In 1996 shortages of Buzz Lightyear cost Disney and Mattell £300 million in lost sales.

➢ **Describe some items of information that would help a manufacturer to accurately predict sales of a particular toy at Christmas time.**

Collecting and analysing data

Data can be collected for a specific purpose, or it may be collected for one purpose and then used for some other purpose. If it is personal data, then care would have to be taken not to contravene the Data Protection Act ('Data must not be used for any reason incompatible with its original purpose').

Tesco's, for example, collects huge amounts of data on customer buying patterns through its Loyalty card. This massive amount of data can be analysed in thousands of different ways to help predict likely sales, or to suggest new marketing ploys. For example, a probably apocryphal tale is told of how a computer analysis of sales data showed that large numbers of disposable nappies were bought by men in their 20s and 30s on Friday evenings. This led the astute manager to position cans of beer in the same area of the store as nappies, on the basis that most men would pop a few cans in their shopping trolley as they were passing. Sales of beer rocketed!

➢ **Discussion: In the example discussed above, sales data is collected directly for the purposes of printing an itemised bill and keeping track of sales and stock levels. The data is used indirectly to target particular customers.**

Think of other examples where data is collected for one purpose initially and then used for a different purpose.

Information as a commodity

Have you ever wondered why YOU in particular, or your family, are targetted for particular mail advertisements? Every time you make a credit card purchase, enter a competition or order goods by phone or mail, information about who you are and the products you bought goes onto a database. This information can then be used to direct advertising to the people who are most likely to be interested in particular products.

Usefulness of data

Data is of poor 'quality' if it is out-of-date, inaccurate or incomplete. Companies who sell their products through direct mail, for example, need up-to-date lists of names and addresses of people who are likely to be interested in their product, and such lists are enormously valuable to them. But unless the list is kept up-to-date, it soon ceases to be of much value. People move away, grow old, die, or change their interests or purchasing habits.

Charities, for example, may sell their mailing lists to other charities, thus raising extra funds for themselves. Without knowing who on the list are regular donors and who is simply a 'one-off' donor of several years ago, the list is probably not very useful. The information can be 'date-stamped' by including for each person not only their address but the date of their last donation.

Coding value judgements

What is a value judgement? The answer is, any description such as 'tall', 'dark', 'handsome', 'green-eyed', 'old'. If you have ever filled in a questionnaire on which you were asked to tick a box rating something from 'Poor' to 'Excellent' you will know how difficult this is.

> ➢ **Fill in the following questionnaire:**

1. *The library facilities at school/college are:*
    Excellent ☐   Good ☐   Fair ☐   Poor ☐

2. *The computing facilities are:*
    Excellent ☐   Good ☐   Fair ☐   Poor ☐

3. *The amount of homework set on this course is:*
    Far too much ☐   A bit too much ☐   About right ☐   Too little ☐

4. *The course is:*
    Very interesting ☐   Quite interesting ☐   Quite dull ☐   Very dull ☐

> ➢ **Discussion: Summarise the responses gathered from the class. Analyse the data and present a summary report.**
>
> **Notice how difficult it is to code such value judgements. To get a more accurate and complete picture, comments, exceptions or reasons need to be included, but these are very difficult to encode and analyse.**

The benefits of I.T.

Information technology systems have become indispensable in many businesses today. The benefits include:

- **Speed of processing.** Modern banking systems, for example, could not function without information technology. An MICR reader can sort and process over 2,400 cheques per minute.

- **Vast storage capacity.** Hundreds of thousands of transactions can be stored on disk for processing and analysing in organisations such as banks, building societies, government departments, hospitals and retail stores.

- **Ability to search and combine data in many different ways.** Retail stores can analyse purchases to identify trends and preferences. The police computers can analyse thousands of different pieces of information to help catch criminals.

- **Instant response.** Real-time systems such as airline reservation systems can give an instant response to a query about seat availability, and update their information as soon as a booking is made.

- **Accurate results.** A computer can calculate the company payroll or the electricity bills for thousands of people with 100% accuracy every time.

- **Communication.** Electronic mail can be used to keep people in different branches of an organisation in touch. Data and information can be sent from one branch to another.

- **Improved company image.** A company can use word processors, desktop publishing and presentation graphics to enhance its image.

Drawbacks of information technology

New systems nearly always have some drawbacks. These could include:

- Job losses among employees;

- New or redesigned accommodation needed for the new setup;

- Faults in the software may mean the new system does not work as planned, which may lead to chaos, loss of customers and low employee morale;

- Inadequate hardware may lead to bottlenecks in the flow of data around an organisation.

Exercises

1. With the aid of an example, describe **one** problem which may arise when coding a value judgement.

(2)
NEAB IT01 Qu 2 1996

2. A college maintains an extensive database of its full-time students. The database contains personal data, the courses students attend, and higher education or employment applications.
   (a) Describe how the college might keep the personal data of the students up to date. (3)
   (b) The college wishes to sell the personal data to a local sports retailer. An agreement is to be written between the college and the retailer. Describe **three** issues, relating to the data, that should be included in the agreement.
(3)
NEAB IT01 Qu 4 1997

3. A telephone company collects the telephone numbers of people who receive calls through a 'Friends and Family' scheme. Under this scheme, subscribers receive discounts on phone calls to numbers they dial most frequently. The customer has to inform the telephone company which numbers are to be included on their 'Friends and Family' list.
   (a) Describe briefly **one** way in which the telephone company could use this data to their advantage.
(2)
   (b) How can the telephone company keep their data up-to-date and accurate? (2)
New question

Chapter 10 – The Professional in I.T.

Careers in I.T.

Are you planning a career in Information Technology or Computing? If so, you will be able to choose from any of over 200 different Information Systems roles, according to the British Computer Society (BCS). Scan any of the quality daily or Sunday newspapers and you will get some idea of the number and types of posts available.

Software Installation and Support Engineer

AutoRite develops and distributes software for use in television newsrooms and studios across the world.
We need a young, enthusiastic science or engineering graduate to join our existing technical team. The post will include installing software at sites around the world, providing support for existing clients and assisting with the testing and documentation of software currently under development.
You will need a good knowledge of Novell, Windows and DOS, and some experience with PC hardware. Previous exposure to the television environment is desirable but not essential. More important is the ability to use your own initiative, to be able to cope under pressure, and to be flexible. You must be willing to travel, sometimes long

responsibility must be taken for ensuring consistency of data. To fulfil these requirements a keen and conscientious approach to detail is essential, to ensure

INFORMIX DATABASE ADMINISTRATOR
You will be responsible for the routine administration, tuning and upkeep of the entire Informix database as well as working closely with the development team.

BMS
Computer Operations Supervisor

Based within a department providing computer systems in a network environment, the postholder will take responsibility for the maintenance of the network and the installation of hardware and software.
The successful candidate will have at least two years' proven experience in a PC and network environment, with a good all-round understanding of databases, word processing and spreadsheets. Ideally with formal computer qualifications, s/he will additionally have well-developed interpersonal and negotiation skills with a customer-focused, flexible approach.

Requirements include an ability to communicate well with a wide range of people, good organisational skills and a thorough knowledge of Microsoft

MicroTec
POST-SALES SUPPORT CONSULTANT
Package up to £22k

MicroTec, based in Bristol, is the market leader in the supply of Management Information Systems to Colleges and Universities.
We are looking for a post-sales support consultant to join our successful team which provides application and technical support to our customers. The ideal person will have a background in either Higher or Further Education administration procedures along with excellent communication skills and a real desire to provide a first class service

Figure 10.1: Careers in I.T.

Personal qualities for I.T. professionals

To rise to the top as an I.T. professional, you will need more than technical knowledge and the right qualifications. A browse through a single day's advertisements for jobs in I.T. will soon throw up commonly required characteristics in prospective employees. Look at the extracts shown in Figure 10.1 and see what you can pick out.

- **Communication skills.** Many jobs such as those of a technical support engineer or systems analyst involve working with non-technical end-users. The ability to listen carefully and understand a user's problem or requirements is one of the most important skills required for a systems analyst. You have to act as a liaison between non-technical users and managers on one hand, and technical people on the other. You must be sensitive to the concerns of managers, programmers, end-users and employees. You must also be able to communicate the information and proposals in clear English in written reports, and give oral presentations when required.

- **Ability to take the initiative.** This is one of the most highly-rated skills for I.T. professionals, according to a recent survey (see case study below).

- **Management skills.** Project leaders, systems analysts, network administrators or database administrators, among others, need to be able to manage schedules, resources and people. They also need to be able to motivate the people working for them and may need to manage change within an organisation.

- **Design skills.** A systems analyst, for example, requires creative and critical thinking as well as the technical knowledge to design new systems.

- **Problem-solving abilities.** Anyone involved with user support, after-sales service or programming will need well-developed problem-solving abilities.

Case study: How to succeed in business

In 1996 DDI, a human resource consultancy, carried out a survey of 218 UK knowledge workers – professionals whose work is PC-based – to identify the skills essential for success. The sample included software developers, technicians, engineers and scientists. The study found that networking, self-management and organisational diplomacy are all seen as necessary skills for star performers.

The study found that managers were much more likely to rate staff highly if they 'take the initiative'. This is defined as being capable of taking risks or being willing to go beyond the call of duty.

Low achievers had a poorer understanding than high flyers of what 'taking the initiative' meant. They were more likely to rate presentation skills and understanding how the company works as crucial. High performers thought these skills important, but not essential.

According to Bridget Blow, a finalist in the 1997 Businesswoman of the Year award: "The really hot people are those who are not just good technically, but also have good interpersonal skills." Help desk staff, for example, have to be good interpersonally as well as having technical knowledge. After all, says, Blow, if you have to cope with a call from the Chief Executive, you had better have the skills to help them.

"Chief executives are usually very busy. If they are calling the help desk, they are probably not having a very good day. The last thing they want is someone who does not understand."

➤ **Discussion: What is meant by 'networking' in the first paragraph above?**

➤ **Give some examples of how**

    (a) **YOU can be taking the initiative in order to achieve top grades at A Level.**

    (b) **a professional on a help desk answering user's enquiries within an organisation could take the initiative.**

The role of professional bodies

All professions have professional bodies which aim to promote professional development and the maintenance of standards within the profession. The leading professional body for I.T. professionals in

Britain is the BCS, and in the US, the Association for Computing Machinery (ACM). Membership of these bodies is usually achieved by examination.

The BCS organises talks all round the country on various aspects of computing which any member of the public is generally allowed to attend, whether or not they are members. You may possibly see an advertisement for such a talk in a local College or University, and you should consider attending since the talks are generally very interesting and given by experienced professionals.

The Industry Structure Model

The BCS has produced a comprehensive set of standards for the training and development of all those working in information systems and related fields. This is called the **Industry Structure Model** and it defines over 200 functions in information systems – including programmers, software engineers, network specialists and managers – at 10 levels of responsibility and technical expertise.

The model can be used to:

- compose customised job descriptions from standardised roles/tasks;
- assess the competence of Information Systems staff;
- establish training needs for individuals and organisations;
- provide training to recognised standards;
- plot career and development paths;
- establish staffing and recruitment needs;
- identify skills shortages.

The Industry Structure Model is delivered as standard PC Windows software.

> ➤ **Task: Get more information on the BCS Industry Structure Model from the Internet, using the Web address www.bcs.org.uk.**

Exercises

1. Professional progression within the I.T. industry requires more than just technical skills. Give **three** other necessary qualities and explain why they are important. (6)

    NEAB IT01 Qu 6 1997

2. A professional organisation for Information Technology practitioners has developed what is referred to as the 'Industry Structure Model'. What is the purpose of this model and how does it work? (6)

    NEAB IT01 Qu 5 1996

3. Describe briefly, giving examples, **three** functions of a professional body such as the British Computer Society. (6)

    New question

Chapter 11 – Codes of Practice

Ethics and computing

Ethics is the science of morals; the study of ethics is the study of how to make choices between right and wrong. Why should we care about ethics? The number of ethical decisions of one kind or another that we face in our personal and professional lives makes it imperative that we care. Some unethical decisions may be illegal; others may have drastic consequences for our lives or careers. Therefore, each of us must care about ethics as a matter of self-interest. In addition, we are all members of society, and ethical decision-making is vital to creating the sort of world in which we want to live.

> ➢ **Discussion: Is 'computer ethics' any different from other kinds of ethics? Is there a difference between**
>
> – **browsing through files on someone's PC, and rummaging through their locker?**
>
> – **sending obscene messages over a computer network, and writing anonymous obscene notes on paper to someone?**
>
> – **using unlicensed software and travelling on a train without paying?**

Factors in ethical decision-making

Ethical decisions, whether or not they involve information technology, are rarely straightforward. There is often not a straight choice between right and wrong – rather, the choice lies between the lesser of two evils. Of course, it is wrong to lie, cheat or steal – but is it wrong to steal food if your child is starving, lie to a friend about how good they look, give a fellow student a helping hand by writing most of his program or essay for him? A poor decision can have a number of undesirable consequences. People may be left hurt or offended, employee morale may be adversely affected, customers may be lost, a company may go bankrupt.

Sometimes the law prescribes whether a certain action is legal. Often an ethical principle is the basis of the Law; for example, the recognition that an individual has the right to ownership of an original work has led to copyright laws being enacted. In other cases, the law does not provide an answer and it is then useful to have a set of guidelines for how to act.

Formal guidelines in the computing industry

When a person accepts employment in any company, he or she accepts moral responsibilities that define appropriate behaviour in that job – responsibilities referred to as professional ethics. Two factors apply to all professionals and influence their actions: professional relationships and professional efficacy ('doing a good job'). Most professions have ethical codes or standards that explain appropriate professional behaviour and efficacious behaviour in various situations, and the computing profession is no exception. Various professional bodies such as the British Computer Society (BCS) and the Association for Computing Machinery (ACM) produce their own Code of Ethics and Professional Conduct. (You can look up the BCS Code of Conduct on the Internet, using the web address www.bcs.org.uk, and then searching for Code of Conduct using the index, or the ACM code of ethics on www.cs.orst.edu/~cook/acm.html .)

The ACM Code of Conduct is shown below:

ACM Code of Ethics

ACM* Code of Ethics and Professional Conduct

1. GENERAL MORAL IMPERATIVES
As an ACM member I will ..

1.1	Contribute to society and human well-being
1.2	Avoid harm to others
1.3	Be honest and trustworthy
1.4	Be fair and take action not to discriminate
1.5	Honour property rights including copyrights and patents
1.6	Give proper credit for intellectual property
1.7	Respect the privacy of others
1.8	Honour confidentiality

2. MORE SPECIFIC PROFESSIONAL RESPONSIBILITIES
As an ACM computing professional I will ..

2.1	Strive to achieve the highest quality, effectiveness and dignity in both the process and products of professional work
2.2	Acquire and maintain professional competence
2.3	Know and respect existing laws pertaining to professional work
2.4	Accept and provide appropriate professional review
2.5	Give comprehensive and thorough evaluations of computer systems and their impacts, including analysis of possible risks
2.6	Honour contracts, agreements, and assigned responsibilities
2.7	Improve public understanding of computing and its consequences
2.8	Access computing and communication resources only when authorised to do so

3. ORGANIZATION LEADERSHIP IMPERATIVES
As an ACM member and an organisational leader I will ..

3.1	Articulate social responsibilities of members of an organisational unit and encourage full acceptance of those responsibilities
3.2	Manage personnel and resources to design and build information systems that enhance the quality of working life
3.3	Acknowledge and support proper and authorised uses of an organisation's computing and communications resources
3.4	Ensure that users and those who will be affected by a system have their needs clearly articulated during the assessment and design of requirements. Later the system must be validated to meet user requirements.
3.5	Articulate and support policies that protect the dignity of users and others affected by a computing system
3.6	Create opportunities for members of the organisation to learn the principles and limitations of computer systems

4. COMPLIANCE WITH THE CODE
As an ACM member I will ..

4.1	Uphold and promote the principles of this Code
4.2	Treat violations of this Code as inconsistent with membership of the ACM

Figure 11.1: The ACM Code of Ethics and Professional Conduct

Codes of practice

The ACM code of Ethics and Professional Conduct above lays out a general code of practice for I.T. professionals. Here is a summary of some of the main points:

1. **Contribute to society and human well-being.** Share your expert knowledge freely with others, and be prepared to help colleagues and others when needed.

2. **Avoid harm to others.** This could include passing on a virus through carelessness or not following company procedures.

3. **Be honest and trustworthy.**

4. **Honour property rights including copyrights and patents.**

5. **Give proper credit for intellectual property.** Do not try and pass off another person's work as your own.

6. **Respect the privacy of others.** For example, if you have authorised access to confidential files of information, do not 'gossip' about this information, or pass on other people's personal information. Do not read other people's e-mail.

Using informal guidelines to make ethical decisions

Informal guidelines can be useful in reaching an ethical decision. Here are some long-standing, broad-based ethical principles to help decide between conflicting demands:

- **The Golden Rule.** Do unto others as you would have them do unto you. Think about the effects of your actions, and put yourself in the position of someone who would be affected.

- **The Greatest Good/Least Harm.** When choosing between courses of action, choose the one which achieves the greatest good for the greatest number of people, and causes the least harm.

- **Kant's Categorical Imperative.** If the action is not right for everyone to take, then it's not right for anyone to take. Think about what would happen if everyone acted as you propose to do.

- **The Slippery Slope Rule.** Actions that bring about a small, acceptable change but that, if taken repeatedly, would lead to unacceptable changes, should not be taken in the first place.

Case study 1

Staff working for a large company called Cyber Electronics frequently complain of various faults on their PCs. Printers that fail to print, software that won't load, files going missing and dollar signs appearing instead of pound signs are among countless faults commonly reported.

Until recently Ben, the software support analyst, was difficult to track down as he was always roaming from room to room, building to building, fixing problems of one sort or another. Recently, however, the company has invested in a software package called ScreenScape which enables the computer support staff to view anyone's screen from their own PC. Ben is now able to spend almost all of his time at his desk, taking calls from users, calling up their screens and advising the user what to do or fixing the problem himself. Users are delighted with the improved service.

One day he happens to mention the improvement to a Senior Manager in the Accounts Department, who is instantly interested. He asks "You mean you can see exactly what any member of staff is doing on his PC at any time?" "That's right", replies Ben. "Well, I'd like a copy of that software installed on my PC. Can you fix that for me? I have a suspicion that one of my staff is involved in something illegal which could be potentially disastrous for this company, but I've never been able to catch her at it. This could be very useful."

Ben is taken aback. "I'm not sure I can do that. I'll have to let you know."

> ➤ **What is the ethical dilemma facing Ben? Should he supply the software to the Senior Manager? What are the conflicting issues here?**

Case study 2

Programs which can read and sift 10 CVs in less than a minute and a half are increasingly replacing humans as the first screening stage in the recruitment process, particularly for big companies which receive hundreds of CVs each week. If you've recently applied for a job with Cable and Wireless, Mercury, ICL or Sainsbury's, chances are it was a computer which determined whether you advanced to the next round in the job hunt.

The simplest programs work by searching for key words, so if the job requires knowledge of a particular software package, the computer will pick out applications which mention this word.

> ➤ **What are the advantages and disadvantages to the employer, and the prospective employee, of using a computer to sift applications? Do you think this is an ethical procedure? Justify your answer.**

Case study 3

Times are bad at B.G. Computer Consultants, with some employees facing redundancy and others who have already been made redundant. Only last week Tom was given 15 minutes to clear his desk before being escorted from the building and his User ID and password removed from the company network. Helen and Ian are fairly confident, however, that their jobs as systems analysts are secure, since they are both working on large contracts. Ian in fact is on the verge of taking out a huge mortgage on a new house. He has often told Helen that if the company ever 'did the dirty on him' as he put it, he would get his own back in no uncertain terms.

One day Helen is working on a presentation. The figures she needs are in a file on the boss's computer, and he is out to lunch. She happens to know his password (unbeknownst to him) and decides to look for the file. Purely accidentally she comes across a memo indicating that Ian is to be made redundant as soon as the contract is completed.

> ➤ **Should Helen warn Ian about his forthcoming redundancy before he commits himself to a mortgage that he won't be able to afford? Who benefits? Who is harmed?**

> ➤ **What changes to company policies are needed to prevent such a situation arising in the future?**

Exercises

1. Use the Internet to look up the British Computer Society's Code of Practice. Describe briefly **four** general areas that you would expect such a Code of Practice to cover. (8)

    New question

2. Describe briefly a situation within an Information Technology environment which could pose a moral or ethical dilemma. Describe briefly **three** informal rules which could help in reaching an ethical decision in how to deal with the situation. (5)

    New question

Chapter 12 – Computer Crime and the Law

Computer crime and abuse

New technologies generally create new opportunities for crime; as soon as one avenue is blocked to the criminal, another one is discovered. As information technology has spread, so too have computer crime and abuse. The Internet, for example, is used not only by innocent members of the public but also by fraudulent traders, paedophiles, software pirates, hackers and terrorists. Their activities include planting computer viruses, software bootlegging, storing pornographic images and perpetrating all sorts of criminal activities from credit card fraud to the most complex multinational money laundering schemes. **Computer abuse** refers to acts that are legal but unethical.

Hacking

Hacking is defined as unauthorised access to data held on a computer system. The extent of hacking is extremely difficult to establish as it is usually only discovered by accident, with only about two percent of security breaches discovered as a result of positive action on the part of security staff. (*Digital Crime* by Neil Barrett, page 40.)

Hacking is often perpetrated by employees of a company who have acquired inside knowledge of particular user IDs and passwords. The ability of such hackers to carry out illegal actions without being detected is often hampered by the audit and monitor software that all computer operating systems supply.

The motive behind hacking can often be mischievous rather than anything more sinister: computing students who are learning about operating systems may take delight in penetrating a University's security system to prove that it can be done, or to gain access to exam questions and answers. The popular image of the hacker as a young, intelligent but perhaps socially inept male is in fact largely accurate.

In November 1997 Matthew Bevan, a 23 year-old programmer obsessed with the X-Files and the search for alien spacecraft, and Pryce, his teenage accomplice, walked free after a 3 year-long case against them collapsed. They had penetrated US Air Force computers, partly motivated by a belief that a captured alien spacecraft was being held secretly at a remote Nevada airbase. They were traced not by infowar techniques but by traditional police methods, when Pryce boasted to an undercover informant of his activities on an Internet chat line and gave him his London phone number. They were charged with three offences under the Computer Misuse Act 1990, but eventually it was decided that they in fact presented no threat to national security and the case was dropped. (Pryce scraped a D in 'A' Level Computing.)

Theft of money

Not all hackers are motivated purely by fascination with technology and the desire to show how clever they are. In a recent case, police in San Diego claimed to have cracked an informal ring of about 1,000 hackers that had obtained credit information from computers at one of the nation's three major credit bureaus, and made fraudulent credit card purchases that may have totalled millions of dollars. In Britain, Roger Cook on the Cook Report on November 18th 1997 showed how easy it is to use special hardware to transfer the details from the magnetic strip on one card to that of another. Other methods of using credit cards fraudulently include stealing them (either from the owner, or in the post before they reach the owner) or getting details from a credit card receipt and using these details to order goods over the phone or Internet.

Theft of data

Data can be stolen by illegally accessing it, or by stealing the computer on which the data is stored. In December 1990 Wing Commander Farquhar's notebook computer was stolen from his car when he left it unattended for a few minutes. It contained the preliminary Allied invasion plan for the impending Gulf war, and could have had potentially disastrous consequences.

Fraud on the Internet

The most common form of fraud on the Internet takes place between traders that appear to be legitimate and innocent purchasers of goods that are offered for sale. A trader could for example represent himself as a particular organisation (say, Selfridges) but in fact be entirely unconnected. They could then take orders and payment for goods and not deliver them.

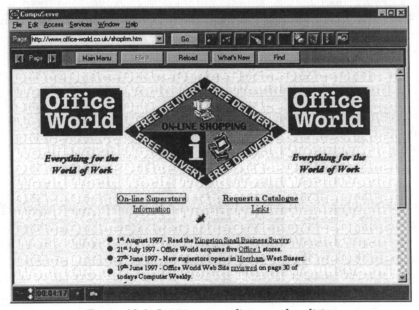

Figure 12.1: Legitimate on-line merchandising

Another type of trade involves the purchase of software, which the buyer provides payment for and then expects to be able to download. The fraudulent trader can take the money and then develop a persistent 'fault' which means that the software arrives scrambled or is not transmitted at all.

Viruses

Viruses are generally developed with a definite intention to cause damage to computer files or, at the very least, cause inconvenience and annoyance to computer users. The first virus appeared at the University of Delaware in 1987, and since then the number of viruses has escalated to over 9000 different variations in 1997. The virus usually occupies the first few instructions of a particular program on an 'infected' disk and relies on a user choosing to execute that program. When an infected program is executed, the virus is the first series of instructions to be performed. In most cases the virus's first action is to copy itself from the diskette onto the PC and 'hide' within obscure files, the operating system code or within unused disk blocks which are then marked as being 'bad' and unavailable for reuse. The virus can then proceed to perform any of a number tasks ranging from the irritating to the catastrophic such as reformatting the hard disk.

Some viruses lie dormant, waiting to be triggered by a particular event or date – the 'Friday 13th' virus being a well-known one. The virus then infects other diskettes, perhaps by modifying operating system programs responsible for copying programs. From there, the next PC to use the diskette will be infected.

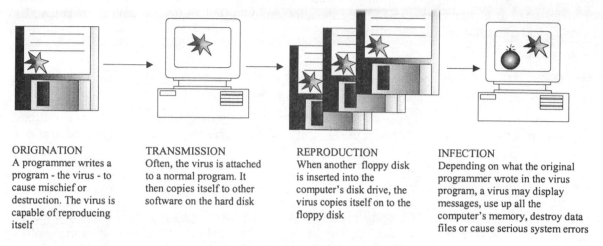

ORIGINATION
A programmer writes a program - the virus - to cause mischief or destruction. The virus is capable of reproducing itself

TRANSMISSION
Often, the virus is attached to a normal program. It then copies itself to other software on the hard disk

REPRODUCTION
When another floppy disk is inserted into the computer's disk drive, the virus copies itself on to the floppy disk

INFECTION
Depending on what the original programmer wrote in the virus program, a virus may display messages, use up all the computer's memory, destroy data files or cause serious system errors

Figure 12.2: How a virus works

'Logic bombs'

A 'logic bomb' is similar to a virus and is sometimes delivered by means of a virus. The 'bomb' can be written to destroy or, worse, subtly change the contents of an organisation's computer systems. However, it does not begin this activity until signalled to do so by the hacker or extortionist, or it may be activated if a cancelling signal fails to arrive. In many cases the bomb itself is not actually planted; a warning message alerting the organisation to the placing of a bomb is usually sufficient to persuade vulnerable institutions to hand over huge sums of money. Estimates suggest that at much as £500 million has been handed to extortionists threatening attacks on computer installations between January 1993 and June 1996.

Electronic emanations ('Tempest')

All screens, just like television screens, work by means of a scanning beam of electrons fired at a fluorescing surface. When the beam is on, a pixel on the screen glows; when it is off, the pixel is unlit. When the beam is switched on, a burst of very low energy radiation is emitted, known as 'Van Eck' radiation. This radiation can be detected by sensitive radio detectors, and in principle this allows the actual contents of a screen to be seen remotely. In practice the signals are very faint and the detector must be very close to pick up anything at all, which increases the possibility of the snooper being detected.

The radiation is widely known about and easily shielded by a surrounding metal grille, routinely used by military installations. The equipment is then said to be 'Tempest' proofed.

Digital crime and the law

The rapid progress of computer technology has led to the need for new laws to be introduced so that all perpetrators of computer crime can be prosecuted. Laws in the U.S. impact on computer users in this country, since the majority of systems and Internet content is American. A general approach to a common standard for Internet-related laws throughout the European Union formed part of a proposed European Commission directive discussed by member states in October 1996.

The Computer Misuse Act of 1990

In the early 1980s in the UK, hacking was not illegal. Some universities stipulated that hacking, especially where damage was done to data files, was a disciplinary offence, but there was no legislative framework within which a criminal prosecution could be brought. This situation was rectified by the Computer Misuse Act of 1990 which defined three specific criminal offences to deal with the problems of hacking, viruses and other nuisances. The offences are:

- unauthorised access to computer programs or data;
- unauthorised access with a further criminal intent;
- unauthorised modification of computer material (i.e. programs or data).

To date there have been relatively few prosecutions under this law – probably because most organisations are reluctant to admit that their system security procedures have been breached, which might lead to a loss of confidence on the part of their clients.

Case study 1

A Sunday Times investigation in 1996 established that British and American agencies were investigating more than 40 'attacks' on financial institutions in New York, London and other European banking centres since 1993. Victims have paid up to £13m a time after the blackmailers demonstrated their ability to bring trading to a halt using advanced 'information warfare' techniques learnt from the military.

Criminals have penetrated computer systems using 'logic bombs', electromagnetic pulses and 'high emission radio frequency guns' which blow a devastating electronic 'wind' through a computer system. They have also left encrypted threats at the highest security levels, reading: "Now do you believe we can destroy your computers?"

In most cases victim banks have given in to blackmail rather than risk a collapse of confidence in their security systems.

➢ **Under which clause of which act could a hacker leaving a threatening message as described above, be prosecuted?**

Software copyright laws

Computer software is now covered by the Copyright Designs and Patents Act of 1988, which covers a wide range of intellectual property such as music, literature and software. Provisions of the Act make it illegal to:

- copy software;
- run pirated software;
- transmit software over a telecommunications line, thereby creating a copy.

Software can easily be copied and bootlegged (sold illegally). In addition, the programming *ideas* and *methods* can be stolen by a competitor. Microsoft was sued (unsuccessfully) many years ago by Apple Computers for copying the 'look and feel' of their graphical user interface. It is possible for an expert programmer to 'reverse engineer' machine code to establish the specific algorithms used, so that they can be copied. Some software manufacturers put 'fingerprints' into the code – little oddities which do not affect the way the program runs – so that if the same code is found in a competitor's program, they can prove that it was illegally copied.

The Business Software Alliance is in 1998 targeting some 20,000 small- and medium-sized companies to ensure that all software being used is correctly licensed. Offences include using 'pirate' copies of software and using software on more machines than is permitted under the terms of the licence.

Figure 12.3: BSA Advertisement 1997

Case study 2

Bill Gates's empire is being jeopardised by Russian software pirates. Microsoft Office '97 is being sold for £3 on the Russian black market, a minute fraction of the normal retail price of £315. In 1996, 91% of software programs being used in Russia were pirate copies.

Gates recently travelled to Moscow in an attempt to persuade those trading in pirated copies of software programs to refrain from doing so. The overall cost of this illegal activity to the software industry is around £300 million each year. However, it is unlikely that this personal appeal will succeed while fines for being caught in possession of pirated materials are insignificant in comparison with the revenue generated from the pirate industry itself, set at over £500,000 per month. As one stallholder reportedly said: "Mr Gates has gone home and we are trading happily – he makes about £18 million a month, so we do not feel too bad about selling these copies to people who cannot afford to buy it."

(Computer Consultant October 1997)

➢ **Who are the stakeholders (the people affected) in this story? Who are the victims? Is the stallholder acting ethically?**

Using computers to combat crime

Although computers are often involved in criminal activities, there is a more positive aspect to computers in crime; they can prove invaluable in the detection and prevention of crime. Detection is very often about collecting and collating huge amounts of information until a key piece of evidence emerges. In the search for Peter Sutcliffe, the 'Yorkshire Ripper', literally millions of hand- or type-written cards were stored in a mass of filing cabinets and desktop rotating card-holders while investigators pored over them and tried to pull together threads from the often conflicting evidence. Sutcliffe himself was interviewed several times but overlooked before the key evidence against him emerged from the mass of data. This case acted as the impetus for the implementation of the 'HOLMES' system (Home Office Large Major Enquiry System).

Databases of fingerprints, stolen vehicles and criminal records are all essential tools in today's fight against crime. Data matching exercises which match, for example, a 'modus operandi' ('style' of crime) with possible suspects can narrow the search field. Analysis of tax returns against the average profits for a particular type of business in a particular area can highlight possible tax fraud.

Exercises

1. The Computer Misuse Act defines three types of offence. With the aid of examples, describe each of these **three** types of offence. (9)

   NEAB IT01 Qu 7 1997

2. The illegal use of computer systems is sometimes known as computer-related crime.
   (a) Give **three** distinct examples of computer-related crime. (3)
   (b) Give **three** steps that can be taken to help prevent computer-related crime. (3)

   NEAB Sample Paper IT01 Qu 4

3. Describe **three** ways in which a person could gain unauthorised access to information stored on a computer. (6)

   New question

4. 'Codes of Practice' exist for professionals within the Information Technology industry separate from any legal requirements.
   Explain, with the aid of an example, the distinction between a legal requirement and a code of practice. (3)

   NEAB Sample Paper IT01 Qu 7

Chapter 13 – Protecting Data

Issues of privacy

Everyone has a right to privacy – the right not to have details about our lives to be held or circulated without our knowledge. Data of a personal nature are regularly collected by numerous different organisations – for example:

- **Employers** hold personnel records that include data on address, age, qualifications, salary, sick leave, dependents and so on;
- **Stores** hold details on credit card payments, account history, items purchased;
- **Banks** hold details on salary, income and withdrawals, direct debits to various organisations;
- **Insurance companies** hold details of property, cars, accidents, claims and health.

The list is endless, and modern technology has made it possible not only to store vast quantities of data about individuals, but to view it from anywhere in the world, and to correlate data held in different databanks to produce a comprehensive profile of an individual.

Case study: TRW Information Service

TRW is a company that sells thirty-five million credit reports each year to 24,000 subscribers in the United States. Every month TRW receives data from thousands of companies containing the status of their customer accounts. They then process and organise this data to build up a comprehensive credit history of each person, so that when a customer wants to buy an item on credit from a store who subscribes to the TRW service, they can carry out an immediate credit check.

The downside is that TRW do not carry out any checks on the accuracy of their data. Each year some 350,000 people register formal complaints about errors in TRW reports and about 100,000 of these result in changes to the data held by TRW. But how many errors pass unnoticed, resulting in people being denied credit completely erroneously?

Threats to information systems

Computer-based information systems are vulnerable to crime and abuse, natural disaster and human error. In this chapter we'll look at some of the ways that an organisation can protect the **integrity** of data (by preventing inaccurate data entry, malicious or accidental alteration), and simple measures that can be taken to protect the **security** of data from theft or destruction.

Data integrity

This refers to the **correctness** of the data. The data held in a computer system may become incorrect, corrupted or of 'poor quality' in many different ways and at many stages during data processing.

1. **Errors on input**. Data that is keyed in may be wrongly transcribed. A batch of transaction data could go astray, or be keyed in twice by mistake.

2. **Errors in operating procedure**. An update program could for example be run twice in error and quantities on a master file would then be updated twice.

3.   **Program errors could lead to corruption of files.** A new system may have errors in it that will not surface for some time, or errors may be introduced during program maintenance.

Standard clerical procedures

To protect against input and operating procedure errors, standard procedures may be documented and followed for both input and output.

Input

- Data entry must be limited to authorised personnel only;
- In large volume data entry, data may be verified (keyed in twice by different operators) to guard against keying errors;
- Data control totals must be used wherever possible to verify the completeness and accuracy of the data, and to guard against duplicate or illegal entry.

Output

- All output should be inspected for reasonableness and any inconsistencies investigated;
- Printed output containing sensitive information should be shredded after use.

> **Discussion: What are 'data control totals'? Give an example of a data control total that could be used by an Examining Board entering marks from students' 'A' Level scripts.**

Write-protecting disks

A simple measure such as write-protecting disks and tapes so that they cannot be accidentally overwritten can be effective in guarding against operator error. Both disks and tapes have write-protect mechanisms.

When the write-protect notch is open, the disk contents cannot be altered

Figure 13.1: Write-protecting a floppy disk

User IDs and passwords

Each user in an organisation who is permitted to access the company database is issued with a user ID and a password, which will normally give them a certain level of access rights set by the database manager. Common rules issued by companies regarding passwords include the following:

- Passwords must be at least 6 characters;
- Password display must be automatically suppressed on screen or printed output;
- Files containing passwords must be encrypted;
- All users must ensure that their password is kept confidential, not written down, not made up of easily guessed words and is changed regularly, at least every 3 months.

> ➢ **Discussion:** **Describe several ways by which a password may become known to an unauthorised person.**

Access rights

Even authorised users do not normally have the right to see all the data held on a company database. In a hospital, for example, receptionists may have the right to view and change some patient details such as name, address and appointments but may not access the patient's medical records. In a stock control system, salesmen may be permitted to view the price, description and quantity in stock of a particular item, but not to change any of the details held.

Access rights to a particular set of data could typically be set to Read-Only, Read/Write, or No Access. This ensures that users within a company can only gain access to data which they are permitted to see, and can only change data on the database if they are authorised to do so.

Likewise, the computer can also be programmed to allow access to particular data only from certain terminals, and only at certain times of day. The terminal in the database administrator's office may be the only terminal from which changes to the structure of a database may be made. An 'access directory' specifying each user's access rights is shown in Figure 13.2.

Access Profile: User ID 26885

Data	Access right	Terminal number	Permitted time	Security level
Customer Number	Read only	04,05	0830-1800	7
Credit Limit	Read Write	04	0830-1800	10
Payment	Read/Write	04,05	1830-1700	7
Credit Rating	No Access			12

Figure 13.2: A security access table as part of a database

Securing against fraudulent use or malicious damage

Organisations are often exposed to the possibility of fraud, deliberate corruption of data by disgruntled employees or theft of software or data which may fall into the hands of competitors. Measures to counteract these risks include the following:

- Careful vetting of prospective employees.

- Immediate removal of employees who have been sacked or who hand in their resignation, and cancellation of all passwords and authorisations.

- 'Separation of duties'; i.e. trying to ensure that it would take the collusion of two or more employees to be able to defraud the company. The functions of data preparation, computer operations and other jobs should be separate, with no overlap of responsibility.

- Prevention of unauthorised access by employees and others to secure areas such as computer operations rooms, by means of machine readable cards or badges or other types of locks.

- The use of passwords to gain access to the computer system from terminals.

- Educating staff to be aware of possible breaches of security, and to be alert in preventing them or reporting them. This can include politely challenging strangers with a "May I help you?" approach, not leaving output lying around, machines logged on, or doors unlocked.

- Appointing a security manager and using special software which can monitor all terminal activity. Such software can enable the security manager to see, either with or without users' knowledge, everything being typed on any screen in a network. It will also record statistics such as number of logins at each terminal, hours of login time, number of times particular programs or databases were accessed and so on. It will even log the security manager's activities!

Protection against viruses

Steps can be taken which minimise the risk of suffering damage from viruses. These include:

- Making sure that all purchased software comes in sealed, tamper-proof packaging;
- Not permitting floppy disks containing software or data to be removed from or brought into the office. (This is a sackable offence in some companies);
- Using anti-virus software to check all floppy disks before use. (This is sometimes known as a 'sheep-dip station'.)

Biometric security measures

Passwords are only effective if people use them properly: if obvious passwords are used, or people tell them to their friends or write them down on a piece of paper blue-tacked to the computer, they are useless. *Biometric* methods of identifying an authorised user include fingerprint recognition techniques, voice recognition and face recognition. One such system uses an infra-red scanner to capture the unique pattern of blood vessels under the skin, and can even differentiate between identical twins by comparing the scan with the one on disk stored for each person.

Case study: Iris recognition technology

The Nationwide Building Society started customer trials in March 1998 of 'iris recognition technology' – cash machines which are capable of recognising an individual's unique 'eye-print'. Special cameras are installed at the counter of the Swindon Head Office branch and at the cash machine. The camera captures a digital image of a person's iris, and from then on, every time a customer uses the cash machine, the system verifies their iris record within seconds.

However, retina verification can be unreliable, as checking the iris requires a person to look into a device at exactly the same angle each time.

Communications security

Telecommunications systems are vulnerable to hackers who discover a user ID and password and can gain entry to a database from their own computer. One way of preventing this is to use a callback procedure so that when a remote user logs in, the computer automatically calls them back at a prearranged telephone number to verify their access request before allowing them to log on.

Data encryption can also be used to 'scramble' highly sensitive or confidential data before transmission.

Disaster planning

No matter what precautions are taken against fire, flood, power surges, and deliberate or accidental destruction of data, the possibility always exists that data will be destroyed. A simple disk head crash can destroy a disk pack in a fraction of a second. System designers must provide a reasonable backup facility that does not degrade the performance of the system and does not cost too much.

The cost of lack of planning for computer failure can be ruinous. IBM estimates that 70% of organisations that experience a failure (caused by fire, flood, power failure, malice etc) cease operating within 18 months. The main consequence of a computer failure is loss of business, but other problems include loss of credibility, cashflow interruptions, poorer service to customers and loss of production.

Periodic backups

The most common technique used to ensure that data is not lost is to make **periodic backups**, by copying files regularly and keeping them in a safe place. This scheme has several weaknesses:

- All updates to a file since the last backup may be lost;
- The system may need to be shut down during backup operations;
- Backups of large files can be extremely time-consuming;
- When a failure occurs, recovery from the backup can be even more time-consuming.

A **benefit** of periodic backups is that files which may have become fragmented by additions and deletions can be reorganised to occupy contiguous space, usually resulting in much faster access time.

An important feature of all backup systems is the safe storage of the backup copies: it is usually necessary to store one backup copy in a fire-proof safe in the building, and another copy off-site.

Recovery procedures

A contingency plan needs to be developed to allow rapid recovery from major disruptions. In addition to file back-up procedures, it is necessary to:

- Identify alternative compatible equipment and security facilities, or implement a service agreement which provides replacement equipment when needed. This may also include putting up temporary office space;
- Have provision for alternative communication links.

Exercises

1. An on-line information retrieval system holds confidential personal data.
   (a) What precautions should be taken to
      (i) minimise unauthorised access
      (ii) detect unauthorised access? (4)
   (b) Why might different users be given different access privileges? (2)
   (c) Explain how the data should be protected from corruption. (4)
   NEAB IT01 Qu 6 Sample Paper

2. A company equips its sales staff with portable notebook computers. The I.T. department feels that a set of 'procedures' is required to ensure the integrity of the data and software held on the notebooks. Suggest **four** different items that the company might include in its set of procedures. (4)
   NEAB IT01 Qu 7 1997

3. Briefly describe the safeguards a company could use for each of the following threats to its computer system.
   (i) Power failure of on-line systems
   (ii) Disk corruption
   (iii) Illegal tapping of data on telephone lines
   (iv) Fire
   (v) Viruses (5)
   NEAB Computing Paper 2 Qu 6 1996

Chapter 14 – Data Protection Legislation

Personal privacy

The **right to privacy** is a fundamental human right and one that we take for granted. Most of us, for instance, would not want our medical records freely circulated, and many people are sensitive about revealing their age, religious beliefs, family circumstances or academic qualifications. In the UK even the use of name and address files for mail shots is often felt to be an invasion of privacy.

With the advent of large computerised databases it became quite feasible for sensitive personal information to be stored without the individual's knowledge and accessed by, say, a prospective employer, credit card company or insurance company to assess somebody's suitability for employment, credit or insurance.

Case study: James Wiggins – a true story

In the US, James Russell Wiggins applied for and got a $70,000 post with a company in Washington. A routine pre-employment background check, however, revealed that he had been convicted of possessing cocaine, and he was fired the next day, not only because he had a criminal record but because he had concealed this fact when applying for the job. Wiggins was shocked – he had never had a criminal record, and it turned out that the credit bureau hired to make the investigation had retrieved the record for a James Ray Wiggins by mistake, even though they had different birthdates, addresses, middle names and social security numbers. Even after this was discovered, however, Wiggins didn't get his job back.

If the pre-employment check had been made *before* Wiggins was offered the job, he would not have been offered it and no reason would have been given. The information would have remained on his file, virtually ensuring that he would never get a decent job – without ever knowing the reason why.

The Data Protection Act

The first concerns about the need for 'data protection' were voiced quite soon after the introduction of computers into commerce and industry, but more than 20 years passed before any legislation came into force. Public pressure for legislation gradually increased in the 70s and early 80s, and with the prospect of 'joining Europe' not too far away, the Government also had to look at the consequences of not conforming with European legislation on data protection. The Council of Europe Data Protection Convention set up in the late 1970s allowed participating countries to refuse to transfer personal information to non-participating countries, and this could have put Britain at a disadvantage in trade and lost international contracts.

The Data Protection Act became law on 12th July 1984. It contains eight **principles**, summarised as follows:

1. Personal data must be obtained and processed fairly and lawfully;

2. Personal data must be held for specified purposes;

3. Personal data must not be used for any reason incompatible with its original purpose;

4. Personal data must be relevant and adequate;

5. Personal data must be accurate and up-to-date;

6. Personal data must not be kept longer than necessary;

7. Personal data must be made available to the individual concerned and provision made for corrections;

8. Personal data must be kept secure. This encompasses two major aspects of data security:

    - Unauthorised access, alteration or disclosure;

    - Unauthorised or accidental loss or destruction of data.

'Personal data' means any data relating to a living person who can be identified from it — for example, by name.

The Data Protection Registrar

The Act established the office of **Registrar**, whose duties include:

- administering a public register of Data Users with broad details of the data held;

- investigating complaints and initiating prosecutions for breaches of the Act;

- publishing several documents that offer guidelines to data users and computer bureaux.

All Data Users have to register, giving:

- their name and address (or that of their company);

- a description of the data held and its purpose;

- a description of the sources from which the data is obtained;

- a description of the persons to whom it is intended to disclose data.

Exemptions from the Act

- The Act does not apply to payroll, pensions and accounts data, nor to names and addresses held for distribution purposes;

- Registration may not be necessary when the data are for personal, family, household or recreational use;

- Subjects do not have a right to access data if the sole aim of collecting it is for statistical or research purposes, or where it is simply for backup;

- Data can be disclosed to the data subject's agent (e.g. lawyer or accountant), to persons working for the data user, and in response to urgent need to prevent injury or damage to health.

Additionally, there are exemptions for special categories, including data held:

- in connection with national security;

- for prevention of crime;

- for the collection of tax or duty.

The rights of data subjects

Apart from the right to complain to the Registrar, data subjects also have a range of rights which they may exercise in the civil courts. These are:

- Right to compensation for unauthorised disclosure of data (arising out of principle number 3);

- Right to compensation for inaccurate data (arising out of principle number 5);

- Right of access to data and to apply for rectification or erasure where data are inaccurate (arising out of principle number 7);

- Right to compensation for unauthorised access, loss or destruction of data (arising out of principle number 8).

Implications of the Data Protection Legislation

Under the current legislation, the use of personal data must be registered, and members of the public have a right, for a small fee, to see what data is held about them by an organisation. However, it is quite legal for an organisation to sell a mailing list for the purpose of direct mailing.

A European Directive was adopted on 24 October 1995 which makes special provision for direct mailing lists. Where data is to be transferred to a third party for the purposes of direct mailing, the subject must be informed and given the opportunity to require that the data be erased. Inevitably, however, there are exceptions, relating for example to the situation where the subject was informed at the time of collection that the data may be transferred at some future date. Many organisations collecting personal data include a check box to be ticked if you object to your data being passed on to other organisations.

Member states have three years to implement this legislation.

> ➢ **Discussion: A supermarket is able to identify through a 'Reward' scheme which customers buy certain products. Does it have to register its use of personal data? Would it be permissible for the company to sell a list of all customers who buy dog and cat food to a Pet Parlour, or a list of customers buying denture cream and corn plasters to a Travel company specialising in holidays for the Over 60s?**
>
> ➢ **Is it permissible for a charity to sell its mailing list to another charity?**

Exercises

1. A company is storing details of its customers on a database. Describe **three** obligations the company has under the Data Protection Act. (6)
    NEAB Computing Paper 1 Qu 7 1997

2. A particular college uses a computer network for storing details of its staff and students and for managing its finances. Network stations are provided for the principal, vice-principal, finance officer, clerical staff and teaching staff. Only certain designated staff have authority to change data or to authorise payments.
    (a) What are the legal implications of storing personal data on the computer system? (4)
    (b) Outline **two** methods of controlling access to the stored data. (4)
    (c) What precautions should be taken to guard against loss of the data? (3)
    New Question

3. State what is meant by the term 'data subject' and outline **two** common criticisms of the Data Protection Act from the data subject's point of view. (5)
    NISEAC Computing Paper 2 Qu 4 1996

4. The manager of a small company wishes to introduce a computer system to keep details of customers.
    Describe the steps which the manager should take to ensure that the system conforms to data protection legislation. (4)
    London Computing Paper 1 Qu 2 1997

Chapter 15 – Health and Safety

Computers and health

Computers can be held responsible for a whole raft of health problems, from eyestrain to wrist injuries, back problems to foetal abnormalities, stomach ulcers to mental collapse. Articles appear regularly in the newspapers relating stories of employees who are suing their employers for computer-related illnesses.

Not so long ago it was thought that the widespread use of these fantastic machines, that could perform calculations and process data with lightning speed and complete accuracy, would free up humans to work maybe only two or three hours a day, while the computer did the lion's share. In fact, people seem to be working harder than ever, trying to keep up with the output of their computers. Human beings are the weak link in the chain, needing food, rest, a social life; prone to headaches, stress, tired limbs and mistakes.

Figure 15.1: Stress at work

Stress

Stress is often a major factor in work-related illness. Simply thinking about computers is enough to cause stress in some people. It is stressful to be asked to perform tasks which are new to you and which you are not sure you can cope with. It is stressful to know that you have more work to do than you can finish in the time available. It is stressful, even, to have too little to do and to be bored all day.

The introduction of computers into the workplace can have detrimental effects on the well-being of information workers at many different levels in an organisation. For example:

- Some companies may use computers to monitor their workers' productivity, which often increases their stress levels. Symptoms include headaches, stomach ulcers and sleeplessness.

- Many people are afraid of computers and fear that they will not be able to learn the new skills required, or that their position of seniority will be undermined by younger 'whizz kids' with a high level of competence in I.T.

- It can be almost impossible for some people to get away from work. Pagers, portable telephones, laptop computers and modems mean that even after leaving the office, there is no need to stop work –

indeed, should you even *think* of stopping work? As a busy executive, can you afford to waste 45 minutes on the train to Ipswich reading the newspaper or just gazing out of the window, when you could be tap-tap-tapping on your laptop, or infuriating your fellow passengers by holding long and boring conversations on your mobile phone?

- 'Information overload' means that managers are often bombarded with far more information than they can assimilate, producing 'information anxiety'. Try typing the words 'Information Overload' into one of the World Wide Web's search engines and within seconds, it will have searched millions of information sources all over the world and come up with thousands of references all presorted so that those most likely to be of interest are at the top.

- A survey of 500 heads of I.T. departments revealed that over three quarters of respondents had suffered from failing personal relationships, loss of appetite, addiction to work and potential alcohol abuse. The continuing developments within I.T. ensure that it is always in the minds of business executives and also that it is blamed for most corporate problems. The very speed of development, for which I.T. is now famous, and the need to keep pace with this is also a major contributing factor to I.T. stress-related illness.

Case study: Information overload

Val Kerridge is an I.T. manager in an Engineering company:

"I have to monitor everything to do with computers that might affect the firm, from fax-modems to new operating systems or network capabilities. I'm always being asked what I think of new hardware or software products, so I feel obliged to read everything – computer magazines, e-mails, user group communications on the Internet, mailshots from suppliers – there was so much it made me ill. I couldn't sleep properly, I had constant headaches and neck pains from staring at a screen, and I never had time to eat properly in a 12 to 14 hour day at the office."

Peter Harris is a management consultant:

"I was away for four days and when I came back, there was a huge pile of mail and faxes and dozens of e-mail messages. I couldn't tell from the titles whether they were important or not, and I spent 10 hours or more in front of a screen dealing with it all. I didn't know what information overload was until I came across the research and then I thought, 'Yes, that's me.'

When I go into organisations I find it very common in all departments. There's too much information and not enough communicating.

I now have a survival strategy. I am very strict with the amount of information I use. I scan it and throw it away or file it. I've learned to say 'No, I don't need that information'".

➤ **Discussion: Do you suffer from computer-related stress? How can it be alleviated?**

Repetitive strain injury (RSI)

RSI is the collective name for a variety of disorders affecting the neck, shoulders and upper limbs. It can result in numbness or tingling in the arms and hands, aching and stiffness in the arms, neck and shoulders, and an inability to lift or grip objects. Some sufferers cannot pour a cup of tea or type a single sentence without excruciating pain.

The Health and Safety Executive say that more than 100,000 workers suffer from RSI. It is not a new disease; Bernard Ramazzini, an Italian physician, noted of scribes and notaries in 1717:

> "The diseases of persons incident to this craft arise from three causes ... constant sitting ... the perpetual motion of the hand in the same manner, and the attention and application of the mind ... constant writing also considerably fatigues the hand and the whole arm on account of the continual tension of the muscles and tendons."

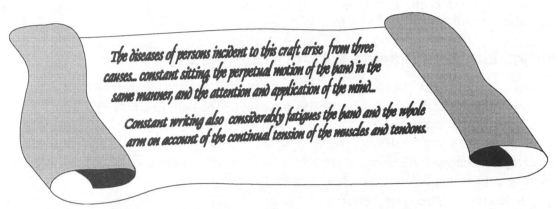

Figure 15.2: Recognition of RSI is not new!

Now, as then, the constant pain "can be removed by no medicines".

Case study: Bank staff 'driven to injury'

Keyboard operators at the Midland Bank's factory-style processing centre at Frimley, Surrey developed severe cases of repetitive strain injury after their work rate was sharply increased, a court was told yesterday.

Five former part-time workers who put cheque details into computers are claiming compensation for upper limb disorders including aches, stiffness and shooting pains in their arms, fingers, wrists, shoulders and necks.

The five former Midland workers, all women, were required to key in transaction records at an intensive stroke rate, on inadequately designed equipment, with a poor working posture and negligible training.

There was a lack of breaks or variation of tasks and there was strong pressure on staff to maintain and increase speed. The fastest operators – who keyed four strokes a second with their right hand, while holding cheques in their left – were awarded gold badges and their names were publicised by the bank.

In 1989, the Midland Bank had to pay £45,000 compensation to an RSI sufferer.

Source: Seumas Milne, The Guardian November 25 1997

➢ **What factors were cited as contributing to the onset of RSI among the employees?**

Eyestrain

Computer users are prone to eyestrain from spending long hours in front of a screen. Many computer users prefer a dim light to achieve better screen contrast, but this makes it difficult to read documents on the desk. A small spotlight focussed on the desktop can be helpful. There is no evidence that computer use causes permanent damage to the eyes, but glare, improper lighting, improperly corrected vision (through not wearing the correct prescription glasses), poor work practices and poorly designed workstations all contribute to temporary eyestrain.

Extremely low frequency (ELF) radiation

In normal daily life we are constantly exposed to ELF radiation not only from electricity mains and computer monitors but also naturally occurring sources such as sunshine, fire and the earth's own magnetic field. Research into the effects of ELF radiation is increasing and seems to indicate that it may be connected to some health problems. Several studies have tried to establish whether there is a link between monitor use and problems in pregnancy such as early miscarriages. The results are not clear-cut, because although some studies seem to show a correlation between an increased rate of miscarriages and long hours spent at a VDU in the first trimester of pregnancy, other factors such as stress and poor ergonomic conditions could have played a part.

Case study: Handsets may be bad for your health

The safety of mobile phones and computer monitors is again being questioned by environmentalists.

Research in France suggests that microwave radiation may not be the only risk to health from computer screens and mobile phones. At the University of Montpelier, chick embryos were subjected to very low-frequency radiation for eight hours a day. Sixty percent died compared with 17 percent in control groups.

And a large survey funded by the European Union, due to be published early next year, is believed by activists to have found a strong link between mobile phone use and cancer.

Green Party activist and bioelectromagnetics expert Roger Coghill believes the threat to health from heavy mobile phone use is so great that handsets should have a warning sticker on them.

Coghill Research Laboratory Web site: www.cogreslab.demon.co.uk

Source:Chris Partridge, The Sunday Times 10 December 1997

Computers, Health and the law

Occupational health and safety legislation in Britain is researched, guided and structured by the Health and Safety Executive (HSE), a government body. An EEC Directive on work with display screen equipment was completed in the early 1990s, with member states required to adapt it to become part of their own legislation. As a consequence, the Health and Safety at Work Act of 1974 incorporated legislation pertaining to the use of VDUs, and the relevant section is now referred to as The Health and Safety (Display Screen Equipment) Regulations 1992.

This legislation is intended to protect the health of employees within the working environment, and employers, employees and manufacturers all have some responsibility in conforming to the law.

Employers are required to

- Perform an analysis of workstations in order to evaluate the safety and health conditions to which they give rise;
- Provide training to employees in the use of workstation components;
- Ensure employees take regular breaks or changes in activity;
- Provide regular eye tests for workstation users and pay for glasses.

Employees have a responsibility to

- Use workstations and equipment correctly, in accordance with training provided by employers;
- Bring problems to the attention of their employer immediately and co-operate in the correction of these problems.

Manufacturers are required to ensure that their products comply with the Directive. For example, screens must tilt and swivel, keyboards must be separate and moveable. Notebook PCs are not suitable for entering large amounts of data.

Screen must **tilt**..

.. and **swivel**

Figure 15.3: Workstations must be ergonomically designed

Classrooom menace: ignore it and you may end up in court

Schools should not only teach children good posture and ensure they take regular screen breaks, but also scrutinise the equipment they provide. Chairs and screens should be adjustable for each child and foot- and back-rests may be needed.

"Some schools may be buying laptops because they are relatively cheap and easy to store but they are terrible for kids and long-term use. The screens are too low and the little workstations sold for them put kids into horrid positions," says Ms Martin, a specialist remedial therapist with extensive experience teaching RSI victims.

Tom Jones, of Thompsons solicitors, the UK's largest personal injury law firm, says schools ignoring RSI may find themselves in court.

"Schools have a duty of care over computer use in the same way they have at a school rugby match."

Source: Caroline Palmer, The Guardian 2 December 1997

The ergonomic environment

Ergonomics refers to the design and functionality of the environment, and encompasses the entire range of environmental factors. Employers must give consideration to

- **Lighting**. The office should be well lit. Computers should neither face windows nor back onto a window so that the users have to sit with the sun in their eyes. Adjustable blinds should be provided.

- **Furniture**. Chairs should be of adjustable height, with a backrest which tilts to support the user at work and at rest, and should swivel on a five-point base. It should be at the correct height relative to a keyboard on the desk.

- **Work space**. The combination of chair, desk, computer, accessories (such as document holders, mouse and mouse mats, paper trays and so on), lighting, heating and ventilation all contribute to the worker's overall well-being.

- **Noise**. Noisy printers, for example, should be given covers to reduce the noise or positioned in a different room.

- **Hardware**. The screen must tilt and swivel and be flicker-free, the keyboard must be separately attached.

- **Software**. Software is often overlooked in the quest for ergonomic perfection. The EEC Directive made a clear statement about the characteristics of acceptable software, requiring employers to analyse the tasks which their employers performed and to provide software which makes the tasks easier. It is also expected to be easy to use and adaptable to the user's experience.

Exercises

1. (i)   Describe briefly **four** computer-related illnesses from which a VDU operator may suffer.   (8)

    (ii) Describe **four** ways in which an employer can help to ensure that VDU operators will not suffer from computer-related illnesses.   (8)

    New question

2. Describe **three** health hazards associated with computer use.   (6)

    NEAB IT01 Sample Paper

3. Under current health and safety legislation pertaining to the use of VDUs, both employers and employees have a responsibility to conform to the law. Describe briefly **three** requirements that employers must conform to and **two** requirements for an employee.   (5)

    New question

Section 2

Information: Management and Manipulation

In this section:

Chapter 16 – Introduction to Computer Systems

Chapter 17 – Internal Storage of Data

Chapter 18 – Operating Systems

Chapter 19 – Categories of Software

Chapter 20 – Software Productivity Tools

Chapter 21 – Capabilities of Software

Chapter 22 – Records, Files and Databases

Chapter 23 – Data Modelling

Chapter 24 – Relational Database Design

Chapter 25 – Database Management

Chapter 26 – Input Devices

Chapter 27 – Data Gathering and Sampling

Chapter 28 – Modes of Processing

Chapter 29 – Storage Devices

Chapter 30 – Dissemination of Information

Chapter 31 – Security of Data

Chapter 32 – Output Devices

Chapter 33 – Configuring Hardware and Software

Chapter 34 – Network Environments

Chapter 35 – Wide Area Networks

Chapter 36 – User Interfaces

Chapter 16 – Introduction to Computer Systems

The components of a computer

All computers, whatever their size or function, have certain basic components. They have input devices for reading data into main memory, a central processing unit (CPU) for processing the data, output devices for printing, displaying or outputting information, and storage devices for permanent storage of programs and data.

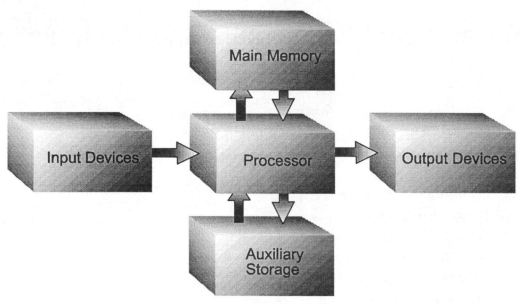

Figure 16.1: Block diagram of a computer system

Types of computer

Computers can be categorised into four types.

1. **Microcomputers**. Desktop personal computers (PCs), laptops, notebook and palmtop computers all fall into this category. They are used in thousands of different organisations; in businesses to increase productivity or to communicate with other areas of the business, in schools and colleges for educational purposes, in hospitals, booking systems and in homes. They vary in cost from a few hundred pounds for a basic model to a few thousand for a powerful PC that can be used to run a network.

2. **Minicomputers**. Minis or midrange computers are often used as multi-user systems, with hundreds of workstations or terminals attached to a central minicomputer. A large supermarket or department store, for example, could run all its electronic point of sale (EPOS) tills from a minicomputer. A police force or a hospital may have a minicomputer at the centre of its operations. They range in price from £10,000 to about £150,000.

3. **Mainframe computers**. Originally all computers were mainframe computers. In the 1960s, a mainframe computer costing hundreds of thousands of pounds, and which occupied the whole of a large, air-conditioned room would typically have been used to calculate the payroll of a large company. It would have had only a fraction of the processing power, speed and storage capacity of one of today's handheld computing devices. However, the capabilities of mainframe computers have increased in line with all other computers, and they are still in much demand by large organisations such as banks, building societies, insurance companies, airlines and government departments. A mainframe may have thousands of terminals attached to it at geographically remote locations, and occupy an entire site with hundreds of disk drives and other hardware units. Frequently, the actual siting of a mainframe computer is kept secret to lessen the danger of a terrorist attack that could cause chaos to an organisation.

4. **Supercomputers.** Supercomputers are the largest category of computer, costing millions of pounds. They are mostly used by scientific and industrial research departments, government agencies such as NASA, the Weather Centre, Stock Exchanges and by very large commercial organisations.

Processing power

The processing power of a computer is measured in terms of its speed of operation, the amount of memory it has, and the number of input/output devices it can handle. All computer operations are under the control of the CPU, which has the following functions:

- It controls the transmission of data from input devices to memory;
- It processes the data held in main memory;
- It controls the transmission of information from main memory to output devices.

Most computers use integrated circuits, or chips, for their CPUs and main memory. A chip is about ½" square and can hold millions of electronic components such as transistors and resistors. The CPU of a microcomputer is called a **microprocessor**. The CPU and main memory of a PC are commonly held on a single board called a main circuit board.

In 1965 Gordon Moore predicted that the capacity of a computer chip would double every year. He looked at the price/performance ratio of computer chips (the amount of performance available per dollar) over the previous three years and simply projected it forwards. He didn't really believe the rate of improvement would last for long, but in fact to this day chip capacity is still doubling every 18 months or so.

Figure 16.2: Intel microprocessors approximately doubling in transistor count every 18 months, in accordance with Moore's Law.

Moore's Law may hold for another twenty years – if it does, a computation that now takes a day will be more than 10,000 times faster and take fewer than ten seconds. Moore himself, speaking in 1997, expressed the opinion that the law is no longer applicable, and that chip technology will peak in about 2017, with processors running at some 1,000MHz.

Main memory

Instructions and data are held in main memory, which is divided into millions of individually addressable storage units called **bytes**. One byte can hold one character, or it can be used to hold a code representing, for example, a tiny part of a picture, a sound, or part of a computer program instruction. The total number of bytes in main memory is referred to as the computer's memory size. Computer memory sizes are measured as follows:

1 Kilobyte (Kb)	=	1000 bytes (or to be exact, 1024 bytes)
1 Megabyte (Mb)	=	1,000,000 (1 million) bytes
1 Gigabyte (Gb)	=	1,000,000,000 (1 billion) bytes
1 Terabyte (Tb)	=	1,000,000,000,000 (1 trillion) bytes

As with processing power, the amount of memory that comes with a standard PC has increased exponentially over the past 20 years. In about 1980, BBC microcomputers with 32K of memory were bought in their thousands for home and school use. In 1981, Bill Gates of Microsoft made his famous remark "640K ought to be enough for anybody". In 1998, a PC with 32Mb of memory is standard, costing around £1,000 including bundled software.

RAM and ROM

There are basically two kinds of memory; Random Access Memory (RAM) which is the ordinary kind of memory referred to above, used for storing programs which are currently running and data which is being processed. This type of memory is **volatile** which means that it loses all its contents as soon as the machine is switched off.

Read Only Memory (ROM) is the other type of memory, and this is non-volatile, with its contents permanently etched into the memory chip at the manufacturing stage. It is used for example to hold the **bootstrap loader**, the program which runs as soon as the computer is switched on and instructs it to load the operating system from disk into memory. To assist software development, some types of ROM are programmable (PROM) and may also be erasable (EPROM).

Cache memory

Cache memory is a type of very fast memory that is used to improve the speed of a computer, doubling it in some cases. It acts as an intermediate store between the CPU and main memory, and works by storing the most frequently or recently used instructions and data so that it will be very fast to retrieve them again. Thus when an item of data is required, a whole block of data will be read into cache in the expectation that the next piece of data required is likely to be in the same block. The amount of cache memory is generally between 1Kb and 512Kb.

Disk storage

All standalone PCs come equipped with an in-built hard disk, the capacity of which is also measured in bytes. A typical storage capacity for a Pentium PC is between 1 and 3 gigabytes. The hard disk is used for storing software including the operating system, other systems software, application programs and data.

Floppy disks consist of a thin sheet of mylar plastic encased in a hard 3½" casing. There are two standard types of disk in use today:

- Double density disks with a capacity of 720Kb;
- High density disks with a capacity of 1.44Mb.

High density disks can be distinguished by the hole punched out in one corner. They also usually have HD written on them.

Figure 16.3: Hard disk and floppy disk

> ➤ **Discussion: Two advertisements for computers are shown below. What do the various terms and abbreviations mean? Is the second computer really worth nearly three times as much as the first?**

Pentium P120 Business PC

◆ Pentium P120 processor ◆ Intel 430VX chipset ◆ 8Mb EDO RAM ◆ 1.2 Gb hdd ◆ 3.5"/1.4Mb fdd ◆ 256K Pipeline Burst Cache ◆ 1Mb graphics card ◆ Windows 95 keyboard and mouse ◆ Desktop case ◆ 14" SVGA monitor ◆ Windows 95

£499 EXC VAT

Figure 16.4: A mail order catalogue advertisement

Pentium II P233 Performance PC

◆ Pentium II P233 processor ◆ Intel 440FX chipset ◆ 32Mb EDO RAM ◆ 3.5 Gb hdd ◆ 3.5"/1.4Mb fdd ◆ 24 x CD-ROM ◆ 512k pipeline burst cache ◆ 2Mb graphics card ◆ Windows 95 keyboard and mouse ◆ Mini Tower case ◆ 15" SVGA monitor ◆ Windows 95 ◆ MS Office SBE ◆ 12 months warranty

£1399 EXC VAT

Figure 16.5: A high specification PC advertised in September 1997

Exercises

1. Find some advertisements for PCs and write down the specifications and prices. Are prices still falling and computers still becoming more powerful? (6)

    New question

2. What is cache memory and why is it used? (2)

    NEAB Computing Paper 1 Qu 1 1995

3. A typical business microcomputer stores all its software and data files on hard disk. It also has a floppy disk drive. Outline **two** different reasons why the floppy disk drive may still be needed. (4)

    NISEAC Computing Paper 1 Qu 1 1994

Chapter 17 – Internal Storage of Data

Digital and analogue computers

In this chapter we will look at how data is actually represented inside a computer. One of the things that many people find most amazing about computers is their seeming ability to understand and interpret all kinds of information fed in via a keyboard, mouse, scanner, microphone or sensor of some kind.

When we refer to computers we usually mean **digital** computers – that is, computers that process data in discrete form as countable numbers. There is another category of computers called **analogue** computers, which process continuously varying data such as speed, height, voltage fluctuations or temperature. A thermostat, for example, is a simple analogue computer.

All digital computers use the **binary** system for representing data of all types – numbers, characters, sound, pictures and so on. A binary system uses just 2 symbols to represent all information. The symbols could be anything like a dot and dash (as in Morse code), + and -, or 0 and 1. The great advantage of the binary system is that the digits 1 and 0 can be represented by electrical circuits that can exist in one of two states – current is either flowing or not flowing, and a circuit is either closed or open, on or off.

A closed circuit allowing current to flow represents 1

An open circuit represents 0

Figure 17.1: Electrical circuits can represent 1 or 0

The ASCII code

A binary digit (1 or 0) is known as a 'bit', short for **BI**nary digi**T**. In most computers today, bits are grouped together in 8-bit **bytes**. A byte can hold 2^8 different combinations of 0s and 1s, which means that, for example, 256 different characters can be represented.

Over the years, different computer designers have used different sets of codes for representing characters, which has led to great difficulty in transferring information from one computer to another. Most personal computers (PCs) nowadays use the ASCII code (American Standard Code for Information Interchange), but many mainframe computers use a code called EBCDIC (Extended Binary Coded Decimal Interchange Code — pronounced EB-SUH-DICK or EB-SEE-DICK according to taste).

ASCII originally used a 7-bit code, but a later version that is now more common uses 8 bits. The 128 different combinations that can be represented in 7 bits is plenty to allow for all the letters, numbers and special symbols, and the extra 128 combinations are used for symbols such as Ç, è, ü, ©, ®, Œ, etc.

> ➤ **Discussion: About how many different combinations of 0s and 1s are required to represent all the keys on a keyboard? (Remember to include uppercase and lowercase letters).**

The ASCII codes are shown below.

Character	ASCII	Char	ASCII	Char	ASCII	Char	ASCII
space	0100000	8	0111000	P	1010000	h	1101000
!	0100001	9	0111001	Q	1010001	i	1101001
"	0100010	:	0111010	R	1010010	j	1101010
£	0100011	;	0111011	S	1010011	k	1101011
$	0100100	<	0111100	T	1010100	l	1101100
%	0100101	=	0111101	U	1010101	m	1101101
&	0100110	>	0111110	V	1010110	n	1101110
'	0100111	?	0111111	W	1010111	o	1101111
(	0101000	@	1000000	X	1011000	p	1110000
)	0101001	A	1000001	Y	1011001	q	1110001
*	0101010	B	1000010	Z	1011010	r	1110010
+	0101011	C	1000011	[	1011011	s	1110011
,	0101100	D	1000100	\	1011100	t	1110100
-	0101101	E	1000101	]	1011101	u	1110101
.	0101110	F	1000110	^	1011110	v	1110110
/	0101111	G	1000111	_	1011111	w	1110111
0	0110000	H	1001000	'	1100000	x	1111000
1	0110001	I	1001001	a	1100001	y	1111001
2	0110010	J	1001010	b	1100010	z	1111010
3	0110011	K	1001011	c	1100011	{	1111011
4	0110100	L	1001100	d	1100100	|	1111100
5	0110101	M	1001101	e	1100101	}	1111101
6	0110110	N	1001110	f	1100110	~	1111110
7	0110111	O	1001111	g	1100111	del	1111111

Figure 17.2: ASCII codes

Parity

For each byte of memory, most computers have at least one extra bit, called a **parity** bit, that is used for error detection. A parity bit can detect if one of the bits in a byte has been inadvertently changed, perhaps because of a chip failure, static electricity or a voltage fluctuation.

Computers use either **even** or **odd** parity. In an even parity machine, the total number of 'on' bits in every byte (including the parity bit) must be an even number. Parity is checked each time a memory location is used. When data is moved from one location to another in memory, the parity bits are checked at both the sending and receiving end, and if they are different or the wrong number of bits are 'on', an error message is displayed.

Figure 17.3: Parity bit

> **Discussion: In an even parity machine, what will be the value of the parity bit for the characters P and Q?**

76

Representing numbers

We have seen that each character has a corresponding code, so that if for example the 'A' key on the keyboard is pressed, the code '01000001' will be sent to the CPU. If the key '1' is pressed, the code '00110001' will be sent to the CPU. To print the number '123', the codes for 1, 2 and 3 would be sent to the printer.

This is fine for input and output, but useless for arithmetic. There is no easy way of adding two numbers held in this way, and furthermore they occupy a great deal of space. Numbers which are to be used in calculations are therefore held in a different format, as **binary numbers**.

Before we look at the binary system, it is helpful to examine how our ordinary decimal or **denary** number system works. Consider for example the number '134'. These three digits represent one hundred, three tens and four ones.

100	10	1
1	3	4

$100 + 30 + 4 = 134$

As we move from right to left each digit is worth ten times as much as the previous one. We probably use a **base 10** number system because we have ten fingers, but essentially there is no reason why some other base such as 8 or 16 could not be used.

In the binary system, as we move from right to left each digit is worth twice as much as the previous one. Thus the binary number 10000110 can be set out under column headings as follows:

128	64	32	16	8	4	2	1
1	0	0	0	0	1	1	0

This represents $128 + 4 + 2 = 134$

> **Discussion: Convert the following binary numbers to decimal:**
>
> | 0011 | 0110 | 1010 | 01000001 | 01000101 |
>
> **Convert the following numbers to binary:**
>
> | 5 | 7 | 1 | 26 | 68 | 137 |
>
> **What is the largest binary number that can be held in 8 bits?**

Obviously, using only one byte (8 bits) to hold a number places a severe restriction on the size of number the computer can hold. Therefore two or even four consecutive bytes are commonly used to store numbers.

Binary arithmetic

One advantage of this method of storing numbers is that arithmetic becomes easy. To see how the 'carry' system works, first count from 1 to 16 in binary. Copy and complete the table below:

Decimal	Binary	Decimal	Binary	Decimal	Binary
0	00000	6		12	
1	00001	7		13	
2	00010	8		14	
3		9		15	
4		10		16	
5		11			

We can now try some binary addition:

$$
\begin{array}{r}
00011001 \\
+ \quad \underline{01010110} \\
= \quad 01101111
\end{array}
$$

> ➤ **Discussion: Convert the above sum to decimal to make sure it is correct.**

> ➤ **Add together the binary equivalents of 7 and 9.**

A discussion of how negative numbers and real numbers (i.e. numbers with a decimal point) are held is beyond the scope of this course. The main thing is to have an appreciation of the fact that numbers which are going to be used in calculations have to be defined as such, and not held as 'text', or individual characters.

Boolean values

So far we have seen how a given binary pattern could represent an ASCII character, a binary integer, or a number held in BCD. A Boolean variable (named after the logician George Boole) is one which can only have one of two values, **true** or **false**, represented by 1 and 0. The database MS Access allows you to define an item of data as a 'Yes/No' field, and this is the same as a Boolean data type, occupying just one bit.

Digitised sound

Sound such as music or speech can be input via a microphone, CD or electronic keyboard with MIDI (Musical Instrument Digital Interface) to be processed by a computer. Since sound waves are continuously variable or **analogue** in nature, an **analogue to digital converter** is needed to transform the analogue input to a **digital** form, i.e. a binary pattern, so that it can be stored and processed. Undesirable sounds such as wrong notes or scratches on an old recording can be edited out before a new digital version is produced.

Sound in analogue form may be represented by wave forms. The height of these wave forms may be sampled at regularly spaced time intervals, with the height being represented by, say, a 16-bit code. The more frequently the samples are taken, the more faithfully the sound will be represented.

Figure 17.4: Converting sound from analogue to digital form

Bitmapped graphics

As well as being used to store numbers and text, binary patterns are also used to store graphics and sound. In a bitmapped system for displaying text and graphics on a VDU, the screen is divided up into a grid, and each square on the grid is called a **pixel** (picture element). A low resolution screen may have 320 by 240 pixels, and a high resolution screen may have 1024 by 1024 pixels or more. A monochrome screen will need just one bit in memory to represent each pixel; if the bit is 1, the pixel is on, and if it is 0, the pixel is off. On a colour screen, each pixel may correspond to one byte in memory, giving a possible 256 colours for each pixel. The memory used is additional to the RAM used for programs and data; it is supplied on a graphics 'card' specific to the type of screen.

If the screen was magnified you would be able to see the individual pixels. The more pixels to the square inch, the higher the resolution and the smoother the image.

Figure 17.5: An image on the screen is composed of thousands of pixels

Exercises

1. State **four** different possible interpretations of a given bit pattern in a computer's memory. (4)
    New question

2. (a) Show how the denary (decimal) numbers 13 and 32 would be represented as 8-bit binary integers. (2)

    (b) Given that the ASCII code for the character 1 is 00110001, show how the text string 1332 would be held in a 4-byte word in a computer's memory. (2)
    New question

3. Music is often recorded digitally. Describe briefly **two** advantages of this method of representing sound. (2)
    New question

4. A PC may be described as having a 1Mb graphics card, meaning that 1Mb of memory is available to represent a full screen image. If a screen resolution of 1024 x 1024 is selected by the user via the 'control panel', how many bytes would be available to represent each pixel on the screen? How many different colours could be represented? (2)

    If more colours are wanted, should the screen resolution be increased or decreased? (1)
    New question

Chapter 18 – Operating Systems

What is an operating system?

Computers require two types of software: **applications software** such as word processing, spreadsheet or graphics packages, and **operating systems software** to control and monitor the running of application programs, and to allow users to communicate with the computer.

The operating system consists of a number of programs which are typically 'bundled' with the hardware; in other words, when you buy a new PC, for example, you will also be supplied with a CD containing the latest version of the Windows operating system. This then has to be installed by running a special installation program supplied on the CD, which will copy the operating system to your hard disk and customise it to your particular hardware configuration.

The part of the operating system that manages the computer's resources (the CPU, memory, storage devices and peripherals) is called the **kernel** (or **supervisor** or **control program**). Each time you switch on your PC, the kernel will be copied from the hard disk into memory, which takes a couple of minutes.

Functions of an operating system

Obviously, the operating system (OS) for a standalone microcomputer system will be very much simpler than that of a supercomputer which is controlling hundreds of terminals and running many different kinds of job simultaneously. Nevertheless, all operating systems perform certain basic functions, including:

- **Memory management**. Most computers nowadays are capable of holding several programs in memory simultaneously, so that a user can switch from one application to another. The operating system has to allocate memory to each application – as well as to itself!

  If the OS detects that there is insufficient memory to load an application that the user has asked for, it may swap another application (or part of it) out to disk temporarily, and reload it when required, swapping something else out to disk. This takes time, which is why increasing memory may have the effect of speeding up the computer's performance.

  The technique of swapping part of the contents of memory out to disk is known as **virtual memory**, because it makes the computer appear to have more memory than it actually does.

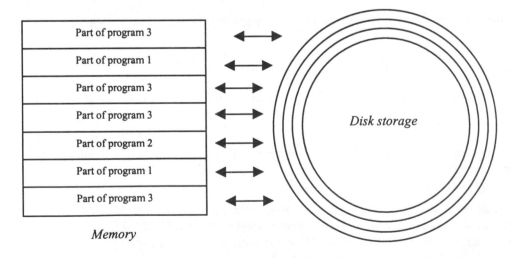

Figure 18.1: Virtual memory

- **Resource allocation and scheduling**. In larger computer systems which are capable of running several programs at once (**multiprogramming**), the OS is responsible for allocating processing time, memory and input-output resources to each one.

- **Backing store management**. The OS controls the transfer of data from secondary storage (e.g. disk) to memory and back again. It also has to maintain a directory of the disk so that files and free space can be quickly located.

- **Interrupt handling**. The OS detects many different kinds of interrupt such as for example a user pressing the Enter key on the keyboard, a printer sending a message that it is out of paper, the real-time clock interrupting to indicate that the processor should be allocated to the next user in a multi-user system, a hardware or software malfunction.

- **Allowing a user to communicate with the computer**. The user gives instructions to the computer to start a program, copy a file, send a message to another user, and so on by typing in commands recognised by the operating system or by using a mouse to point and click in a graphical user interface such as Windows 95.

Utility programs

As well as the basic operating system, the systems software available to users includes numerous **utility programs**, such as:

- **Virus checkers** which check disks and memory for viruses and delete them if detected;

- **Security and accounting** software which checks user IDs and passwords, counts and reports the number of attempts made to log on under each user ID, the amount of processor time used at each session, total login time and so on;

- **File management utilities** which attempt to repair corrupted files, reorganise files on disk so that free space is 'defragmented' (which can improve performance), 'zip' (compress) files so that they occupy less space if for example you want to make a backup copy of a large file onto a floppy disk.

The DOS operating system

Two operating systems currently dominate the microcomputer world; Windows and the Apple Macintosh operating system.

In 1981, IBM purchased from a tiny company called Microsoft Corporation an operating system which it called PC-DOS (Personal Computer Disk Operating System) for its new microcomputer. Bill Gates, the head of Microsoft, retained the right to sell the same operating system to other computer companies, under the name MS-DOS (Microsoft Disk Operating System), with the result that it rapidly became the most popular operating system in the world, with over 150 million copies sold worldwide.

DOS tells the computer how to format, read and write information on either floppy disks or hard disks. It manages peripheral devices such as the printer and keyboard, and controls the execution of application software. It also specifies how many files can be held in a disk directory, what constitutes an acceptable file or directory name, the number of bytes that can be on a disk, the number of bytes of memory usable by a program.

The command-driven interface

DOS is essentially a command-driven interface, meaning that the user has to type in commands in exactly the correct syntax to perform any operation. This allows complex commands to be entered to customise the operating system for a particular user, and experienced users may be able to perform operations faster using DOS than by using a mouse and menus or icons in a Windows interface.

A DOS prompt appearing on a blank screen shows which drive and directory are current, e.g.
C\WINDOWS>

To change drive, the user types the characters shown in bold
C\WINDOWS>**A:** and the prompt changes to
A:>

To display a directory of files held on A, the user types the word **DIR**
A:>**DIR** and a directory is shown. Figure 18.2 shows a similar dialogue.

```
                        MS-DOS Prompt

C:\ACCOUNTS>cd\

C:\>cd work

C:\WORK>dir

 Volume in drive C is MS-DOS_5
 Volume Serial Number is 13FC-1E25
 Directory of C:\WORK

.               <DIR>            24/03/98    22:14
..              <DIR>            24/03/98    22:14
ANAGRAM  DOC          11,264 15/12/95     9:23
MAILMRGE DOC         603,136 21/01/98     9:55
MERGE1   DOC           7,680 30/12/97     8:48
        5 file(s)           622,080 bytes
                         16,572,416 bytes free

C:\WORK>_
```

Figure 18.2: MS DOS Command line interface

The Apple Macintosh graphical user interface (GUI)

While Microsoft were developing their DOS operating system, the Apple Computer Corporation were working on a completely different way of communicating with a microcomputer. In 1984, Apple brought out their most powerful PC, the Macintosh, complete with the WIMP interface that has now become universal. WIMP stands for Windows, Icons, Mouse and Pull-down menus or alternatively, Windows, Icons, Menus, Pointer – and the term 'user-friendly' was more or less invented to describe this approach.

The Macintosh could do things that the IBM PC could not, such as having more than one application open at once, each in its own 'window', and transferring data between applications.

Unfortunately for Apple, from being the most popular PC in the late 1970s, they rapidly fell behind IBM even after the success of their graphical user interface. What went wrong? The major problem lay in the lack of software packages written especially for the Mac. Apple, unlike IBM, owned both the hardware and the operating system, and refused to license the operating system to any other company, so that while sales of PC 'clones' mushroomed, Apple retained a much smaller niche market. Software developers concentrated on developing software for PCs running MS-DOS because this was a much larger market, even though the operating system was inferior to Apple's.

DOS with Windows

It was not long before Microsoft, headed by Bill Gates, began to develop its own Windows interface. The early versions of Windows, including Windows 3.1 and 3.11, were not full operating systems. They provided an operating environment or *graphical user interface* (GUI) that operated under the control of DOS, acting as a kind of bridge between the user and DOS. Because Windows 3.11 is not an actual operating system, DOS has to be loaded into memory first when the machine is switched on.

One primary objective of Windows 3.1 was to allow **multi-tasking**, allowing a user to have several applications running simultaneously and to switch between them. With multi-tasking, there is no need to close one application before starting another. The concept is analogous to working at a desk; you might start to write a report, then decide to check your diary and make a phone call, and use your calculator to work out a couple of figures to include in the report.

Several desktop 'accessory' programs are supplied with Windows, including:

1. **Calculator;**
2. **Calendar** for displaying a calendar in month or day format and setting alarms to 'beep' at specific times;
3. **Notepad** for writing brief notes;
4. **Card file** for keeping a card index, say of names and addresses;
5. **Clock** for displaying the current time;
6. **Paintbrush**, a simple drawing package;
7. **Write**, a simple word processing package;
8. **Clipboard** for temporarily saving anything such as text, a graphic, spreadsheet or screenshot, temporarily in memory so that it can be pasted into another application;
9. **Terminal**, for communicating with another computer.

Figure 18.3: The Windows 3.11 Graphical User Interface

Windows 95 – a full operating system

Windows 95 (and its successor Windows 98), unlike previous versions of Windows, is in itself a full operating system offering true multi-tasking, and taking full advantage of the 32-bit architecture of newer PCs. This means, effectively, that applications will run faster under Windows 95 than under Windows 3.11. Other improvements include a completely redesigned interface, and the ability to use long file names rather than being restricted to 8 characters.

Figure 18.4: Windows 95 Interface

Windows 95 also provides 'Plug and Play' support designed to make it easier to install peripherals such as a new printer. The device merely needs to be plugged in and the user can then select 'Add New Hardware' from Control Panel in the Settings menu to be taken through a few easy steps for the device to be automatically configured with the appropriate driver. That is the theory anyway but many users view such tasks with a degree of trepidation and scepticism and refer to the procedure as 'Plug and Pray'.

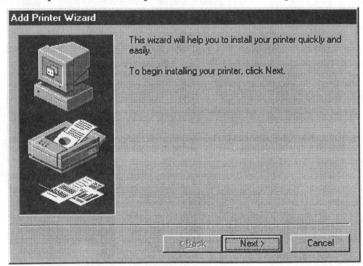

Figure 18.5: Installing a new printer under Windows 95

UNIX

UNIX is a general-purpose, multi-user, multi-tasking operating system written in C, which has been around since the early 1970s. Unlike other operating systems, UNIX is available on a wide variety of platforms, which is to say that it can be used on computers from many different manufacturers. This means that users can select hardware from different manufacturers and use the same software on different types of hardware, which is not the case with other operating systems traditionally supplied with the hardware.

Exercises

1. At present there are many different computer operating systems in existence. If operating systems were standardised, give **one** different benefit for each of the following:

    (a) the user of computers;

    (b) the manufacturer of computers;

    (c) developers of software for computers.

    Give **one** technical reason why this is not likely to happen. (4)
    AEB Computing Paper 1 Qu 8 1993

2. Describe **three** housekeeping utilities normally provided with the operating system for a single-user personal computer. Your description should include a typical task for which each utility is used. (6)
    NEAB Computing AS Paper 1 Qu 9 1996

3. Most microcomputers store the system date and time internally. Describe briefly **three** circumstances in which a user may find this useful. (6)
    New question

4. In recent years there has been a move from command driven interfaces to WIMP driven interfaces.

    (a) Compare and contrast command and WIMP driven interfaces. (3)

    (b) Discuss factors which have led to the development and increased use of WIMP driven interfaces. (2)
    SEB Computing Studies Paper 1 Qu 9 1995

5. Disk directories record information about the files that are stored on disk. State **three** items of information that, typically, would be recorded. (3)
    AEB Computing Paper 2 Qu 4 1997

6. From the experienced user's viewpoint, give **three** functions of an operating system. (3)
    NEAB IT02 Specimen Paper Qu 5

7. Give **two** reasons why additional memory might be useful to the user of a PC. (2)
    New question

Chapter 19 – Categories of Software

Categorising software

Software is the general term used to describe all the programs which run on a computer. There are three general categories of software: systems software, applications software and general-purpose software. This categorisation is not rigid, however, and some people would say that general-purpose software and applications software can be lumped together. You will soon discover that very little in computing is black and white; whatever you read, someone will soon come up with an apparently contradictory statement on most topics, leaving you to choose your own truth!

Systems software

In the last chapter we looked at the functions of an operating system, which must be installed on every computer and is independent of any applications that a user may wish to run. The operating system comes under the general heading of **systems software**, as do the utility programs mentioned in the last chapter. Here is a list of some of the different types of systems software.

1. **Operating system.**   Already discussed.
2. **Utility programs.**   These are programs designed to make life easier for computer users. Utility programs perform common tasks that thousands of computer users need to do at one time or another, such as search for lost files, sort files of data into a particular sequence, copy disk files to magnetic tape for backup purposes and so on.

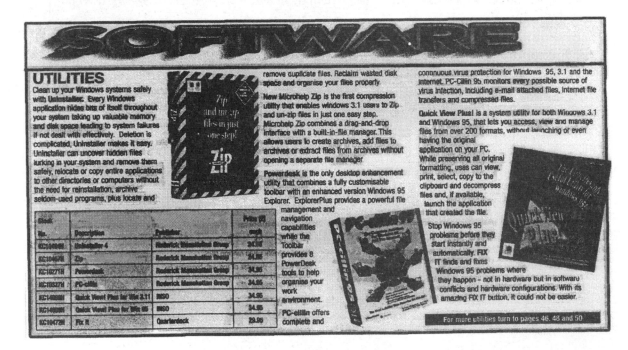

Figure 19.1: Common utility programs

3. **Programming language compilers/interpreters.** Compilers and interpreters are different types of program used to translate the statements in a programming language such as Pascal, Visual Basic or C into a form that the computer can understand.

4. **Performance monitoring software.** This is used to monitor, analyse and report on the performance of a computer and its components. It can provide information such as the overall utilisation of the processor and number of disk accesses over a given period of time. In a mainframe environment, this can assist management in monitoring the current and future hardware requirements.

5. **Communications software.** In a mainframe environment, communications software is executed on a separate, dedicated processor ('front-end processor') and controls the flow of data to and from remote locations.

Applications software

Applications software is written to perform specific tasks such as order entry, payroll, stock control or hospital appointments. The software may be designed specifically for one particular company, ('bespoke software') and written especially for them using a programming language or software such as a database management system. Alternatively, the software may be purchased 'off the shelf'.

General purpose software

All common application packages such as word processing, desktop publishing, spreadsheet, database, computer-aided design (CAD) and presentation graphics packages fall into this category. Most general purpose software is sold as a package, including a CD containing the software and manuals to help you get started and to be used as a reference.

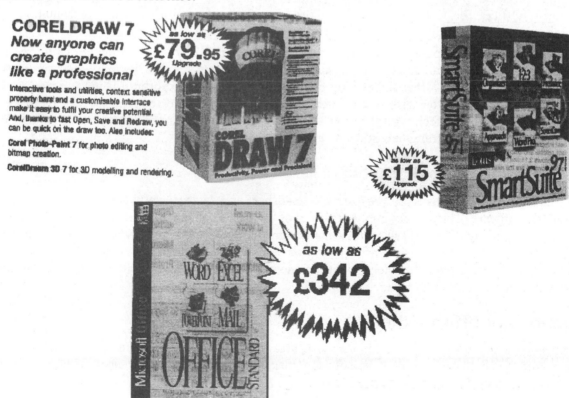

Figure 19.2: General purpose software

Who uses application packages?

Employees at every level in an organisation have access to computers and may use so-called 'productivity tools'. There are three main groups of user:

1. **Managers and executives** who need information in the form of summaries, graphs or reports to help them make decisions, keep track of day-to-day operations or give presentations.

2. **Software specialists** whose job it is to customise the software so that it performs the required tasks correctly. This may be a fairly simple matter of installing and customising word processing software, writing macros to automate common tasks and ensuring that the correct printer driver is installed. On the other hand it may involve spending weeks or months writing a complex database application.

3. **Data entry operators** who enter data to be processed by the application.

People at all levels of the organisation may use software such as word processors.

Integrated packages and software suites

The main productivity tools used by organisations include word processing, spreadsheets, databases, presentation graphics and communications software to enable users to communicate with each other either locally or across the world in an international company.

Integrated packages which combined features from all five of these products were once very popular, because they offered capabilities from all these packages in a single product at a relatively low price, and data could be transferred between applications. However, a single integrated package (e.g. Microsoft Works) has fewer and less sophisticated features than are found in separately-purchased packages.

Today, complete **software suites** such as Microsoft Office or Lotus SmartSuite offer four or more software products packaged together at a much lower price than buying the packages separately. Microsoft Office, for example, includes Word, Excel, Access, a multimedia presentation graphics package called PowerPoint and Microsoft Mail.

Terminology in the computer world soon becomes fuzzy and MS Office is sometimes referred to as an integrated suite. The advantage of buying such a suite of programs is that the individual applications are completely compatible so that there is no difficulty importing or exporting data from one package to another, if for example you wish to put a spreadsheet in a word processed report. Also, the packages all have the same look and feel, with the same shortcut keys used for various operations (such as Ctrl-S for Save) and this makes learning new software an easier task.

Generic and specific software

Note that software such as word processing, spreadsheet and database software is sometimes referred to as **generic** software. This simply implies that any of the dozens of spreadsheet packages, for example, can be made to do many different tasks, and is not designed specifically for one type of application. The other type of application software such as a payroll or stock control system mentioned above, or a software package such as a program to help fill in an income tax return, is in contrast **specific** because it is designed to do one particular task.

Bespoke or off-the-shelf?

When an organisation decides to computerise an area of its business, a decision has to be made whether to buy an off-the-shelf package or have software specially written. The advantages of buying an off-the-shelf package include the following:

- It is generally a less expensive solution;
- It may be possible to speak to other users of the package for their evaluation before spending money;

- The software can be bought and installed straight away;
- The software is tried and tested and likely to contain fewer bugs than newly written software;
- The software is usually well documented;
- Training may be available in common software packages.

Conversely, there are also advantages in buying tailor-made software:

- The software is designed to do exactly what the user wants;
- The software can be written to run on specified hardware;
- The software can be integrated with existing software;
- There may not be a suitable software package on the market.

Exercises

1. Describe the difference between applications software and systems software, giving an example of each. (4)

    NEAB IT02 Qu 2 1996

2. When purchasing software, it is often possible to buy either an 'integrated package' or separate application packages that run under a common operating system environment.

    (a) What is meant by the term 'integrated package'? (2)

    (b) What applications would you normally expect an 'integrated package' to offer? (4)

    (c) What are the relative advantages and disadvantages of an 'integrated package' over a collection of separate applications packages running under a common operating system environment? (4)

    NEAB IT02 Sample Paper Qu 2

3. Give **three** points a user should consider before deciding to purchase a software package. (3)

    NEAB AS Computing Paper 1 Qu 1 1996

4. Describe **three** housekeeping utilities normally provided with the operating system for a single-user personal computer. Your description should include a typical task for which each utility is used. (6)

    NEAB AS Computing Paper 1 Qu 8 1996

5. There is a trend for general purpose packages to include additional features normally found in different classes of package. A word processing package with a graphics capability is an example of this trend.

    (a) Give **two** reasons for this trend. (2)

    (b) What are the implications of this trend for:

    > the users of the package;
    > the hardware required to run the package;
    > data compatibility? (3)

    SEB Computing Studies Paper 1 Qu 6 1995

Chapter 20 – Software Productivity Tools

Types of productivity tools

This is a general term sometimes used to describe the application packages that are used to perform operations that are an integral part of day-to-day business operations. The most common ones are word processors, spreadsheets, database management systems and electronic mail. These four applications form the basis of both integrated packages and software suites from many different software manufacturers, and all have many features in common.

Word processing

A word processing package is a program or set of programs used to enter, edit, format, store and print documents. A document may be anything from a simple memo to a complete book. In addition to data entry and editing facilities, word processors have several important features:

- **Spelling and grammar checker**. Each word in a document can be checked against words held in the package's dictionary, and in some packages misspelt words and grammatically incorrect sentences are underlined. If the original word is correctly spelt but was highlighted by the spell checker, it can be added to the dictionary.

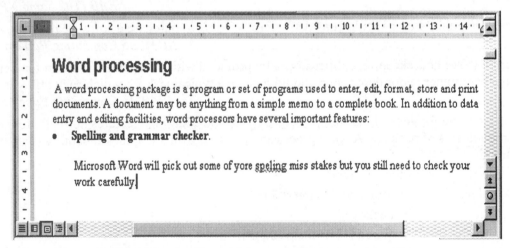

Figure 20.1: a spelling checker underlines misspelt words

- **Automatic creation of index and table of contents**. Any word in the text can be marked for inclusion in an index. Headings and subheadings in a given style can be included automatically in a table of contents, which can be updated at any time.

- **Import files**. Tables, photographs, graphics and even video and sound files can be imported from other sources and inserted in a document.

 A sound icon

To play the sound, double-click its icon. (This could be used to insert a verbal message or some music in a document, for example.)

- **Mail Merge**. A document and a list of names and addresses can be merged to produce personalised letters. (see Figure 20.2)

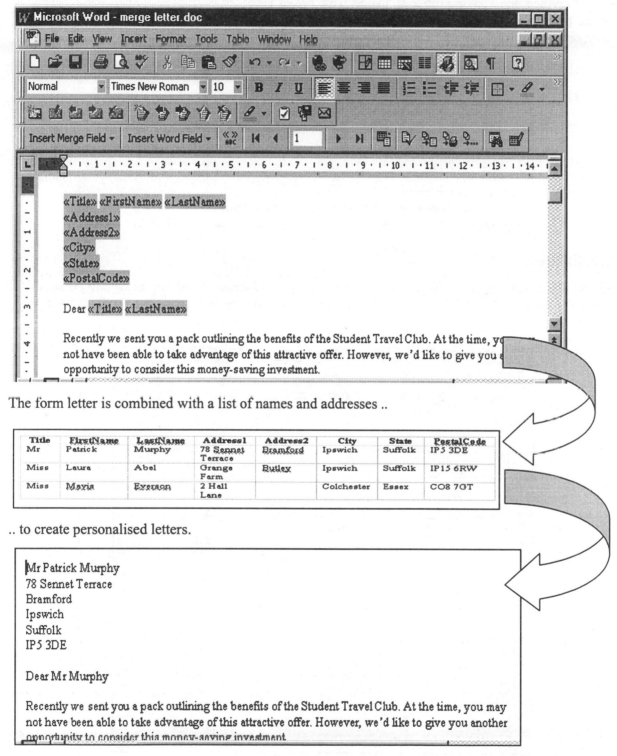

The form letter is combined with a list of names and addresses ..

Title	FirstName	LastName	Address1	Address2	City	State	PostalCode
Mr	Patrick	Murphy	78 Sennet Terrace	Bramford	Ipswich	Suffolk	IP5 3DE
Miss	Laura	Abel	Grange Farm	Butley	Ipswich	Suffolk	IP15 6RW
Miss	Maria	Everson	2 Hall Lane		Colchester	Essex	CO8 7GT

.. to create personalised letters.

Mr Patrick Murphy
78 Sennet Terrace
Bramford
Ipswich
Suffolk
IP5 3DE

Dear Mr Murphy

Recently we sent you a pack outlining the benefits of the Student Travel Club. At the time, you may not have been able to take advantage of this attractive offer. However, we'd like to give you another opportunity to consider this money-saving investment.

Figure 20.2: Mail merge

- **Creation of templates** with preset text styles, margins, formatting, letterheading, etc.

- **WYSIWYG** capability. This acronym stands for 'What You See Is What You Get', and refers to the ability to display on screen exactly what you will get when the text is printed. Many word processors have more than one viewing mode so that in page layout view, for example, you can see a page as it will be printed, and in 'normal' view can see and edit text but not see imported pictures or text laid out in columns.

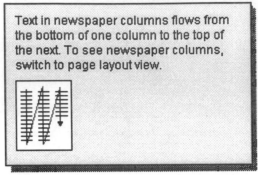

Figure 20.3: Columns can be viewed in 'Page Layout' view in MS Word

Spreadsheets

Spreadsheets packages allow a user to create worksheets (spreadsheets) representing data in column and row form. Spreadsheets are used for any application that uses numerical data, such as budgets, cash flow forecasts, profit and loss statements, student marks or results of experiments.

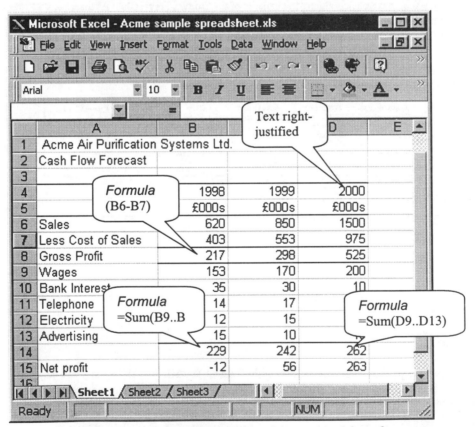

Figure 20.4: Spreadsheet containing numbers, text and formulae

Spreadsheet features

Spreadsheets offer the following facilities:

- Format cells, rows and columns, specifying for example, the alignment of text, number of decimal points, height and width of cell;

- Copy cell contents to other locations, with automatic adjustment of formulae from say B9 to C9, D9 etc.;

- Determine the effect of several different hypothetical changes of data; this facility is termed 'what-if' calculation;

- Insert, move or delete rows and columns;

- Use functions such as SUM, AVERAGE, MAX, MIN in formulae;

- Create a simple database and sort or query the data to produce a report of, say, all females earning over £20,000 for a list of employees;

- Write macros to automate common procedures;

- Create templates – spreadsheets with formats and formulae already entered, into which new figures may be inserted;

- Create 'multi-dimensional' spreadsheets using several sheets, and copy data from one sheet to another;

- Create many different types of charts and graphs (see Figure 20.5).

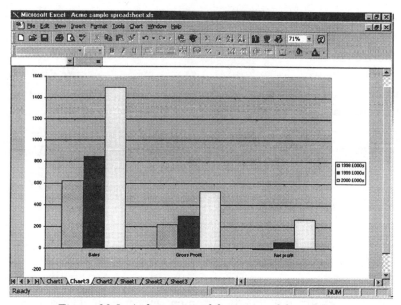

Figure 20.5: A chart created from spreadsheet figures

Databases and Electronic Mail

These two applications are each discussed elsewhere (see chapters 22-25, 6) and are not covered here.

> ➤ **Discussion: Many integrated suites share common features such as menus, toolbars and shortcut key combinations to perform common tasks. Do you know some of these shortcuts? Do you know how to display toolbars that are not currently on the screen? Do you make use of the 'Help' menu when you are stuck?**

Application generators

An application generator is a piece of software, often database-oriented such as MS Access or Paradox, which allows a user to develop an application such as a Stock Control or Accounts system without having to do very much programming. The software will automatically generate the code from tables, forms and reports specified by the user. Such software could be extremely useful in, say, a Recruitment department of a large company that wants to keep track of applicants, where they come from, what qualifications they have, and so on in order to plan future recruitment campaigns.

Report generators

A report generator is a piece of software that allows a business user who may have little knowledge of programming to specify the format and content of a printed report to be composed using values from a database or calculations performed by a computer. Visual Basic, for example, uses a report generator called Crystal Reports which can generate reports automatically. In the programming language RPG (Report Program Generator), the user designs reports using statements similar to programming language statements. In Access, 'wizards' are used to generate reports without having to write any code.

Exercises

1. A particular word processing package is described as having a WYSIWYG (what you see is what you get) output capability. Give the advantages of using such a package rather than one which does not possess this capability. (3)

   NEAB IT02 Qu 1 1996

2. A mail-order book club holds its customer data on a computer file. The club wishes to contact its customers who have not ordered a book for one year or more. Briefly describe the stages involved in the necessary mail merge. (3)

   NEAB Computing AS Qu 2 1995

3. A cell in a typical electronic spreadsheet can contain a data value or a formula. Describe briefly **two** other types of cell contents. (6)

   NISEAC Computing Paper 1 Qu 5 1996

4. One common business application package is the spreadsheet. Give **two** different reasons why a spreadsheet package is particularly useful as a decision-making tool. (2)

   AEB Computing Paper 1 1996

5. Modern spreadsheets make use of macros.

   (a) What is a macro? (3)

   (b) Write a macro to move the cursor from its current position to the first empty cell (from the top) in the first column of a spreadsheet. (3)

   NEAB Computing Paper 1 Qu 7 1996

6. (a) The following is an example of an advertisement appearing in a computing magazine:

   "For sale: 386 16MHz microprocessor with 4Mb RAM, 180Mb hard disk, mouse and installed operating system and user software (including DTP, Clip Art and integrated software). Best offer secures."

   (i) Describe the main features you would expect to find in each of the DTP, Clip Art and integrated software offered with this microcomputer. (9)

   (ii) What operational difficulties might arise with the software already installed on this microcomputer if the original disks are not available? How might these difficulties be prevented? (6)

   NISEAC Paper 1 Qu 15(a) 1995

Chapter 21 – Capabilities of Software

Object Linking and Embedding (OLE)

Using OLE, it is possible to share information between programs. For example, if a report is being written in Word which requires the use of a spreadsheet or chart created in Excel, the spreadsheet can be either linked to, or embedded in, the document.

In the Word menu, selecting Insert, Object and then 'Create from file' in the next window brings up the following screen:

Figure 21.1: Linking a file to another document

The spreadsheet 'Sample Stats.xls' is then linked into the report.

Mortimer College A Level Statistics 1997-98							
Cumulative Percentage of Candidates at each grade							
	A	B	C	D	E	N	U
1997	8.35	18.22	37.00	58.63	74.19	88.99	100.00
1998	9.11	24.55	53.07	73.66	92.28	98.81	100.00

Figure 21.2: This spreadsheet is linked to the original in Excel

About linked and embedded objects

The main differences between linked objects and embedded objects are where the data is stored and how it is updated after you place it in the destination file.

Figure 21.3: The difference between linked and embedded objects

Use **linked** objects if:

- you want the information to reflect any changes to the original data, or
- file size is a consideration.

With **a linked object**, the original information remains stored in the source file. The destination file displays a representation of the linked information but stores only the location of the original data. The linked information is updated automatically if you change the original data in the source file. For example, if you select a range of cells in a Microsoft Excel workbook and then paste the cells as a linked object in a Word document, the information is updated in Word if you change the information in your workbook.

In contrast, an **embedded object** becomes part of the destination file. Because an embedded object has no links to the source file, the object is not updated if you change the original data. You can still edit a spreadsheet or other object embedded in Word, though, by double-clicking it to open and edit it using Excel.

The need for portability of data

Portability is the ability to run the same program on different types of computer. It can also refer to the ability to transfer a file from one computer to another.

For all sorts of reasons, it's important to be able to transfer data between applications and between computers of the same or different types, perhaps using different operating systems. For example:

- You're writing a report in Word and you want to be able to insert an Excel spreadsheet in the report.
- You're using a desktop publishing system and you want to be able to import some graphics from a drawing package.
- You're doing a research assignment and want to download articles from the Internet on 'Computers and Dolphins'.
- You want to e-mail your friend on a Unix machine in Hull from your PC in Southampton, and send her a scanned photograph she requested.

Files (binary, text or graphical) can be downloaded from the Internet using **ftp** (File Transfer Protocol) – software that can copy files between different types of computer.

Problems with portability

There are several reasons why files may not be portable.

- A document created using one word processing package (e.g. Word) commonly cannot be read by a different word processing package (e.g. Word Perfect) running on the same computer. Different formatting codes are used by different packages; for example, the information that a word or paragraph is in bold text must be stored along with the actual text, but exactly how this information is coded varies between packages.

  For this reason, most word processing packages allow documents to be stored in 'Text only' format. This strips out all the formatting information and any graphics, leaving only the text, which can be read into a different package and reformatted.

- A document created on one computer using a particular word processor appears differently on the screen of another computer running the same word processing package.

  Some word processors (e.g. Word Perfect) lay out a document based on the printer that is being used. If the document is transferred to another computer, and a different printer specified, the document may appear with a completely different layout, with line breaks and page breaks appearing in different places.

Another reason why a document may appear differently on a different computer is that it may not have the same fonts (typefaces) installed. An alternative font will be substituted, which usually changes the layout.

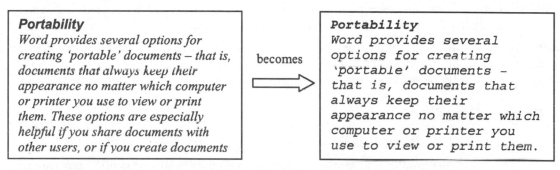

Figure 21.4: Transferring a document to another computer can change its appearance

Upgradability

Software manufacturers commonly bring out upgrades about every two years, to the intense annoyance of many customers who soon find themselves either using out-of-date software or having to pay for the upgrade. Software upgrades frequently cause some or all of the following problems:

- Documents or applications produced by the upgraded software are not 'downwardly compatible'. In other words, a document written in Version 6 can usually be read in Version 7, but not vice versa. Usually, the newer version allows the user to save the file as a 'Version 6 file' so that it can be read by the earlier version.

- The new version is likely to contain new features non-existent in earlier versions, so that data or formatting may be lost if it is converted to the earlier version for another user.

- The upgraded software frequently needs more memory, more disk space and a faster processor to work efficiently, meaning that hardware has to be upgraded.

On the other hand, of course, the march of progress brings its advantages and a new version often brings impressive improvements in ease of use, functionality and speed.

> ➢ **Discussion: A College has several independent local area networks in different open-access rooms, each with its own file server. Periodically the oldest computers are replaced with the most up-to-date hardware available. Why does the College continue to run older versions of software on the new computers?**

Criteria for selecting a software package

The most important factor in evaluating software is how well the software meets your needs, but there are many other factors to consider as well.

1. Compatibility with existing hardware. Will the software run on existing equipment?

2. Compatibility with existing software. Can files from other packages be imported or exported to and from the new package to other packages?

3. Quality of documentation.

4. Ease of learning. How good is the on-line help? Are tutorials available?

5. Ease of use. Is the package easy to use? Are there shortcuts for advanced users?

6. Technical support. Is this available, and at what cost?

7. Upgrade policy. Will future upgrades be available at a discount? Can files created in older versions be used without change?

8. Speed. How long does it take to perform complex but frequently performed operations such as database queries. Some database packages, for example, are very fast with small amounts of data but grind to a halt when presented with several thousand records.

9. Cost. This may involve simply the cost of an individual package. If the package is to be used throughout an organisation, the cost of a licensing agreement that specifies how many copies of the software may legally be made, or how many users can use it on a network, has to be investigated.

Evaluating software

Before selecting a particular software package you could:

- Read reviews of it in a computer magazine. Magazines commonly compare similar software packages on dozens of different criteria;

- Consult other users who have experience of the type of software you are thinking of purchasing;

- Perform benchmark tests (performance tests) to see how fast various packages perform a number of different tasks. Computer magazines often publish the results of benchmark tests.

Software reliability

As software becomes increasingly complex, it becomes more and more difficult to test. Batch systems, where the data is entered together in a batch, processed and output produced, are relatively easy to test. Test files can be created and expected results of all processing calculated and compared with actual results. If something is wrong, the program can be fixed and the same set of tests run again.

With GUI interfaces and on-line systems, however, this type of testing is not possible. It may be impossible to recreate the conditions under which a program crashed. The difficulties arise because:

- There is no single, well-defined flow of events at the user interface;

- It is often impossible to restore a database to the condition it was in before a bug was detected. In a client-server environment, the data may be held on different servers and across networks;

- Rapid, iterative and continuous development techniques mean that software continues to develop and new, weekly versions of systems are released by programmers. Testing simply cannot keep pace with these rapid changes;

- Users often use new software in ways which were not anticipated by the software engineers who wrote the system. When the system finally crashes, ("I was just trying to add a new record and it crashed") it is impossible to retrace the sequence of events that caused the crash;

- Performance testing is difficult to set up. An on-line, multi-user system that works well when tested with 1,000 records and 2 users may fall over when a million records are added and hundreds of users are simultaneously accessing the database.

The development of de facto standards

Some technologies don't depend on widespread acceptance for their value. A device that automatically opens a garage door when you point at it and press a button may be very useful even if you're the only person in the world who has one. But for products that depend on communications or collaboration between different organisations, much of a product's value comes from its widespread acceptance. There is no point owning a new type of CD player that plays full-length videos on a TV screen, if no one has recorded the videos that you want to watch. Likewise, there is no point buying a computer that is much faster than any other, and has a better user interface, unless it will run the software that you want to use. You're better off with the slower one that will do the job.

> ➢ **Discussion: Why do all keyboards have the same layout of letters, i.e. QWERTY along the top line? Would it be a good idea to adopt a new standard?**
>
> ➢ **In England we push a light switch down to turn the light on. In the U.S. 'Up' is On. These are 'de facto' standards – standards that have evolved.**
>
> ➢ **Think of some 'de facto' standards applicable to PCs.**

De facto standards are developed by the marketplace rather than by law.

Case study: Microsoft's MS-DOS

In the summer of 1980 two emissaries from IBM came to Microsoft – then a tiny, unknown company – to discuss a personal computer they said IBM might or might not build. Working with the IBM design team Microsoft encouraged IBM to build one of the first computers to use the 16-bit microprocessor chip, the Intel 8088. The move from 8 bits to 16 bits meant that the PC would be able to support up to one full megabyte of memory – 256 times as much as an 8-bit computer. Microsoft granted IBM the royalty-free right to use their MS-DOS operating system for a one-time fee of about $80,000. In other words, they practically gave it away – but their goal was not to make money from IBM but to license the operating system software to other companies who made IBM-compatible machines.

Consumers bought the IBM PC with confidence, and by 1982 third party software developers began turning out applications to run on it. Each new customer and each new application added to the IBM PC's strength as a de facto standard for the industry, until almost all of the newest and best software was written for PCs running MS-DOS. A positive-feedback cycle began to drive the PC market, so that within three years, almost all other personal computers (Apple being the main exception) had disappeared. Many new companies such as Eagle and Northstar (ever heard of them?) thought people would buy their new computers because they offered something different and slightly better than the IBM PC. They were wrong. The IBM PC had become the hardware standard.

Common operating systems

Microsoft did not rest on its laurels with MS-DOS. In 1983, they announced that they planned to bring out a new graphical user interface named Windows. In fact Apple brought out a graphical operating system before Microsoft in 1984, on its new Macintosh, but Microsoft worked closely with Apple and brought out new software – Word and Excel – for the Macintosh. The Macintosh had a first-class operating system with the first graphical user interface, but they refused (until 1995) to let anybody else make computer hardware that would run it. Microsoft operating systems, on the other hand, are offered today by over 1,000 different manufacturers.

Microsoft has been able to offer compatibility because hardware manufacturers have agreed not to allow modifications to the operating system.

In the spring of 1988, IBM joined other computer manufacturers to promote UNIX, an operating system that had originally been developed at AT&T's Bell Labs in 1969. Over the years, modifications and enhancements have been made to UNIX by different computer companies. The many differences between versions have made software compatibility harder and have held back the widespread acceptance of UNIX. Only a few software companies could afford to develop different versions of their software for a dozen different versions of UNIX, and computer software stores could not afford to stock all the different versions even if they did.

Exercises

1. Most word processors provide users with the facility to save a document as 'text only' as well as in the 'usual' format. Explain briefly the difference between the versions of a document stored in each of these two ways giving **one** reason why the 'text only' option is provided. (6)

    NISEAC Computing Paper 1 Qu 6 1995

2. Given an existing hardware platform, selecting the most appropriate software package for a specific application can be a difficult process.

    (a) Describe the criteria and methods you would use to select the most appropriate software package for a specific application. (16)

    (b) Users may encounter problems when software manufacturers upgrade a software package. With reference to specific examples describe **two** such problems. (4)

    NEAB IT02 Specimen Paper Qu 9

3. A freelance reporter who regularly contributes articles to various newspapers and magazines is considering which word processing package she should purchase. A friend has said that 'most modern applications packages enable users to produce files which are portable'.

    With the aid of specific examples discuss this statement. Include in your discussion:

    - An explanation of what portability means in this context;
    - Why portability is important;
    - How the Information Technology industry can encourage this portability. (16)

    NEAB IT02 Qu 10 1996

4. Explain briefly what is meant by the term *software portability*. (4)

    NISEAC Computing Paper 1 Qu 4 1994

5. (a) Give **three** examples of conventions or *de facto* standards that users expect to find when using a graphical user interface such as Windows. (3)

    (b) A new type of microcomputer with superior facilities to anything currently on the market may from time to time appear. Explain why it is unlikely to be successful. (5)

    New question

Chapter 22 – Records, Files and Databases

Hierarchy of data

An effective information system provides users with timely, accurate and relevant information. This information is stored in computer files, which need to be suitably organised and properly maintained so that users can easily access the information they need.

We'll look at the way that data is represented and structured in a computer, starting with the very lowest level.

BIT All data is stored in a computer's memory or storage devices in the form of binary digits or **bits**. A bit can be either 'ON' of 'OFF' representing 1 or 0.

BYTE Bits are grouped together, with a group of 8 bits forming a byte. One byte can represent one character or, in different contexts, other data such as a sound, part of a picture etc.

There are different codes used for representing characters, one of the most common being ASCII (American Standard Code for Information Interchange). Using 8 bits it is possible to represent 256 (2^8) different characters.

FIELD Characters are grouped together to form **fields**. Data held about a person, for example, may be split into many fields including ID Number, Surname, Initials, Title, Street, Village, Town, County, Postcode, Date of birth, Credit Limit and so on.

RECORD All the information about one person or item is held in a **record.**

ID Number:	432768
Surname:	King
Initials:	DF
Title:	Mr
Street:	2 Burghley Crescent
Town:	Bath
County:	Avon
Post code:	BA3 5WT
Date of Birth:	14/8/78
Credit Limit:	£250

FILE A file is defined as a collection of records. A stock file will contain a record for each item of stock, a payroll file a record for each employee and so on.

DATABASE A database may consist of many different files, linked in such a way that information can be retrieved from several files simultaneously. There are many different ways of organising data in a database, and many different database software products for use on all types of computer from micros to mainframes.

Database Management Systems (DBMS)

A Database Management System is a set of programs that permits an organisation to centralise data, create database files, manage them efficiently and access the data when required. Using a DBMS, users can create new database files, add, delete, alter, and sort data, make enquiries and print reports. The DBMS will allow many users to simultaneously access the central database, and restrict access for each user to those parts of the database that they are entitled to view or change. MS Access has many of the features of a DBMS.

Flat file and file management systems

File management systems (such as the one which forms part of the integrated package MS Works) have been around for a number of years and differ from true Database Management Systems in that the data stored in one file cannot easily be linked to data stored in another file. These so-called 'flat files' are useful for storing data such as a list of contact names and addresses, a list of student grades or details of a video collection. A spreadsheet can be used as a flat file database, with a column representing a field and a row representing a record.

Video number	Title	Country	Date released	Classification	Star
1	A Few Good Men	U.S.	1992	15	Tom Cruise
2	The Mask	U.S.	1994	PG	Jim Carrey
3	The Flintstones	U.S.	1994	U	John Goodman
4	Trainspotting	U.K.	1996	18	Ewan McGregor
5	Crocodile Dundee	AUS	1986	15	Paul Hogan
6	Titanic	U.S.	1998	12	Leonardo DiCaprio
etc					

Creating a database file

Before you can begin to store data in a database file, you have to specify the format of a record in the file. Each record in the file will have the same format or structure, specified by defining the characteristics of each field in a record. You must specify:

1. The **order** in which the fields are stored in the record;
2. The **name** of each field;
3. The **field type**. The database software will offer a number of field types including:
   - Text (also referred to as Character or Alphanumeric);
   - Numeric (integer, or real with a specified number of decimal points);
   - Date (in a number of different formats);
   - Yes/No (or True/False);
   - Memo (for writing notes about a client, for example);
4. For some types of field such as a text field, the field length. This should be large enough to hold the maximum expected length of data – for example, 20 characters could be allowed for a surname.

Once the structure of the database file has been specified, the empty file can be given a name and saved.

The significance of field types

Does it really matter whether you specify a date or numeric field as a text type, or a field such as a telephone number as numeric? The answer is YES – for several reasons.

- Certain field types are automatically validated when the user enters data. Thus, if you specify a field named Date of Birth as a date field, the software will not allow a user to enter 31/2/76 because this is not a valid date. If you have specified the field as a text field, no automatic validation is possible.

- Similarly, if a field is defined as currency or numeric, the user will not be able to enter a non-numeric character in the field by mistake.

- On the other hand, it is unwise to define a telephone number as numeric because a user may want to leave a space or hyphen between the area code and the rest of the number, and a numeric field will allow only numbers and a decimal point to be entered

- Numeric fields are held differently inside the computer from text fields, and if the field will be involved in any type of calculation, it MUST be defined as numeric (or date, or currency) or an error will be reported when the computer tries to perform the calculation.

- The length specified for a text field should also be chosen carefully and documented for future reference. If a student ID, for example, is defined as 6 characters in one file and 10 characters in another file, errors will occur when the two files are linked through this common ID number.

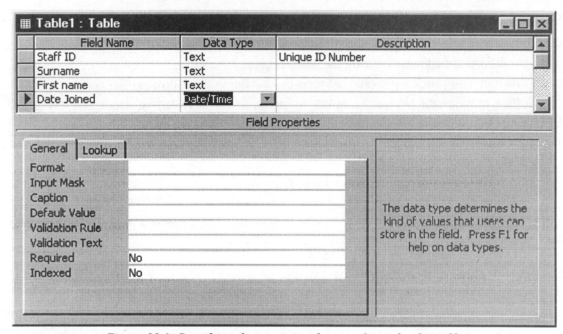

Figure 22.1: Specifying the structure of a record in a database file

Primary key

Each individual row or record in a database file needs to be given a unique identifier, and this is termed the **primary key**. It needs to be carefully chosen so that there is no possibility of two people or items being confused; Surname, for example, is no use as an identifier. The primary key sometimes consists of more than one field: for example several stores in a national chain may each have a store number, and each store may have Departments 1,2,3 etc. To identify a particular department in a particular store, the primary key would be composed of both Store number and Department number.

> **Discussion: What would be a suitable primary key for: a book in a bookshop?**
> **a book in a library?**
> **a hospital patient?**
> **a car owned by a car-hire firm?**

Validation of input data

Almost every field in a database can be put through some type of **validation** to ensure that data entry is accurate. There are several types of validation check that can be specified, for example:

- Presence check – must data be entered in this field?

- Range check – is there a low/high limit? (e.g. the date must be greater than or equal to today's date in a theatre booking file, the price of a new car from a particular manufacturer must be between £6,000 and £30,000 in a car sales database.)

- Format check – must the data be in a particular format? (e.g. a new car registration must be 1 letter, 3 digits and 3 letters. A course code at a particular college must be 2 letters followed by 5 digits.)

- Is there a list of valid values? (e.g. Sex can be either M or F.)

Exercises

1. Most database management packages allow conditions to be associated with the fields of a record. These conditions are specified during the design stage.

   An application using such a package has records containing the following fields:

   Part_number, description, number_in_stock, unit_cost, value_of_stock.

   Explaining your decision, choose from these fields:

   (a) one which must be unique;

   (b) one which must be calculated;

   (c) one which is always required (mandatory). (3)

   AEB Computing Paper 1 Qu 4 1997

2. A file of pupil records has fields that contain a school number, a name, a date of birth and year of entry to the school. A typical example is

   234; Holmes S; 13 02 83; 1995

   (a) Describe data types for each of these fields. (4)
   (b) Describe validation checks that could be made on the data as it is entered. (5)

   New question

Chapter 23 – Data Modelling

Traditional file approach

Most organisations began information processing on a small scale, buying a computer for perhaps one or two individual applications, and then computerising other departments one by one. Applications were developed independently, and files of information relevant to one particular department were created and processed by dozens or even hundreds of separate programs. This situation led to several problems:

- **Data redundancy.** The same data was duplicated in many different files. For example, details of a salesman's name, address and pay rate might be held on a payroll file for calculating the payroll. The same data may be held on a file in the Personnel department along with a lot of other personal data, and in the Sales Department which has a program to keep track of each salesman's record and performance.

- **Data inconsistency.** When the same items of data are held in several different files, the data has to be updated in each separate file when it changes. The Payroll Department, for example, may change the commission rates paid to salesmen but the Sales Department file may fail to update its files and so be producing reports calculated with out-of-date figures.

- **Program-data dependence.** Every computer program in each department has to specify exactly what data fields constitute a record in the file being processed. Any change to the format of the data fields – for example, adding a new field or changing the length of a field – means that every program which uses that file has to be changed, since the file format is specified within each program.

- **Lack of flexibility.** In such a system, when information of a non-routine nature is needed, it can take weeks to assemble the data from the various files and write new programs to produce the required reports.

- **Data was not shareable**. If one department had data that was required by another department, it was awkward to obtain it. A second copy of the file could be made, but this would obviously soon lead to problems of inconsistency. If the same file was used, it would almost certainly be necessary to add extra fields for the new application, and that would mean the original programs would have to be changed to reflect the new file structure.

Figure 23.1: Data files in a traditional file organisation ('flat files')

The database approach

In an attempt to solve these problems, the concept of a database was born.

A **database** is defined as a collection of non-redundant data shareable between different applications.

All the data belonging to the entire organisation would be centralised in a common pool of data, accessible by all applications. This solved the problems of redundancy and inconsistency, but two major problems remained to be addressed.

- **Unproductive maintenance**. Programs were still dependent on the structure of the data, so that when one department needed to add a new field to a particular file, all other programs accessing that file had to be changed.

- **Lack of security**. All the data in the database, even confidential or commercially sensitive data, was accessible by all applications.

The Database Management System (DBMS)

A DBMS is a layer of software inserted between the applications and the data, which attempts to solve these problems. Two essential features of the DBMS are:

- Program-data independence, whereby the storage structure of the data is hidden from each application/user;

- Restricted user access to the data – each user is given a limited view of the data according to need.

Figure 23.2: The DBMS acts as an interface between application programs and data

The conceptual data model

The first stage in designing a database is to identify and state what data needs to be held. Figure 23.2 shows some of the data items that may be required for some of the applications required by an organisation such as a Department store.

From the statement of data requirements a **conceptual data model** is produced. This describes how the data elements in the database are to be grouped. Three terms are used in building a picture of the data requirements.

1. An **entity** is a thing of interest to an organisation about which data is to be held. Examples of entities include Customer, Employee, Stock Item, Supplier.

2. An **attribute** is a property or characteristic of an entity. Examples of attributes associated with a Customer include Customer ID, Surname, Initials, Title, Address, Credit Limit.

3. A **relationship** is a link or association between entities. An example is the link between Dentist and Patient; one dentist has many patients, but each patient only has one dentist.

This conceptual data model is created without specifying what type of database system will eventually be used to implement the system.

Types of relationship

There are only three different 'degrees' of relationship between two attributes. A relationship may be

*   **One-to-one**   Examples of such a relationship include the relationship between Husband and Wife, or between Householder and Main Residence.

*   **One-to-many**   Examples include the relationship between Mother and Children, between Customer and Order, between Borrower and Library Book.

*   **Many-to-many**   Examples include the relationship between Student and Course, between Stock Item and Supplier, between Film and Film Star.

Entity-relationship diagrams

An entity-relationship diagram is a diagrammatic way of representing the relationships between the entities in a database. To show the relationship between two entities, both the **degree** and the **name** of the relationship need to be specified. E.g. In the first relationship shown below, the **degree** is *One-to-one*, the **name** of the relationship is *Drives*:

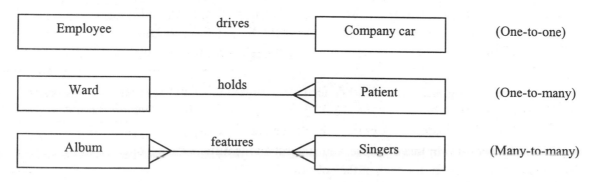

Figure 23.3: Entity relationships

Sometimes it can be tricky to establish the degree of the relationship. For example, several employees may use the same company car at different times. A single employee may change the company car that he uses. The relationship will depend upon whether the data held refers to the current situation, or whether it is a historical record. The assumption has been made above that the database is to record the current car driven by an employee.

Example:

The data requirements for a hospital in-patient system are defined as follows:

A hospital is organised into a number of wards. Each ward has a ward number and a name recorded, along with a number of beds in that ward. Each ward is staffed by nurses. Nurses have their staff number and name recorded, and are assigned to a single ward.

Each patient in the hospital has a patient identification number, and their name, address and date of birth are recorded. Each patient is under the care of a single consultant and is assigned to a single ward. Each consultant is responsible for a number of patients. Consultants have their staff number, name and specialism recorded.

State four entities for the hospital in-patient system and suggest an identifier for each of these entities.

Draw an entity-relationship diagram to show the relationship between the entities.

Answer:

Entity	Identifier
WARD	Ward number
NURSE	Staff number
PATIENT	Patient identification number
CONSULTANT	Staff number

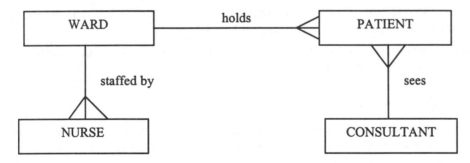

Exercises

1. A library plans to set up a database to keep track of its members, stock and loans.
    (a) State an identifier for each of the entities MEMBER, STOCK and LOAN. (3)
    (b) Draw an entity-relationship diagram showing the relationships between the entities. (3)
    New question

2. What is meant by program-data independence in the context of a database management system? (2)
    AEB Computing Paper 2 Qu 2 1994

3. A vet has a database to keep track of the animals seen at the surgery.
    (a) Name **two** entities in this database, and suggest an identifier for each one. (2)
    (b) Name **four** attributes for each of the entities. (4)
    (c) What is the relationship between the two entities? (You may use a diagram). (2)
    New question

Chapter 24 – Relational Database Design

What is a relational database?

There are several different types of Database Management System available. The most common type of DBMS is the **relational database**, widely used on all systems from micros to mainframes. In a relational database, data is held in tables (also called relations) and the tables are linked by means of common fields.

Conceptually then, one row of a table holds one record. Each column in the table holds one field or attribute.

e.g. A table holding data about an entity BOOK may have the following rows and columns:

BOOK

Accession Number	Dewey Code	Title	Author	Date published
88	121.9	Let's Cook!	Chan, C	1992
123	345.440	Electricity	Glendenning, V	1995
300	345.440	Riders	Cooper, J	1995
657	200.00	Greek in 3 weeks	Stavros, G	1990
777	001.602	I.T. in Society	Laudon, K	1994
etc				

Figure 24.1: A table in a relational database

There is a standard notation for describing a table in a relational database. For example, to describe the table shown above, you would write

> BOOK (<u>Accession Number</u>, Dewey Code, Title, Author, Date Published)

Note that:

> The entity name is shown in uppercase letters;
>
> The key field (unique identifier) is underlined;
>
> The attributes are shown in brackets, separated by commas.

Linking database tables

Tables may be linked through the use of a common field. This field must be a key field of one of the tables, and is known as a **foreign key** in the second table. An example best illustrates this.

In a library database, two entities named BOOK and BORROWER have been identified. An entity-relationship diagram may be used to describe the relationship between these two entities.

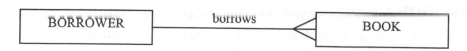

Figure 24.2: One-to-many relationship between BORROWER and BOOK

The BORROWER table can be described using standard notation as follows:

BORROWER (<u>Borrower ID</u>, name, address)

In order to link the two entities, the key field Borrower ID needs to be added to the BOOK table as a *foreign key*. The BOOK table can be described as

BOOK (<u>Accession Number</u>, Dewey Code, Title, Author, Date Published, *Borrower ID*)

Note that a foreign key is shown in italics.

In practice, since only a very small proportion of books are on loan at any one time, it would be sensible to have a third table holding data about books on loan, who had borrowed them and when they were due back.

The entity-relationship diagram would then look like this:

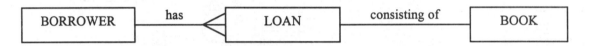

Figure 24.3: Entity-relationship diagram for a library database

> **Discussion: What would be the attributes of the LOAN table? Does it have any foreign keys?**

Normalisation

Normalisation is a process used to come up with the best possible design for a relational database. Tables should be organised in such a way that:

- No data is unnecessarily duplicated (i.e. the same data held on more than one table).
- Data is consistent throughout the database (e.g. Mr Bradley's address is not recorded as The White House, Sproughton on one table and as 32 Star Lane in another. Consistency should be an automatic consequence of not holding any duplicated data.)
- The structure of each table is flexible enough to allow you to enter as many or as few items (for example, books borrowed by a particular person) as you want to.
- The structure should enable a user to make all kinds of complex queries relating data from different tables.

We will look at three stages of normalisation known as first, second and third normal form.

First normal form

Definition: A table is in first normal form if it contains no repeating attributes or groups of attributes.

Let's look at a simple example of two entities STUDENT and COURSE. A student can take several courses, and each course has several students attending. The relationship can be represented by the entity-relationship diagram.

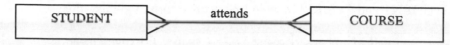

Figure 24.4: The many-to-many relationship between entities STUDENT and COURSE

Sample data to be held in the database is shown in the table below:

STUDENT

student number	student name	date of birth	sex	course number	course name	lecturer number	lecturer name
12345	Heathcote,R	20-08-77	M	EC6654	A-Level Computing	T345267	Glover,T
22433	Head,J	13-02-77	F	EC6654	A-Level Computing	T345267	Glover,T
				HM7756	A-Level Music	T773351	Reader,B
				AD1121	Pottery	T876541	
66688	Hargrave,R	13-09-54	M	BM3390	HNC Business	T666758	Newman,P
				HM7756	A-Level Music	T773351	Reader,B

The two tables STUDENT and COURSE will be represented in standard notation as

STUDENT (<u>student number</u>, student name, date of birth, sex)

COURSE (<u>course number</u>, course name, lecturer number, lecturer name)

The question now is, how can the relationship between these two tables be shown? How can we hold the information about which students are doing which courses?

The two tables need to be linked by means of a common field, but the problem is that because this is a many-to-many relationship, whichever table we put the link field into, there needs to be *more than one* field.

e.g.   STUDENT (<u>student number</u>, student name, date of birth, sex, *course number*)

is no good because the student is doing several courses, so which one would be mentioned?

Similarly,   COURSE (<u>course number</u>, course name, lecturer number, lecturer name, *student number*)

is no good either because each course has a number of students taking it.

One obvious solution (and unfortunately a bad one) springs to mind. How about allowing space for 3 courses on each student record?

STUDENT (<u>student number</u>, student name, date of birth, sex, *course1, course2, course3*)

> **Discussion: Why is this not a good idea?**

What we have engineered is a repeating attribute - anathema in 1st normal form. In other words, the field course number is repeated 3 times. The table is therefore NOT in first normal form.

It would be represented in standard notation with a line over the repeating attribute:

STUDENT (<u>student number</u>, student name, date of birth, sex, $\overline{\text{course number}}$)

To put the data into first normal form, the repeating attribute must be removed. In its place, the field course number becomes part of the primary key in the student table. The tables are now as follows:

STUDENT (<u>student number</u>, student name, date of birth, sex, <u>course number</u>)

COURSE (<u>course number</u>, course name, lecturer number, lecturer name)

> ➤ **Discussion: What is a primary key? Why does course number have to be part of the primary key?**

The two tables STUDENT and COURSE now in first normal form, look like this:

STUDENT

student number	student name	date of birth	sex	course number
12345	Heathcote,R	20-08-77	M	EC6654
22433	Head,J	13-02-77	F	EC6654
22433	Head,J	13-02-77	F	HM7756
22433	Head,J	13-02-77	F	AD1121
66688	Hargrave,R	13-09-54	M	BM3390
66688	Hargrave,R	13-09-54	M	HM7756

COURSE

course number	course name	lecturer number	lecturer name
EC6654	A-Level Computing	T345267	Glover,T
HM7756	A-Level Music	T773351	Reader,B
AD1121	Pottery	T876541	
BM3390	HNC Business	T666758	Newman,P

> ➤ **Discussion: Why is this a better way of holding the data than having one table with the following structure?**
>
> **STUDENT (student number, student name, date of birth, sex, *course1, course2, course3*)**
>
> **If student Head, J decides to take up A Level Art, what changes need to be made to the data?**
>
> **How will we find the names of all students doing A-Level Computing?**
>
> **What are the weaknesses of this table structure?**

Second normal form – Partial key dependence test

Definition: A table is in second normal form (2NF) if it is in first normal form and no column that is not part of a primary key is dependent on only a portion of the primary key.

This is sometimes expressed by saying that a table in second normal form contains no partial dependencies.

The tables above are not in second normal form. For example, Student name is dependent only on Student number and not on Course number. To put the tables into second normal form, we need to introduce a third table (relation) that acts as a link between the entities Student and Course.

The tables are now as follows:

STUDENT (student number, student name, date of birth, sex)

STUDENT_TAKES (student number, course number)

COURSE (course number, course name, lecturer number, lecturer name)

Dealing with a Many-to-Many relationship

As you get more practice in database design, you will notice that *whenever* two entities have a many-to-many relationship, you will *always* need a link table 'in the middle'. Thus

will become

Figure 24.5: A 'link' table is needed in a many-to-many relationship

Third normal form – Non-key dependence test

Definition: A table in third normal form contains no 'non-key dependencies'.

Looking at the COURSE table, the lecturer name is dependent on the lecturer number, not on the course number. It therefore needs to be removed from this relation and a new relation created:

LECTURER (<u>lecturer number</u>, lecturer name)

The database, now in third normal form, consists of the following tables:

STUDENT (<u>student number</u>, student name, date of birth, sex)

STUDENT_TAKES(<u>student number</u>, <u>course number</u>)

COURSE (<u>course number</u>, course name, lecturer number)

LECTURER (<u>lecturer number</u>, lecturer name)

This is the optimum way of holding the data, with no attributes being duplicated anywhere. In any database work that you do, you should always make sure you have designed the tables in such a way that they are in THIRD NORMAL FORM.

Comparing a flat file system with a relational database

From the example above you will have seen that a relational database is able to create **links** between tables representing different entities such as STUDENT and COURSE, through the use of **foreign keys**. *A flat file system is not able to create links between tables* and is therefore only useful for very simple databases which contain information about just one entity. It is impossible to 'normalise' a database in a flat file system, since this involves correctly establishing links between tables.

Flat file systems do not have any of the sophisticated features of a full DBMS such as the ability to set individual user access rights, or allow several people to access the database at the same time.

Exercises

1. Data on patient prescriptions are held by a GP's surgery in the following form:

PRESCRIPTION

Patient ID	Patient Name	Date of Birth	Address	Date of prescription	Drug ID	Drug Name	Dosage	Manufacturer
111	Naylor E	12-9-76	76 Church St, Hull	2-9-96 5-12-96 3-4-97	AS12 AS12 BS03	Aspirin Aspirin Migril	2 tablets 3 tablets 2 tablets	Bayer Bayer Wellcome
123	Jones R	23-9-55	23 Bay Ave Hull	5-12-96	AR14	Arnica	2 tablets	Boots
234	Leech M	4-8-77	Reckitt Hall Cottingham	3-5-97	AS12	Aspirin	2 tablets	Bayer

(a) Draw an entity-relationship diagram showing the relationships between the entities PATIENT, DRUG and PRESCRIPTION. (3)

(b) Describe the three relations needed to hold the data in a relational database in second normal form. (7)

New question

2. The manager of a video hire shop uses a relational database management system to operate the business. Separate database files hold details of customers, video films and loans. Customers can hire as many films as they wish.

   (a) For **each** of the files mentioned above identify the key fields and list other appropriate fields that would be required to enable this system to be maintained with minimum redundancy. (6)

   (b) Describe **three** advantages of using a relational database rather than a flat file information storage system. (6)

   NEAB IT02 Qu 7 1996

3. The data requirements for a booking system are defined as follows.

   An agency arranges booking of live bands for a number of clubs. Each band is registered with the agency and has its name (unique) recorded, together with the number of musicians, the type of music played and hiring fee. Each band is managed by a manager. A manager may manage several bands. Each manager is assigned an identification number and managers have their name, address and telephone number recorded. Each club is assigned an identification number and clubs have their name, address and telephone number recorded.

   The agency records details of each booking made between a band and a club for a given date. A band will never have more than one booking on any particular date.

   (a) In database modelling, what is:

      (i) an attribute; (1)

      (ii) a relationship? (1)

   (b) Four entities for the booking system are Manager, Club, Band and Booking.

      (i) Suggest an identifier, with justification, for **each** of the entities Manager, Club and Band. (3)

      (ii) Describe **four** relationships involving the entities Manager, Club, Band and Booking that can be inferred from the given data requirements. (4)

   (c) A relational database is to be used. Describe tables for the following entities underlining the primary key in each case:

      (i) Manager; (2)

      (ii) Band; (4)

      (iii) Booking. (5)

   AEB Computing Paper 2 Qu 12 1996

4. A company sports centre uses a database management system to operate a membership and fixture system. Normally members register for at least three sports, although they can play any of the sports offered by the centre. Fixtures against many other organisations are arranged in a wide range of sports involving a large number of teams.

   (a) Name **three** database files you would expect to find in this system. (3)

   (b) For each of the database files you have named, list the fields required to enable this system to be maintained with minimum redundancy. (6)

   (c) Draw a diagram to show the relationship between the database files named in part (a). (3)

   (d) Describe **three** reports that the system might be required to produce. (3)

   (e) The manager of the centre intends to send out personalised letters to each of the members. This is to be done using the mail-merge facility offered by a word processor in conjunction with the database. Explain how this is achieved. (4)

   NEAB IT02 Qu 10 Specimen Paper

Chapter 25 – Database Management

Introduction

The pooling of information, software, and computer power is very useful but it does involve potential problems. There is the danger that one user will damage or change data used by other people without their knowledge; there is the question of how to protect confidential information; there may be problems if more than one person tries to change the same item of data at the same time. If a hardware failure occurs, everyone using the database is affected, and recovery procedures must ensure that no data is lost.

In order to minimise the potential hazards, a group known as **database administration** (or a person in charge of the group, known as the **database administrator**) is responsible for supervising both the database and the use of the DBMS.

Database Administration (DBA)

The DBA's tasks will include the following:

1. The design of the database. After the initial design, the DBA must monitor the performance of the database, and if problems surface (such as a particular report taking an unacceptably long time to produce), appropriate changes must be made to the database structure.

2. Keeping users informed of changes in the database structure that will affect them; for example, if the size or format of a particular field is altered or additional fields added.

3. Maintenance of the **data dictionary** (see below) for the database, and responsibility for establishing conventions for naming tables, columns, indexes and so on.

4. Implementing access privileges for all users of the database; that is, specifying which items can be accessed and/or changed by each user.

5. Allocating passwords to each user.

6. Providing training to users in how to access and use the database.

The data dictionary

The data dictionary is a 'database about the database'. It will contain information such as:

* What tables and columns are included in the present structure;
* The names of the current tables and columns;
* The characteristics of each item of data, such as its length and data type;
* Any restrictions on the value of certain columns;
* The meaning of any data fields that are not self-evident; for example, a field such as 'course type';
* The relationships between items of data;
* Which programs access which items of data, and whether they merely read the data or change it.

The Database Management System (DBMS)

The DBMS is an application program that provides an interface between the operating system and the user in order to make access to the data as simple as possible. It has several other functions as well, and these are described below.

1. **Data storage, retrieval and update.** The DBMS must allow users to store, retrieve and update information as easily as possible, without having to be aware of the internal structure of the database.
2. **Creation and maintenance of the data dictionary.**
3. **Managing the facilities for sharing the database.** The DBMS has to ensure that problems do not arise when two people simultaneously access a record and try to update it.
4. **Backup and recovery.** The DBMS must provide the ability to recover the database in the event of system failure.
5. **Security.** The DBMS must handle password allocation and checking, and the 'view' of the database that a given user is allowed.

Querying the database

Different database systems all have their own way of performing **queries** to extract data from the database. However all perform similar functions, allowing the user to:

- Combine into one table the information from two or more related tables;
- Select the fields that are to be shown in the 'Answer' table;
- Specify criteria for searching on; e.g. find the names and addresses of all club members whose subscriptions are due;
- Save the query so that it can be executed whenever necessary;
- Save the 'Answer' table so that it can be displayed or used as the basis for a report or a mail shot, for example.

The figure below shows a **query by example** window in the Access database.

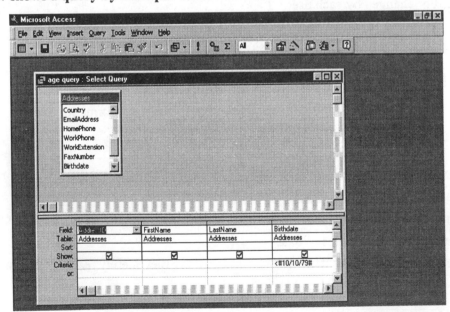

Figure 25.1: Query by Example

Using SQL

When a user constructs a query using a **query by example** form like the one shown above, the resultant query is automatically coded by Access into statements in **SQL**, or **Structured Query Language**. This is a data manipulation language that has been supported by many mainframe and minicomputers and more recently by PCs as well. The SQL for the query performed above, for example, can be viewed using a menu option in Access and is as shown below:

```
SELECT Addresses.AddressID, Addresses.FirstName, Addresses.LastName,
Addresses.Birthdate
FROM Addresses
WHERE (((Addresses.Birthdate)<#10/10/79#));
```

Some types of query cannot be performed using QBE (query by example) and SQL has to be used. It is also sometimes convenient to amend a query by changing the SQL directly instead of going back to the QBE form.

The basic retrieval facility in SQL is the **select** statement, which consists of three clauses in the general form

> **select....**
>
> **from ....**
>
> **where ....**

The **select** clause specifies columns to be extracted from the table or relation in the **from** clause. The **where** clause specifies the condition that must be met for items to be selected.

For example, to find all the female students in the **STUDENT** table given below we could enter

> **select** Student-name
>
> **from** STUDENT
>
> **where** Sex = 'F'

STUDENT

Student-name	Student ID	Date-of-birth	Sex
Heathcote,R	12345	20-08-73	M
Head,J	22433	13-02-73	F
Hargrave,R	66688	13-09-54	M
Daley,C	87656	24-12-72	M

Using indexes

A DBMS will allow the application developer to create an index for any field in the database, whether or not that field is unique. All the indexes are then held in memory while the database is open to allow fast retrieval of data. For example, suppose the following records were added in the sequence shown by the record number:

Record number	Student ID	Surname	Firstname
1	5321	Bates	Joseph
2	1963	Scully	Anne
3	4218	Chatterjee	Sara
4	3727	Fidler	Lillian
5	2858	Deacon	Michael

If the Student ID field is indexed, the index will have entries as follows:

Student ID	Record number
1963	2
2858	5
3727	4
4218	3
5321	1

Why index?

Indexing a particular field will speed up access to data, but will slow down record updating since every time an indexed field is changed, the index entry will have to be changed as well. When a new record is added, all indexes have to be updated. It makes sense, in general, to index any foreign keys in a table, and any fields like surname or department that you frequently need in alphabetical order in a report. It is also a good idea to index fields that you often use in a query criteria; e.g. to quickly find all club members whose subscriptions are overdue, the Due Date field needs to be indexed.

Indexed fields other than the primary key field are known as **secondary keys**.

Sorting

Records in a database can be sorted into any sequence that you specify, but sorting large tables can be a very time-consuming business. You may for example want one report in order of a date field, and another report from the same table in alphabetical order of surname within department. Sorting is always much faster when performed on an indexed field, so in this example you could have three indexed fields, namely date, department and surname.

Database security

Data held in databases needs to be kept secure from hackers and industrial spies, and from hazards such as disk crashes, fire, floods and so on. Methods include:

- **Taking regular backups**, daily or twice daily with the backup disks or tapes being stored in a fire-proof safe, with at least one copy off-site.

- **Transaction logging**, where information about every updating transaction is recorded on a separate transaction file. A before-image and an after-image of any record being updated is saved so that if part of the database is destroyed by a disk failure, an up-to-date copy can be created from the backup copy together with the transaction log, using a utility program.

- Using **passwords** to restrict entry to authorised users. Each user may be assigned particular access privileges such as Read-Only, Read-Write or No Access to particular areas of the database.

Exercises

1. Use a **select** clause to find all the lecturers on salary grade 13 in the **LECTURER** table below.

    LECTURER

Lec-name	Payroll-number	Department	Salary-grade
Glover,T	T345267	Computing	13
Reader,B	T773351	Humanities	23
Newman,P	T666758	Business	12

    (3)
    New question

118

2. A college library uses a relational database management system to operate a membership and loans system. Staff and students can borrow as many books as they wish at any given time.

    (a) Name **three** database tables that you would expect to find in this system. In each case, identify the columns and keys required to enable this system to be maintained with minimum redundancy. (6)

    (b) Draw an entity-relationship diagram to show the links between the database tables named in part (a). (3)

    (c) Describe the capabilities of the relational database management system that might be used to identify and output details of overdue loans. (6)

    NEAB IT02 Qu 7 1997

3. (a) Briefly explain the principal differences between a relational database and a flat file system. (4)

    (b) What is meant by data consistency, data redundancy and data independence? (3)

    (c) Describe **two** distinct security procedures you would expect to find in relational database management systems. (2)

    (d) Describe **three** functions of a database administrator. (3)

    New question

Chapter 26 – Input Devices

Keyboard data entry

The keyboard is the most common input device, suitable for a wide range of applications from entering programs to typing all kinds of documents using a word processor, or entering personal details of customers or patients at a hospital, etc. Data entered at a keyboard is commonly copied from a source document, and as such has disadvantages:

- It is easy to make **transcription** errors – that is, copy the data wrongly from the document.
- It is time-consuming.
- Data entry operators who enter data all day every day are prone to **repetitive strain injury** (RSI), a condition which renders them unable to do any further data entry or even perform everyday tasks such as pouring a cup of tea.

Voice data entry

The user speaks the text into a microphone and special software such as IBM's VoicePad or Dragon's Naturally Speaking interprets the text and displays it on a screen, where it may be edited using the keyboard and exported to a word processing package such as Word. The accuracy of the voice recognition system is improved by 'training' it to a particular user's voice – an embarrassing process of speaking a given set of a few hundred short sentences to your computer, repeating any that are not accurately interpreted.

Figure 26.1: Voice recognition: not always 100% accurate!

Scanners and OCR

An optical scanner can be used to scan graphical images and photographs, and software can then be used to edit or touch up the images. Scanners can also be used to read typed or even hand-written documents and OCR (Optical Character Recognition) software can then be used to interpret the text and export it to a word processor or data file. Scanners are also used to input large volumes of data on preprinted forms such as credit card payments, where the customers account number and amount paid are printed at the bottom of the payment slip.

Case study: Automating college enrolment

Enrolling thousands of college students on hundreds of different courses is a year-long administrative headache for colleges. Unravelling the mysteries of what students and staff have written on the enrolment forms and then entering all this information onto computer, checking it and resolving it can take weeks. One college has slashed this time and eliminated many of the errors by investing in a scanning solution from Formic.

Formic has a proven track record in scanning survey questionnaires using graphical imaging and intelligent character recognition technologies which produce clean, validated data with minimal human intervention. Its new ACE product (Automated College Enrolment) links a scanner with a digital camera and identity card printer to offer immediate and complete enrolment in the presence of the student.

Students select their courses with the help of teaching staff, who then attach official peel-off stickers to the form. Stickers are preprinted with course names and barcodes for reliable scanning. This simple procedure has eliminated much administrative frustration of trying to identify which course a student really meant to enrol for, and made it impossible for students to enrol on courses that do not exist.

Students present themselves at the enrolment desk for their form to be scanned by computer. Handwriting is converted to letters and numbers, answers are checked and validated against a postcode database. This way, all omissions and inconsistencies are picked up and resolved while the student is still there. Finally, a plastic identity card is produced bearing the student's name, enrolment number and smiling face in full colour etched securely into its tough surface. The same digital picture is stored for use later. The whole process typically takes two to three minutes from start to finish.

Source: Tim Macer, Formic magazine

➤ **Discussion: What are the benefits of the scanning system? What output could be obtained from the information gathered at enrolment time? What other use could be made of the digital photographs?**

Key-to-disk systems

In organisations where large amounts of data are collected on forms which then have to be keyed in for later processing (a **batch processing** system) an entire computer system consisting of a processor, dozens of terminals and central disk storage may be dedicated entirely to data entry. One terminal is nominated as the supervisor's terminal, from whose screen the supervisor can see exactly what every data entry operator is working on and how many keystrokes per hour and how many errors everyone is making. Completed batches of data are stored on disk from where they are either downloaded to the main computer over a communications link, or transferred to magnetic tape which is physically removed and taken to the main computer room.

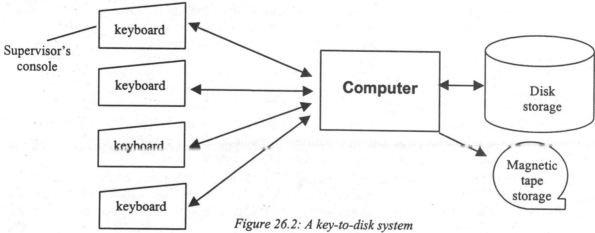

Figure 26.2: A key-to-disk system

Using a key-to-disk system, each data entry operator calls up the data entry program for her particular batch of data (e.g. payroll data entry, Council Tax payments, student grant applications) and keys in the data, which is automatically validated by the computer program.

When the batch of data has been entered and stored on disk, the source documents are passed to a second data entry operator who switches her machine to **verify** mode and keys in the data a second time. The keystrokes are compared with the data already stored on disk and any discrepancy causes the machine to beep so that the error can be corrected.

Mouse, joystick, light pen, touch screen

The mouse and its variants such as a trackball is well known to all users of PCs. A light pen is a device which incorporates a light sensor so that when it is held close to the screen over a character or part of a graphic, the object is detected and can be moved to create or modify graphics.

A touch screen allows the user to touch an area of the screen rather than having to type the data on a keyboard. They are widely used in tourist centres, where tourists can look up various local facilities and entertainments, in fast food stores such as McDonald's for entering customer orders, in manufacturing and many other environments.

(See *Case study: Pubs get a new round of touch tills* in Chapter 61.)

Magnetic Ink Character Recognition (MICR)

All banks use MICR for processing cheques. Along the bottom of a cheque the bank's sort code, customer account number and cheque number are encoded in special characters in magnetic ink. The amount of the cheque is encoded in magnetic ink when it is handed in at a bank. The cheques can then be processed extremely fast by high-speed MICR devices that read, sort and store the data on disk. MICR has several advantages for processing cheques:

- It is hard to forge the characters;
- The characters can be read even if the cheque is crumpled, dirty or smudged;
- The characters are readable by humans, unlike bar codes.

Magnetic stripe

Cards with magnetic stripes are used as credit cards, debit cards, railway tickets, phone cards and many other applications. The magnetic strip can be encoded with up to 220 characters of data, and there are over 2.4 billion plastic card transactions every year in Britain, with 83% of adults owning at least one card. Nevertheless, three factors threaten to destroy the lucrative business that high street banks have made out of plastic: crime, the cost of cash and competition. In 1996 card fraud cost the banks £97.1 million, with £13.3 million of it from fake magnetic stripe cards. The 220 characters are simply too easy to copy, which is why the stripes will eventually disappear and be replaced by a chip, which is almost impossible to fake.

Smart cards

Smart cards look similar to plastic cards with a magnetic stripe, but instead of (or as well as) the magnetic stripe, they contain a 1-millimetre square microprocessor embedded in the middle, behind a small gold electrical contact. Instead of swiping the card, you plug it into a reader.

Chip cards cost only about £1 to produce, and can hold millions of characters of data. Banks plan to introduce a 'supercard' which in addition to debit and credit facilities, can be loaded with digital cash so that smaller items such as bread, milk and newspapers can be bought without the need to carry cash. BT will adapt local payphones in a trial area to load the cards, and NCP car parks will accept the cards. When your card runs out of digital cash, you reload it from a cashpoint machine.

The Mondex card was introduced in Swindon in 1994 for a trial period, and incorporates the 'electronic purse' idea but no debit or credit facilities. However even this card has proved not to be entirely tamper-proof, which leaves open the possibility that dishonest users could simply load their cards with as much money as they like.

Figure 26.3: the Mondex smart card

> ➤ **Discussion: It has been suggested that other information such as kidney donor record and driving licence could be held on the same chip card that allows you to withdraw cash and pay for goods.**
> ➤ **What would be the benefits of doing this?**
> ➤ **What other information would it be useful to hold on a card of this sort?**

Optical Mark Recognition (OMR)

An optical mark reader can detect marks made in preset positions on a form. It is widely used for marking multiple-choice exams and market research questionnaires.

Bar code reader or scanner

Bar codes appear on almost everything we buy. The pattern of thick and thin bars represents the 13-digit number underneath the bar code. There are four main pieces of information on a bar code;

The first two (or sometimes three) digits indicate in which country the product has been registered. The code for the UK and Ireland is 50.

The next five digits represent the manufacturer's code – Cadbury's for example is 00183.

The second group of five digits represents the product and package size, but not the price.

The last digit is a check digit, which is calculated from the other digits in the code and ensures that the barcode is keyed in or read correctly.

Figure 26.4: A product bar code

> ➤ **Discussion: A supermarket has a file of all stock items, which is on-line to the point-of-sale terminals at each checkout. What data is held on the stock file? What processing takes place when an item is scanned by the barcode reader? What is the output from the process?**

Hand-held input devices

Portable keying devices are commonly used in such applications as reading gas or electricity meters, where the meter reader displays the next customer name, address and location of meter on a small screen, then reads the meter and keys in the reading. At the end of the day all the readings can be downloaded via a communications link to the main computer for processing.

Digitiser (Graphics tablet)

Professional quality illustrations can be drawn on a digitiser, which is a flat rectangular slab of material onto which a stylus is placed. The position of the stylus can be detected by the computer. As well as or instead of a stylus, a 'puck' may be used to click on a special template which covers part of the tablet. (See Figure 26.5.)

Graphics tablets come in a wide range of resolutions and types, from those used by primary school children to create drawings, to those used by engineers and architects in conjunction with computer-aided design (CAD) software. The graphics tablet shown in Figure 26.6 is a high-resolution tablet that translates x-y dimensional data into readable format and transfers it to a computer.

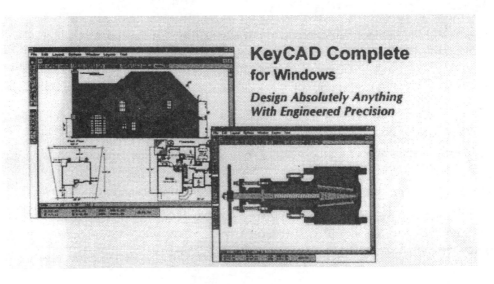

Figure 26.5: KeyCAD software can be used in conjunction with a graphics tablet

Photograph courtesy of Kye Systems UK Ltd

Figure 26.6: A graphics tablet with puck and stylus

Exercises

1. "In the future computer keyboards will be obsolete as every computer will be capable of direct speech input".

   State whether or not you agree with this claim and give **two** distinct reasons to support your answer.

   (2)

   AEB Computing Paper 1 Qu 1 1994

2. Most banks now dispense cash via Automated Teller Machines (ATMs). After inserting a plastic card which is read by the ATM, the customer types requests and responses on a special keypad.

   (a) Describe fully the procedure that the customer follows when making a cash withdrawal.   (2)

   (b) The information on the card is encoded onto a magnetic strip. Name **three** customer attributes that are stored on the strip.   (3)

   AEB AS Paper 1 Qu 2 1996

3. The use of Point of Sale (POS) terminals in supermarkets is now commonplace. What is meant by *Point of Sale*?

   Suggest **two** advantages to the customer of POS terminals connected to the central computer.   (3)

   AEB AS Paper 1 Qu 3 1994

4. Describe briefly an appropriate application for each of the following methods of input:

   (i) MICR

   (ii) Key-to-disk

   (iii) Video camera

   (iv) Touch screen

   (v) Smart card   (10)

   New question

5. (a) Why is MICR used in preference to OCR in cheque processing systems? (1)

   (b) Why is OCR used in preference to MICR in invoicing systems? (1)

   (c) (i) What is Optical Mark Reading (OMR)?

   (ii) Give **one** situation where OMR might be used. (2)

NEAB Computing Paper 2 Qu 3 1997

6. A particular company operates a manual clocking on and off system in which each employee has a time card. At the start and end of a shift, each employee takes their card out of an envelope beside the time clock, places it in a slot where the current time and date are stamped in ink on the card and replaces the card in the envelope. Each Friday evening the cards for the week are collected and replaced by new ones for the next week. The details from each card are used to work out how many hours each employee has worked so that each employee's pay can be calculated. Workers are paid one week in arrears.

A computerised system is being proposed in which the time clock will be replaced by an on-line device through which each employee will pass a swipe card instead of clocking in or out. In addition, employees will be able to use the swipe cards to purchase refreshments at a number of on-line automatic dispensers. The cost of these refreshments will be deducted from each employee's pay.

   (a) The current manual system gives rise to a number of problems. Describe **three** different problems which may arise and suggest one way in which each problem could be eliminated while still using the current time clock and cards. (6)

   (b) List the details which will be recorded on the swipe card and suggest **two** other uses to which the swipe card might be put. (6)

   (c) Describe **two** significant problems the proposed system may give rise to and suggest a way in which each of these problems might be resolved. (6)

   (d) Outline **three** advantages the proposed system will bring to the company's payroll system. (6)

NISEAC Computing Paper 1 Qu 13 1996

Chapter 27 – Data Gathering and Sampling

Data capture

In the last chapter we looked at different input devices and situations in which they would be appropriate. The particular method used to capture data will be chosen because it offers advantages in terms of speed, accuracy, and/or cost.

Methods of 'direct data capture' which cut out the need to key in data from input documents are likely to have all these advantages, and so are becoming more and more common. However, we are a long way off from escaping the chore of filling in forms of one sort or another, a large number of which will then have to be keyed into a computer system.

> ➢ **Discussion: Name (a) some applications which use direct data entry, eliminating the need for keying in data and (b) applications which require data to be keyed in.**

Types of error

Figure 27.1 shows an example of an order form filled in by customers of a mail order company.

Figure 27.1: A Mail Order form

The information from this form will be keyed in to the computer and then processed to produce a set of documents including a delivery note and invoice for the customer, as well as updating stock and sales records. There are several possible sources of error before the data are processed:

- The customer could make a mistake, entering the wrong product codes, adding up the total cost wrongly, forgetting to enter their address or card expiry date, etc.;

- The person keying in the data could make a **transcription** error, keying in the wrong product code or quantity, misreading the customer's name, adding an extra couple of 0's to the total price by keeping a finger down too long, and so on;

- A form could be blown into the bin by a sudden draught as a fan starts up or someone flounces out, slamming the door – or the operator might decide the writing was so bad it simply wasn't worth the effort of struggling with, and bin it;

- A bored keypunch operator, chatting to a colleague, could enter the same form twice without realising it;

- A faulty connection between hardware components such as the processor and the disk drive could mean that some characters are wrongly transmitted.

Now clearly a mail order company would not stay in business very long if this was how the operation worked! So what can be done to minimise the possibility of error?

Batch processing

In a batch processing system, documents such as the sales orders described above are collected into batches of typically 50 documents. A **data control clerk** has the responsibility of:

- counting the documents;

- checking each one visually to see that the customer has entered essential details such as their name and address, card details if that is the payment method, and total payable;

- calculating a control total of some crucial field such as Total Payable, for the entire batch of 50 documents;

- calculating **hash totals** of other fields such as size or quantity (see below);

- filling in a batch header document which will show, for example:

  ❑ batch number

  ❑ number of documents in batch

  ❑ date received

  ❑ control total

  ❑ hash total

- logging the batch in a book kept for this purpose.

A hash total is a sum of values calculated purely for validation purposes. For example, if the sizes of all garments ordered on a batch of forms (12, 10, 12, 34, 36, etc.) are added together and the total entered on the batch header and keyed in, the computer will be able to perform the same calculation and if the figures don't match, then the batch must have an error in it somewhere.

Control totals and hash totals have a similar purpose: the data from the batch header is keyed in as well as the contents of all the documents in the batch, and the computer performs the same summing calculations that the data entry clerk made manually. If there is any discrepancy, an error is reported and the batch is rechecked. The difference between the two types of total is only that a hash total has no meaning, whereas a control total (e.g. number of documents in the batch) does.

The stages in batch processing are discussed in the next chapter.

Validation checks

As the data is being keyed in, a computer program controlling the input can perform various validation checks on the data. For example:

1. **Presence check.** Certain fields such as customer number, item code, quantity etc must be present. The data control clerk may have visually checked this but the program can perform a second check. Also, if this is a new customer, a number could be automatically assigned.

2. **Format check** (also called **picture check**). For example the code perhaps has a pattern of 2 letters followed by 4 numbers. The quantity and price must be numeric.

3. **Range check.** The expiry date of a card must have a month number between 1 and 12, and the date must be later than today's date.

4. **File lookup check.** If the customer has filled in their customer number, the computer can look this up on the customer file and display the name and address. The data entry operator can check that it tallies.

5. **Check digit check.** (see below).

6. **Batch header checks.** The total number of records in the batch should be calculated by the computer and compared with the figure on the batch header. The control totals and hash totals are also calculated and compared.

Check digits

Code numbers such as a customer number, employee number or product number are often lengthy and prone to error when being keyed in. One way of preventing these errors occurring is to add an extra digit to the end of a code number which has been calculated from the digits of the code number. In this way the code number with its extra check digit is self-checking.

The best-known method of calculating check digits is the modulus-11 system, which traps over 99% of all errors. The calculation of a check digit is shown below.

1. Each digit of the code number is assigned a 'weight'. The right hand (least significant) digit is given a weight of 2, the next digit to the left 3 and so on.

2. Each digit is multiplied by its weight and the products added together.

3. The sum of the products is divided by 11 and the remainder obtained.

4. The remainder is subtracted from 11 to give the check digit. The two exceptions are:
   - If the remainder is 0, the check digit is 0, not 11.
   - If the remainder is 1, the check digit is X, not 10.

Example:

To calculate the check digit for the number 1587:

Original code number	1	5	8	7
Weights	5	4	3	2
Multiply digit by its weight	5	20	24	14
Add products together	5 + 20 + 24 + 14 = 63			
Divide by 11	5 remainder 8			
Subtract remainder from 11	11 - 8 = 3			

Check digit = 3. The complete code number is 15873.

To check that a code number is valid, it is not necessary to recalculate the check digit completely. If the check digit itself is assigned a weight of 1, and the products of the digits (including the check digit) and their respective weights are calculated, their sum will be divisible by 11 if the check digit is correct.

All books have an ISBN number which have a modulus-11 check digit. Try checking whether the ISBN number 1-85805-170-3 is valid. (Ignore the hyphens.)

Verification

Verification is the process of entering data twice, with the second entry being compared with the first to ensure that it is accurate. It is common in batch processing for a second data entry operator to key in a batch of data to verify it. You have probably come across another example of verification when setting a password; you are asked to key the password in a second time to ensure that you didn't make a keying error the first time, as it is not echoed on the screen.

Detecting transmission errors

In order to guard against the possibility of data being wrongly transmitted between the various hardware components of a computer, a **parity bit** is added to each character. In an even parity machine, the total number of 'On' bits in every byte (including the parity bit) must be an even number. When data is moved from one location to another, the parity bits are checked at both the sending and receiving end and if they are different or the wrong number of bits are 'On', an error message is displayed.

Thus a character code of 1101010 will have a parity bit of 0 appended to it, and a character code of 1101110 will have a parity bit of 1 appended.

Data is transmitted over a transmission line between computers in **blocks** of say 256 bytes. A **checksum** may be calculated by adding together the numeric value of all the bytes in a block, and this sum transmitted with the data, to be checked again at the receiving end.

Accuracy and validity

When primary data is collected for surveying prospective customers or following the launch of a new product, for example, the research organisation has to be careful that the sample of the population chosen to be asked questions accurately reflects the whole population. If for example the researcher collects data from random members of the public in a town between 10am and 12 noon each morning for a week, they are probably going to interview mainly pensioners or people not currently employed.

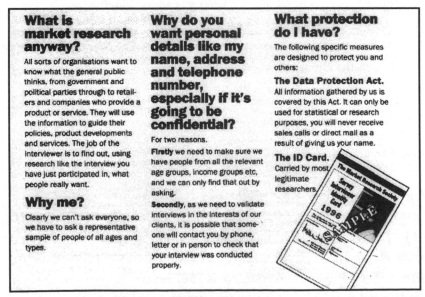

Figure 27.2: A Market Research Society card

> ➤ **Discussion: Think of examples of situations where incorrect sampling rates lead to accurate data but inaccurate information.**
>
> ➤ **Look back at the order form shown in Figure 27.1. Is it possible that some of the data entered on the form could be *valid* but *inaccurate*?**

Exercises

1. *(see case study below)*

Case study: Market research survey

The National Readership Survey is a survey about the newspapers and magazines people read (and the ones they don't), how much television they watch, and how much they listen to the radio. The research is used by publishers and editors to help them identify, for instance, what people of different ages are interested in, so they can produce newspapers and magazines to suit their readers.

The people to be interviewed (35,000 annually) are a cross-section of the population, and in order to make sure that a representative sample is chosen, interviewees are asked questions about their age, occupation, income and other descriptive details. They are also asked for their name and telephone number. Each interviewer is equipped with a battery-powered laptop computer with a single floppy disk drive and a modem. The program for each particular survey is posted to them in advance together with a list of addresses to visit and a list of questions to ask. The interviewer types the respondent's answers straight into the computer from where the data is saved onto the floppy disk. Each evening the data is transferred by telephone link to the company's mainframe computer. The data is analysed and distributed within two weeks of collection.

> ➤ **Questions:**
>
> a. How can a householder be sure that the interviewer is genuinely employed by a Market Research Organisation? (1)
>
> b. Name **two** advantages of entering data straight into the computer rather than onto hand-written forms. (2)
>
> c. Describe briefly **two** advantages and **two** disadvantages of using laptop computers that have only a single floppy drive and no hard disk. In each case say whether the advantage or disadvantage is to the market research company or to the interviewer. (4)
>
> d. The interviewees' names, addresses and telephone numbers are stored on the mainframe computer system, but held separately from the answers given in the interview and not linked to them in any way. Why are interviewees asked to supply this information? Explain why names and addresses are held separately from the rest of the data. (3)
>
> e. The survey includes questions on which sections (home news, foreign news, sport, computers, finance etc) people read in newspapers and also questions on major purchases made by members of the household over the past year or two. How would this information be useful to the organisations which use the data? (2)

2. A well designed information system should be able to check that input data is valid, but it can never ensure that information is accurate.

    (a) Explain the distinction between accuracy of information and validity of data. Illustrate this distinction with a suitable example. (4)

    (b) Describe **two** ways in which data capture errors may arise, together with techniques for preventing or reducing these errors. (4)

    NEAB IT02 Qu 6 1997

3.   In large scale batch systems which process several thousand documents daily, the data may be entered using an off-line key-to-disk system. The system may be used to validate as well as verify the data. Outline the processes of verification and validation.   (4)

AEB AS Computing Qu 6 1996

4.   Name and describe two validation checks that could be used when a product code number is input.

(4)

AEB AS Computing Qu 2 1997

5.   A school uses an information system to store details of students' examination entries and results. As part of this system a program is used to check the validity of data such as candidate number, candidate names and the subjects entered.

(a)   Suggest **three** possible validation tests which might be carried out on this data.   (3)

(b)   Explain, with an example, why data which is found to be valid by this program may still need to be verified.   (2)

NEAB IT02 Qu 5

6.   With the aid of an example, distinguish clearly between a batch/control total and a hash total.   (4)

NISEAC Computing Paper 2 Qu 3 1996

7.   Distinguish clearly between the purpose of a check digit and a parity bit.   (4)

NISEAC Computing Paper 2 Qu 1 1996

8.   Briefly explain what is meant by verification during data entry in batch processing systems.   (2)

NEAB Computing Paper 2 Qu 2 1997

9.   An international chain of department stores uses an information system to assist in marketing their produce by forecasting public demand for certain products.

(a)   Suggest **two** factors which might be considered when planning a sampling strategy for forecasting public demand.   (2)

(b)   Describe a situation where an inappropriate sampling rate could lead to accurate data but inaccurate marketing information.   (2)

NEAB IT02 Qu 3 1997

Chapter 28 – Modes of Processing

Processing methods

There are several different ways in which data can be processed, the main distinction being made between **batch processing** and **pseudo real-time processing**. You will also see or hear the terms **on-line processing**, **interactive processing** and **transaction processing** – unfortunately in computing these terms tend to be used rather loosely and seem to mean different things to different people. All these types of processing involve processing transactions, so what exactly is a transaction?

Transactions

Transactions are events which need to be recorded in connection with the production, sale and distribution of goods and services.

Many organisations have to keep track of thousands or millions of transactions every day. Every time you withdraw cash from a cashpoint machine, for example, you are performing a transaction that has to be recorded and, at some point in time, used to update the balance in your account. Some banks do not update the balance until late at night when all customers' balances are updated. Other banks use a system which updates the bank balance straight away. That is the basic difference between a batch system and a pseudo real-time system.

Other examples of transactions include:

- Buying an item in a store;
- Paying a gas bill;
- Taking out a library book;
- Applying for a driving licence;
- Enrolling on a college course;
- Applying for a University place;
- Notifying a new employer of your full name, address and bank account details;
- Clocking in and out from work.

> ➢ **Discussion: Which of the above transactions need to be processed straight away, and which can wait for a few hours or even days? Think of some more examples of transactions.**

Master files and transaction files

A **master** file is a collection of records holding information about an entity such as a person or good. For example, an employee payroll master file will contain a record for each employee, with dozens of different fields holding an employee's surname, first name, several lines of address, department, date joined, pay rate, tax code, national insurance number and bank account number. These are all fields which will not change very often – maybe once or twice a year. In addition, there will be fields which change regularly – fields such as gross pay to date (since the start of the tax year), tax paid to date, N.I. contributions to date.

A **transaction** file holds information about events occurring in the organisation. Notice that in the case of an employee payroll file, there will be basically two different kinds of transactions. There will be the weekly or fortnightly transaction file containing information about hours worked which will be used to calculate each employees wages or salary. Every so often there will be other transactions to process – additions, changes and deletions to the file.

- When a new employee is hired, a new record must be added;
- When an employee leaves, their record is (eventually) deleted;
- An employee may change address, bank account, etc.

> ➤ **What fields might be included on a record in a stock file in a supermarket? What different types of transaction will cause data on the master file to be changed?**

Batch processing

With batch processing, a group of similar transactions are collected together over a period of time and processed in one operation. The transactions may be input to the computer over a period of time (as with cashpoint machine withdrawals) or they may be collected together as pieces of paper (like orders sent by customers to a mail order firm). These documents are then batched as described in the last chapter before being entered into the computer. Either way, the actual processing of the transactions is delayed until a convenient time, which may be later the same day, at night, or once a week, for example.

> ➤ **Discussion: Look again at the examples of transactions given above. What processing needs to be carried out in each of these examples?**

Stages in batch processing

In a typical, large-scale batch system where data is collected on paper documents (such as applications for renewal of a TV or driver's licence) the following stages are gone through:

1. The paper documents are collected into batches of say 50, checked, control totals and hash totals calculated and written on a batch header document.
2. The data is keyed in off-line (i.e. to a separate computer system used solely for data entry, not the main computer) and validated by a computer program. It is stored on a transaction file.
3. The data is verified by being entered a second time by a different keypunch operator. Any discrepancies are followed up and corrected.
4. The transaction file is transferred to the main computer. This may be a matter of carrying a magnetic tape from one room to another, or it may be transferred electronically between computers.
5. Processing begins at a scheduled time – maybe overnight when the computer is not busy dealing with on-line users. All the processing steps (beginning with step 6) can take place without operator intervention.
6. The transaction file may be sorted into the same sequence as the master file (using a sort utility program) since this may speed up the processing of the data.
7. The master file is updated.
8. Any required reports are produced.

Interactive processing

In interactive processing, data is entered and processed straight away. Organisations such as insurance companies are often able to make changes to a customer's household insurance, for example, while the customer is on the phone. The insurance clerk simply calls up details of the customer's policy on the screen, and types in any required changes which immediately update the customer's record. A report of the change would be automatically generated and a copy sent to the customer.

Some interactive systems allow queries to be made, but cannot process transactions right away. Examples include:

- Cashpoint machines which allow you to query your balance and withdraw cash but do not update the balance until late at night;

- Point-of-sale terminals which can access a stock file to look up the description and price of an article when the bar-coded label is scanned, but do not alter the quantity in stock when a sale is made. (This is done later in batch mode.)

Pseudo real-time processing

Real-time processing occurs when a computer responds instantly to events occurring. The term is normally used in the context of, say, a computer controlling the flight of an aeroplane where on-board computers respond instantly to changes in wind speed, air pressure and so on. In data processing of a more mundane nature (selling tomatoes in Sainsbury's or borrowing a library book) a system where the computer records a transaction and more or less immediately updates the master file is termed 'pseudo real time' because a delay of a few seconds is quite acceptable, unlike genuine real-time processing.

An example of a pseudo real-time processing system is the British Airways Booking System which is operated by a central computer at Heathrow linked to thousands of British Airways agents in the U.K. and overseas. A person wanting to book a seat can enquire at any airline office or travel agent about a flight on a particular day, and the booking clerk can call up details on a screen. A booking can be made if a free seat is available, or alternative choices offered. Such systems need to have methods of ensuring that the same seat is not booked simultaneously by two different agents at different terminals. (This would be a function of a *database management system*.)

Criteria for choice of processing mode

The choice of whether to use a batch processing system or a pseudo real-time system depends on such factors as:

- Whether the information obtained from the system needs to be completely up-to-date at all times.

- The scale of the operation. Batch systems are well suited to very high volumes of data, when it becomes economical to have an off-line key-to-disk system for data entry.

- Cost. A real-time system is generally more expensive because of the more complex backup and recovery procedures required to cope with power failures or breakdowns in hardware.

- Computer usage. The advantage of a batch system is that it can make use of spare computer capacity overnight or at times when the computer would otherwise be idle. Batch processing is often carried out on mainframe computers.

Many applications use a combination of batch and interactive processing.

Exercises

1. A chain of estate agents has eighty branches. Daily transactions relating to house sales, purchases and enquiries are processed using a batch system based on a mainframe computer at head-office.

   (a) Outline the flow of data through such a batch processing system. (4)

   (b) The company is considering changing from the batch system to an interactive system. Describe the advantages and disadvantages of moving to an interactive system. (4)

   NEAB IT02 Qu 3 1996

2. A proposal has been put forward by a school's management to introduce a computerised system for recording pupils' attendance. Two different systems are under consideration:

   - The register books currently in use will be filled in manually as they are now, and these registers will be batch processed.

   - Pupils will record their own presence directly into the computer system.

   (a) Describe briefly what is meant by **batch processing** in this context. (2)

   (b) Suggest, with a reason, how often the batch processing should take place. (2)

   (c) Suggest and justify a method by which pupils could record their own presence into the system. (3)

   (d) Describe **one** advantage and **one** disadvantage of the proposed batch system over the other proposal. (2)

   New question

3. The management of a company which sells goods to customers by mail order is considering computerising the sales accounts of its customers.

   The system would record details of new orders, issue invoices, and record payments received from customers. In particular the management is considering whether to implement a batch processing system or an on-line transaction processing system.

   (a) State **two** advantages of batch processing and **two** advantages of on-line transaction processing. (4)

   (b) Describe **four** criteria which should be considered when choosing the processing method. (4)

   (c) State **three** validation checks which should be made to ensure that customers' accounts are correctly updated when payments are received. (3)

   (d) Describe **two** steps which should be taken to protect against the consequences of the system failing. Explain and justify how often these steps should be taken. (4)

   London Computing Paper 1 Qu 9 1996

Chapter 29 – Storage Devices

Primary and secondary storage

A computer's main memory (RAM) is known as **primary storage**. In order to execute a program, the program instructions and the data on which it is to operate have to be loaded into main memory. Primary storage, however, is **volatile**; when the computer is switched off, all the contents of memory are lost. This is one good reason to perform frequent saves to disk when working on, for example, a word processed document.

A more permanent, **non-volatile** form of storage is required by all computer systems to save software and data files. Magnetic tape, magnetic disks, CD-ROM (Compact Disk Read Only Memory), and microfilm are all examples of what is known as **secondary storage**.

File processing concepts

Data stored on secondary storage is typically stored in **files**, with a file of data being defined as a collection of records. A payroll file, for example, will contain a record for each employee, and a stock file will contain a record for each stock item. The manner in which these files are **processed** depends on whether every record in the file is to be processed one after the other, or whether individual records will be processed in no particular sequence. These two methods of processing are known as sequential and random processing.

Sequential processing. Each record in the file is read. If only the 200th record on the file needs altering, the first 199 records must be read anyway, and left as they are. Sequential processing is very fast and efficient for an application such as payroll where every record needs to be processed because every person in the company will be paid.

Random processing. Each record on the file has its own address, which can either be calculated from its unique key, or held in a separate Index, so the record can be directly accessed. This type of processing is essential if for example you want to look up the price of an item of stock on a file of 20,000 items.

These two types of processing are similar to the different ways in which you would access a particular song on a cassette tape and on a CD. On a tape, you have to wind forward until you find the song you want, whereas on a CD, you just select the track and press the correct button. Note, however, that whereas you can 'process' a CD sequentially (listen to all the tracks from beginning to end) you cannot go directly to a particular song on a tape.

Similarly, some files need to be processed sequentially on some occasions, and randomly on others.

> ➤ **Discussion: Many files need to be processed sequentially on some occasions and randomly on others.**
>
> **When would the following files need to be processed (a) sequentially? (b) randomly?**
>
> **(i) Payroll file   (ii) Electricity billing file   (iii) Library book file**

Floppy disks

The standard 3½" floppy disk is a thin, flexible plastic disk coated in metal oxide, enclosed in a rigid plastic casing. There are two varieties of these disks:

- A high density disk has a storage capacity of 1.44 Megabytes. It can be distinguished from the lower capacity disk by an extra hole in one corner (in addition to the write-protect hole), and it often (though not always) has the letters HD inscribed near the protective metal sleeve.

- A double density disk has a storage capacity of 720 Kilobytes.

Both types of disk have a write-protect hole with a built-in tab which can be positioned to leave the notch open, which write-protects it so that it cannot be written to. Positioning the tab so that the hole is closed enables the disk for writing.

No hole in this corner indicates a double density disk, capacity 720Kb

Write-protect tab

Recording window with sliding cover

Figure 29.1: A floppy disk

How data is stored

A diskette consists of two surfaces, each of which contains typically 80 concentric circles called tracks. Each track is divided into sectors. Microcomputer disks are soft-sectored: the sectors are not present when you buy a new floppy disk, but are defined when you first format the disk. If you reformat a disk that already has data on it, all the data will be erased (although you can also do a 'quick format' which erases only the file directory).

The tracks near the centre store the same amount of data as the outer tracks – the data is recorded more densely near the centre.

Tracks

Sector

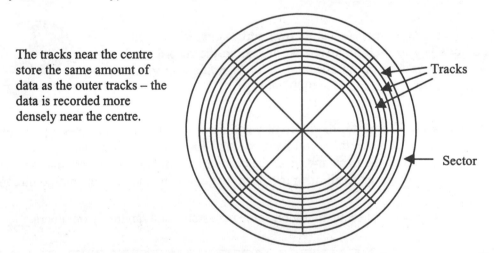

Figure 29.2: Tracks and sectors on a magnetic disk

Hard disks for microcomputers

The hard disk used with PCs consist of one or more disk platters permanently sealed inside a casing. Hard disks typically have a capacity of between 500Mb and 5Gb. (1Gb = 1,000Mb.)

Each surface has its own read-write head. The heads are mounted on a single spindle so they all move in and out together.

Figure 29.3: A microcomputer hard disk drive

External hard drives which can be plugged into a microcomputer are available as extra storage.

Hard disks for minis and mainframes

For large-scale applications storing huge amounts of data, several hard disk units will be required. The disks may be either fixed (sealed inside the unit) or removable. Fixed disks are faster, more reliable, and have a greater storage capacity.

As with other types of disk, data is stored on concentric tracks, with tracks being divided into sectors. All the tracks that are accessible from one position of the read-write heads form a **cylinder**; data is recorded cylinder by cylinder to minimise movement of the read-write heads, thereby minimising access time.

Figure 29.4: A disk drive

Magnetic tape

Data is recorded in 'frames' across the tape, with one frame representing one byte. The frames form tracks along the length of the tape, with 9 tracks being common, giving 8 data tracks and one parity track.

```
                              1 0 1        Track 1
------------------------------1-1-1----------------------------------
                              0 1 1
                              0 0 0
                              1 1 0
                              1 1 0
                              0 0 1
                              0 0 1
------------------------------0-0-1----------------------------------
                              0 0 1        Parity track
```

Figure 29.5:Tracks on a magnetic tape

Magnetic tape is a serial medium, meaning that an individual record can only be accessed by starting at the beginning of the tape and reading through every record until the required one is found. Likewise, it is impossible to read a record, amend it in memory, then backspace to the beginning of the block and overwrite the old record. Therefore, updating a magnetic tape file always involves copying the file to a new tape with the amendments made.

Uses of magnetic tape

Tape is a cheap and convenient medium for backup, and is also used for **archiving** past transactions or other data that may be needed again, such as for example, weather records collected over a number of years.

Cartridge tape drives are in common use for backing up the hard disk of personal computers, being much more convenient than using dozens of floppy disks. Cartridge tapes storing up to 7Gb can be bought for under £10, or about £50 for a 20Gb capacity tape.

> ➢ **Discussion: Discuss the relative advantages of hard disks, floppy disks and magnetic tape.**

CD-ROM

CD-ROMs can store around 680Mb of data, equivalent to hundreds of floppy disks. The data may be in text form, or may be in the form of graphics, photographic images, video clips or sound files. Although they do not transfer data as fast as a hard disk drive, their speed is increasing every year and is acceptable for most applications.

As the name suggests, the disks are read-only. When the master disk is created, a laser beam burns tiny holes in the surface of the disk, which (unlike a magnetic disk) has a single spiral track divided into sectors. To read data from the disk, a laser beam is reflected off the surface of the disk, detecting the presence or absence of pits which represent binary digits.

WORM disks

Write Once, Read Many optical laser disks look similar to CD-ROM disks, but they are often gold rather than silver in colour. An end-user company can use these disks to write their own material, typically for archiving or storing say, graphic or photographic images which will not be changed.

These disks are also widely used for pirated software; whereas silver CDs are pressed in factories, gold CDs are usually written one at a time on PCs in garages and back bedrooms. A £5 blank disk can hold £20,000 worth of software and sell for £50 to £80, and they are sometimes used by less reputable PC manufacturers who install the software on their PCs to make a more attractive deal for the unknowing customer. However, because there is a lot of competition among pirates, these CDs sometimes carry viruses which can cause havoc on a hard drive.

Magneto-optical disks

Magneto-optical disks integrate optical and laser technology to enable read and write storage. A 5½" disk can store up to 1000Mb. These disks may in the future replace current magnetic disks, but at present the technology is still developing and the disks are too expensive, slow and unreliable to be in widespread use.

Microfiche

COM (Computer Output on Microfilm) devices are used to prepare microfiche, a 4" by 6" hard-copy film that is sometimes seen in libraries and bookshops being used for reference purposes. Each microfiche sheet is divided into as many as 270 frames each containing a page of information which can be read using a special viewer. COM is also extensively used for archiving material such as old cheques or income tax returns.

COM system   4' X 6'
Microfiche   Microform viewer

Figure 29.6: Computer Output to Microfilm

> ➤ **Discussion: What are some of the applications of CD-ROM? Why is CD-ROM particularly suitable for these applications?**

Exercises

1. Why do many software manufacturers now prefer to sell their software on CD-ROM rather than on floppy disk?

   (2)
   NEAB Computing Paper 1 Qu 1 1997

2. Give **one** appropriate use with clear justification for:
   (a) floppy disks;
   (b) hard disks;
   (c) CD-ROMs

   (6)
   AEB Computing Paper 1 Qu 9 1997

3. WORM (Write Once Read Many times) is an acronym sometimes used for certain types of data storage.

   Give **one** example of this type of storage and describe a typical use for your example.

   Give **one** feature of WORM type of storage which makes it appropriate for the example you have given.

   (3)
   AEB Computing Paper 1 Qu 5 1995

4. Although large disk storage devices are now readily available for computer systems, the use of magnetic tape is still widespread.

   Describe **two** distinct uses of magnetic tape and explain its suitability in each case. (4)
   London Computing Paper 1 Qu 8 1995

5. (i) Describe, with the aid of a diagram, the layout of data on one surface of a magnetic disk pack.

   (2)

   (ii) Why is data storage on a magnetic disk pack organised in cylinders? (2)

   (iii) Why is it necessary to format a magnetic disk before it can be used? (2)
   NEAB Computing AS Qu 7 1995

Chapter 30 – Dissemination of Information

Characteristics of good information

Computers are capable of producing unimaginable amounts of information in a fraction of a second – unfortunately, humans can only digest about four or five brief points in a 45 minute presentation, as you will be well aware if you have been attending classes regularly. To be useful to a manager who will use computer-produced information to make decisions, information needs to be:

- Relevant;
- Complete;
- Accurate;
- Clear;
- Timely – the information must be available when it is needed, which may be immediately, or in time for a monthly meeting, for example;
- Concise – the principle of **reporting by exception** is very important in management information systems – in other words, only items that need some action on them are reported;
- In an appropriate sequence.

> **Discussion: A manager in a fast food store wants to know how many days of sickness employees have had over the past 3 months. The data is available in the following form:**

REPORT FOR WEEK ENDING 13/12/97

Employee Name	Date	Hrs Scheduled	Hrs Worked	Reason for Absence
Andrews, M	10/12/97	7	7	
Andrews, M	11/12/97	5	4.5	
...				
...				
Goode, L	12/12/97	7	7.5	
Goode, L	13/12/97	8	0	Sick
...				

(rest of records for Goode, L followed by other employee records in alphabetical order)

> Would this be a suitable report to present to the manager? What are its faults? Check the list given above for 'characteristics of good information' and suggest improvements.

Presenting management information

The way that information is presented can be almost as important as the information itself. Information can be presented in numerous different ways:

- On computer printouts, using the principle of exception reporting for brevity and clarity;

- On a VDU. It could take the form of a report or a 'slide show' produced using a presentation graphics package, for example;

- Desktop published, incorporating company logo, graphs, diagrams, photographs etc;

- Orally – 'over the grapevine', by telephone or in formal presentations;

- Using videoconferencing to enable several people at separate locations to participate in meetings and information exchange;

- Over a company-wide Intranet – an internal network which all employees have access to and on which important information can be posted.

> ➢ **Discussion: Think of other ways in which information can be disseminated to employees in an organisation.**

The intended audience

The way that information is presented will depend to a large extent on who it is intended to reach. Information on products and sales intended for customers will be presented in a different way from information intended for wholesalers or the company accountant.

Graphs and charts

Graphs and charts are an effective way of presenting information and highlighting problems or trends. A **bar chart**, for example, shows a trend at a glance. (Figure 30.1.)

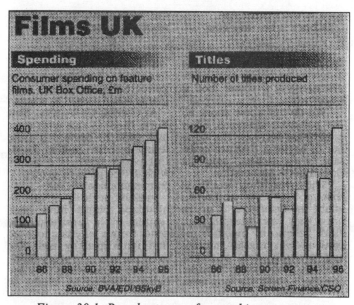

Figure 30.1: Bar charts are often used in newspapers

A **line graph** may be a good way to highlight seasonal sales figures.

A **pie chart** can be a good way of showing how a total is made up, but is not effective if there are too many segments. The one shown in Figure 30.2 could be used to emphasise the amount of money spent on domestic services at Oxford Colleges.

Oxford Colleges		
Expenditure 1995/96		
	£m	%
Academic	33	29
Catering	10	8
Domestic services	30	27
Administration	13	12
Buildings	22	19
Other	6	5

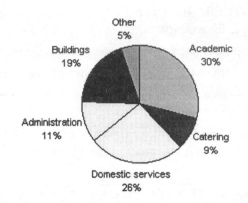

Source: Oxford Magazine

Figure 30.2: A pie chart illustrating a table of figures

Guidelines for presentations

A presentation could for example take the form of a talk accompanied by overhead projector transparencies or slides, or a slide show prepared in PowerPoint or a similar graphics package. Either way, the information on each screen or slide should be:

- Simple – no more than 5 or 6 clearly legible lines, in clear English;

- Brief – bullet points are a good communication tool;

- Visually appealing – don't use too many different fonts, or all uppercase letters. Graphs and charts are useful where numeric information has to be imparted.

Exercises

1. Prepare a presentation on one of the topics in your I.T. syllabus, to be delivered in class.

2. A manufacturing company intends to use an information system to store details of its products and sales. The information system must be capable of presenting the stored information in a variety of ways. Explain, using **three** distinct examples, why this capability is needed. (6)

   NEAB IT02 Qu 4 1997

3. A company has a computerised accounting system which produces a detailed monthly report in tabular form. This report is distributed to all the company's managers. The managers have difficulty in extracting information to enable them to make decisions.

   Briefly describe *two* ways of presenting the information in the report so that individual managers can use it more easily. (4)

   London Computing Paper 1 Qu 7 1996

Chapter 31 – Security of Data

Privacy and security

Personal data about employees and customers is held by almost every company, large and small.

Under the Data Protection Act (see Chapter 14), every organisation that stores personal data about members of the public or employees has a duty to keep the data 'secure'. This not only implies that the data must be kept safe from prying eyes, and ensuring that the data does not fall into the hands of the wrong people. It also means that data must be secured against accidental loss or destruction. It is impossible to protect computer systems completely from the dangers of accidental corruption of data, fire, hurricanes, earthquakes and terrorist attacks, so it is in the interest of every computer user to make regular backups.

Keeping data secure

The various threats to information systems were discussed in Chapter 12. They include:

- Illegal access to data ('hacking');
- Malicious destruction of data by planting a virus or altering the data in some way;
- Accidental destruction of data.

In this chapter we'll concentrate on backup strategies. Refer back to Chapter 13 for other methods of protecting data.

Disaster planning

The cost of lack of planning for computer failure can be ruinous. IBM estimates that 70% of organisations that experience a failure (caused by fire, flood, power failure, malice etc) cease operating within 18 months. The main consequence of a computer failure is loss of business, but other problems include loss of credibility, cashflow interruptions, poorer service to customers and loss of production.

Case study: Safe as Houses

One summer evening last year, the heart of Tony Pidgeley's computer system was stolen. "Someone walked into the office at 6pm and walked away with the network server. Incredible!" he says.

The consequences could have been catastrophic for Pidgley's construction business. "We would have lost everything – all our accounts and land acquisition programmes," he says.

The firm was saved from disaster by a small cartridge no bigger than a couple of cigarette packets. Inside was a tape containing a backup copy, made the previous evening, of everything on the server's 1Gb hard disk. All that was lost was one day's data input, which was re-keyed in a couple of hours. The firm's PC dealer worked through the night to set up a replacement server, and insurance covered the hardware cost.

The firm's backup is run every evening. It takes most of the night, but this does not matter since it can run unattended. The next day, somebody takes the tape home, in case fire or flood should destroy the entire office. Once a month, a tape is checked to make sure the backup is working properly.

Source: Paul Bray, The Sunday Times 19 October 1997

➢ **Discussion: What are the main points of Tony's backup strategy?**

Many companies have comprehensive emergency plans, and even after suffering severe bomb or fire damage, can be up and running after a day or two. They generally subscribe to disaster recovery services offered by companies specialising in this field. Smaller companies may not need such elaborate backup and recovery procedures, but a backup system is still vital.

Backup strategies

The simplest backup strategy for a small business is to copy the contents of a computer's hard disk at the end of each day to a tape or removable disk.

However, it is not necessary to copy software programs except when they are changed, so a better solution is to keep data files in separate directories from the software and selectively back up only certain directories.

If this still results in backing up huge quantities of data, it can be reduced by backing up only those files which have changed since the last backup – an 'incremental backup'. Backup devices come with special software that helps you to select which files to copy, when and how.

Backup hardware

- For small quantities of data, removable disks are the simplest. Iomega's Zip drive costs around £100 and takes 100Mb disks similar to floppy disks costing £10 each.

- SuperDisk drives from manufacturers such as Panasonic take 120Mb disks and can also read ordinary 1.44Mb floppy disks.

- For larger backups, magnetic tape is the preferred medium. Low-cost tape drives such as Hewlett-Packard's Colorado range and Iomega's Ditto range costing around £100 use 2Gb tape cartridges costing around £20. An 8Gb drive costs around £250.

- A rewriteable optical disk drive costs around £280 and holds about 650Mb.

- RAID (Redundant Array of Inexpensive Disks) – see below.

Backing up on-line databases

When a database is on-line and being constantly updated, precautions have to be taken to ensure that data is not lost in the event of hardware failure such as a disk head crash. Methods used include:

- **Transaction logging.** Information about every updating transaction is recorded on a separate transaction file. A *before-image* and an *after-image* of any record being updated is saved so that if part of the database is destroyed by a disk failure, an up-to-date copy can be created from the backup copy together with the transaction log using a utility program.

- **Using RAID (Redundant Array of Inexpensive Disks).** These devices use a technology which enables data to be written simultaneously to several disks. Three copies of the database may be held, two in the same room and one at a remote location, and all three copies are kept completely up-to-date. Then if one disk fails, the data is still safe on the other two disks.

Factors in a backup strategy

When a company is planning its backup strategy, there are several factors to be taken into account. For example:

- **Frequency of backups.** Many organisations, such as a school or college, find it sufficient to back up data once or twice a day. On-line databases (for example in a hospital or airline booking system) need to be backed up constantly to prevent any loss of data.

- **Backup medium.** Magnetic tape is cheap, compact and can store large amounts of data, and is used by many organisations to back up data from hard disks every night. Smaller amounts of data may be backed up on removable disks using a Zip drive.

- **Location of backup storage.** The data needs to be held in a secure location in case of fire or burglary. Many organisations have a fireproof safe for the latest backups, with another set of backups being stored off-site.

- **Number of generations to be kept.** A typical strategy is to:
  - keep the daily backups for a week;
  - keep Friday's backup for a month;
  - keep one backup each month for a year;
  - give each tape or disk a serial number and keep a log book, to prevent mix-ups.

- **Responsibility for implementing the backup strategy.** Although the regular backup routine may be performed by a computer operator or an office worker, a senior manager should have overall responsibility for ensuring that all aspects of the backup strategy are properly implemented.

- **Testing of recovery procedures**. At regular intervals the effectiveness of the backup strategy needs to be tested to ensure that the organisation can recover quickly from loss of data. It would be rather tragic to discover that the magnetic tapes that were supposed to store the backup data were in fact blank!

Exercises

1. A computer system, that is normally in use 24 hours a day, holds large volumes of different types of data on disk packs. The main types of data stored are:
   - Applications software that changes only occasionally during maintenance;
   - Data master files that are updated regularly every week;
   - Transaction files which are created daily;
   - Database files which are changing constantly.

   It is vital that these different types of files can be quickly recovered in the event of file corruption.

   Outline a suitable back up strategy for each of these types of file explaining what data is backed up and when, the procedures to be followed, and the media and hardware needed. (8)

   NEAB IT02 Sample Paper Qu 8

2. Describe briefly **three** different types of threat to data held in a computer system, and methods to combat each of these threats. (6)

   New question

3. A small company holds records of customer accounts, invoices and payments, stock records and mailing list on a hard disk on one of three networked PCs. Describe procedures that they should adopt to ensure that this data is not lost or corrupted. (10)

   New question

Chapter 32 – Output Devices

Printers

Printers come in all shapes and sizes, and the type of printer chosen will depend on several factors such as:

- **volume of output** – for high volumes, a fast, heavy-duty printer is required;

- **quality of print required** – business letters and reports to clients, for example, will require a high quality print, probably on special headed stationery;

- **location of the printer** – if the printer is going to be situated in a busy office, the noise that it makes is an important consideration;

- **requirement for multiple copies** – some printers cannot produce multiple copies;

- **requirements for colour** – does the output need to be in colour?

Dot matrix printer

A dot matrix printer is an **impact printer**, producing its image by striking the paper through a ribbon. Its print head consists of a number of small pins, varying between 9 and 24 depending on the manufacturer. A 24 pin print head will produce a better quality of print than a 9 pin print head because the dots are closer together.

As the print head moves across the page, one or more pins strike the ribbon and make a dot on the paper. The figure below shows how the letter F is produced.

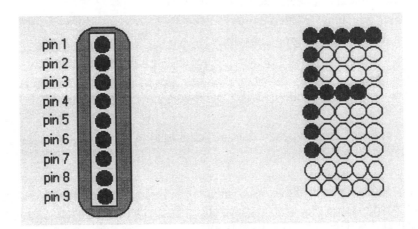

Figure 32.1 — Dot matrix print head

In order to produce 'near letter quality' (**NLQ**) print, a line is printed twice, with the print head being shifted along very slightly in the second printing so that the spaces between the dots are filled in. The disadvantage of this technique is that the document then takes approximately twice as long to print. Many dot matrix printers are 'bidirectional', meaning that they can print in either direction, thus eliminating the need to start printing each line from the left hand side of the page.

Dot matrix printers are extremely versatile, with most of them able to print in condensed, standard and enlarged mode, in 'bold' or normal print.

Many dot matrix printers have a graphics mode that enables them to print pictures and graphs by activating individual print head pins separately or in combination to produce any shape or line. With appropriate software any typeface can be produced, and using a special 4-colour ribbon (red, yellow, blue and black), colour output for, say, a graphical presentation can be produced. However the quality of colour is not as good as that produced by other types of colour printer.

One of the main drawbacks of a dot matrix printer is its noise; in an office environment it can be an irritating distraction. Covers can be obtained to cut down the noise, but it is still audible.

Ink jet printers

Ink jet printers are a popular type of non-impact printer, with prices ranging between £150 and £1500; a popular colour inkjet printer such as Hewlett Packard's DeskJet 690C costs around £150. They are compact and quiet, and offer resolution almost as good as a laser printer. However, they are slow in operation; on average 3 pages per minute are printed, but a complex combination of text and colour can take several minutes for a single sheet.

Inkjet printers such as the HP Deskjet fire a droplet of ink at the page by boiling it in a microscopic tube and letting steam eject the droplet. Heating the ink can damage the colour pigments and matching the ink chemistry to the broad range of papers used in the office is a technical challenge. Large areas of colour can get wet, buckle, and the ink may smear. Printing an ink jet colour page can cost as much as 75p if all colour inks are supplied in a single cartridge; more thrifty printers will use separate red, blue, yellow and black cartridges which can be individually replaced. Although ordinary photocopy paper can be used, special smooth-coated paper may produce a more satisfactory result.

Figure 32.2: A Canon Bubble Jet Printer BJC7000

Laser printers

Laser printers are becoming increasingly popular, with prices dropping rapidly to under £500 for a PostScript printer suitable for desktop publishing applications. Laser printers use a process similar to a photocopying machine, with toner (powdered ink) being transferred to the page and then fused onto it by heat and pressure. A laser printer produces output of very high quality at a typical speed in the region of ten pages per minute, and is virtually silent in operation. The main running expenses are the toner, which costs about £75 for a cartridge lasting for around 5,000 copies, and a maintenance contract which is typically up to £300pa.

A high quality colour laser printer may cost between £4,000 and £5,000.

Plotters

A plotter is an output device used to produce high quality line drawings such as building plans or electronic circuits. They are generally classified as pen (vector plotters) or penless (raster plotters). The former use pens to draw images using point-to-point data, moving the pen over the paper. Pen plotters are low in price and hold a large share of the plotter market.

Penless plotters include electrostatic plotters, thermal plotters and laser plotters. They are generally used where drawings of high densities are required, for example drawings of machines, printed circuit boards or maps. Colour electrostatic plotters are increasingly being used in, for example, assembly drawings of machines and building plans, making them easier to read and understand.

Photograph courtesy of Hewlett Packard Company

Figure 32.3: Hewlett-Packard plotters

Visual display unit (VDU)

A VDU has three basic attributes: size, colour and resolution. It has its own fixed amount of RAM associated with it to store the image being displayed on the screen, and the amount of RAM it has will determine the resolution and the maximum number of colours that can be displayed. Note that:

- The resolution is determined by the number of pixels (addressable picture elements) used to represent a full-screen image;

- the number of colours that can be displayed is determined by how many bits are used to represent each pixel. If only one bit is used to represent each pixel, then only two colours can be represented. To display 256 colours, 8 bits per pixel are required, and to display 65,536 (i.e. 2^{16}) colours, 16 bits (2 bytes) per pixel are needed. It is usually possible to adjust both the resolution and the number of colours - *if a high resolution is selected you won't be able to have as many colours because of the memory limitations of the VDU.*

For example, if a resolution of 800x600 pixels is selected together with 65,536 colours, the amount of video RAM required will be 800x600x2 bytes = 960,000 bytes, i.e. almost 1Mb. If 1Mb is all the video RAM supplied by the manufacturer, the resolution cannot be increased to say, 1000x800 unless the number of bytes used to represent each pixel is reduced, thus limiting the number of colours which can be displayed.

On a PC, the number of colours and the resolution of the screen can be adjusted on the Display option of the Control Panel.

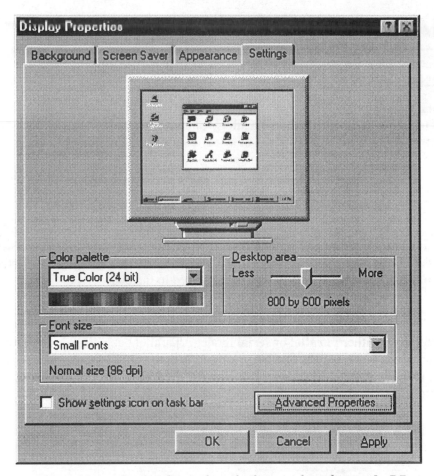

Figure 32.4: Adjusting the number of colours and resolution of a PC

Exercises

1. A printer fails to work or perform as the user expects when a document has been sent to be printed. The user has checked that the on-line light of the printer is illuminated and the printer paper is correctly inserted. Give **two** other possible reasons why the printing process failed. (2)

    AEB Computing Paper 1 Qu 1 1997

2. Explain the relationship between the resolution of a screen and the number of colours that it can display. (3)

    New question

Chapter 33 – Configuring Hardware and Software

Communicating with the CPU

Data, addresses and control signals are transferred between the various components of a computer by means of **buses**. The name originates from the analogy of carrying many people at once around town in a double-decker, but in this case is simply a set of wires connecting components. There are two sorts of buses:

- **internal buses** which connect the various registers and internal components of the CPU
- **external buses** which connect the CPU to main memory and to the input-output units.

Input and output units vary enormously in their speed, mode of operation, code conversion requirements and so on, and so cannot be connected directly to the CPU by means of a simple bus. Instead, each device comes with its own **interface unit**, which in turn is connected to the bus.

Parallel and serial data transmission

Data may be transferred in either **parallel** or **serial** mode. A parallel bus with 8 lines can transfer one byte at a time, whereas a serial bus transfers one bit at a time. A commonly used serial interface is the 25-pin RS232C interface, used for example to connect an external modem to the CPU. A mouse commonly uses a 9-pin serial interface.

Figure 33.1: Different types of serial interface connectors

Although only one line is used for transmitting data, other lines are needed for control signals, timing signals, secondary data channels, grounding and so on. Some lines are not used at all.

Transferring data in parallel mode is obviously faster than transferring in serial mode because 8 bits are transferred simultaneously, but parallel connections can only be made over a short distance of two or three metres. Printers and scanners normally use parallel interfaces when the printer is close to the computer. Many printers have both types of connector so that if for example the parallel port on your computer is being used to connect a scanner, you could use the serial port for the printer.

Buffering

A buffer is an area of memory used for holding data during input or output transfers to and from I-O devices. Because the CPU can process data thousands of times faster than, say, a printer can print it, input and output are handled independently of the main processor. Once an I-O operation is initiated, a special I-O channel takes control of the operation, leaving the CPU free for other tasks.

Information that is to be printed is placed in a print buffer which may be several megabytes long, located either in the computer or the printer, or both. A laser printer, for example, comes with its own memory buffer of say 1 or 2 megabytes.

Spooling

Spooling is a technique used to speed up communication between devices which operate at differing speeds. Output to a printer, for example, may be spooled (written) to disk, which is a high-speed device. When the printer becomes free, the output will be printed. This technique enables several users on a network to share a single printer without their output getting muddled up. Each user's output is spooled to a different position on the disk, and printed using a queuing system.

Installing hardware devices such as a printer

When you add a new device such as a printer, scanner, mouse, soundcard or videodisk player to a computer system, you have to install a piece of software called a **device driver** to control the device. For example, when you attach a new printer to a computer, you have to do the following before you can print anything:

- Install the printer-driver file for the printer;
- Select the port you want to assign the printer to.

A printer-driver file is a piece of software that specifies information about the printer, including details about printer features, descriptions of fonts (sizes and styles) and control sequences that the printer uses to produce various formats. When you give an instruction to print, the driver translates the information about fonts, formatting, highlighting etc. into a form that the printer can understand.

TrueType fonts

Printers differ in their abilities to use fonts, graphics, spacing, alignment and character formats. The appearance of a printed document is affected by three factors:

- Whether you can specify fonts and formats in your application;
- The font and format choices you make;
- The fonts and formats your printer can print.

Some applications attempt to display fonts on the screen as you would see them on the printed page. However, unless you use TrueType fonts, the document may not look the same when it is printed as it does on the screen. If you use TrueType fonts, all Windows applications will display the fonts on the screen exactly as they appear when printed. In addition, documents become more portable; they look the same printed on different printers, as long as you use the same application and print at the same resolution.

Configuring software

When you install a new piece of software, it often requires some customisation – in other words, it needs to be **configured** to your requirements. When you install the latest version of Windows on your PC, for example, you may need to:

- configure the keyboard layout for English rather than American usage;
- configure the default date display from mm-dd-yy to dd-mm-yy;
- alter the time delay before a screen saver appears.

(From Windows Explorer, look up *Configure* in the Help system and you will see dozens of different ways of configuring Windows, from adjusting the cursor blink rate or the size of the Recycle Bin to enabling print sharing on your computer.)

Other examples include communications software which needs to be configured to a particular modem, and games software which may need to be configured to respond correctly to a joystick.

Exercises

1. Many computers have both serial and parallel ports. Data can be sent to a printer from either port.
    (a) Describe serial and parallel transmission of data. (2)
    (b) Given that both a printer and a computer have a serial and parallel port, state **one** factor that would influence a user's choice of connection between a computer and a printer. Justify your answer. (2)
    (c) A printer is a slow device compared to a central processing unit. Describe **two** techniques that can be used to compensate for the difference in speed between a printer and a central processing unit. (4)
    SEB Computing Paper 1 Qu 10 1996

2. (a) Describe the process of producing a printout when a print spooler is used. (3)
    (b) Explain why a print spooler is desirable in
        (i) a multi-user system,
        (ii) a single-user system. (4)
    NEAB Computing Paper 1 Qu 10 1996

3. When installing or configuring a particular word processing package, the documentation states that the correct printer driver must also be installed. What is a printer driver, and why is it necessary? (4)
    NEAB IT02 Qu 2 1997

Chapter 34 – Network Environments

Communications networks

A Local Area Network (LAN) is a collection of computers and peripherals confined to one building or site, connected together by a common electrical connection. A LAN can be connected to other LANs, or to a Wide Area Network (WAN).

A WAN connects computers or networks over a wide geographical area; for example different sites, towns or continents.

Advantages and disadvantages of networks

A network has several advantages over a collection of stand-alone microcomputers:

- It allows the sharing of resources such as disk storage, printers, image scanners, modems and central servers;

- It allows sharing of information held on disk drives accessible by all users;

- It is easier to store application programs on one computer and make them available to all users rather than having copies individually installed on each computer;

- It allows electronic mail to be sent between users;

- It is easier to set up new users and equipment;

- It allows the connection of different types of computer which can communicate with each other.

The main **disadvantages** of networks are:

- Users become dependent on them; if for example the network file server develops a fault, then many users will be unable to run application programs. (On many sites, a back-up file server can be switched into action if the main server fails).

- If the network stops operating then it may not be possible to access various hardware and software resources.

- The efficiency of a network is very dependent on the skill of the system manager. A badly managed network may operate less efficiently than stand-alone machines.

- It is difficult to make the system secure from hackers, novices or industrial espionage.

- As traffic increases on the network the performance degrades unless it is properly designed.

Network topologies

The **topology** of a network is its physical layout — the way in which the computers and other units (commonly referred to as **nodes**) are connected. Common topologies include **star**, **bus** and **ring**, discussed below.

Star network

Each node in a star network is connected to a central **host computer** which controls the network. This is a common topology for a wide area network in large companies which have a mainframe computer at the Head Office, and computer facilities (perhaps linked together in a LAN) at each branch. It has the advantage that each node is independent of the others so a fault at one branch will not affect the other branches. On the other hand if the main computer goes down, all users are affected.

Figure 34.1: A star network

Bus network

This is a typical topology for a LAN, with all the devices on the network sharing a single cable. Information can be transmitted in either direction from any PC to any other. The problem here is that several stations may want to transmit down the same line simultaneously, and there has to be some strategy for deciding who gets the line. A popular scheme called **Ethernet** uses a collision system known as '**carrier sense multiple access with collision detection**' (CSMA-CD). Before a station begins to transmit, it checks that the channel is not busy; if it is, it has to wait before transmission can begin. Once it begins transmission, it listens for other nodes also beginning transmission. If the transmitted message collides with another, both stations abort and wait a random period of time before trying again.

This system works well if the channels are not too heavily loaded. On the other hand if sixteen students sit down at sixteen computers all at once and all try to load software from the network's hard disk, the whole system more or less grinds to a halt!

File/Print server

Figure 34.2: A bus network

Ring network

In a ring network, a series of computers is connected together and there is no central controlling computer. Each computer may communicate with any other computer in the ring, with messages being specifically addressed to the destination computer. Using the 'token ring' system, a 'message token' (actually a unique character sequence) is passed from node to node, and each node has a designated time at which it can remove the token and either add a message together with the addresses of the receiving node and sending node, (and some control bits) or take a message from it. A receiving device acknowledges the receipt of a message by inverting a 1-bit field.

Figure 34.3: A ring network

Server-based vs. peer-to-peer networks

In *client-server architecture*, different devices on the network are treated as clients or servers. The client devices send requests for service, such as printing or retrieval of data, to specific server devices that perform the requested processing. For example, the client devices might consist of twenty workstations in a room, and the server devices might be a laser printer and a computer dedicated to managing the network (the file server).

Peer-to-peer architecture is an alternative to client-server for small computer networks. In peer-to-peer, each workstation can communicate directly with every other workstation on the network without going through a server. Peer-to-peer is most appropriate when the network users mostly do their own work but occasionally need to share data or communicate with each other. One disadvantage of this arrangement is that if the workstation from which a user wishes to retrieve data is switched off, the data cannot be retrieved!

Any sort of network requires maintenance – someone has to be responsible for ensuring that:

- Response time is adequate;
- Hardware is upgraded when necessary;
- The required software is loaded;
- Software is upgraded when necessary and users are kept informed of changes;
- A system of regular backups is adhered to;
- Network security is maintained.

The differences between the client-server and peer-to-peer networks are summarised in the table below:

Server-based networks	Peer-to-peer networks
Example: Novell's NetWare	*Example: Microsoft Windows for Workgroups*
A central backing store is available to all users.	Storage facilities are distributed throughout the network.
Software is centrally held and shared. The server distributes the programs and data to the other microcomputers in the network (the 'clients') as they request them. Some processing tasks are performed by the desktop computer; others are handled by the file server. This is termed '**client-server**' architecture. The use of servers provides the network with more speed and power, but adds expense and complication.	Copies of software may be held on individual machines. Peer-to-peer networks provide basic network services such as software, file and print sharing, and are less expensive and less difficult to administer than those set up with servers. They are most appropriate for smaller businesses that do not need the power and speed of client-server architecture.
User IDs, passwords and access levels are controlled by the central computer.	Security is not centrally controlled.
Backup facilities are centralised; data and information held centrally are backed up regularly.	Backup is the responsibility of individual computer users.
All users are reliant on the service provided by the central facility. If the central computer goes down, all users are affected.	No reliance on a central computer.
All communication takes place through the central computer. Computers on the network may be of different types (from different manufacturers) and the central node computer controls the communications protocol.	The individual computers on the network must have software to control communication with other computers of the same or different types on the network.

Figure 34.4: Comparison of client-server and peer-to-peer networks

Exercises

1. A local surgery uses a number of stand-alone computer systems to manage patient records, appointments, staff pay and all financial accounts. The surgery manager is considering changing to a local area network.

    (i) Compare the relative advantages of stand-alone and local area network systems.   (6)

    (ii) Describe, with the aid of diagrams, **two** alternative network topologies.   (6)

    NEAB IT02 Qu 9 1996

2. What is meant by the term 'peer-to-peer network'? Describe briefly **two** advantages of this type of network over a server-based network.   (6)

    New question

Chapter 35 – Wide Area Networks

Principle of electronic data communication

Data communication involves sending and receiving data from one computer or data processing device to another. Applications using for example e-mail, supermarket EPOS (electronic point of sale) terminals, cash dispensers, facsimile, and video conferencing are all examples of this.

When the devices are close together, for example in the same building, they can be linked by means of cables. However, when devices are separated by more than a few hundred yards, data has to be sent over a communications link (e.g. telephone line) and extra equipment such as a modem is required.

Wide area networks

A wide area network is a collection of computers spread over a wide geographical area, possibly spanning several continents. Communication may be via microwave, satellite link or telephone line, or a combination of these. The use of global networks (including the Internet) has increased enormously over the past few years, owing to:

- Changeover of telephone networks from old-style analogue to high-speed digital technology;
- Reduction in cost of connecting to and using networks;
- Improved compression techniques which allow faster transmission of text and graphics.

Communications links

In the UK, British Telecom, Mercury and other telecom operators provide services and data links. Telephone lines may be either:

- Public lines, on which the cost of sending data depends on the length of time taken;
- Private or leased lines, for which there is a fixed annual fee and the line can be used as often as needed for no extra cost.

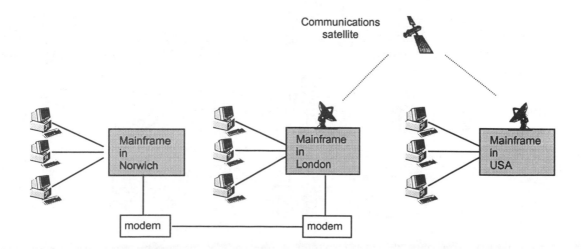

Figure 35.1: Satellite transmission

Communications media

Communication may take place over a combination of different media:

- Twisted pair (copper cable), used in much of the telephone network;

- Coaxial cable – high quality, well insulated cable that can transmit data at higher speeds;

- Fibre optic cable through which pulses of light, rather than electricity, are sent in digital form;

- Microwave – similar to radio waves. Microwave stations cannot be much more than 30 miles apart because of the earth's curvature as microwaves travel in straight lines. Mobile telephones use microwave radio links.

- Communications satellite, using one of the hundreds of satellites now in geosynchronous orbit about 22,000 miles above the earth. (Geosynchronous orbit means that they are rotating at the same speed as the earth, and are therefore stationary relative to earth.)

ISDN lines

The amount of data that can be sent over a line depends partly on the **bandwidth**, which is the range of frequencies that the line can carry. The greater the bandwidth, the greater the rate at which data can be sent, as several messages can be transmitted simultaneously.

A network that is capable of sending voice, video and computer data is called an **Integrated Services Digital Network (ISDN)**, and this requires a high bandwidth.

Bridges and gateways

A **bridge** is a connection between two local area networks. Wide area networks may be connected through a system of **gateways**, a gateway being a computer which acts as a point of connection between different networks.

Figure 35.2: Local area networks connected to a central computer

Modems

Telephone lines were originally designed for speech, which is transmitted in analogue or wave form. In order for digital data to be sent over a telephone line, it must first be converted to analogue form and then converted back to digital at the other end. This is achieved by means of a modem (MOdulator/ DEModulator) at either end of the line.

Figure 35.3: A modem converts digital signals to analogue and vice versa

Synchronous and asynchronous transmission

With **asynchronous** transmission, one character at a time is sent, with each character being preceded by a start bit and followed by a stop bit. A parity bit is also usually included as a check against incorrect transmission. This type of transmission is usually used by PCs, and is fast and economical for relatively small amounts of data.

In **synchronous** transmission mode, timing signals (usually the computer's internal clock) control the rate of transmission and there is no need for start and stop bits to accompany each character. Mainframe computers usually use synchronous transmission. It is less error-prone than asynchronous transmission.

Data compression

Data compression is frequently used when transmitting large quantities of data, thereby reducing the number of blocks transmitted and hence the cost. It basically works by replacing repeated bytes by one copy of the byte plus a count of the repetitions.

Protocol

In order to allow equipment from different suppliers to be networked, a strict set of rules (**protocols**) has been devised covering standards for physical connections, cabling, mode of transmission, speed, data format, error detection and correction. Any equipment which uses the same communication protocol can be linked together.

It is also possible to link equipment using a special translation device called a protocol converter to link, for example, a PC to a mainframe. This overcomes problems of incompatibility such as:

- different types of transmission – the PC may use asynchronous transmission, and the mainframe synchronous transmission;
- different character representations – PCs commonly use ASCII to represent characters, whereas many mainframes use a different code such as EBCDIC (Extended Binary Coded Decimal Interchange Code);
- different error detection and correction methods (such as extra check bits that are calculated and added to each block of data, to be checked on receipt).

Factors affecting rate of data transmission

- The speed of the modem. Different modems provide different data transmission rates, varying typically between 9K bps (bits per second) to 56K bps.

- The nature of the transmission line. A digital line such as an ISDN line has a much higher transmission speed than an analogue line.

- The type of cable used. Twisted pair cable has a transfer rate of about 10Mbps, whereas fibre optic cable is about 10 times as fast.

- The type of transmission, synchronous or asynchronous.

Exercises

1. (i) Describe briefly **three** factors which affect compatibility between different computer systems.

   (6)

   (ii) Describe briefly **three** factors which may affect the performance of a local area network.   (6)

   New question

2. A newspaper has a multiaccess system which supports 200 terminals. As the number of users increases, there is a gradual degradation of performance which rapidly worsens as the number of users approaches 150.

   (a) Explain the gradual degradation of performance.   (2)

   (b) Explain the rapid worsening of performance and suggest how this could be remedied.   (4)

   EDEXCEL Computing Paper 2 Qu 4 1996

3. Before using a computer network or multi-user computer system a user must log on. Give **two** reasons why it is necessary to log on.

   (2)

   NEAB Computing Paper 1 Qu 2 1994

4. Two people working on a new piece of software both work from home, and frequently need to send data and files to each other via e-mail. Describe briefly **two** ways in which they could minimise the data transmission charges.

   (4)

   New question

Chapter 36 – User Interfaces

Introduction

The '**human-computer interface**' is a term used to describe the interaction between a user and a computer; in other words, the method by which the user tells the computer what to do, and the responses which the computer makes.

It's important not to allow the word 'computer' to limit your vision to a PC sitting on an office desk. You also need to think in terms of a person getting cash from a cash machine, a pilot of a jumbo jet checking his instrument panels, the operator of a high-volume heavy duty photocopier, a scientist monitoring a chemical reaction, a musician composing a symphony using appropriate hardware and software.

> ➢ **Discussion: Name some other tasks for which computers are used, and for which special purpose interfaces are required.**

The importance of good interface design

A good interface design can help to ensure that users carry out their tasks:

- **Safely** (in the case of a jumbo jet pilot, for example);
- **Effectively** (users don't find they have video'd two hours of Bulgarian clog dancing instead of the Cup Final);
- **Efficiently** (users do not spend five minutes trying to find the correct way to insert their cash card and type in their PIN and the amount of cash they want, and then leave without remembering to extract their card);
- **Enjoyably** (a primary school pupil using a program to teach multiplication tables).

Well designed systems can improve the output of employees, improve the quality of life and make the world a safer and more enjoyable place to live in.

> ➢ **Discussion: In the early days of cash machines, it was found that users sometimes forgot to remove their cards after withdrawing their cash. What simple change was made to eliminate this fault?**

Designing usable systems

In order to design a usable interface, the designer has to take into consideration:

- **Who** will use the system. For example, will the users be computer professionals or members of the general public who may be wary of computers? For an educational program, will the users be young, for example primary school children, or teenagers on an A Level course? Will the system have to cater for both beginners and experienced users?
- **What tasks** the computer is performing. Is the task very repetitive, does the task require skill and knowledge? Do tasks vary greatly from one occasion to the next? A travel agent who spends most of the day making holiday bookings will require a different interface from an office worker who needs to be able to switch between word processing, accounts and accessing the company database.

- **The environment** in which the computer is used. Will the environment be hazardous (in a lifeboat setting out to rescue a stricken vessel), noisy (in a factory full of machinery), or calm and quiet (some offices)?
- **What is techologically feasible** (is it possible to simply dictate a letter to a word processor instead of typing it in?)

Interface styles

There are a number of common interface styles including:

- Command line interface;
- Menus;
- Natural language;
- Forms and dialogue boxes;
- Graphical user interface (GUI).

Command-line interface

The command-line interface was the first interactive dialogue style and is still widely used in spite of the availability of menu-driven interfaces. It provides a means of expressing instructions to the computer directly using single characters, whole word commands or abbreviations.

With this type of interface very little help is given to the user, who has to type a command such as, for example, **Format a:** to format a disk. Commands enable a user to quickly and concisely instruct the computer what to do, but they do require the user to have a knowledge of the commands available and the syntax for using them. How for example do you format a double density disk rather than a high density disk? *(Answer: **Format a:/n:9/T:80**)*

> ➤ **Discussion: Identify TWO situations in which a command-driven interface would be appropriate.**

Menus

There are several different types of menu interface, outlined below.

1. **Full screen menu.** This type of menu is often used as the 'front end' of an application. It stays on screen until the user makes a choice.

Figure 36.1: Full screen menu

2. **Pull-down menu.** This type of menu is displayed along the top of the screen, and when the user clicks on an item, a submenu appears. The menu is always present whatever screen the user is looking at in the application.

Figure 36.2: Pull-down menu

3. **Pop-up menu**. The menu pops up in response to, say, a click of the right mouse button on a particular area of the screen.

Figure 36.3: Pop-up menu

Natural language

It is a very attractive idea to have a computer which can understand natural language – 'plain English' in other words. *'Please, dear computer, format this double-density disk for me and don't give me obscure error messages which I can't understand'* seems an eminently civilised way of communicating with a PC. Unfortunately, the ambiguity of natural language makes it very difficult for a machine to understand. Language is ambiguous in a number of different ways. Firstly, the syntax, or structure of a sentence may not be clear – for example consider the sentences

James and Henrietta are married.

A salesman visited every house in the area.

The man hit the dog with the stick.

Are James and Henrietta married to each other? Was there only one salesman involved in the house-to-house sales operation?

Secondly, many English words have more than one meaning. How many ways can the word 'match' be interpreted?

Advantages and disadvantages of natural language dialogue

Advantages:

*   Most natural form of dialogue for humans — no need for training in a specialised command language;
*   Extremely flexible and powerful;
*   The user is free to construct his own commands, frame his own questions, etc.

Disadvantages:

- People find it difficult to stick to strictly grammatical English;
- A well designed 'artificial language' can often say the same thing more concisely than 'natural language';
- A smooth, natural language can easily mislead the naive user into believing the computer is much more intelligent than it actually is.

Forms and dialogue boxes

When a user is required to enter data such as, for example, sales invoices or customer names and addresses, it is common to have a 'form' displayed on the screen for the user to fill in. The following points should be noted when designing forms of this type:

- The display should be given a title to identify it;
- The form should not be too cluttered – spaces and blanks in a display are important;
- It should give some indication of how many characters can be entered in each field of data;
- The user should be given a chance to go back and correct any field before the data is accepted;
- Items should appear in a logical sequence to assist the user;
- Default values should wherever possible be prewritten onto the form so that a minimum of data entry is required;
- Full exit and 'help' facilities should be provided – for example, users could enter '?' in a field if they require more information;
- Lower case in a display is neater and easier to read than upper-case;
- 'Attention-getting' devices such as blinking cursors, high-intensity, reverse video, underlining etc should not be over-used.

Dialogue boxes are a special type of form often associated with the Windows environment; an example shown below is the dialogue box which appears when the instruction to *Print* is given in Word 7.

Figure 36.4: Dialogue box

The WIMP interface

WIMP stands for Windows, Icons, Mouse and Pull-down menus.

A **window** is an area on the screen through which a particular piece of software or a data file may be viewed. The window may occupy the whole screen, or the user can choose to have several windows on the screen with a different application running in each one. Windows can be moved, sized, stacked one on top of the other, opened and closed. A Windows environment mimics a desktop on which a worker may have several books or pieces of paper spread out for reference.

An **icon** is a small picture representing an item such as a piece of software, a file, storage medium (such as disk or tape) or command. By pointing with a mouse at a particular icon and clicking the mouse button the user can select it.

Microsoft Windows enables the user to run several different software packages such as MS Word (a word processor), MS Excel (a spreadsheet), MS Paint (a graphics package) simultaneously and to move data and graphics from one package to another. Software packages written by other manufacturers, such as Aldus PageMaker, have been written to run under Windows because of the convenience to the user of this easy-to-use environment.

Advantages of a common user interface

All the software packages mentioned above use a consistent interface and have a similar 'look and feel' so that a user familiar with one package can quickly learn a second. For example, in each package a single click of the mouse button **selects** an item, and a double click **activates** the item. In each package, the methods for opening, closing, sizing and moving windows is identical. The advantages can be summarised as:

- Increased speed of learning;
- Ease of use;
- Confidence building for novice users;
- Increased range of tasks solvable by experienced users;
- A greater range of software accessible to the average user.

Speech input (voice recognition)

The ultimate in user-friendly interfaces would probably be one in which you could simply tell your computer what to do in ordinary speech. Two distinct types of voice recognition system are emerging; small vocabulary command and control systems and large vocabulary dictation systems.

- **Command and control systems** can be relatively small and cheap because they need only a small, tightly defined vocabulary of technical terms. Such systems are coming rapidly into use as automatic call-handling systems for applications such as bank account enquiries. In PC systems, voice command can be used to bring up files, control printing and so on, effectively replacing the mouse. In some systems the computer is 'trained' by an individual user pronouncing a given vocabulary of words; it then stores a recording of the user's speech pattern for each word or syllable.

- **Large vocabulary dictation systems** can handle whole sentences and extensive vocabularies but need much greater processing power and memory space. These systems use elaborate probability distributions to estimate which word the accoustic pattern it has picked up is most likely to be, partly by looking at other words in the developing sentence and predicting what sort of word (noun or verb, for example) is likely to be used. Various voice recognition packages after suitable 'training' will take dictation at 70 words per minute and get about 97% of them correct. Voice recognition is however still an expensive technology and widespread use is some way off.

> ➤ **Discussion: Name some other situations in which voice input would be appropriate.**

Speech/sound output

A speech synthesis system works as follows:

Individual words and sounds are spoken into a microphone by a human being and recorded by the system, thereby training it to speak. Output that would normally be printed can then be spoken, so long as the word is contained in its vocabulary. Sometimes words which are not recognised are spelt out.

Such a system has limited use but could for example be used by a bank computer connected by telephone line to customers' homes and offices. The customer could key in his account number using the telephone keypad, and the computer could then access his account and speak out the customer's account balance.

Exercises

1.   *see case study below*

Case Study: Putting patients in the picture

New software is about to go on trial in doctors' surgeries to enable patients to see a picture of their condition on screen. An attractive interface features drawings of the human body overlaid with 'hotspots'. The cursor can be moved to the part of the body under investigation and clicked to reveal information. If for example the patient has a problem in the knee, the doctor clicks on the appropriate spot and a menu of options is displayed on the screen. Information can then be obtained on medical history, examinations, investigations, diagnosis, referrals and procedures.

The interface was designed to salvage a £19m coding system for the health service, whereby 245,000 medical conditions were given unique computer codes. The system was difficult to use because in order to do a keyboard search for a particular condition, everything including spaces and syntax had to be typed in with 100% accuracy. With the new system a complete list of possible diagnoses and treatments is available at the touch of a button. In addition, patients are much better informed because they can see a picture of the problem.

Three doctors and two programmers have worked on the interface, called Visual Read, for two years in their spare time.

➤ **Questions:**

   a.   What name would you give to this type of interface?   (1)

   b.   Describe **one** advantage of the software to   (i) the doctor;

                                            (ii) the patient.   (2)

   c.   Why do you think the NHS spent £19m on a coding system for medical conditions? What use could such a scheme be put to, apart from the one described in the case study?   (4)

   d.   Describe briefly **two** possible problems with the software that may come to light during testing in surgeries.   (2)

   e.   The development team consisted of three doctors and two programmers. Identify the likely strengths and weaknesses of such a team.   (4)

   f.   "If the system works as well as it is supposed to, the doctor will be superfluous." State whether you agree or disagree with this statement, giving **two** reasons to support your answer.   (2)

2. A college uses a range of software packages from different suppliers. Each package has a different user interface. The college is considering changing its software to one supplier and to a common user interface.

   (a) Give **four** advantages of having a common user interface. (4)

   (b) Describe **four** specific features of a user interface which would benefit from being common between packages. (4)

   (c) Discuss the issues involved, apart from user interfaces, in the college changing or upgrading software packages. (8)

   NEAB IT02 Qu 8 1997

3. A railway station has a computer-based timetable enquiry system for use by passengers. Enquiries are entered from a keyboard and displayed on the screen-based form illustrated below.

   > Destination:
   > Date of Travel:
   > Latest arrival time:

   Details of the train times are displayed at the bottom of the screen.

   (a) The exact format of the input required for this system is not clear. Redesign the form to make it clear. (4)

   (b) Some users of the enquiry system find it difficult to use. Suggest **three** ways in which it could be made easier to use. (3)

   London Computing Paper 2 Qu 4 1995

4. Briefly describe **three** important features of a well-designed user interface. (6)

   NISEAC Paper 2 Qu 7 1996

5. A different human-machine interface would be needed for each of the following users:

   (i) a young child in a primary school;

   (ii) a blind person;

   (iii) a graphic artist.

   For each user describe and justify an appropriate human-machine interface. (9)

   NEAB Computing Paper 1 Qu 9 1994

Section 3

Developing I.T. Solutions

In this section:

Chapter 37 – Tackling a Minor Project
Chapter 38 – Specification and Analysis
Chapter 39 – Design
Chapter 40 – Implementation and Testing
Chapter 41 - Documentation

Chapter 37 – Tackling a Minor Project

Syllabus requirements

At the time of writing, the NEAB Information Technology syllabus requires candidates to undertake two 'minor projects'. For each of these projects, you are expected to tackle a task-related problem of limited scope, each of which, with few exceptions, can be implemented using a single piece of generic applications software such as a database, spreadsheet or desktop publishing package. (The exception might be for example, using scanning or drawing software to create an image to import into a desktop published document. You should not, on the other hand, export data from a database to a spreadsheet, or vice versa, or use data from an Access database to produce a mail-merge letter in Word. This type of data exchange would be suitable for the major project.)

There are certain expectations from each type of software, for example:

Word processing software

Remember that the emphasis for the project is on *developing a solution* to a reasonably substantial problem posed by an end-user. You need to select a problem that can be broken down into subtasks, each of which can be implemented using your chosen package. You will need to use a powerful word processing package such as Word 7 or Word 97 that has sufficient advanced facilities to carry out some non-trivial tasks. For example, your project could be to produce all the templates needed for a club or a small business to send out letters and invoices to members or customers. The project might also involve holding a list of names and addresses so that you could send a mail shot to a selected group, for example a reminder notice to people who had not paid their subscriptions or invoices.

Automating the processes using the macro language might be demonstrated using a User Data Entry form, with macros attached on entry and exit. Finally, the project might attempt to fully customise the solution by tailoring the toolbars and drop-down menus.

You can use a word processing package to:

- Create a company 'ident'; that is, a logo and typeface for letter headings, invoices, fax cover sheets, With Compliment slips and business cards which gives the company or club a recognisable identity.

- Create templates for some/all of the above. Templates can be set to be read-only so that data is added to a document based on the template and not stored with the template itself.

- Create an internal data source containing names and addresses, subscriptions due, whether paid, etc.

- Create a mail-merge letter containing fields. You should explore the advanced features of the software that allow you to insert formulas and IF fields.

- Insert FILLIN fields to enable the user to fill in, say, a subscription rate (Family, Adult or Junior) for each member of a club.

- Insert a table into a document that contains formulae – for example, to add up the individual lines in an invoice, add VAT and calculate a total amount due.

The important thing is to be aware that all these things can be done in Word, and then to carefully analyse the user's requirements and use whatever features of the software are required to perform the tasks involved.

A word of warning – a simple mail-merge letter using a single file of data just won't make the grade, and nor will an application to allow a user to print out business cards.

Steer clear of word-processing software except to write up your project documentation, unless you have a good idea from a real user with a genuine need that can be broken down into several subtasks.

Database software

Databases must be relational and used in a fully relational manner. This implies that your system must contain at least two related tables. Typically, you should choose a project which gives you scope to perform some or all of the following tasks:

- Draw an entity-relationship diagram;
- Normalise your data;
- Design your table structures, giving due consideration to field lengths and types, validation and default values;
- Create relationships which enforce referential integrity;
- Create and tailor forms and subforms to provide a pleasing and easy-to-use interface for the user;
- Perform multi-table queries;
- Perform some processing or calculation on the input data to produce information;
- Display or print reports, perhaps summarising data or displaying data that has been calculated, sorted or processed in some way;
- Write macros and code modules to customise your database;
- Provide a menu of options (a 'switchboard') as a front end to your application;
- Provide the user with on-line help.

Software such as Works is not suitable for a minor project, since it does not have a full range of advanced facilities available.

Figure 37.1: A sample opening menu for a database project

Spreadsheet software

A spreadsheet application must consist of more than a single sheet containing labels, numbers and formulae into which the user types data. It could well involve the use of:

- A template which can only be altered by an authorised user, while other users would load the template, enter their own data and save the spreadsheet as a worksheet rather than altering the original template;

- A separate area of the spreadsheet set aside for data entry, making use of a User Input dialogue box and validation of input data. Data would then be automatically transferred to a different area for processing;
- Pivot tables for management analysis;
- Multiple scenarios of best, likely and worst case;
- Use of Goal Seek and solver;
- Locking sheets (with some cells unprotected) to prevent unwanted modification;
- Outlining and other auditing tools;
- Table lookup functions;
- Cell naming. Rather than having formulas such as =D2*E2, it is more meaningful to have a formula such as =Qty*Unit_Price;
- Macros to control input, processing and output. Auto Open and Close macros;
- A front-end menu to allow the user to select different options;
- Command buttons to perform various tasks;
- Use of control boxes such as list box, check box and radio buttons;
- On-line help for the user.

Desktop publishing

It is difficult to score good marks using a desktop publishing package. The essence of the project is that it should not be simply a passive document, for example a beautifully produced newsletter or theatre program. It should have some element of interactivity with an end-user – for example, a template which a user can use over and over again with different text and graphics. The project needs to make use of advanced features of the package and must give scope for the full range of activities (Analysis, Design, Testing etc.)

A DTP project needs to be based on a repeatable need and must not be a one-off. This then gives you the scope to provide test data, such as testing out with different texts or different articles.

It is extremely important to:

- Have a real end-user (even if this is your teacher);
- Establish the aims and objectives;
- State why a DTP solution is appropriate;
- Consider the user's requirements very carefully; for example in this case the layout, appearance, colour restrictions, paper size, how many copies will be printed, how it will be folded;
- Establish how the printing will be done and by whom, how the document will be supplied to the printers (i.e. the human printer, not the LaserJet! disk or hard copy?), whether the printer will be scanning in photographs using high resolution equipment, etc.
- Design a test strategy and test plan;
- Evaluate the final solution against the objectives;
- Write technical and user manuals on how to use your template – NOT on how to use desktop publishing software.

Presentation packages

In the main, packages such as PowerPoint are unsuitable for a minor project. There is simply not enough scope for a high-scoring project.

Authoring packages

A package such as Authorware can be used to produce an interactive tutorial, and has plenty of scope for advanced features to be used but as the package costs around £800 for a single copy probably very few centres or candidates would have access to such software.

If you have used sound, video or animation in your project and it is hard to show evidence of how it works in the report, you may as a last resort include a video with the project. Do NOT send a disk.

Internet Web pages

It is relatively easy to produce a Web page using Microsoft software, and so unless you can develop a functional site on the Internet that records hits and collects e-mail responses or answers to on-line questionnaires, this is likely to score only low marks.

Each of the minor projects must be produced using a **different** generic type of software package. If you use the same software for both projects, the best one will be given a mark and the other will score zero. Also, you should avoid using Access for a database project, and then Excel for a second database project, using its database functions. Similarly, avoid using a word processing package for one project and a desktop publishing package for the other, because the skills demonstrated are likely to be too similar. Also, neither of these packages really offers the scope to fully demonstrate skills in analysis, design and testing in the same way as say a database or spreadsheet project.

Planning the time schedule

Once you have decided on a project, one of the first things you should do is draw up a timetable of when each stage is going to be done and completed, so as to ensure it is handed in before the deadline.

There are many different possible schedules. If your teacher has more or less suspended theory classes to allow you to work flat out on your project, it should be possible to complete it within 6 to 8 weeks. This assumes that you will have 3-5 hours per week of class time, and at least as much again outside class. Even if you don't have a computer at home, and the open-access facilities at school or college are limited, do remember that there is a huge amount of work to be done away from the computer. You can:

- plan your schedule;
- interview the user;
- design the application;
- draw data flow diagrams (Context Level 0 and Level 1);
- read books to find out about the advanced features of the software;
- design your test strategy and test plan.

If you are planning to complete both projects by the end of the second term (typically mid-March), for marking and submission to the Examining Board by the May 1st deadline, then you need to start your first project no later than the beginning of November. It needs to be handed in the first or second week back after Christmas. That gives you about 8 weeks to get the second project completed.

If this sounds like an impossibly tight schedule, you might consider postponing the submission of the minor projects until the second year. In that case, your teacher could set you a deadline of the end of February for the first project, and the end of the summer term for the second project. Naturally, theory classes would then take place alongside project work. This does not prohibit you from sitting the first two theory papers at the end of the first year.

The project requirements

Your project should include:

- A clear statement of the problem;
- An analysis of the problem with a discussion of the end-user's requirements, with a list of objectives and performance criteria;
- An implementation using a software package;
- A test strategy, test plan and test results cross-referenced to the test plan;
- An evaluation of how well the final system met the objectives and performance criteria;
- Documentation showing how all the above were achieved;
- A user guide and technical manual.

In the next few chapters each of these aspects will be tackled in more detail. The NEAB project mark scheme is given in Appendix B.

Chapter 38 – Specification and Analysis

Selecting a project

For the minor project it is acceptable for your teacher to identify a problem for computerisation and act as the end-user. However you are very strongly encouraged to find your own project since this is much more likely to give you the opportunity to show your capabilities in a clearly original way. It's very important that the project is not teacher-led, with the whole class ending up with more or less identical solutions. Even if you find a particularly good way of overcoming some problem encountered in a class project, you're not likely to get any credit if the rest of the class has copied your techniques.

Try and find an application that you have personal knowledge of, or that you can investigate further. Parents can be a good source of ideas, or perhaps you belong to a club of some kind that could use a computerised membership system. The lab technician might like a computerised stock control system, or the school librarian may have an idea for computerising some aspect of the library. Do not be too ambitious – don't try and redo Tesco's stock control or the payroll system for British Gas. It is perfectly acceptable to ask the end-user for their priorities, be selective and model just a small slice of the user's problem.

Investigating the user's requirements

Analysis involves finding out:

- How the current system works;
- What the problems are with the current system, including any client dissatisfaction;
- What the user's requirements are for a new system;
- What constraints there are on hardware, software, time-scale.

In order to do this, you need to prepare a list of questions and interview the user. Ask to see any (source) documents that are currently used, and if possible include a copy of them in an Appendix.

Establishing the objectives

It is very important to write a clear statement of the objectives, both **qualitative** and **quantitative**. An example of a qualitative objective is:

"It should be easy for the user to locate a particular customer invoice".

An example of a quantitative objective is:

"It should be possible to locate any customer invoice in under 30 seconds".

Having a clear list of objectives will not only make the design of the system more straightforward, it will also enable you to evaluate the implementation by comparing its performance point-by-point with the objectives.

Documenting data flows

A data flow diagram shows how data moves through a system and what data stores are used. It does not specify what type of data storage is used or how the data is stored.

The following four symbols are used in data flow diagrams:

External entity – data source or data destination, for example people who generate data such as a customer order, or receive information such as an invoice.

Process – an operation performed on the data. The two lines are optional; the top section of the box can be used to label the process, the middle to give a brief explanation, the bottom to say where the process takes place. Make the first word an active verb – e.g. **validate** data, **adjust** stock level.

Data store – such as a file held on disk or a batch of documents

Data flow – the arrow represents movement between entities, processes or data stores. The arrow should be labelled to describe what data is involved

Example: A theatre uses a computerised booking system to keep records of customers, plays and bookings. A customer may make a booking in person, by telephone or by preprinted form. The booking clerk first has to check whether there are any seats free for the performance. If there are, the clerk reserves the seats, then checks whether the customer's details are already on file, and if not, types them in. The tickets are then printed out and handed or sent to the customer. Payment is made either in cash or by credit card.

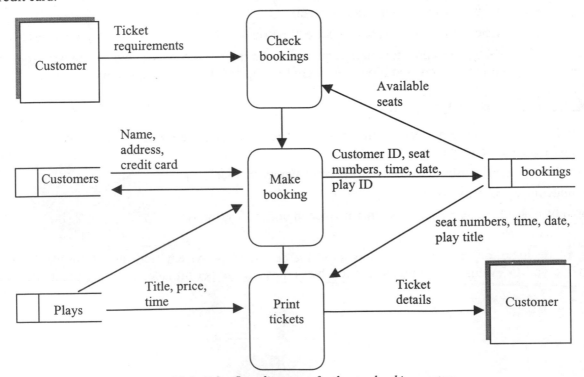

Figure 38.1: Data flow diagram of a theatre booking system

Writing up the analysis

A possible framework for the analysis is given below:

---

1. Introduction

    1.1   Background
Describe and name the user and/or type of organisation (club, library, garage, etc) the project is to be written for and give some background information about the organisation.

    1.2   Statement of the problem
Give an overview of the problem that you intend to solve.

2. Investigation

    2.1   The current system

Include a summary of the main points of an interview if appropriate. Identify the data flows and tasks being performed, and summarise these in a data flow diagram.

    2.2   Problems with the current system

3. Requirements of the new system

    3.1   General objectives

    3.2   Specific objectives – quantitative

    3.3   Specific objectives – qualitative
A list of performance criteria given here can be systematically addressed at the evaluation stage.

4. Constraints

    4.1   Hardware
Describe the hardware that is available both for development and at the end-user's organisation, or wherever the system is to be implemented.

    4.2   Software
Name the software you have available to use (including the version number) and briefly describe its main capabilities.

    4.3   User's I.T. skills and knowledge
Give some indication of the level of the end-user's I.T. skills, and what possible effects this could have on the design.

    4.4   Areas not included in computerisation
If your project is a subsystem of a much larger system, make clear what parts of the whole system are included in your project.

Do vary this format according to the demands of your own particular project – don't try and force it into a format which does not fit. This is only a starting point from which you can branch out.

Chapter 39 – Design

Design tasks

Designing a system involves the following tasks:

- Considering possible methods of solution and justifying your final choice;
- Identifying the required output from the system;
- Identifying the input data;
- Specifying the processing that needs to be carried out;
- Splitting the tasks into a number of subtasks, divided into input tasks, processing tasks, output tasks and user interface tasks (no more than six or seven main tasks);
- Devising a test strategy and test plan;
- Planning a schedule of activities to ensure that the project is finished by the deadline – and sticking to it!

Justification of chosen solution

You should consider the use of different software packages and briefly say why, for example, you think a spreadsheet would be more appropriate than a database, or vice versa. Also state why your computerised system is going to be better than simply improving the current manual system.

Database design (for a database project)

Identify the entities involved and the relationships between the entities and draw an entity-relationship diagram. A database project should involve at least three related tables. A sample entity-relationship diagram is shown below.

Figure 39.1: An entity-relationship diagram

Data descriptions

For each item of data you should specify:

- Name;
- Data type (integer, real, text etc);
- Length (if text);
- Default value (if any);
- Validation.

For a database project, you can use a form with headings similar to those shown below for each table in the database.

TABLE NAME:

Attribute name	Data type	Length	Default value	Description, validation, comments

Figure 39.2: Suggested headings for a table layout form in a database project

For a spreadsheet project, you should specify the purpose and contents of each sheet:

SHEET NAME:

Row/Column heading	Data description and format	Comment	Example
Book code	Unique 6 character code	Acts as a link between sheets "Book" and "Sales"	AC0073, CM0021
Total sales	The total month's sales of a book		=sum (d5..d11)

Figure 39.3: Designing a spreadsheet

Input

Design all your input screens on paper; decide on headings, placement of any buttons, and approximate position of data fields. Try to maintain a consistent style for aiding user navigation, such as buttons returning to the Main Menu or Switchboard all placed in the same position on the page in every form.

For each sheet in a spreadsheet project show:

- General layout;
- Which cells will be locked or protected;
- Links to other sheets;
- Fonts, shading etc.

Output

List the reports or other output (e.g. mailing labels, information available on screen). You should design each report or screen on paper, listing the data items that will appear. It does not have to be done on squared paper with every character shown, but you should give thought to whether a report is to be tabular or not, whether labels are to be printed 2 or 3 across the page, and so on. You can always change the design if you later find you have made some mistakes – such changes can be documented and justified as part of your report.

Menu design

If your system has a menu structure, draw a chart showing how various submenus relate to each other. An example is shown below.

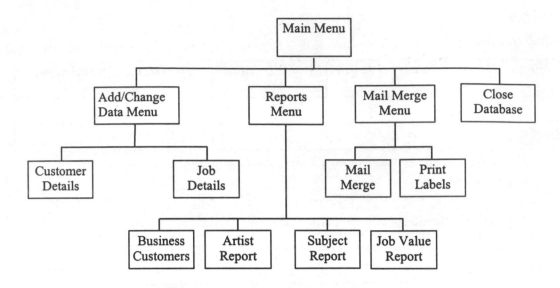

Figure 39.4: A sample menu structure chart

Identifying subtasks

At this stage you should be able to identify and list a number of subtasks to be achieved. If the list includes writing modules or macros, you should specify these, explaining the steps in each. You should describe objects (e.g. forms, macros, command buttons) in sufficient detail so that using your description, a competent person should be able to implement your design. A database project, for example could include the following tasks:

1. Create Club Member table;
2. Create Fixtures table;
3. Create form for adding/editing members;
4. Create form for adding/editing fixtures;
5. Create query to find all members with unpaid subs;
6. Create report listing fixtures;
7. Write macro to find a particular member's record.

Etc.

Test plan

The test plan may be included here or in the Testing section. It will be discussed in the next chapter.

A final note – a good design should be so rigorous that another person could implement it from your documentation!

Plan of action

You should write down a schedule showing how you intend to complete each subtask and finish the project by the deadline – and stick to it! A sample is given below.

Schedule

Week no. / date	*Subtask*	*Comment*
1. 3/11/98	Design database structure, tables, forms, reports and menu structure. Document the design	What was actually achieved this week. Any problems or difficulties.
2. 10/11/98	Create tables. Create prototype input forms using Wizards	Need to find out how to validate fields. Form/subform for Order form doesn't work properly.
etc		

Figure 39.5: A sample work schedule

Writing up the design

A possible framework for the design is given below:

1. **Consideration of possible solutions**

    Include a justification of your chosen software

2. **List of subtasks to be performed**

    The list will include the implementation, testing, documentation and evaluation of the various parts of the system.

3. **Database/Spreadsheet design**

    3.1   Entity-relationship diagram (for a database)

    3.2   Data descriptions

4. **Input**

    Design of input forms and screens

5. **Output**

    Design of reports and other output

6. **Menu design**

7. **Macro/Module design**

8. **Test plan**

9. **Plan of Action**

    A schedule showing for each week of the project, what task(s) will be completed.

Chapter 40 – Implementation and Testing

Organisation is the key

You will almost certainly be learning more about the software as you go along. There are many things you can do to ensure a successful implementation.

1.   Buy a binder to hold everything to do with your project, divided into sections so that you can quickly find what you are looking for. A floppy plastic binder of the type that holds papers securely through punched holes is most suitable.

2.   Have your design documentation in front of you and follow it; if you find it needs to be adjusted, remember to do so, and make a note of why this was necessary.

3.   Have at least two spare floppy disks and make a backup after every session at the computer. Having 2 backup disks means that you can leave the most recent backup alone and overwrite the previous 'generation'. It is impossible to be too conscientious about backups; sooner or later you will lose the current version, quite possibly through no fault of your own – but blaming the dog, Microsoft or the school network won't bring your project back!

4.   Keep a diary and leave 15 minutes at the end of every class to write up what you did and what problems you encountered. This will help you at the beginning of the next class.

5.   Test each form, report, macro etc. thoroughly as you go, and make a note of these tests for your test plan.

6.   Buy a good book on the software you are using, and spend time actually READING it. Try out the exercises and improve your knowledge of the advanced features of the software.

The implementation

The implementation is the actual software solution that you create, using whichever package you have chosen to use. It is very tempting to proceed straight to the implementation stage without doing any design work first, but try not to do this. *Write down* the menu structure, *design* the data structures/fields/tables, the input and the output screens or reports. *Construct a list* of subtasks. Then you will be able to see what parts of your project you need help with. It is very hard for a teacher to help students who have nothing written down and have only the vaguest idea of what they are trying to achieve.

If you are using the computer facilities at school or college, there is a lot of work you can do at home. You can:

- Read software guides to learn how to overcome any problems you have encountered;
- Refine your design;
- Create sets of test data;
- Draw up a test plan;
- Work on your documentation;
- Plan how you are going to make the best use of your next practical session.

If you are using computer facilities at home, then all these tasks can be done during practical sessions. If you can plan your time effectively, you will be able to complete the project in the time allowed.

Testing objectives

The objectives of testing are to prove that:

- All parts of the system work correctly, no matter what data is input;
- All parts of the system as originally specified are present.

In drawing up a test plan, you should bear in mind the following rules proposed by Glen Myers in his book 'The Art of Software Testing'.

1. **Testing is a process of executing a program with the intent of finding an error.**
2. **A good test case is one that has a high probability of finding an as yet undiscovered error.**
3. **A successful test is one that uncovers an as yet undiscovered error.**

In other words, it is not sufficient to think up a few tests which you are fairly sure will not make your program crash or give a wrong result; you must use tests and test data which have been carefully thought out to test all parts of the program.

Steps in software testing

1. Module testing

As you complete each module of your program, it needs to be thoroughly tested. Even if you can't test every combination of paths, you can test the important paths, the extreme cases, valid and invalid data, and so on. For the purposes of your project, you should aim to demonstrate that you have tested systematically and that your testing is **reasonably** exhaustive. A maximum of 20 to 30 pages of actual test runs which cover major processes and show a variety of test data (i.e. extreme, correct, incorrect) is quite sufficient.

2.   System (or integrated) testing

When all the modules have been written and the whole system put together, system testing can begin.

At this stage, you should ideally test your system with a realistic volume of data. If the system is designed to hold details of 5000 stock items, and you have never tested it with more than 8, there is no way of knowing how it will perform after installation unless you test it. Obviously, you will not have the time to enter 5000 different records, but it would be reasonable to enter about 20 items of data.

Drawing up a test plan

For the module testing, draw up a test plan of preferably no more than two or three pages which shows that you have chosen your test data carefully, tested each module, and know what the results ought to be. A suggested table for a test plan is given below.

Test No	Test Data	Purpose	Expected Result	Comment /Verified
1	Enter incorrect password 'ABC'	Test password	Only password 'ABF' accepted	
2	Enter Customer ID abc	Test invalid digits	Not accepted	
3	Enter new customer with ID 456, 'Jones K.'	Test 'Add new customer' function	Jones added to database	

Figure 40.1: A suggested format for a test plan

Sometimes it is impossible to show evidence that a test works correctly; in those cases, have your supervisor carry out the test and authenticate the result in the 'Comments/Verified' column. You could also use this column to reference the page number on which your test evidence is shown, or to make notes to yourself of any tests that did not work correctly.

Selecting tests for the test plan

Try to choose tests that test the more complex aspects of your system, such as calculations, command buttons that perform updating or open up a form with data already in it, and so on. Masses of tests for really trivial validations that are performed automatically by Access (such as a date in the correct format) are fairly pointless.

If, for example, you are testing a mail-merge, it is not necessary to include all the printouts as evidence. A better test would be to see whether your system can insert a new name into the list and then just print out one more letter, rather than printing the whole lot again.

You may well have to amend or add to your initial test plan as the program develops, but you will find it very helpful to have a written plan at all stages, even if you keep adjusting it.

Similarly, if you design your system tests **before** you start coding, you will be forced to think about how this phase will be carried out, what will have to be done to make system testing possible, and how to ensure that it will be successful. The earlier you can foresee any problems, the easier they will be to solve.

Presenting the test results

Your test results should be presented in an Appendix, and cross-referenced to your test plan. They will normally take the form of test runs, screen dumps and file dumps. You may need to explain exactly what data was input. Use a highlighter pen to emphasise the key point about a screenshot, and annotate the output by hand to show what the test proves. Be selective, and consider it a challenge to make it as easy as possible for a reader to confirm that test results were as expected. As a general rule, include the absolute minimum essential to get the point across.

Test runs and screenshots with no annotation and no cross-referencing to the test plan are virtually useless!

Figure 40.2: Presenting the test results

Chapter 41 – Documentation

Introduction

The report that you hand in at the end of your project contains all the evidence of the work you have done over the past few months. No matter how careful your analysis, how appropriate the design, how clever the macros or modules and how thorough the testing; if the written evidence is not there to prove it, you will not achieve a good mark.

It will take longer than you expect to complete the documentation. It will pay you to write the documentation in parallel with the other stages of the project and not leave it all to the end. Then, when you have finished the implementation and testing, you will be able to go through it all, proof reading, adding a table of contents, page numbers, and appendices.

Remember that the project is going to be seen by a reader who may have no knowledge of the background to the project. Try to be highly aware of the reader when writing the documentation.

Should the documentation be word-processed?

The short answer is YES. It should also be thoroughly spell-checked, both using the spell-checking facility provided by the word processor, and by reading it through slowly and carefully.

> They're know miss steaks in my project report cause I used special soft wear witch checked my spelling. However it cannot correct arrows inn punctuation and it will not fined words witch are miss used but spelled rite. An it wont catch the sentence fragments witch you have forgotten to.

Figure 41.1: Don't rely too heavily on your spell-checker

Word processing skills

There are some crucial word-processing skills which you need to acquire in order to present a really professional-looking final report. This document must do justice to the effort you have so far put into your project; it is all that the examiner will see, and even if you feel you have perhaps not achieved as much as you could have, a well-presented report will help.

Use the Help system to learn new skills, including:

- **Setting styles for the various level of headings and text in your document.** (All the tips below apply to MS Word.) The 'Normal' template comes with built-in styles for Heading 1, Heading 2, Heading 3 and Normal text. You may like to alter the font, size, style and justification of these, or set up new styles of your own.

- **Creating a Table of Contents.** If you have used styles consistently throughout your document, you can create a Table of Contents automatically. Put your cursor where you want the Table of Contents to appear, select Insert, Index and Tables from the menu bar and then select Table of Contents. It can be updated at any time by selecting it and pressing F9.

- **Inserting headers and footers.** The project title and the page number can be placed in either a header or footer. Select View, Header and Footer from the menu bar.

- **Inserting a page break whenever you want one.** Press Ctrl-Enter.
- **Using numbered points and bullet points.** Use the tools on the toolbar.
- **Creating tab stops.** Never use the space bar to indent; nothing will line up when you print the document. Learn to use the tab stops on the ruler line, and the Tab key (above Caps Lock on the keyboard) to tab.
- **Inserting tables.** Use the Table menu.
- **Inserting screenshots.** When you want to take a screenshot to include in your User Manual, for example, press Alt-Print Screen to copy the current window to the clipboard. Then switch to your Word document and use Edit, Paste. A better way is to use a screen capture utility program to copy your screens to a file, from where they can be linked to your document using Insert, Picture, From File. Screen capture utilities are available as shareware.

Putting it all together

Your project documentation should be neatly bound in such a manner that it can be read without a major unbinding job. A ring binder is too large and heavy to be conveniently posted, so investigate the shelves of W.H.Smith or any stationery shop to find something suitable.

Do not put each page (or several pages together) in a plastic sleeve; it makes the project report heavy, expensive to post, and inconvenient for marking.

The title page

The title page should include the title of the project, your name and centre, school or college. It could also include the date you submitted the project and your candidate number, if appropriate.

Table of contents

This is a must. Include in it the sections and numbered subsections, together with page numbers. Every page in your project should be numbered for easy reference; you can add page numbers by hand at the end to pages of test data, for example.

Analysis

A suggested framework for the Analysis section is given at the end of Chapter 39. Remember to include a write up of preparation for interview (such as a list of questions), and a summary of the main points gleaned during the interview. Do not include a transcript of the interview. A questionnaire, if you have used one, can be included together with a summary of responses. Your own observations of the current system, and deductions, are worth including also. If your analysis included reading about other similar systems, or trying out other similar software packages, for example, then that can be written up here.

Design

Headings for the design section are given in Chapter 39. Look carefully at these and make sure you have covered all aspects of the design in your documentation. Your test strategy should be included in this section. You must aim to show that you have worked out what tests need to be performed and what results you expect. If you number the tests, it will make it easier to cross-reference them to the actual test runs.

Testing

Testing is a vitally important part of the project. The test data and test plan should all be included in this section. The Testing Section should also contain a test plan analysis to show that it does test all parts of the system. Then, in the Systems Maintenance section, you can refer to any unusual results or unsolved problems.

Test runs may be included in an Appendix. **The test runs should be cross-referenced clearly to the test plan**, and be presented in such a way that the reader can see at once what a specific page of output is designed to show. Devising appropriate tests, organising and cross-referencing screen dumps and printed output can take a great deal of time and ingenuity. There is no point including several pages of output with no explanation of what test it relates to or how the output proves that a certain section of the program is working correctly. Make hand-written annotations on the output and use highlighter pen to show significant results.

There is a great temptation to skimp on this section of the project; the feeling is "Right! I've finished the programming and I'm pretty sure it all works. Here's a disk – you try it...". Unfortunately the devising and implementation of the test plan is your job, not the examiner's!

Documenting the implementation

The implementation stage needs documenting but is not a guide on how to use the software package. It should relate to the solution, and describe what was actually built. Don't repeat anything here that you have written elsewhere, though.

Technical documentation

This section is aimed at an I.T. specialist who would be maintaining or enhancing the system. It could include the following:

- A brief description of each object in the system, i.e. form, report, query, module;
- A summary of the purpose of each macro or module, and when it is used;
- An explanation of the features you have used, and a description of how you tailored the package to suit the user's requirements;
- Limitations of the system;
- Discussion of unresolved problems or odd test results;

You will also be awarded marks in this section for macro code, if your project has involved writing macros, SQL or other code as part of the customisation of a software package. The listing should be a genuine printout rather than a word-processed document, and should be clearly annotated by hand wherever this helps to explain what is happening. It needs to be made easily understandable, for example by:

- using meaningful variable names;
- stating the purpose of each variable unless it is self-explanatory;
- using comments to state the purpose of each procedure;
- using comments where necessary to explain the logic of a particular section;
- grouping procedures in a logical order so that it is easy to find your way around a long program;
- using indentation to clarify the extent of loops and condition statements;
- using blank lines between procedures to separate them.

System-generated code such as that produced by wizards or recorded macros should be clearly labelled as such.

User manual

This section is aimed entirely at a non-technical user and should use ordinary English rather than 'computer-speak'. For example, do not say 'Boot up the system' when 'Switch on the computer' will achieve the same result.

Presentation is all-important here. Use whatever facilities your word processor has to enhance the appearance of the document, spell-check it carefully and read it through to make sure it flows well and makes sense. It should be a 'stand-alone' document and could even be bound separately from the rest of the project.

Your user manual should include:

- a table of contents;
- an introduction, stating what the system is about and who it is for;
- examples of actual screen displays such as menus, data input screens and output screens;
- samples of printed output;
- an explanation of what each option on a menu does;
- any special instructions on how to input data – for example the format of a date field, or the range of accepted values in an amount field;
- an explanation of any manual procedures such as batching or recording data manually;
- error messages that may be displayed and what to do in that event;
- error recovery procedures – for example what to do if you realise you have made a wrong data entry, or the power goes off in the middle of an update;
- perhaps a hot-line help number.

If you have used a package, explain how to use the system you have created, rather than explaining how to use the software package in general terms. It is a good idea to test out your user manual on the user or a colleague to see if they can follow your instructions without any extra help from you.

Evaluation

The evaluation is an important part of the project accounting for some 20% of the total mark. It should be clearly related to the list of specific objectives written in the Analysis section. The more clearly you have stated the objectives, the easier it will be to evaluate how well your system achieved them.

If the project has been written for a real user, it is a good idea to include the user's comments in this section, perhaps in the form of a letter written on official headed paper and signed by the user. If any suggestions have been made for amendment or improvement, include these as well, whether or not you have managed to incorporate the suggestions. Add your own suggestions for improvement and possibilities for future development. Do take note that a fake letter from your best friend or a glowing letter from an uncritical parent stating how marvellous your system is, flying in the face of all the evidence, is not likely to gain you any marks.

Be honest about the shortcomings of the project; if it is not complete, maybe this is because it was over-ambitious and you should say so. You will not, however, score many marks for criticising the hardware, software, staff or lack of time. One of the skills to be learned in writing a project is to finish it on time in spite of all the difficulties you may encounter!

Honesty pays – if the project has some apparent failures, turn these into successes and gain credit showing what was learnt, documenting what was being attempted, what the outcome was and what difficulties were experienced. Your teacher can authenticate hardware and software difficulties that were beyond your control.

Section 4

Information Systems in Organisations

In this section:

Chapter 42 – Organisational Structure

Chapter 43 – Management Information Systems

Chapter 44 – The Information Systems Life Cycle

Chapter 45 – Implementation of Information Systems

Chapter 46 – Information Systems Strategy

Chapter 47 – Executive and Decision Support Systems

Chapter 48 – Expert Systems

Chapter 49 – Information

Chapter 50 – Data Collection

Chapter 51 – The Management of Change

Chapter 52 – Security Policies

Chapter 53 – Disaster Recovery

Chapter 54 – Implementation of Legislation

Chapter 55 – User Support

Chapter 56 – Training

Chapter 57 – Project Management

Chapter 42 – Organisational Structure

How organisations work

Organisations are entities comprising a range of human and technological resources which are managed, organised and coordinated to accomplish goals. The goal of a business organisation is usually to generate a profit; other types of organisation may have quite different objectives such as the preservation of the environment, military conquest or gaining religious converts.

> ➤ **Discussion: What are the goals of the following organisations? A College of Further Education, a hospital, the BBC, McDonald's, Greenpeace?**

The three fundamental resources of any organisation are

- People;
- Organisation;
- Technology.

The success of an organisation is determined by how well it manages and controls these three resources (the 'pillars' of an organisation), the components of which include the following:

People	*Organisation*	*Technology*
Career	Strategy	Hardware
Education	Policy	Software
Training	Mission Statement	Telecommunications
Employee Attitudes	Culture	Information Systems
Employee Participation	Management	
Employee Monitoring	Bureaucracy	
Work Environment	Competition	
	Environment	

Figure 42.1: The three pillars of an organisation

Ingredients for success

A survey commissioned by the Department of Trade and Industry in 1997 came to the following conclusions about the most successful UK companies.

Winning UK companies:

- Are led by visionary, enthusiastic champions of change;
- Unlock the potential of their people
  - Creating a culture in which employees are genuinely empowered and focused on the customer;

- Investing in people through good communications, teamwork and training;
- Flattening and inverting the organisational pyramid;
- Know their customers
    - Constantly learning from others;
    - Welcoming the challenge of demanding customers to drive innovation and competitiveness;
- Constantly introduce new, differentiated products and services
    - By deep knowledge of their competitors;
    - Encouraging innovation to successfully exploit new ideas;
    - Focusing on core businesses complemented by strategic alliances;
- Exceed their customers' expectations with new products and services.

Nine out of ten of the winning UK companies studied exhibited these characteristics of innovation best practice.

Source: DTI 'Winning' Report 1997

Focus on people

Successful companies view people as a key resource rather than simply as a cost - the competition may copy the product but it cannot copy the people. One of the main tasks of management, therefore, is to enable each person in an organisation to fulfil his or her full potential.

As one MD puts it, "motivated staff will be ten times more productive than unmotivated staff". There is a clear recognition that it is employees who most often meet with the company's customers and that "when customers meet an employee they meet the whole organisation and often judge the whole on that basis".

Training is seen as a key component in achieving empowerment of the individual and in maintaining focus on the customer in order to remain competitive. Not only is training "the epicentre of empowerment", with as much as 100% of employees' time spent on it, but successful companies "use education as a competitive weapon".

Focus on organisation

Business organisations have four internal functions which they must manage and control:

- The **Production** group produces the goods or services;
- The **Sales and Marketing** group sells the product;
- The **Personnel** or **Human Resources** group hires and trains workers;
- The **Finance and Accounting** group seeks funds to pay for all these activities and keeps track of the accounts.

Traditionally, an organisation is structured in a pyramid fashion, as in Figure 42.2.

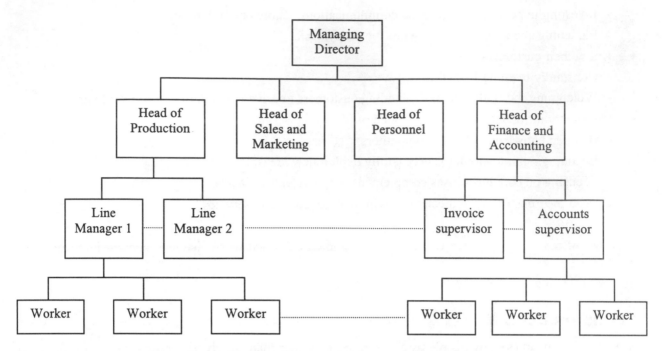

Figure 42.2: The traditional organisational structure

In the late 1990s, changes in working practices resulted in 'flatter' organisations, with layers of middle management disappearing in an effort to eliminate the stifling effects of hierarchy and bureaucracy. As the DTI 'Winning' report says:

"Five years ago the corporate structure was like a pyramid with very steep sides, in fact one could say a stalactite. Now it is more like a plate of peas. The number of levels in an organisation is cut to as few as possible. In some instances there are only three levels within the organisation: Directors, Managers and People".

Turning the organisational pyramid upside down emphasises that customers, markets and competition are crucial to business success, and employees are in the front line, being the major point of contact between the organisation and the customers.

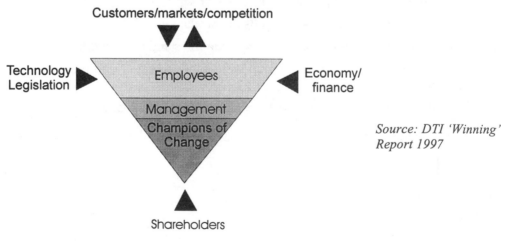

Source: DTI 'Winning' Report 1997

Figure 42.3: A different view of organisational structure

External pressures on an organisation

Surrounding the organisation is an environment of customers, competitors, government regulators, pressure groups and other interested parties, all of which have an influence on how the business is run and what policy decisions are made. (See Figure 42.4.)

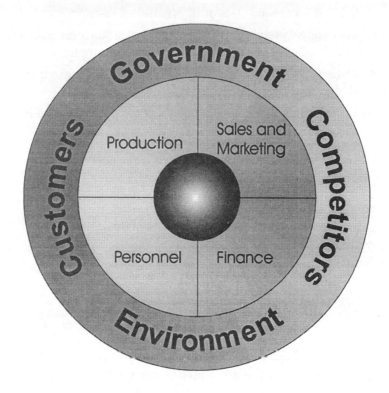

Figure 42.4: The activities of a business organisation

Case Study: Preservation vs. the people

In November 1997 the Guardian carried an article describing the four-year battle over local authority plans to replace the chairlift serving the ski centre of Aviemore with a funicular railway. Conservationists compare it with driving a motorway through Stonehenge while local people say it will bring much-needed jobs and money to the area. The RSPB together with the World Wide Fund for Nature (WWF) have fought the plan to develop a glen that offers one of the most breathtaking views in Scotland, home to the rare black grouse and scene of Landseer's famous tribute to the stag, "Monarch of the Glen". For the people of Strathspey, the funicular railway holds the key to their economic future, and the Government is prepared to contribute £9 million to the £17 million scheme.

➤ **Discussion: This is a good illustration of the external pressures that can be brought to bear on the decision-making process within an organisation. Anyone with an interest in a business is called a "stakeholder". Who are the stakeholders in this case?**

Focus on technology

In the first year of this course you learned about various computer technologies. In this module, you'll learn how technology can be used in building and using information systems in organisations. Technology is the third 'pillar' of a successful organisation.

Organisations and information systems

Most organisations are hierarchical; they are arranged in ascending order of power, pay and privilege. The three major levels in an organisation are production workers, information workers and management workers.

Each level in an organisation has its unique class of information system:

- Data or transaction processing systems serve the needs of production workers who must deal with thousands, or even millions, of transactions with customers and suppliers.

- Knowledge work systems serve the needs of clerical and professional people to process and create information and knowledge.

- Management information systems serve management's needs to control and plan the organisation.

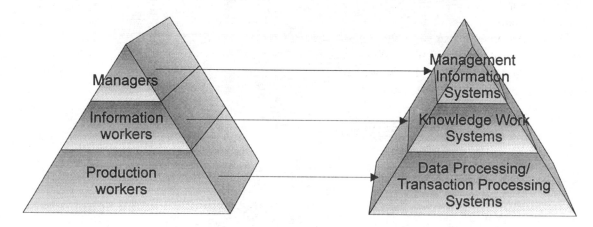

Figure 42.5: Organisations and Information Systems

Organisations, then, do not have just one information system; they may have hundreds. Each of the basic types of systems is described below.

Data processing systems

A data processing system is also known as a **transaction processing system**. Every time you buy an item in a supermarket, withdraw some cash from your bank account, make a hospital appointment or sign up for a college course, a **transaction** has occurred. Transactions are all the events that are recorded when goods or services are bought, sold, distributed or dealt with in some manner.

There are two kinds of transaction processing system:

- Batch systems, whereby transactions are collected over a period of time (say a day or a week) and processed together;

- On-line systems where the data is processed as soon as it is collected.

When there is no immediate urgency for a response or up-to-the-minute information, a batch processing system is often suitable. The TV Licensing Authority, for example, may collect requests for TV licences and process them in batches of 50 or 100 at a time. An airline reservation system, on the other hand, requires up-to-date information on what seats are available, so an on-line system must be used. Such a system is also known as a 'pseudo real-time' system. The word 'pseudo' indicates that processing takes place effectively but not absolutely immediately: a delay of a couple of minutes is normally acceptable.

> ➢ **Discussion: What type of transaction processing (batch or on-line) would be suitable for**
> **following?**
>   **A mail-order company taking orders by telephone or mail;**
>   **A credit-card company processing sales transactions;**
>   **A bookshop using electronic point-of-sale tills to keep track of sales and stock;**
>   **A hospital appointment system.**

Knowledge work systems

'Information workers' are of two general types: office clerical workers and sales personnel, and behind-the-scenes professionals such as accountants, lawyers, doctors and engineers.

Knowledge work systems are used by information workers to help deal with problems requiring knowledge or technical expertise. Word processing programs, spreadsheets, databases, computer-aided design packages and project management software all fall into this category. In addition, software and hardware that enables groups of people to find out information, communicate or work together as a team, even though they are geographically separated, is of vital importance in large organisations. Networks, web browsers, e-mail facilities and the use of video conferencing are examples of such technology.

Figure 42.6: Global communications network

Management information systems

Management information systems are designed to help managers monitor and control organisational performance and plan for the future. This type of information system is discussed in more detail in the next chapter.

Exercises

1. What are the major functions and levels in an organisation? How do the information systems used in an organisation relate to those functions and levels? (6)

    New question

2. An organisation generally consists of different levels, employing production workers, knowledge workers and management.

    Give an example of each of these types of worker in a named organisation. (4)

    New question

er 43 – Management mation Systems

Introduction

Over the past two decades, a transformation to an information society has been taking place, and computers and telecommunications technologies have revolutionised the way that organisations operate. We live in an information age, and no business of any size can survive and compete without embracing information technology. Information has come to be recognised as a resource of fundamental importance to an organisation, in the same way as the more traditional resources of people, materials and finance.

It is not enough to be merely 'computer-literate' in order to become an expert in information systems. It is also necessary to understand how to apply modern technology in a business, commercial or other environment to achieve the goals of the organisation.

Information systems vs. data processing systems

In the last chapter we looked at the different levels of information system in an organisation.

Remember that a data processing system is simply one which records the day-to-day transactions taking place within an organisation. An information system is one which uses this data and turns it into useful information. For example:

- Data on items sold is collected by the **data processing system**, using a barcode scanner and an EPOS system, and stored on a computer file;

- An **operational information system** then reads this data and produces a list of items that need reordering;

- A **management information system** may analyse the sales data to highlight sales trends and use this information to plan a new marketing campaign, adjust price levels or plan an increase or reduction in production facilities.

Internal and external information

Much of the information used by management concerns the **internal** operations of the company. However, **external** information about the environment in which the organisation exists is crucial to all organisations. This may include

- Intelligence gathering about competitors' activities;

- Information about population shifts;

- Economic and social factors;

- Government legislation.

This type of information is of great importance to managers who are trying to shave production costs, find new markets, develop new products, or have strategic decisions to make about the future direction of the company. Information is collected in many ways – through conversations and interpersonal 'networking', reading newspapers, trade reviews and magazines, attending conferences and meetings, browsing the Internet. A **formal information system** relies on procedures for the collecting, storing, processing and accessing of data in order to obtain information.

> ➤ **An international car manufacturing company maintains a database holding details of every car that will be made over the next ten years by every other car manufacturer in the world. This data is collected through agencies specialising in information gathering, through trade fairs and reviews, 'leaks' and even industrial espionage.**
>
> **A special department exists to collect and collate this information. One of the manager's jobs is to read every relevant magazine, newspaper article and communication every morning, highlight anything of importance and pass the pile of paper round the department for the others to read prior to the database being updated.**

The role of a management information system

The role of a management information system is to convert data from internal and external sources into information that can be used to aid in making effective decisions for planning, directing and controlling the activities for which they are responsible. An organisation may have dozens of different information systems, some of which are useful for the day-to-day operational decisions, and some of which are used in making tactical and strategic decisions.

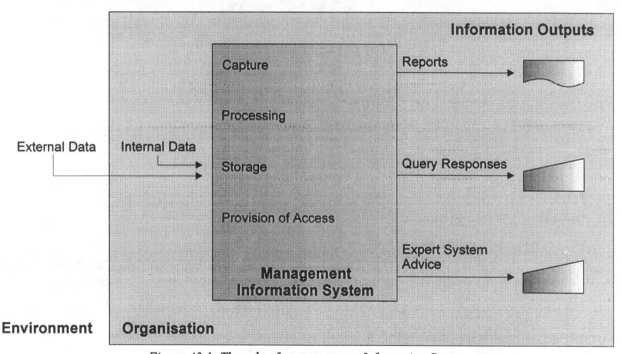

Figure 43.1: The role of a management Information System

What managers do

To understand how information systems can benefit managers, we first need to examine what the functions of management are and the kind of information they need for decision-making.

The five classical functions of managers (described more than 70 years ago) are:

1. **Planning.** Managers plan the direction a company is to take, whether to diversify, which areas of the world to operate in, how to maximise profit.

2. **Organising**. Resources such as people, space, equipment and services must be organised.

3. **Coordinating**. Managers coordinate the activities of various departments.

4. **Decision-making**. Managers make decisions about the organisation, the products or services made or sold, the employees, the use of information technology.

5. **Controlling**. This involves monitoring and supervising the activities of others.

Management information systems must be designed to support managers in as many of these functions as possible, at different levels (operational, tactical, strategic) of an organisation.

> ➤ **Discussion: How could a MIS help college managers at various levels to carry out activities of planning, organising, coordinating, decision-making and controlling?**

A study in 1973 by Henry Mintzberg found that managers divided up their time as shown in the pie chart below. He described the work of a manager as consisting of hundreds of brief activities of great variety, requiring rapid shifts of attention from one issue to another, very often initiated by emerging problems. Half of the activities of chief executives lasted less than 9 minutes.

Figure 43.2: How managers spent their time in 1973

> ➤ **Discussion: Today's managers still spend their time divided between many activities. Do you think there are any activities which managers spend more time on than they did in 1973?**

Types of decision

Management decisions can be classified into two types – *structured* and *unstructured*. Structured decisions are repetitive, routine and involve a definite procedure for handling them. Unstructured decisions on the other hand are decisions which require judgement, insight and evaluation. They are often important decisions and there is no set procedure for making them.

> ➤ **Discussion: Categorise the following decisions to be made by a department store manager as structured or unstructured:**
>
> **In which town shall we open the next branch?**
>
> **How many extra staff shall we hire to cope with the Christmas rush?**
>
> **What shall we do about an employee who has had 30 sick days in the last 6 months?**
>
> **Should we try and increase the number of customers who hold a store card?**

Stages of decision-making

Making unstructured, non-routine decisions is a process that takes place over a period of time, and consists of several stages. Think of any important decision that you may have to make, like whether to go on to University or get a job, which college or University to attend, what course or career to follow. You will probably reach any of these decisions over a period of time, having gathered together information from various sources and listened to friends, parents or careers advisers.

The manager who has non-routine decisions to make typically goes through the following stages:

1. **Recognition that there is a problem.** An information system is useful at this stage to keep managers informed of how well the department or organisation is performing and to let them know where problems exist. The principle of exception reporting is especially important in this stage – in other words, only situations which need some action are reported. (For example, customers with outstanding accounts, a sudden drop or increase in sales compared with the same period last year or a rash of staff resignations.)

2. **Consideration of possible solutions.** More detailed information may be needed at this stage, or possibly tools such as a spreadsheet which can model the effect of different solutions such as price increases or decreases, staff pay increases etc.

3. **Choosing a solution.**

4. **Implementing the solution.** This may involve setting up a new management information system to report on the progress of the solution.

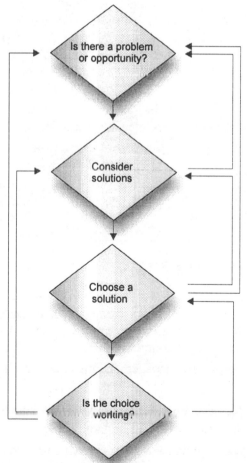

Figure 43.3: The decision-making process

Most decisions do not proceed smoothly from one stage to the next, and backtracking to a previous stage is often required if a chosen solution turns out to be impossible or new information comes to light which offers alternative choices.

Making structured decisions – often of an operational nature – is made easier by having an information system which provides the information necessary to make the correct decisions.

> ➤ **Discussion: A car company gathers information about its customer base through many sources, including market research surveys. One company has discovered that it has relatively few customers in the 18-30 age range. How can this information be used by the company to improve its sales?**

Case study: Buying a new car

If you want to purchase a new car from a Ford dealer, chances are that the make and model you want, in the right colour with the right accessories, is not in stock. It's just too expensive to have cars with every possible combination of options sitting in the parking lot waiting for a customer. In the past, it's been almost impossible for dealers to track down exactly the model that a customer wants.

With the new information system, the dealer can type the details of the required car into a terminal connected to the main Ford plant at Dagenham. The information will then come back to tell the dealer whether there are any cars available of that specification, and exactly where they are. They may be on the Ford parking lot, or there may be only two available, one at a dealer's in Perth and the other in Bournemouth. There may be none available – in which case Ford will make one for you, though this may take some time.

Plant production managers are also connected to the system, and so they know exactly what cars have been ordered and can adjust production to reflect demand every day.

> ➤ **Discussion: This is an example of a management information system. How does it help**
>   **– the dealer?**
>   **– the customer?**
>   **– the manufacturer?**

Desirable characteristics of a MIS

Formal information systems are useful at every level of an organisation. Operational systems provide answers to specific, routine questions on screen or through regular daily, weekly or monthly reports. A senior manager is likely to need information which comes to light from a new way of analysing the available data, or information from external sources.

Systems designers need to try to design management information systems which have the following characteristics:

- They are flexible, allowing for many different ways of analysing data and evaluating information;
- They are capable of supporting a range of skills and knowledge;
- They help managers get things done through interpersonal communication with other members of the organisation;
- Because managers are busy people who switch rapidly between different tasks, they should not require extensive periods of concentration;

- They should make it easy to interrupt the work and return to it at a later time;
- They should protect a manager, as far as possible, from information overload.

Exercises

1. (a) What is the purpose of a Management Information System? (1)

    (b) Why is such a system required by managers of an organisation? (1)

    (c) Give **one** example of the use of a Management Information System within an organisation, clearly stating its purpose. (2)

    NEAB IT04 Qu 1 1997

2. Explain with the aid of **two** different examples how information systems can assist managers and improve managerial decision-making. (6)

    New question

3. The Personnel Manager of a large chemical company is concerned that not enough students are applying for sponsorship prior to going to University. She has asked Giles, one of her staff, to look through all the applications received over the past three years and enter details of each applicant's GCSE and A Level grades, gender, type of school or college, area of the country and other relevant information into a database.

    (a) How can this data be analysed to help plan a new student recruitment campaign? (3)

    (b) What other information could applicants be asked to provide which might provide additional useful information in planning the campaign? (2)

    New question

4. List **three** desirable features of a management information system, stating in each case why the feature you have specified is useful. (6)

    New question

Chapter 44 – The Information Systems Life Cycle

Overview of the systems life cycle

Large systems development projects may involve dozens of people working over several months or even years, so they cannot be allowed to proceed in a haphazard fashion. The goals of an information system must be thoroughly understood, and formal procedures and methods applied to ensure that the project is delivered on time and to the required specification.

The systems life cycle methodology approaches the development of information systems in a very methodical and sequential manner. Each stage is composed of certain well-defined activities and responsibilities, and is completed before the next stage begins. This approach was popular in the 1960s and 70s, when systems were largely transaction-processing systems and had a much heavier reliance on programming than most modern information systems, which are database-oriented.

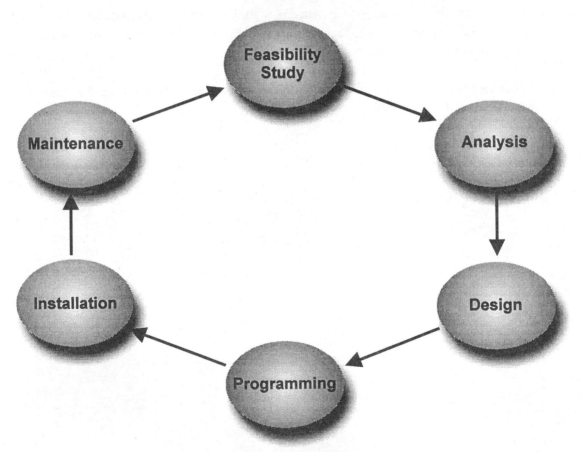

Figure 44.1: The systems life cycle

> ➤ **Discussion: In your experience of practical work on information technology projects, is this a good representation of the process of implementing a system from scratch? If not, why not?**

The waterfall model

The systems life cycle approach to development is also known as the 'waterfall model', and a variation on the basic diagram of 44.1 is shown in Figure 44.2.

Note that the arrows go up and down the 'waterfall', reflecting the fact that developers often have to rework earlier stages in the light of experience gained as development progresses.

A project milestone terminates each stage of a life-cycle-oriented approach. At this stage, the 'deliverable' resulting from that stage – such as the documentation for the analysis or the design, or the program code or finished database application, is *signed off* by all concerned parties and approval is given to proceed. The 'concerned parties' usually include the end-users, the management and the developers, as well as other experts such as database administration personnel. This sequence continues until the evaluation stage has been completed and the finished system is delivered to the end-users.

In this model, the end-user has very little say in the development process, which is carried out by technical specialists such as systems analysts and programmers. He or she is presented with the finished system at the end of the development cycle and if it is not quite what was wanted, it is generally too late to make changes. Therefore, it is extremely important that the system requirements are very clearly specified and understood by all parties before being signed off.

Such levels of certainty are difficult to achieve and this is one of the major drawbacks of the 'waterfall model'.

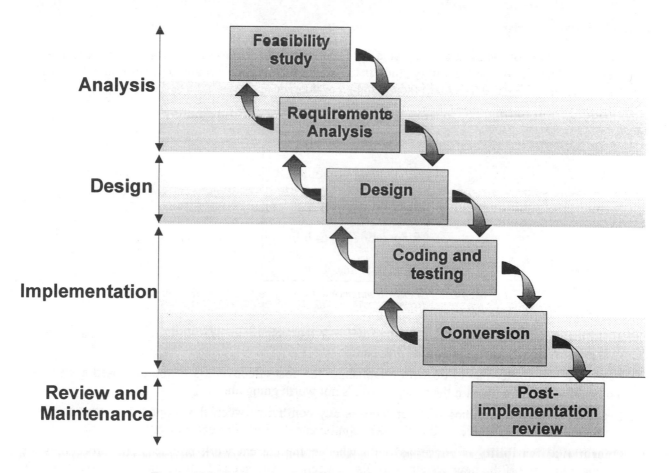

Figure 44.2: Systems development life cycle (the 'Waterfall model')

What prompts a new system?

The development of a new information system is a major undertaking and not one to be undertaken lightly. Wal-Mart, an American discount store, spent $700m on its new computerised distribution system in the 1980s. Tesco, Sainsbury's and Marks and Spencer have spent massive sums of money on their computer systems in the past decade. Businesses must adapt to remain competitive. Some of the reasons for introducing a new system may be:

1. **The current system may no longer be suitable for its purpose**. Changes in work processes, expansion of the business, changes in business requirements or the environment in which the organisation operates may all lead to a reassessment of information system requirements.

2. **Technological developments may have made the current system redundant or outdated**. Advances in hardware, software and telecommunications bring new opportunities which an organisation cannot ignore if it is to keep ahead of its rivals.

3. **The current system may be too inflexible or expensive to maintain**, or may reduce the organisation's ability to respond quickly enough to customer's demands.

As we reach the end of the millennium, many businesses with old systems that may be susceptible to the 'millennium bug' are taking the opportunity to install a new system which will provide better information, rather than spend money on having external consultants patch up their old system.

Feasibility study

This is the first stage of the systems life cycle. The **scope** and **objectives** of the proposed system must be written down. The aim of the feasibility study is to understand the problem and to determine whether it is worth proceeding. There are five main factors to be considered:

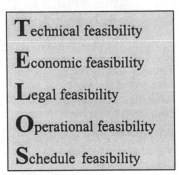

Technical feasibility

Economic feasibility

Legal feasibility

Operational feasibility

Schedule feasibility

Figure 44.3: TELOS – a mnemonic for the five feasibility factors

- **Technical feasibility** means investigating whether the technology exists to implement the proposed system, or whether this is a practical proposition.

- **Economic feasibility** has to do with establishing the cost-effectiveness of the proposed system – if the benefits do not outweigh the costs, then it is not worth going ahead.

- **Legal feasibility** determines whether there is any conflict between the proposed system and legal requirements – for example, will the system contravene the Data Protection Act?

- **Operational feasibility** is concerned with whether the current work practices and procedures are adequate to support the new system. It is also concerned with social factors – how the organisational change will affect the working lives of those affected by the system.

- **Schedule feasibility** looks at how long the system will take to develop, or whether it can be done in a desired time-frame.

The completion of this stage is marked by the production of a feasibility report produced by the systems analyst. If the report concludes that the project should go ahead, and this is agreed by senior managers, detailed requirements analysis will proceed.

Requirements analysis

The second phase of systems analysis is a more detailed investigation into the current system and the requirements of the new system.

Gathering details about the current system will involve:

- Interviewing staff at different levels of the organisation from the end-users to senior management.

- Examining current business and systems documents and output. These may include current order documents, computer systems procedures and reports used by operations and senior management.

- Sending out questionnaires and analysing responses. The questions have to be carefully constructed to elicit unambiguous answers.

- Observation of current procedures, by spending time in various departments. A time and motion study can be carried out to see where procedures could be made more efficient, or to detect where bottlenecks occur.

The systems analyst's report will examine how data and information flow around the organisation, and may use **data flow diagrams** to document the flow. It will also establish precisely and in considerable detail exactly what the proposed system will do (as opposed to how it will do it) It will include an in depth analysis of the costs and benefits, and outline the process of system implementation, including the organisational change required. It must establish who the end-users are, what information they should get and in what form and how it will be obtained.

Alternative options for the implementation of the project will be suggested. These could include suggestions for:

- Whether development should be done in-house or using consultants;

- What hardware configurations could be considered;

- What the software options are.

The report will conclude with a recommendation to either proceed or abandon the project.

Case study: Computer-dating the customer

When it started a century ago, marketing treated all customers the same. By the 1960s, marketers were able to break that anonymous mass into segments. Now customer databases allow them to treat customers as individuals. They may know consumers' names and addresses, what they buy, what they have stopped buying and even how they respond to a rise in the price of dog food.

For big multinational retailers, this is the equivalent of going back to the days of the individual store owner who knew and greeted each customer personally. The benefits are potentially huge: instead of spending millions on advertising beamed at people who may be indifferent or even hostile to it, retailers can use databases to help them hang on to their existing customers and persuade them to buy more. But it is not trouble-free: databases are expensive to collect and analyse, and some customers may see such individual marketing as an invasion of their privacy.

Talbot's, a 385-store women's clothing chain based in Massachusetts, has compiled a database of 7m names that includes information about customers' sizes. This has enabled them to forecast more accurately which sizes will sell in particular stores. It also asks all customers for their post codes when they pay, to help it plan new store openings. The effort seems to be paying off. For the past five years the company has been opening around 50 new stores a year.

Source: The Economist 4 March 1995

> ➤ **Discussion: A system like the one above would have cost millions of dollars to install. What were the major costs? What were the benefits?**

System design

The design specifies the following aspects of a system:

- The hardware platform – which type of computer, network capabilities, input, storage and output devices;
- The software – programming language, package or database;
- The outputs – report layouts and screen designs;
- The inputs – documents, screen layouts and validation procedures;
- The user interface – how users will interact with the computer system;
- The modular design of each program in the application;
- The test plan and test data;
- Conversion plan – how the new system is to be implemented;
- Documentation including systems and operations documentation. Later, a user manual will be produced.

Implementation

This phase includes both the coding and testing of the system, the acquisition of hardware and software and the installation of the new system or conversion of the old system to the new one.

The installation phase can include:

- Installing the new hardware, which may involve extensive recabling and changes in office layouts;
- Training the users on the new system;
- Conversion of master files to the new system, or creation of new master files.

Methods of conversion

There are several different methods of conversion:

- **Direct changeover.** The user stops using the old system one day and starts using the new system the next — usually over a weekend or during a slack period. The advantage of this system is that it is fast and efficient, with minimum duplication of work involved. The disadvantage is that normal operations could be seriously disrupted if the new system has errors in it or does not work quite as expected.
- **Parallel conversion.** The old system continues alongside the new system for a few weeks or months. The advantage is that results from the new system can be checked against known results, and if any difficulties occur, operations can continue under the old system while the errors or omissions are sorted out. The disadvantage of parallel conversion is the duplication of effort required to keep both systems running, which may put a strain on personnel.
- **Phased conversion.** This is used with larger systems that can be broken down into individual modules that can be implemented separately at different times. It could also be used where for example only a few customer accounts are processed using the new system, while the rest remain for a time on the old system. Phased conversion could be direct or parallel.

- **Pilot conversion.** This means that the new system will be used first by only a portion of the organisation, for example at one branch or factory.

> ➤ **Discussion: For each of the following examples, state with reasons what type of conversion method would be suitable.**
>
> (a) A bakery is introducing a system to input orders from each salesperson and use this data to calculate how much of each product to bake each day, and also to calculate the salesperson's commission.
>
> (b) A chain store is introducing EPOS terminals connected to a mainframe computer which holds details of stock levels and prices.
>
> (c) A public library is introducing a computerised system for the lending and return of books.
>
> (d) A large hospital is introducing a computerised system for keeping patient records and appointments.
>
> (e) A College is introducing a computerised timetabling and room allocation system.
>
> (f) A Company manufacturing electronic components is introducing an integrated system for production control, stock control and order processing.
>
> (g) A Local Authority is introducing a computerised system for the collection of a new type of tax.

Post-implementation review

An important part of the implementation is a review of how the new system is performing, once it has been up and running for a period of time. Minor programming errors may have to be corrected, clerical procedures amended, or modifications made to the design of reports or screen layouts. Often it is only when people start to use a new system that they realise its shortcomings! In some cases they may realise that it would be possible to get even more useful information from the system than they realised, and more programs may be requested. The process of **system maintenance**, in fact, has already begun, and the life cycle is complete.

System maintenance

All software systems require maintenance, and in fact the vast majority of programmers are employed to maintain existing programs rather than to write new ones. There are differing reasons for this, and different types of maintenance.

- **Perfective maintenance.** This implies that while the system runs satisfactorily, there is still room for improvement. For example, extra management information may be needed so that new report programs have to be written. Database queries may be very slow, and a change in a program may be able to improve response time.

- **Adaptive maintenance.** All systems will need to adapt to changing needs within a company. As a business expands, for example, there may be a requirement to convert a standalone system to a multi-user system. New and better hardware may become available, and changes to the software may be necessary to take advantage of this. New government legislation may mean that different methods of calculating tax, for example, are required. Competition from other firms may mean that systems have to be upgraded in order to maintain a competitive edge.

- **Corrective maintenance.** Problems frequently surface after a system has been in use for a short time, however thoroughly it was tested. Some part of the system may not function as expected, or a report might be wrong in some way; totals missing at the bottom, incorrect sequence of data, wrong headings, etc. Frequently errors will be hard to trace, if for example a file appears to have been wrongly updated.

Prototyping

The waterfall model of the system life cycle has major shortcomings and often bears little relation to what happens in practice. One reason for this is that it doesn't allow for modifications to the design as the project proceeds, with both user and developer learning as they go along. Users frequently have difficulty in explaining their requirements at the start of a proposed system since they do not know what is possible and cannot visualise how the final system will work. This can result in a system which does not really match their requirements. (See Figure 45.2.)

Using the **prototyping** approach, a model of a new system is built in order to evaluate it or have it approved before building the production model. Applied to software projects, this means, for example, using special software to quickly design input screens and create a program to input and validate data. This gives the user a chance to experience the 'look and feel' of the input process and suggest alterations before going any further. The earlier a user is involved, the easier it will be to make changes.

Figure 44.4: The prototyping approach

Benefits of prototyping

The benefits of prototyping are:

- Misunderstandings between software developers and users can be identified when the prototype is demonstrated;
- Missing functions may be detected;
- Incomplete or inconsistent user requirements may be detected and can be completed or corrected;
- A prototype version will be quickly available to demonstrate the feasibility and usefulness of the proposed system to management;
- The prototype can sometimes be used for training before the final system is delivered.

Prototyping may be used in a number of different ways, and various terms have been coined to describe them:

- **Piloting** – using a prototype to test the feasibility of a design proposal;
- **Modelling** – building to develop an understanding of the user's requirements;
- **Throw-away prototyping** – both piloting and modelling are 'throw-away prototypes': once they have achieved their purpose the real system is built;
- **Evolutionary prototyping** – each prototype built represents a step closer to the final solution.

Exercises

1. A feasibility study will often be carried out at an early stage of system development. As well as finding out if the proposal is technically possible the study will also consider economic and social feasibility.

    In the context of a feasibility study describe **one** cost, **one** benefit and **three** possible social effects that would be considered. (5)
    AEB AS Computing Qu 7 1996

2. Often the most critical phase in the systems life cycle is the changeover from the old system to the new one. This may be implemented by *parallel running* or by *pilot running*. Briefly describe these installation methods. (3)
    AEB AS Computing Qu 4 1997

3. State **three** different methods of fact finding available during the systems analysis stage of the systems life cycle, and for **each** of these three methods, give **one** reason for its use. (6)
    AEB Computing Paper 1 Qu 11 1996

4. State and briefly describe **two** different types of program maintenance. (2)
    NEAB Computing Paper 2 Qu 1 1995

5. Describe **five** main stages in the full life cycle of a computerised system. (10)
    NEAB Computing Paper 1 Qu 11 1995

6. Some of the steps in computerising an existing manual system are:
    *   systems analysis
    *   systems design
    *   programming
    *   testing
    *   changeover to the new system
    *   operation and maintenance.

    (a) Describe **three** aspects of the existing manual system which would have to be investigated so that the analysis could be carried out. (3)

    (b) Briefly describe **four** tasks which will be performed during the design process. (4)

    (c) Explain how it is possible for all the individual component modules to pass their tests and yet for the system still to fail. (3)

    (d) The changeover to the new system from the manual system can be achieved in three ways:
    (i) immediate change;
    (ii) running the manual and computerised systems in parallel;
    (iii) gradually introducing the new system a subsystem at a time.

    In **each** case, state an application for which the technique is most appropriate. (3)

    (e) Briefly describe the responsibilities of the systems analyst once the system is operational. (2)
    London Paper 1 Qu 13 1994

Chapter 45 – Implementation of Information Systems

What is implementation?

Implementation is the process of preparing people for the introduction of a new system and actually introducing it. Preparation work can start early in the systems development life cycle, even preceding the development stage. A major new system runs a high risk of failure if its implementation is not very carefully planned and the organisational changes that will be required not fully recognised and allowed for. A fully developed system may be regarded by its developers as a success because it 'works', and yet never become operational, or fall into disuse after a short trial period.

Successful implementation

As part of your course you will probably analyse, design and develop an information system for a real user. This will include scheduling the various stages of implementation, and evaluating its success. You are in fact doing on a small scale what the developers of any system, large or small, have to do. So what are the criteria for judging the success of a system? Here are some possible measures:

- **High level of use.** Is the new system actually used? New systems for recording student results, registering students' presence using swipe cards, or constructing timetables and scheduling classroom use may all be introduced but not be widely accepted. A new customer information system may never become operational because users discover it simply takes too long to enter the data.

- **High level of user satisfaction.** Do users like the system? Large companies may identify products and services provided by the information systems unit (such as e-mail or Intranet services, network services, new software) and ask users to fill in questionnaires to gauge their level of satisfaction with each product or service.

- **Accomplishment of original objectives.** A comprehensive list of objectives should have been stated in the Analysis stage of system development. Have these objectives been satisfactorily achieved? The objectives may be, for example, to perform certain tasks such as recording student grades or sending out invoices in a shorter time than before, to increase market share of a particular product or to produce more accurate estimates of building costs.

- **Appropriate nature of use.** A high level of use is not always an indication that a system is a complete success. Witness the man who called a PC manufacturer to complain that his coffee-mug holder had broken. The puzzled service engineer, on quizzing the customer, finally realised he was referring to the CD drive. Software, too, can be used inappropriately if training is not given.

- **Institutionalisation of the system.** A successful system will be taken on board enthusiastically by users and used in new and changing ways, evolving to meet new demands.

> ➢ **Discussion: Think of some large-scale information systems that have been successfully implemented. What makes these systems so successful?**

Why do information systems fail?

Information systems fail for many reasons at any stage of the systems life cycle.

1. Analysis

- Not enough time and money is spent researching the problem, and objectives are poorly defined, so that benefits will be hard to measure.

- The project team is not properly staffed, with team members being allocated only when available so that they cannot dedicate themselves to the task, resulting in a lack of continuity and commitment.

- Users are not sufficiently involved.

- Analysts have poor communication skills and do not ask the right questions or extract the necessary information to establish what the problems are with the current system or what the requirements of the new system are.

2. Design

- Users have little involvement and the design therefore does not reflect their requirements.

- The system is designed to meet current needs but is not flexible enough to respond to changes in the business environment.

- Management is not involved in the design, or makes excessive and inappropriate demands with no real understanding of information technology and its capabilities.

- Major changes to clerical procedures are planned with no regard to the impact on staffing or the organisation.

3. Programming

- The amount of time required for programming is grossly underestimated.

- Programmers lack the necessary skills: too much time is spent on coding and not enough on proper program design.

- Programs are not properly documented and so disruption occurs when any of the team leaves.

- Not enough resources such as computer time are allocated.

4. Testing

- The project team does not develop a proper test plan.

- Users are not sufficiently involved in testing. They do not help by creating test data and tests with expected results specified.

- Acceptance tests are not devised, conducted and signed off by management.

5. Conversion

- Insufficient time and money is allocated for converting the data to the new system.

- Training is not given to the users, or is only started when the system is installed.

- User documentation is inadequate.

- Performance evaluations are not conducted.

With so much to go wrong, it seems quite amazing that so many systems are successfully implemented! The key lies in careful planning and heavy involvement from both users and management combined with technological expertise.

Case study: Tiptree Book Distributors

Tiptree is a book distributor holding books from many different publishers in its huge warehouse and distributing them to bookshops and libraries around the country as orders come in. One of the largest distributors in Britain, it has 10 acres of warehousing and 25 million books in the warehouse, and in 1994 won the British Book Awards Distributor of the Year. It was able to guarantee that any order received would be dispatched by the following day.

Tiptree wanted to ensure that it stayed at the top – and had plans to put in place a computerised warehousing system that would be so much more efficient that all orders would be filled the same day. Under the manual system, when an order was received from a bookshop, warehouse staff would have to travel all over the warehouse finding the correct titles to put in the box. Then to fill the next order they might have to go right to the far end of the warehouse again.

The new computerised system would hold a map of where every book was positioned in the warehouse. The orders would be entered into the computer, which would work out the most efficient way for books to be picked off the shelves and put onto a new conveyor belt system. The system automatically issued an invoice, advising if books were out of stock. The dimensions and weight of each book were entered so that the computer could automatically pick the right sized box to pack the books in, and double-check the consignment was correct by weighing the box before heat-sealing it and dispatching it.

The system worked perfectly during trials. Tests were carried out with every aspect of the hardware, software and warehouse equipment functioning as they would when the system went live. Tiptree's management was so confident of success that they decided to use a 'direct conversion' method of implementation – stop using the old system one day, and start up the new system the next.

Almost immediately, things started to go wrong.

The warehouse staff did not appreciate the need to pick the books off the shelves exactly as instructed by the computer. If the books were awkward to reach, they would take them from a more convenient shelf. This meant that the computer's map showed the correct pallet of books as being out of stock and in need of replenishment, and the incorrectly dispatched pallet as being still on the shelf when in fact it had gone.

After a few weeks, the computer's map became hopelessly inaccurate. The problem was made worse because as the system deteriorated and customers began to complain about books not being delivered, warehouse staff started to circumvent the computer system and take books off the shelf themselves for immediate dispatch. At this point there were no reliable manual stock records for backup, and it also transpired that the map had not been completely accurate in the first place because staff hadn't transferred data from the old manual system to the new computerised system completely accurately.

With the stock records now corrupted, staff were unable to find books to put onto the conveyor belt within the two-hour period allotted by the computer. After this time the books were marked out of stock and the customers did not receive their orders. Meanwhile, some perfectly packed orders were rejected by the computer system because they were underweight. This turned out to be because the programmers had not allowed for the fact that paperback books lose moisture in a warehouse and so weigh a few grams less. Also, some warehouse staff had mistakenly keyed in the dimensions of the box instead of the book, so the computer thought that only one book would fit into a large box. To add to the problem, the computer would allocate a box to be filled with books it thought were in stock but which could not be found anywhere.

One retailer received six pallets of one title, another received three beautifully packed, heat-sealed boxes which contained no books at all. Waterstone's in Croydon opened a large box that should have contained many titles to find inside a single book: *Chaos* by James Gleick.

As the managing director of Tiptree said: "It took 27 years to build up a reputation as the best distributor in the country, and 7 weeks to lose it".

The story has a happy ending – by 1995 the system was yielding the promised rewards and 98% of orders were dispatched the same day as they were received, and the systems have become a model for the book trade.

(Adapted from Tony Collins' account of this implementation in his book 'Crash')

➢ **Discussion: What were the major errors in the implementation of Tiptree's system? Could these have been avoided? Think of at least three things they could have done differently in order to ensure a smooth changeover from the old system to the new one.**

Factors in successful implementation

Some recognised factors in successful system implementation are shown in Figure 45.1.

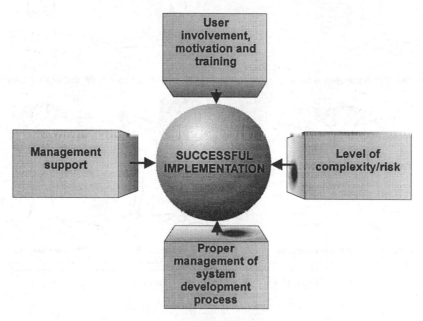

Figure 45.1: Factors in successful system implementation

These factors are considered in more detail below:

1. **User involvement, motivation and training.** If users are involved right from the start of a project, they have more opportunity to state their priorities and have some influence on the end result. Their expertise may lead to a better system being developed. Secondly, they are more likely to react positively to the finished system if they have had an active part in its development.

2. **Level of complexity and risk.** The larger the project, the greater the risk. Some projects are relatively straightforward and others are so highly complex that the requirements may change even before the project is completed. If the implementation team is inexperienced or lacks the required technical expertise, this adds to the likelihood of failure.

3. **Proper management of the system development process.** A project that is not properly managed is likely to suffer from:

   • Cost overruns;

   • Delays in completion;

   • Technical problems resulting in poor performance;

- Failure to achieve expected benefits.

4. **Management support**. New systems that have the backing of management are more likely to succeed because they are more likely to be positively perceived by both users and technical staff. Also, sufficient funds are more likely to be made available. Changes in work habits and any organisational realignment associated with the new system are likely to be implemented more successfully with management backing.

Figure 45.2: Problems of communication

Exercises

1. The management of a company wishes to introduce a computerised diary/scheduling package which is known to be compatible with the existing software base. With the aid of examples, give **three** factors which could influence the success or failure of this exercise. (6)

   NEAB IT04 Qu 2 1997

2. A theatre plans to introduce a computerised booking system. Apart from the ability to take bookings and print tickets, describe **two** other possible benefits to the theatre management. Describe briefly three ways in which the success of the new system can be measured. (5)

   New question

3. (a) Name **five** stages of the systems life cycle. (5)

   (b) At each stage of the cycle, things can go wrong which ultimately mean that the system is not successfully implemented. Describe briefly **one** possible cause of failure at **each** stage of the life cycle. (5)

   New question

4. Give **two** reasons why major information system projects which are scheduled to take several years to develop have a higher risk of failure than smaller I.T. projects. (2)

   New question

Chapter 46 – Information Systems Strategy

Introduction

All businesses, from the smallest sole trader to the largest multi-national concern, need to have a long-term plan of where they are headed – a business strategy, in other words. Over the next few years, will the business expand or stay the same size? Will it develop new markets for existing products, or expand its product line? Should it aim to take over one or more of its supplier's or customer's businesses, or sell part of the business to a competitor?

Without a business strategy, a business may drift along for some time but it is unlikely to be successful in the long term. A strategy is needed for the following reasons:

- There needs to be an agreed set of objectives for the whole company so that the activities of individual departments are coordinated to serve these objectives.

- Resources have to be allocated to departments to buy new equipment, property and machinery, or to allow new products to be developed or advertised. Such expenditure can only be made effectively if there is an overall plan for the direction the business is moving in.

- Organisations have responsibilities to their 'stakeholders' – for example employees, owners, shareholders, banks and customers. The stakeholders will have a particular interest in seeing that the corporate strategy takes into account their interests.

A SWOT analysis (Strengths, Weaknesses, Opportunities, and Threats) may be used to identify internal and external factors that will have an impact on the business. (Figure 46.1)

Figure 46.1: Formulating a business strategy

Formulating an information system strategy

An information systems strategy is just one part of the overall business strategy and must be developed within the context of the overall corporate objectives, which it will be designed to support. Expansion or development of an information system will inevitably involve:

- The allocation of significant resources;
- Changes in the way that certain parts of the business operate.

The emphasis in formulating the strategy is on determining the information needs of the business, rather than on how the information is to be provided. It must be led by the needs of the business and not by technology. However, an awareness of developments in technology will enable a business to find new ways of gaining competitive advantage.

The general organisational structure, the personalities of managers and other employees and the technology available will all play a part in determining the information system strategy.

Figure 46.2: Factors influencing an information systems strategy

The following is an extract from Ford's Graduate Recruitment brochure in 1998:

> **'Ford is looking for quantum improvements in cost, timing, productivity and customer satisfaction. The way to achieve this is through people, processes and technology. Most important are the people, because without a highly motivated workforce, willing to embrace change, none of this will happen. We need processes that are lean, robust and nimble, changing the way we do business, and we need leading edge technology to implement these processes.**
>
> **Our manufacturing and product engineering operations are two areas of the business undergoing significant change and Advanced Information Technology is the key to enabling that change. It is reducing cycle times, improving quality standards, and allowing us to respond more flexibly to changing customer needs.'**

> ➤ **Discussion: What impact does Ford's information systems strategy have on their recruitment strategy? What sort of people are they looking for in their Business Systems Department?**
>
> ➤ **What benefits do they hope that I.T. will bring to the organisation?**

End-user computing

The 'end-user' is the person who uses the information produced by a management information system. Traditionally, the MIS professionals developed all the computer applications, and end-users were provided with the output in the form of reports. Today's computing environment is very different: end-users now typically develop systems themselves to satisfy a large proportion of their own informational requirements. For example, a manager may use a spreadsheet to work out the forecast for the next quarter. A marketing manager may develop a database application to help plan a marketing strategy for a new product. Teachers develop their own applications to track students' progress and print out results.

The management of end-user computing is one aspect of the overall MIS strategy of an organisation. The dividing line between what systems should be developed by the MIS professionals and what is more efficiently developed by the end-users themselves is not at all well-defined. Some managers think the best strategy is to exert strict control over end-user development (the 'monopolist' approach), while others see benefits in encouraging it to expand (the 'laissez-faire' approach). This allows the creativity and capabilities of end-users to be exploited to their full potential, and means that users' needs can be met without having to wait for funds or time to become available for a professional to develop or upgrade a system, or add a much-needed function to an existing system.

The policy also has major disadvantages:

- **Ineffective use of resources.** Many organisations spend more than half their total I.T. budget on end-user computing, so cost-justification is essential.

- **Incompatible hardware and software between departments.** Hardware and software may be incompatible between departments. It is generally more economical to purchase a site licence for software than to have individual departments buying their own packages.

- **Poorly designed and documented systems.** Some systems may be developed by people who are less than expert in analysis, design and implementation, leading to systems which are difficult to use or allow invalid data to be input. Such systems may fall into disuse when the developer leaves.

- **Threats to data security and privacy.** Controls over what data is held, and who has access to it, may be missing.

I.T. for competitive advantage

There are four major forces exerting pressure on a business:

- Bargaining power of customers;
- Bargaining power of suppliers;
- New and better products appearing which make the organisation's product obsolete;
- New competitors entering the market.

Figure 46.3: Pressures on an organisation

Strategies can be adopted to counteract these pressures, and maintain competitive advantage, for example by:

- Keeping costs lower than those of competitors;
- Producing better products than competitors;
- Creating new or different products that no one else produces;
- Locking suppliers or customers in to the organisation's products or services, for example by supplying excellent after-sales service.

> ➢ **Discussion: Information technology can help in all these aspects. Think of some examples of how technology can be used to keep costs down (see also case study below), or how it has been used in new products over the past ten years.**

Case study: Just-in-time at Wal-Mart's

Wal-Mart's is an American discount store that was among the first to use I.T. for competitive advantage in the 1980s. Many of Wal-Mart's strategies were born of necessity. 'Sometimes it was difficult getting the bigger companies – Proctor and Gamble, Kodak, whoever – to deliver to us, and when they did, they would dictate how much they would sell us and at what price', Walton said later. This forced him to set up his own distribution system. In 1969, with just 32 stores, he built his first warehouse so he could buy goods in volume.

In the past each store manager would order goods to replace those sold, relying on suppliers to deliver them direct to the shop – a hit-and-miss system that took up potential selling space for storage and often left shops out of stock. As Wal-Mart developed its distribution centres in the 1970s, it introduced two innovations. The first was 'cross-docking': goods were centrally ordered, delivered to one side of the distribution centre, and then transferred to the other side for delivery to an individual shop, along with the other goods the shop had ordered. This meant that one full lorry would make frequent trips to each store, instead of several half-empty ones visiting less often. To make this system work well, the firm had to keep track of thousands of cases and packages, making sure they were delivered to the right shop at the right time.

That was where computers came in. By the early 1980s Wal-Mart had not only set up computer links between each store and the distribution warehouse; through a system called EDI (electronic data interchange), it also hooked up with the computers of the firm's main suppliers. The distribution centres themselves were equipped with miles of laser-guided conveyor belts that could read the bar codes on incoming cases and direct them to the right truck for their onward journey. The final step was to buy a satellite to transmit the firm's enormous data load. The whole system covering all the firm's warehouses, cost at least $700m, but it quickly paid for itself.

The first benefit was just-in-time replenishment across hundreds of stores. This has since been refined further, using computer modelling programs to anticipate sales patterns. The second benefit was cost. According to Walton, Wal-Mart's distribution costs in 1992 were under 3% of sales, compared with 4.5 - 5% for the firm's competitors – a saving of close to $750m in that year alone.

Source: The Economist 4 March 1995

> ➢ **Discussion: Note how Wal-Mart's I.T. strategy was driven by its business strategies. What problems did Wal-Mart need to overcome to gain competitive advantage? In what ways does information technology help them?**

Exercises

1. Name **three** major resources of an organisation that will influence its business information strategy.
    (3)
    New question

2. An educational publishing company publishes about 100 different titles which are sold by direct mail and through bookshops. Describe briefly **three** alternative strategies which the company might adopt to increase its profit. For **each** of these strategies, show how information technology could help to carry them out.
    (6)
    New question

3. Describe briefly **three** factors within an organisation that can contribute to the successful implementation of an information system strategy.
    (3)
    New question

4. A national charity which provides housing for homeless people has a Head Office in London and 12 branch offices in other parts of the country. The management is currently developing an information systems strategy to help them achieve their objectives, which are to increase donations and ensure that the money raised is spent effectively. Describe briefly **four** ways in which information technology could be used to help them achieve their objectives.
    (8)
    New question

5. Name **four** external 'threats' to a commercial organisation, giving an example of each. Describe with the aid of an example in each case how information technology can be used to counteract these threats.
    (8)
    New question

6. The recruitment department of a large company has an MS Access database which was developed by an information systems professional, to help them keep track of students on sponsorship schemes.

    A student on the scheme is currently spending 3 months in the department, and has found that there is a need for some extra reports, and that it would also be useful to keep details of sponsored students' 'mentors' on the database. As she recently gained a Grade A in Advanced Level I.T. and acquired a good knowledge of Access in the process, she is able to add some extra options to the main menu, and also correct some minor bugs which have annoyed the recruitment personnel for some time.

    Describe, with reference to the above scenario, **two** advantages and **two** disadvantages of a management strategy that allows users a large degree of freedom to develop their own applications.
    (8)
    New question

Chapter 47 – Executive and Decision Support Systems

Categories of business information system

A typical organisation will have three broad levels of decision-making – strategic (executive) level, management level and operational level. Each level has different information requirements, and the business information systems fall into these three main categories: *executive*, *decision support* and *operational* systems.

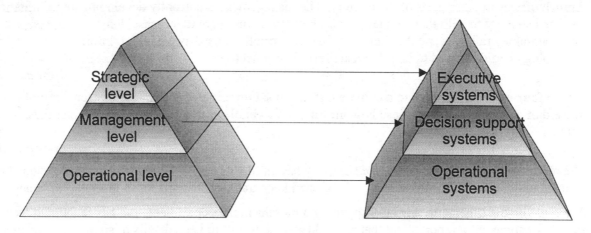

Figure 47.1: Levels of information system within an organisation

Operational systems such as payroll, accounting, stock control and purchase order processing are highly automated and any decisions within these systems are usually made according to a formula. For example, a supermarket stock control system will decide how many hot dogs to order automatically from a formula involving the current quantity in stock, the reorder level and the reorder quantity for that particular item.

Decision support systems are used by managers to help them make decisions to ensure the smooth and efficient running of the business. A decision support system, for example, might help a manager to spot that the sales of hot dogs go up when there is a long spell of fine weather, and therefore to adjust the formula in the operational system which calculates the reorder quantity.

Executive information systems are used to help senior managers make strategic decisions such as whether to open a new distribution centre for goods because the supplies of items such as hot dogs are unreliable or delivery too slow.

Turning data into information

Within an organisation, data is captured, processed and turned into useful information. Thus in the example of the supermarket stock control system, sales data is captured at the tills, typically by scanning the bar code on each item. This data can be stored on a database and processed in many different ways to produce information which can be used at each of the three levels described above.

- The total quantity remaining in stock is adjusted each time an item is sold. At the **operational level**, the system can then generate a reorder report listing all the items that need reordering, and how much to order.

- At the **decision support systems level**, information can be gathered on how often the store runs out of stock of particular items, or has to throw away unsold perishable goods. This information can be used to adjust reorder levels.

- At the **executive information systems level**, the data can be fed into a computer model which can calculate the effect on profits of adopting different strategies such as changing the distribution system or opening a store in another area.

Figure 47.2: Turning data into information for different levels of an organisation

Decision support systems

In chapter 43 we discussed two different kinds of decisions: **structured** decisions, which tend to be of an operational nature, and **unstructured** decisions, which are more likely to be high-level management decisions. A decision support system cannot make a decision for a manager, but it can offer him or her access to information that will help make the correct decision.

For example, suppose the marketing manager in an organisation is given the task of planning the marketing strategy for a new brand of toothbrush. The type of information that would be required would probably include:

- **Customer information.** Information could be collected from customers using questionnaires and market surveys, to ascertain what they thought were important features in a toothbrush, how often they changed their toothbrush and so on.

- **Information about the competition.** Information could be collected on new products, pricing strategies, sales and advertising of rival products.
- **Sales reports.** Information on sales of similar products will be helpful in forecasting demand.
- **Feedback from advertising campaigns.** This can be used to plan future advertising campaigns or modify the marketing strategy.

A simple decision support system could take the form of a spreadsheet which the user can employ to test out the effects of various courses of action – 'what if' analyses. Data on sales levels and various pricing policies can be entered to determine the optimum price and marketing strategy. More sophisticated decision support systems employ special software, usually database-oriented, which can include a variety of data to build a model of a situation. The more internal and external data that is collected and input to the system, the more likely it is that the software will be able to realistically model the likely outcome of a particular course of action.

> ➢ **Suppose you have to decide on the best method of transport for a school trip to France. What information will need to be collected? Is there any software that could help you make the final decision?**

Executive information systems

Executive information systems are designed to help higher management spot a problem, opportunity or trend. They enable managers to sit at their own desks and access increasingly detailed levels of data in order to try and analyse problems or opportunities. Such a system needs to be user-friendly and capable of producing various forms of output such as exception reports, graphs and charts.

Figure 47.3: Relationship between EIS and DSS

Information flow

Information flows through an organisation through both formal and informal information systems. Informal ways of gathering information include face-to-face conversations, meetings, telephone conversations, reading newspapers and magazines, listening to radio and television and surfing the Internet.

Information is also circulated through company newsletters, memos and notice boards. The problem with newsletters and memos is that readers often have so much information to absorb that they quickly forget it.

Formal methods of disseminating information around an organisation include the following:

- Computerised information systems which allow users to query databases over a company-wide network. Internal data is often collected in the first instance through transaction processing systems. External data can be collected, for example, through agencies such as Dun and Bradstreet which produces an on-line electronic data service called 'DataStream' to both business and academic organisations.

- Software packages such as Lotus Notes enables people at different locations to have the same document on their screens and work on it together. Appointments can be held on the systems so that meetings can be arranged at a time when everyone is free.

- E-mail allows correspondence and files to be transmitted throughout an organisation as well as to others outside the organisation.

- Company-wide Intranets are networks which work on the same principle as the Internet but are for use within the organisation. Information can be disseminated throughout an organisation via the Intranet rather than in the form of written memos and newsletters.

Exercises

1. A school is planning the introduction of a computer-based attendance system for classes and registration groups. The purpose of the system is to produce information for the following end-users:
    - Class teachers
    - Tutors/Head of Year
    - Senior managers (e.g. Deputy Head)
    (a) Describe **three** alternative ways of collecting the information for the system. (6)
    (b) For each of the different end-users describe, with the aid of an example, information that the system might produce in relation to their requirements. (6)
    NEAB IT04 Qu 3 1997

2. (a) Describe, with the aid of examples, the difference between **formal** and **informal** methods of communication within an organisation. (4)
    (b) Describe briefly **two** ways in which information technology can be used to help improve communication between different levels of an organisation. (4)
    New question

Chapter 48 – Expert Systems

Definition

An expert system is a computer program that attempts to replicate the performance of a human expert at some specialised reasoning task. Also known as **knowledge-based systems**, expert systems are able to store and manipulate knowledge so that they can help a user to solve a problem or make a decision.

The main features of an expert system are:

- It is limited to a specific domain (area of expertise);
- It is typically rule-based;
- It can reason with uncertain data (the user can respond "don't know" to a question);
- It delivers advice;
- It explains its reasoning to the user.

An expert system has the following constituents:

- The 'knowledge base' that contains the facts and rules provided by a human expert;
- Some means of using the knowledge (the computer program, commonly known as the 'inference engine');
- A means of communicating with the user (the 'human-computer interface').

Programming the knowledge base

Computer languages such as PROLOG (PROgramming LOGic) have been developed for the creation of expert systems. Using PROLOG, the facts and rules are written down using the special syntax of the language, and the user can then type in a query which the program will attempt to answer.

The following is an example of part of a simple knowledge base which will deliver advice on whether a person may legally drive a certain class of vehicle.

```
1        age (edward  20)
2        age (robert  19)
3        age (flora  17)
4        age (emma  17)
5        age (andrew 16)

6        minimum_age (motor_cycle 16)
7        minimum_age (car  17)
8        minimum_age (heavy_goods_vehicle 20)

9        passed_test (edward  heavy_goods_vehicle)
10       passed_test (andrew  motor_cycle)
11       passed_test (emma  car)

12       has_provisional_licence (andrew)
13       has_provisional_licence (robert)

14       permitted_to_drive (X  V) If passed_test (X  V)
15       permitted_to_drive (X  V) If has_provisional_licence (X) And
                age (X  A) And
                minimum_age (V  L) And
                A >= L
```

In this syntax:

fact 1 means that Edward is 20 years old;

fact 6 means the minimum age for driving a motor-cycle is 16;

fact 10 means Andrew has passed the driving test for a motor-cycle;

fact 12 means that Andrew has a provisional driving licence;

rule 14 means that a person X may drive a vehicle V if person X has passed the test for a vehicle of class V;

rule 15 means that a person X may drive a vehicle V if person X has a provisional licence and is old enough to drive a vehicle of class V.

The query

?permitted_to_drive (flora car) means "Is it true that Flora is permitted to drive a car?"

The program would first look at rule 14 and then scan the facts to see if Flora has passed the test. The answer is "no", so rule 15 is examined. The facts are scanned again to check if Flora has a provisional licence. No relevant fact is found so the program returns the answer "no".

The query

　　　?permitted_to_drive (robert motor_cycle)

will return the answer "yes" using Rule 15 and facts 2, 6 and 13.

The query

　　　?permitted_to_drive (emma V)

will return the answer "car" using rule 14 and fact 11.

Case study: ELSIE the expert system

ELSIE is an expert system that was built in the 1980s for use in the construction industry, is still in widespread use today, and is continually being refined and improved. It is designed to take over many of the more mundane aspects of the job of a quantity surveyor. When a customer approaches a construction company to have, say, a new office block built, hundreds of questions first have to be answered with regard to the size of the building, the number of storeys, the type of central heating required, the number of elevators, the type of cladding (e.g. brick or stone), the state of the proposed building site (level or sloping, wet or dry, clay or rock etc.) The quantity surveyor then takes all these factors into consideration and comes up with an estimate.

ELSIE is an expert system that runs on a PC and is organised in a simple menu-driven format with well-presented screen layouts. It can be used by people with no previous computer experience, and takes the form of a question-and-answer session. When the user has input the answers to all the questions, the system gives a total cost for the building, with a detailed breakdown. The user can then go back and change the answers to certain questions to see what the effects would be of selecting, for example, a less expensive form of heating, or having an extra storey and more car-parking space on the site. The knowledge base also contains current building regulations for all areas of the country to ensure that the proposed building stays within the law.

ELSIE can perform calculations in a matter of seconds that would previously have taken days or even weeks of a quantity surveyor's time.

Expert system shells

An expert system shell is a special software program that allows a user to build an expert system without having to learn a programming language. It provides a straightforward user interface both for the expert to enter the facts and rules, and for the end-user to use the completed expert system to solve a problem.

A shell is basically an expert system without a knowledge base. It provides the developer with the inference engine, the user interface and the means of inputting the 'knowledge'. Many shells enable the developer to present examples with the correct conclusions and the system automatically builds the rules. Thus, for example, a medical team building an expert system could type in the symptoms of hundreds of patients with 'upper abdominal pain' with a known diagnosis of kidney stones, gallstones, stomach ulcers, cancer and so on for each one. The software will then calculate the significance of each symptom so that presented with a new case, it can give one or more diagnoses with an indication of the probability of each being correct.

> ➢ **Discussion: Many expert systems have been developed for medical diagnosis (see 'Expert systems in Medical Diagnosis' in Chapter 4). What are the advantages and disadvantages of such systems?**

Uses of expert systems

Expert systems are used in a wide range of applications such as:

- **Medical diagnosis.**
- **Fault diagnosis** of all kinds – gas boilers, computers, power stations, railway locomotives. If your gas boiler breaks down, the service engineer may well arrive with a laptop computer and type in all the symptoms to arrive at a diagnosis, and then use the system to find out the exact part numbers of any replacement parts required for your particular model of boiler.
- **Geological surveys** to find oil and mineral deposits.
- **Financial services** to predict stock market movement or to recommend an investment strategy.
- **Social services** to calculate the benefits due to claimants.
- **Industrial uses** such as the expert system ELSIE described above.

Benefits of expert systems in organisations

Expert systems can be used to assist decision-makers in much the same way as an experienced colleague. They cannot entirely replace the decision-maker but they can dramatically reduce the amount of work that a person has to do to solve a problem.

Some of the *organisational* benefits of expert systems are:

- An expert system can complete some tasks much faster than a human – for example performing all the calculations required to estimate the costs of a construction project – which will enable an immediate response to be made to a client.
- A reduction in the downtime of an expensive piece of equipment when an expert system is able to quickly diagnose the fault.
- The error rate in successful systems is often very low and may be lower than that of a human being.
- Recommendations will be consistent: given the same facts, the recommendation will always be the same and completely impartial.

- An expert system can capture the scarce expertise of a well-qualified professional who may leave or retire, and can be used at locations where the human expert is not available – say, for geological surveys or medical expertise in remote areas.

- An expert system can be used as a repository for organisational knowledge – the combined knowledge of all the qualified experts in an organisation – which makes the organisation less dependent on an individual's knowledge, which may be lost when they leave.

- Expert systems can be useful for training employees.

Limitations of expert systems

- Expert systems can make mistakes, just as humans do, but even a low error rate in the diagnosis of a disease, for example, may cause people to mistrust a computer system.

- Expert systems do not 'learn from their mistakes' – new knowledge has to be entered into the knowledge base as it becomes available.

- It can be difficult to acquire all the required knowledge from the human experts in order to build the expert system. Expert systems work best when the problem is very well defined and the facts and rules associated with the problem can be clearly stated.

- The use of expert systems within an organisation can result in a decline in the skill level of some of the people using the systems. If a large part of the task is handled by an expert system, employees may not acquire the experience or knowledge that gives them a 'feel' for the task.

- Over-reliance on an expert system may stifle creative thinking and lead to the advice delivered being slavishly followed. For example an expert system which delivers advice on whether a client should be given a loan may come to a different conclusion from a human adviser who can spot exceptional circumstances that the expert system does not take into account.

Comparison of expert systems and decision support systems

Both decision support systems and expert systems are tools used to help in the decision-making process. The table below compares the two types of system.

	Expert system	**Decision support system**
Objective	Reproduce knowledge of a human expert	Assist a human decision maker
Organisational level	Mainly operational	Mainly managerial
Major purpose	Automating the reasoning or calculations of a human expert	Aiding decision-making
Query direction	System queries the human	Human queries the system
Knowledge base	Knowledge base of facts, rules and judgements	Database of facts, largely numeric
Explanation capability	Extensive	Very limited
Type of problem	Limited domain (area)	Wide variety of problems

> ➤ Discussion: Southampton Football Club is experimenting with an expert system to decide on the monetary value of each player in the Club, based on number of goals, assists, contacts with the ball, age etc. It has been found to give a largely accurate estimate of the value of players who have been transferred in the past.
>
> ➤ What are the benefits to the management of using such a system? What factors are not likely to be taken into account by this system in assessing the desirability of selling or buying a player?

Exercises

1. *(see case study below)*

Case study: Protecting endangered species

The annual turnover in live animals, skins and animal products of endangered species is astonishingly even greater than the money made from the illegal arms trade, amounting to £3 billion per year – second only to illegal drugs trading.

At airports such as Heathrow, Customs Officers are often faced with the task of identifying the particular species of animal or reptile that, say, a handbag has been made from – not an easy task when there are over 35,000 different species of snake alone, each with a different level of protection. The item often has to be sent to a Zoo or Natural History Museum, where an expert counts the number of scales and other features and cross checks this with reference material, a process which can take up to 3 weeks.

Help is now at hand in the form of 'Nemesis', a computer system that can identify the species that a product is made from. A camera attached to a computer takes a photograph of the product, and the computer program compares the features with its database and displays the name of the species on the screen. The more skins it sees, the more accurate it becomes, a process known as 'training' the system.

At the moment, it only stores information on the 15 most traded snake skins, but the developers hope that it will eventually be able to identify all species, and will also be used on furs.

> ➤ Questions:
>
> (a) The system described could be said to be an 'artificially intelligent' system, performing a task that would require intelligence if performed by a human. What distinguishes an 'artificially intelligent' system from an 'expert system'? (2)
>
> (b) Give another example of an 'artificially intelligent system'. (1)
>
> (c) What does 'training' an artificially intelligent system involve? (2)
>
> (d) What are the likely consequences of the use of a fully developed system of this kind? (3)

2. Expert systems are suitable for many different categories of application. Give **two** different categories and, for each category, **one** typical application. (4)

AEB Computing Paper 1 Qu 8 1996

3. One of the essential components of an expert system is a knowledge base.

Using suitable examples, describe the nature and structure of the data held within a knowledge base. (4)

London Computing Paper 2 Qu 8 1997

4. Expert systems and decision support systems are both used to help in solving problems or making decisions. Describe briefly **four** differences between these two types of system. (4)

New question

Chapter 49 – Information

Introduction

The theme running through this entire course is information: ways of acquiring it, distributing it and using it at the various different levels of an organisation. In this chapter we'll take a closer look at the characteristics of information.

Sources of information

Information can be gathered from a number of different sources. It may be:

- Internal information produced by processing transactions within the organisation;
- External information collected by buying it from agencies or other organisations, reading trade magazines and newspapers, visiting trade shows, Internet databases, government and other statistics.

Levels of information

In the 1960s and 70s, computers were largely used for applications such as payroll, or for scientific and engineering applications where their ability to perform rapid and accurate calculations was an obvious benefit. But today, computers are invaluable because of the information that they can provide to assist and improve decision-making. There are three main reasons why information is needed in organisations:

1. A record of daily events and transactions must be kept so that the company can operate. For example, employees must be paid and records kept of gross pay, tax paid, pension payments and so on; customer orders must be recorded, invoices must be sent out and payments recorded, stock levels must be adjusted. This type of information is called **operational information**.

2. Middle managers in an organisation need information to help them manage effectively. For example, a supermarket manager needs to know how fast particular items move, how quickly stock can be replenished, how well a particular new product is selling, at what times of day or week the store is most crowded. This type of information is referred to as **tactical information**.

3. Historical information, environmental information and information about new businesses moving into the area may be used to build computer 'models' which help to forecast future changes or needs. For example, if a new car manufacturing plant is to open in a particular area, this may have an impact on local supermarkets because more workers and their families may move into that area. This type of information is referred to as **strategic information**.

Quality of information

Useful information should have certain attributes. It should be:

- **Brief.** The information needs to be as concise as possible: too much detail can result in overlooking vital facts. A stock report giving the amount sold and quantity in stock of every one of a hundred thousand items is not useful to a manager who needs to know which are the top selling items or the items which are not selling enough; a summary or aggregate of data is needed. Reports which only list items on which some action may be required are known as **exception reports**.

- **Accurate.** Information which is inaccurate is likely to lead to poor decisions being made and a loss of confidence in the source of the information. Sometimes information can only be given with a certain probability that it will be correct: for example, a farmer may rely on the weather forecast to plan when to harvest a field of wheat, but the forecast is unlikely to be 100% accurate.

- **Up-to-date.** Sometimes information needs to be up to the minute, for example in a booking system or ordering system where a customer needs to know whether a certain item is available. In other cases, it may not matter if the information is not up to the minute; a theatre manager reviewing the season's ticket sales does not necessarily need the figures for last night's performance.
- **Timely.** Reports must reach the right person at the right time.

Case study: Mortgages – a changing market

The senior management of a Building Society is considering changing the criteria used by branches to decide whether a customer may be given a mortgage. Traditionally, when a customer takes out a mortgage to buy a house, fixed payments are made over a period of say 25 years to repay the loan. Before a loan can be agreed, customers have to prove that they have a certain level of regular income, have been in employment for a certain period of time and are likely to remain so for the foreseeable future. However, changing patterns of work mean that many workers, particularly in the computing industry, are self-employed, working mostly on short contracts, and cannot therefore demonstrate that they are in steady employment with one employer, even though they may earn considerable sums from each contract and are in much demand.

The information gathered might lead to other decisions being made, for example a more flexible type of mortgage could be introduced whereby a customer could vary the repayments depending on their income at the time.

➢ **Discussion:**
- **What sort of data about contract workers in general would need to be collected to help the management with their change in policy?**
- **How could this data be collected?**
- **Who would collect the data?**
- **What sort of processing would be carried out on the data?**
- **What information could be produced?**
- **Would this information be operational, tactical or strategic?**

Channels of communication

Formal information systems at an operational level are categorised by having well defined procedures for the flow of data and information between the people who need it, often in the form of reports or other documents produced by the system. Sales orders in a manufacturing company, for example, may come in to the Sales Department, copies are passed to the Production Department, who will order parts from the Stock Department, who may need to order parts from a supplier, and so on.

How well data and information flows through an organisation will depend on several factors, including:

- The nature of the information – whether it is routine operational information or 'ad hoc' information requested intermittently by managers;
- The organisational structure – for example, the size of the organisation and the number of management 'layers';
- The amount of processing that has to be carried out on the data, and the frequency of processing;
- The geographical distance between the different parts of an organisation.

Case study: Guides need information

The Guide Association is a voluntary organisation with 700,000 members, one tenth of whom are adult leaders. Leaders are registered as members at one of nine regional offices in the U.K. Each region is responsible for the registration process, and each has a different PC custom-built member registration database system. There is a head office for the UK where programmes of activities and international events are developed for guides throughout the UK, and from which training for leaders is co-ordinated. This central office has no information on the membership because they are registered regionally.

The central office wants to provide more exciting opportunities to more members, and to be able to consult more widely with the membership at large. In order to achieve this and to plan for the future, there is a need to be able to access the regions' information.

Currently the central office has a Novell network, and is currently installing e-mail links to the regional offices. The regional offices have historically paid for their own I.T. equipment, and therefore having taken advice locally, have all installed different hardware and software.

An I.T. strategy is being developed which aims to improve communication and data sharing within the Association, and to enhance the management information available.

➤ **Discussion: What are the problems in getting the information to the Head Office of the Guide organisation? How can these problems be solved?**

➤ **Think of some ways in which the head office will be able to make use of the information it can access once the new system is in place.**

Keeping everyone informed

The Department of Trade and Industry (DTI) commissioned a survey in 1997 of 'best practices' in over 100 different 'winning UK companies'. They note that in these organisations:

> 'Communication takes place in many directions throughout an organisation, and is always a two-way process. Just as the leaders of a company communicate their vision of where the company is going, they welcome and encourage feedback and ideas from all their employees, for they recognise that all have something to offer: "one proposal from each of our 100 employees is better than 100 proposals from one super boss". Communication takes the form of regular team briefings, frequent internal newsletters and regular contact with customers. In addition, senior management frequently gets out to meet employees by walking around the organisation and talking with individuals, encouraging the team concept of "us" rather than the divisive "them" and "us".'

Source: 'Winning' (A DTI report 1997)

The bar chart below summarises the different ways that information is disseminated around the organisations surveyed.

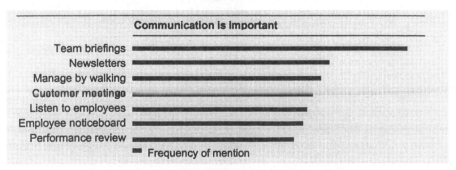

Figure 49.1: Methods of communication

Marketing information

One of the most valuable assets that many companies hold is the information they have collected about their customers. As well as names and addresses, they may collect information about their incomes, their professions, how much they spend, what products they are most likely to be interested in and so on. There are several ways this information can be collected:

- Every time a customer makes a purchase or orders a catalogue, their name and details are added to a customer database.

- When customers make a purchase and fill in a guarantee card, they are frequently asked to provide a lot of information about products they own, their income group, number of children and so on.

- People visiting a company's Web site can be asked to 'register' by providing a lot of personal information before gaining access to the site.

- Companies may buy mailing lists from other companies selling related products. For example, a company selling seeds, bulbs and shrubs may buy a list from a manufacturer of garden furniture.

Keeping a mailing list up-to-date is a major task – it is estimated that companies in the UK waste over £37m a year on 'gone-aways' – people who have died or moved with no forwarding address, and whose letters are returned. Companies do not usually remove 'gone-aways' from their lists: they mark them as such, and leave them on the database. If they subsequently buy a list from another organisation, they can run a program to identify names which appear on both lists, and thus avoid the problem of reinserting names they had previously deleted.

Some people object to their names being passed on, and questionnaires usually include a box to tick if the customer does not want this to happen. However, the data is often collected without the customer's knowledge, simply by making a purchase in a shop, so there is no guarantee that your name, address and purchasing habits are not on databases all over the world.

Exercises

1. The management of a company complains that the Management Information System (M.I.S.) continually fails to produce the appropriate information at the right time. The person responsible for the M.I.S. responds by blaming the 'inadequate data and information flow' within the company and requests a review of 'data and information flows'.

   (a) State **six** factors which influence the flow of information and data within an organisation.　　(6)

   (b) With the aid of examples, describe **three** techniques which could be used to review the current information flows.　　(6)

   NEAB IT04 Qu 8 1997

2. "The quality of management information is directly related to its timing."

   (a) Discuss this statement paying particular reference to:

   - The different purposes for which the information may be required;

   - The relative merits of speed versus accuracy.　　(6)

   (b) In planning the information flow within a system, where are the delays likely to occur and why?　　(6)

   NEAB IT04 Qu 9 Sample Paper

3. Many retail organisations have developed large databases of customer information by buying data from each other.

   (a) Describe **two** possible uses these organisations could make of the data they purchase.　　(4)

   (b) Some customers may object to data held on them by one organisation being sold to another organisation. Describe some of the arguments which either of these retail organisations may use to justify this practice.　　(4)

   NEAB IT04 Qu 2 Sample Paper

Chapter 50 – Data Collection

Using bar codes

Bar coding is one of the most popular ways of capturing data, with the most common application being in shops and supermarkets where all items are bar coded. In spite of the high initial investment, it is estimated that a 2% investment of costs in information technology leads to a 6% saving in costs.

The major benefit of using bar codes at point of sale is that management is provided with very detailed up to date information on key aspects of the business, enabling decisions to be made quicker and with more confidence. For example:

- Fast-selling items can be identified quickly and automatically reordered to meet demand;

- Slow-selling items can be identified, preventing a build-up of unwanted stock;

- The effects of repositioning a given product within a store can be monitored, allowing fast-moving more profitable items to occupy the best space;

- Historical data can be used to predict seasonal fluctuations very accurately.

Bar code scanners are relatively low cost and extremely accurate: only about one in 100,000 entries will be wrong.

Photograph courtesy of Scanner Technologies

Figure 50.1: A bar code scanner

Other uses of bar codes

Bar codes can be used in a wide range of applications that require fast and accurate data entry. These include:

- **Warehousing**. Bar coded containers of raw materials are stored in racks of bins which are also bar coded. When goods are put into the warehouse, the computer system instructs an automatic crane to retrieve the nearest available empty bin. The filled bin is then returned to an empty location. The crane relies entirely on bar codes to move goods in and out.

- **Transport and distribution**. All major road freight carriers now use bar codes. Individual packages are bar coded as are depot consignments. The exact location of any package is known at any one time together with details of the type of service used. Individual customers can be billed quickly and missing parcels traced more easily.

- **Manufacturing**. Very accurate data relating to work in progress can be obtained using bar codes as the data entry method. Management can obtain up to date data on the progress of unfinished goods, enabling bottlenecks and over-production to be reduced and production efficiency to improve.

- **Marketing**. Many polling companies now use bar coded multiple choice questionnaires to enter data quickly and accurately. Survey times can be dramatically reduced.

- **Medical**. Bar codes are commonly used to identify blood and other samples. Hospital patients' and outpatients' records are increasingly bar coded for fast retrieval and better accuracy.

- **Libraries**. Bar codes are used to record loans and provide more information on stock.

- **Banking, insurance and local government**. Bar codes are used extensively for accurate document control and retrieval. Many cheque book covers, insurance claim files and council tax forms are bar coded.

Magnetic stripe cards

Cards with a magnetic stripe are widely used for applications ranging from railway cards to customer loyalty cards. The information provided when someone signs up for a loyalty card with Sainsbury's, Tesco, Boots or W.H.Smith, for example, plus a few months of shopping records, can provide a detailed portrait of customers' habits.

The day is not far off when you will be able to wake up on Saturday morning (or whichever is your regular shopping day) to an e-mail from Sainsbury's suggesting what you need to buy this week.

Linking customers and suppliers through EDI

Electronic data interchange (EDI) is the electronic transmission of business data, such as purchase orders and invoices, from one firm's computerised information to that of another firm. Since EDI transmission is virtually instantaneous, the supplier's computer system can check for availability and respond quickly with a confirmation.

Figure 50.2 (a): Before EDI

Figure 50.2 (b): After EDI

Speed and reliability are major advantages of EDI. It does away with re-keying data, increases accuracy and eliminates delays. Data such as 'A' Level results are now commonly transmitted direct to schools and colleges rather than being sent by mail. Using a service such as BT's CampusConnect, schools and colleges are able to download the results in encrypted form up to two days before their official release date; at one minute past midnight on results day, they are sent a password which allows them to decode the results. Having the results on computer also makes it far easier for the schools and colleges to collate exam results and produce the various statistics and performance indicators required by the DfEE for national league tables.

Smart cards

Smart cards containing a microchip are likely to replace cash over the next five years. Cash-loaded smart cards are already undergoing trials in several British cities and university campuses.

Case study: A smarter way to pay

Students at Aston University are all issued with a plastic smart card. That one card gets the students through security checks into any area they need to visit. It can also be used to buy lunch at any one of the campus refectories or bars and acts as a student ID and library card.

If a student's cash balance gets low, it can be replenished at a bank or through a hole-in-the-wall machine that acts like a cashless ATM. There is a £5 minimum and £100 maximum cash capacity on the card.

➢ **Discussion: As students move around the campus, data can be collected about where they have been, what they have bought, what books they have borrowed from the library and so on. This data could be processed in many different ways to provide all sorts of management information. Think of some useful reports that could be produced, and ways in which this information could be used.**

➢ **What would be the benefits and drawbacks of smart cards replacing cash in the UK? It would theoretically be possible to know exactly how much cash each individual spent – would this be desirable, or an invasion of privacy?**

Keying in data

The keyboard is still widely used for data input in spite of the drawbacks of inaccurate data transcription (copying from a paper form), comparatively slow data entry and the risk to the health of employees who spend all day at a keyboard.

Banks, for example, no longer process routine transactions (such as paying in cheques) in branches. Instead, the work is sent to giant processing centres where the staff do nothing but key in data.

"It's like a factory", said one Barclay's worker. "There's just crates and crates of work everywhere. They call them customer service centres, but you never see a customer".

The trend is raising health and safety concerns among the banking unions. Four employees at one Midland Bank processing centre are currently taking their employer to court claiming they developed repetitive strain injury (RSI) after being required to key in 2000 cheque details per hour.

In order to ensure the accuracy of the data entered, it is commonly **batched** and **verified** – that is, entered twice by different operators with the second version being automatically compared with the first version and any discrepancies brought to the operator's attention. (See **batch processing** in Chapter 27.)

Other high volume data entry applications include processing results of customer research questionnaires. (See case study below).

Case Study: Bradford & Bingley

In January 1998 the Bradford and Bingley, Britain's second biggest Building Society, mailed a questionnaire to its two million members asking them for personal details about their employment status, financial position and so on. Customers were also asked whether they agreed or disagreed with the statement "I appreciate the value of the long-term benefits provided by a mutual building society as against a one-off windfall from a converting society."

Figure 50.3: A customer research questionnaire
(Reproduced with permission from Bradford & Bingley Building Society)

> ➤ **Discussion: What would be the best method of inputting data from the returned questionnaires?**
> ➤ **Studies have shown that on average one error occurs every 300 key presses. If the data is keyed in, approximately what percentage of forms will contain an error? Do these errors matter? How can they be spotted and corrected?**
> ➤ **What sort of analyses could be performed on the data to provide management with useful information about their customers? How could the management use this information?**

Exercises

1. A college collects data from incoming students which includes the students' subjects and grades at GCSE level. These grades are processed and used to predict an expected grade at A level. It is found that some of the grades given by students are less than accurate. Describe methods of data capture and entry which minimise this problem. (6)

   NEAB IT04 Qu 5 Sample Paper

2. A large supermarket has fifty checkout points. Each is equipped with a point of sale incorporating a bar code reading device and is linked to a computer in the stock room.

   The supermarket is one of a number of similar supermarkets, all supplied from a central warehouse.

   Each night the supermarket's computer is connected to the computer in the warehouse to pass on the requirements for the supply of stock.

   Fresh food is ordered direct from local suppliers each day according to demand.

   (a) (i) Identify **three** points at which data is captured for this system.

   (ii) Describe **two** methods of capturing this data. (5)

   (b) Explain why the supermarket management might encounter difficulties if it relies only on sales data captured at the point of sale, as a basis for restocking the shelves. (2)

   (b) Occasional failures of equipment occur which might affect:

   - Point of sale terminals;
   - The supermarket computer;
   - The communication links;
   - The warehouse computer.

   Discuss how the system could be designed to cope with failures, without causing a serious loss of data, or making it impossible for the supermarkets to operate. (8)

   London Computing Paper 1 Qu 9 1997

3. In a particular computerised payroll system data is keyed in from timesheets. In the context of this application distinguish between data verification and data validation. (4)

   NISEAC Computing Paper 1 Qu 1 1997

4. State **two** advantages to the supermarket and **two** advantages to the customer of the use of bar code scanning equipment. (4)

   NISEAC Computing Paper 1 Qu 1 1996

5. Briefly describe **two** direct data capture methods stating one application for which each is appropriate. (6)

   NISEAC Computing Paper 1 Qu 7 1995

Chapter 51 – The Management of Change

Outcomes from I.T. investments

A study carried out in the UK in 1996 by OASIG, a special interest group concerned with the organisational aspects of I.T., came to the following alarming conclusions:

- 80-90% of systems do not meet their performance goals;
- About 80% of systems are delivered late and over budget;
- Around 40% of developments fail or are abandoned;
- Fewer than 40% fully address training and skills requirements;
- Fewer than 25% properly integrate business and technology objectives;
- Just 10-20% meet all their success criteria.

Source: OASIG Study 1996

This study drew on the expertise of leading management and organisational consultants and researchers, and covered approximately 14,000 organisations in all major sections of the economy, including a comprehensive range of I.T. systems.

Valuing the workforce

The increasing complexity of interactions between business, work and technological changes is a source of an immensely difficult set of problems for everyone who manages, uses and develops I.T. systems. These complexities are made even more difficult to resolve when organisations are faced with competitive and economic pressures. The emphasis on minimising costs and increasing efficiency sometimes means that not enough weight is given to other values and goals, and insufficient attention is given to human and organisational factors.

When cost savings are the dominant criteria on which I.T. investments are judged, people become perceived as costs rather than as assets; as units of production rather than motivated beings who add value to products and services; as sources of error rather than assets whose experience and creativity differentiate one organisation from another.

Job cuts, described euphemistically as 'downsizing' or 'delayering' are often perceived as a major goal of a new I.T. project. Naturally, employees are unlikely to participate enthusiastically in a new system that they perceive is a one-way ticket to unemployment.

Reasons why I.T. systems fail

Common causes of the failure of new I.T. systems are:

- There is too much emphasis on technological factors and the capabilities of the latest hardware. Trying to use the latest hardware, unproven by time and the experience of other organisations, is very risky.
- Senior managers are often vague about exactly what the objectives of a new system are. They may fail to understand fully the business opportunities and the difficulties arising from new I.T. systems, justifying the investment on the grounds of cost reduction alone.

- This narrow viewpoint means human and organisational factors are often ignored. The way things are done and the jobs of individual users will be changed and this needs to be carefully explained and managed. Most senior managers do not have a good enough understanding of the links between technological and organisational change.

- Users are often not involved or invited to participate in the design or development of a new system and as a result are resentful and obstructive when they could make the difference between success and failure.

- Users may have been given unrealistic expectations of the new system so that even if it is a success judged by the performance criteria, they may be disappointed and feel that the effort was a waste of time. The benefits to the business may be overestimated by management, unintentionally or for political reasons.

- Costs are often underestimated.

- The time that the new system will take to develop is often underestimated.

- The new system may be over-ambitious. The more complex the system, the greater the risk of failure.

Case study: London Ambulance Service

It was never going to be easy computerising the largest ambulance service in the world, while at the same time profoundly changing an organisation that had existed since before the Second World War. Today, the service covers about 600 square miles with a population of 6.8 million residents, increasing steeply during the daytime. In January 1993 it employed 22,700 people including 200 managers and 326 paramedics. 300 emergency ambulances and over 400 patient transport vehicles struggled to cope with between 1,300 and 1,600 emergency calls a day.

In the early 1990s, the service was experiencing internal problems, with the staff resenting management's imperious attitude towards them, and management resenting the staff's resistance to change. In 1990 there was a major pay dispute and, in preparation for government health reforms, 53 senior and middle managers were made redundant. It was against this background of instability, organisational change and employee resentment that plans for a new computerised system were made. It was claimed that "it would be the first of its kind in the UK", and would involve "a quantum leap in the use of technology" – two phrases that should have caused a chill of foreboding in anyone remotely connected with I.T. projects.

The objectives of the new system included the following:

1. Call-taking, accepting and verifying incident details, including location;
2. Determining which ambulance to send;
3. Communicating details of an incident to the chosen ambulance;
4. Positioning suitably equipped and staffed vehicles in places where they were most likely to be needed, so minimising response times to calls.

Under the manual process, when a 999 call was received the details were written down together with the location and a map reference. The form was put on a conveyor belt by one of the 200 people working in the department, and at the other end a resource allocator identified duplicate calls and, taking into account the location of ambulances from information radioed in, dispatched the nearest or most suitable one. The whole process took about 3 minutes.

Much of this process could be computerised, but part of the process depended on the judgement and experience of the dispatcher. But the end-users were not involved in the computerisation – there was little consultation of employees and many saw it as a way of downgrading their jobs and forcing them to accept unwelcome changes. They regarded it with distrust from the start. Training on the new system was given, but so far in advance of implementation (as the deadlines for implementation slipped) that many had forgotten how to use it by the time it was introduced.

In January 1992 a limited trial took place, which demonstrated a number of problems.

- Ambulance crews did not always report where they were and what call they were handling, and the computer required a perfect knowledge of where every vehicle was.

- Transmission blackspots and software error resulted in inaccurate location fixes of ambulances.

- The system could not cope with established working practices such as an operator allocating a different vehicle from the one allocated by the system.

- Problems with hardware, especially slow system response times during busy periods.

Despite recognition of all these problems, deployment of the full system went ahead on October 26 1992, with disastrous consequences. As the hours went by, the system knew the correct location of fewer and fewer ambulances. Neither did it know what equipment they carried or the particular skills of the crew on board. Several ambulances were dispatched to single minor incidents, and real emergencies were ignored. The staff had been told to minimise voice communications and lost complete control of the system. During the three-week period which followed, an eleven year-old girl died of renal failure after waiting 53 minutes for an ambulance. The irony was that she lived only two minutes from a hospital where she was a regular patient, and the only available ambulance was sent to a caller who turned out to have a headache.

The 80-page report which was produced after a three-month enquiry stressed that:

- such a system needs to be fully resilient and reliable, with fully tested levels of backup;

- the system must have total ownership by both management and staff, and staff must have confidence in its reliability;

- the system must be developed in a time scale and at a cost that allow for consultation, quality assurance and testing;

- the system should be introduced in a stepwise, modular approach;

- retraining of staff should be carried out thoroughly on the system, and the timing of the training should be such that 'skills decay' does not occur;

- a suitably qualified and experienced project manager should be appointed to ensure the close control and coordination of all parts of the system.

A full and fascinating account of this disaster is given in 'Crash' by Tony Collins. (See booklist in Appendix C.)

> **Discussion: Change needs to be properly managed. What could the management have done differently to avoid this disastrous computerisation?**

Managing change successfully

Generally, the introduction of a major new I.T. system needs to be preceded by a review of the organisational structure and current working practices. Trying to change too much at once is a sure step to disaster – and change cannot be successfully managed by imposing it on a reluctant organisation.

All the users of a proposed new system, from the shop-floor workers through to senior management, need to be involved and included in consultations. Ideas and misgivings should be listened to and proposed changes explained.

The benefits of a new system should be explained but not exaggerated – unrealistic expectations of what a new computerised system will do can lead to disappointment.

Training must be given to all those involved, not only in how to use the technology but also in the new organisational procedures and the consequences of not using the new system correctly.

Case study: Pindar

Andrew Pindar is the fourth-generation chairman of Pindar, a printing firm recently nominated as one of Britain's finest users of best-practice management. Pindar's main business is printing BT phone directories and industrial catalogues. Pindar described his early problems:

"Walking around Pindar, I encountered a feeling of frustration and dissatisfaction among the workforce. One could almost feel a certain hostility in the air, born no doubt out of a resentment and a feeling that management just did not understand the everyday issues and pressures heaped upon them by a hierarchy that never bothered to explain the logic behind directives. On the other hand, we had a management that could not understand why the workforce was not satisfied, in fact grateful, for being employed."

Andrew concluded that Pindar had to change, and he hired Time Manager International to put in place its Putting People First programme. Early enthusiasm soon dissipated, however. "I had a romantic notion that people would come along with me", he says, "and understand what we'd agreed at board and strategy meetings. I never appreciated that obstacles could be put in place, not by worker-bees, but by senior managers. They felt territory-threatened."

Pindar redoubled his efforts "My resolve was greater than their resistance." He staged the first of several all-worker conferences, and described how Pindar were putting in place foundations that would create maximum understanding, which would create commitment as their core philosophy.

The directories' workforce is a mixture of typesetters and graphics-arts graduates. Its database had a £1.5m upgrade a year ago, and now stores 300 billion bytes. "We are looking to replace it in October, with a £3m or £4m facility," says Rick Lumby, managing director of the Directories division. This will enable customers to dial into the Internet to amend ads.

Lumby says "When Pindar first got involved in technology in the early 50s, we had 20 employees. Now we have almost 1000. Has technology done us out of business? When we started doing telephone directories, we had 17 people working on them. We now have more than 200. Along the way, certain jobs have been automated out of existence. We've always changed for the sake of improving the job we do – because if we don't do it, somebody else will."

Source: John Lawless, Sunday Times 25 January 1998

➢ **Discussion: What factors contribute to the successful management of change at Pindar?**

Today's leaders, tomorrow's dinosaurs?

The coming of age of the Internet has posed enormous challenges to existing companies. At the same time it has given exciting opportunities to new companies which have been able to build up from scratch using the new technology. Thus it is not Waterstone's or WH Smith which is transforming the book business, but new companies such as Amazon and iMVS. It is much harder for an established company to change because if they start to sell books over the Internet, this will adversely affect their High Street stores. Grabbing new opportunities threatens the value of their existing investments. On the other hand, if they do not change, they may be put out of business. So it was the newcomer, Direct Line, which transformed the insurance market rather than Guardian Royal or General Accident. These companies did not want to upset the insurance brokers who account for most of their business.

Many established companies are vulnerable: who needs banks, travel agents and shops like Marks and Spencer or Debenhams when you can get lower prices, better information and more choice from your armchair? Last year, for example, 11% of all new cars in the US were bought on the Internet. To many US car buyers, dealers are becoming simply pick-up points.

Managers have to adapt to this revolution or they will soon be logging on to www.unemployment.com.

Implications of change

The introduction of new technology or a change in the way an organisation does business will inevitably impact upon everyone in the organisation. Consideration will have to be given to:

- Possible redundancies and the effect of this on the rest of the workforce;
- Teaching and learning new skills;
- A change in organisational structure;
- Changes in employment patterns and conditions;
- Changes in internal procedures.

Exercises

1. An information system was introduced into an organisation and was considered a failure. The failure was due to the inability of the organisation to manage the change rather than for technical reasons.

   With the aid of examples describe **three** factors which influence the management of change within an organisation. (6)

   NEAB IT04 Qu 10 1997

2. It is not uncommon for designers involved in the introduction of information systems to encounter resentment and opposition from existing employees.

   Discuss the reasons for this response and describe steps that can be taken by the system designer to reduce this resistance. (10)

   NEAB IT04 Qu 10 Sample Paper

3. A small firm of solicitors is considering the introduction of an Information Technology system to improve the efficiency of its operations. One of the directors of the firm has expressed some concerns over the effects on the organisation of the introduction of the system.

   Describe **five** possible concerns the director may have, and the arguments that may be used to persuade her to accept the new system. (10)

   NEAB IT04 Qu 7 Sample Paper

4. "Companies must adapt to new technology, or go out of business." Discuss this statement, with the aid of examples. (6)

   New question

Chapter 52 – Security Policies

Threats to security and integrity

Today's organisations are dependent on their information systems, and most could not survive the devastating effects of their destruction. Threats to information systems include human error, computer crime, natural disasters, war or terrorist activities and hardware failure. (See Table 52.1)

Threat to security/integrity	Example
Human error	Mistakes in data entry
	Program errors
	Operator errors (e.g. loading wrong tape)
	Not Year 2000 compliant
Computer crime	Hacking (unauthorised access) and stealing data
	Modifying data illegally
	Planting viruses or 'logic bombs' (code which remains inactive until triggered by an event such as a certain date becoming current, or an employee's record being marked 'Fired'.
Natural disasters	Fire, earthquake, hurricane, flood
War and terrorist activity	Bombs, fire
Hardware failure	Power failure
	Disk head crash
	Network failure

Table 52.1: Threats to security of information systems

Risk analysis

"Those who think they have no time for bodily exercise will sooner or later have to find time for illness", said Edward Stanley, the 15th Earl of Derby. This quote could be paraphrased:

"Those who think they have no time or money to put in place a security policy will sooner or later have to find both the time and money for unplanned disaster recovery – and it will cost a lot more."

A corporate I.T. security policy is a strategic issue, and as such is for company directors and senior managers to sort out, rather than something which can be left to technical staff. The first step in defining a security policy is to establish a clear picture of what the risks are and what the company stands to lose if disaster strikes. This **risk analysis** could include finding answers to questions such as:

- What is the nature of the data being stored in the system?
- How is the data used?
- Who has access to the system?
- Is all software Year 2000 compliant?
- How much money does the company stand to lose if the data is lost, corrupted or stolen?

Layers of control

Computer systems must be made secure to protect valuable data, and different 'layers' of security can be implemented, as shown in Figure 52.2.

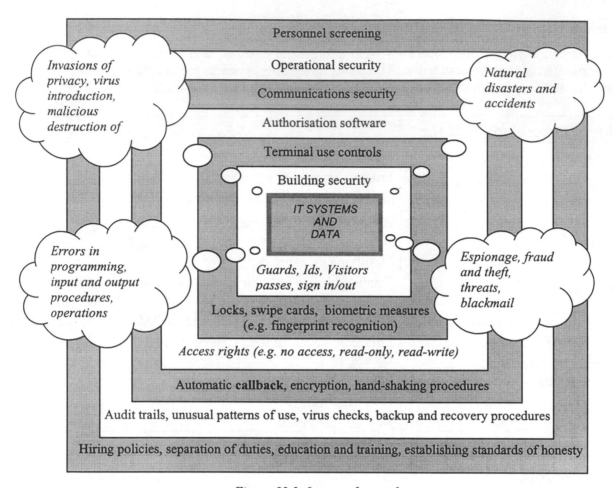

Figure 52.2: Layers of control

Building and equipment security

Building security can include measures to protect the premises from break-ins or unauthorised visitors, as well as from natural disasters such as fire and flood. Locks and window grilles, guards on the gate, rottweilers patrolling the fences, earthquake-proof construction, smoke alarms and automatic fire extinguishers are all possibilities.

Once in the building, even genuine employees and visitors may be restricted as to the areas they are permitted to visit. Employees may have ID cards with a bar code, magnetic strip or chip which allow access to particular areas. Visitors may be issued with passes. The visitor's pass shown in Figure 52.3 uses special ink which becomes visible 12 hours or so after being issued, and then displays 'EXPIRED' in red ink all over the card.

Biometric methods include fingerprint, handprint and iris recognition. These can be used to gain access either to a room or to a particular terminal. The Chancellor of the Exchequer, Gordon Brown, was presented in 1997 with a new dispatch box containing a laptop computer which required him to register a fingerprint before he could sign on. History does not relate whether he actually uses it.

Figure 52.3: A company visitor's pass

Authorisation software

Authorisation software includes the use of User Ids and passwords. The problem with passwords is that users tend to be careless with them – they use obvious words like FRED and PASSWORD, write down passwords, tell them to friends, and keep the same password for too long. A recent report on computer security revealed that for a number of years the chairman of a large company used CHAIRMAN as his password. Some companies insist that passwords are changed every month or so. Passwords are held on the computer system in encrypted form, with no way of decrypting them.

Access rights will be assigned to each user depending on their position in the organisation. A user may have different rights such as Read Only, Read-Write or No Access to different parts of a database. For example a worker in the Personnel Department may be able to change employee names and addresses but may not have access to salary details.

Communications security

Databases may be vulnerable to outside hackers. Methods of combatting such illegal access include **callback**, where the computer automatically calls back a predetermined telephone number when a user attempts to log in, **handshaking** and **encryption**.

A 'handshake' is a predetermined signal that the computer must recognise. For example, the computer may generate a random number and the user may then be required to multiply the first and last digits and add the product to the current month number. Of course this could pose a problem to people with shaky mathematical skills but it is generally more secure than a simple password, because it is never the same twice, and every user has their own algorithm.

Operational security

During daily operations, careful checks of logs showing terminal usage and any unusual behaviour should be regularly carried out. Many PC LAN security packages now include **audit controls**. Audit controls track what happens on a network, for example:

- which users have logged on, where from and for how long;
- how many times a server has been accessed;
- what software has been used;
- which files have been accessed by which users;
- how many unsuccessful attempts were made to log on from any terminal (to detect hackers trying to guess the password).

Anti-virus software can be installed on all PCs, and employees forbidden to bring in disks from outside the organisation. Viruses can also be introduced by downloading files from the Internet, so to guard against spreading a virus from one of these files, many firms run anti-virus software every night. This isolates all files containing a virus in a special directory and leaves a warning message on the screen.

Backup and recovery procedures form part of disaster planning which is discussed in the next chapter.

Audit trail

An **audit trail** is a record that allows a transaction to be traced through all the stages of processing, starting with its appearance as a source document and ending with its transformation into output.

Public companies have to have all financial records audited by external accountants every year, and the system must create an audit trail that makes it possible to see how each figure on a report is arrived at. No accounting system allows a financial record simply to be altered without a transaction being stored which can be checked. The auditor typically selects source documents, traces associated entries through intermediate computer printouts, and examines the resultant entries in summary accounts.

Personnel safeguards

Many studies show that users and computer personnel within an organisation are far more likely to breach security than outsiders. Security may potentially be breached by anyone from computer operators and programmers right up to company directors. Motivated by revenge, financial gain, fanaticism or irrational behaviour, employees are sometimes well-placed to plant a virus, steal or corrupt data, set up false accounts or attempt to extract money by extortion by threatening to destroy vital files.

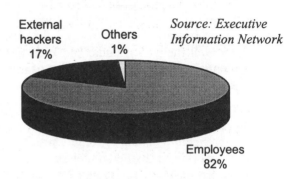

Figure 52.4: Who commits computer crime?

Motivating employees to be alert to security breaches and giving publicity to security measures may serve as a deterrent to computer crime.

Separation of duties is an important principle in maintaining security of data – no employee should perform all the steps in a single transaction. This makes it more difficult for a single individual to perpetrate fraud or theft.

Corporate I.T. security policy

Once the risks to I.T. systems and data have been established, policies can be determined which will be effective without costly overkill. There is often a conflict between wanting to make systems as secure as possible, but at the same time accessible to authorised users. For this reason University, college and school systems tend to be relatively insecure, because one of their most important requirements is to be easily accessible by students.

Once policies have been developed, they need to be implemented. The best security policy in the world is no use if people do not abide by it, and the key here is education – all employees should be made aware of the security policies and mechanisms put in place to ensure that they are adhered to. Instilling norms of ethical behaviour with respect to the use of information and information systems is an important management responsibility.

A typical security policy will cover the following aspects:

- **Awareness and education;**
    Training and education requirements
    Timetable for training/education

- **Administrative controls;**

  Formal procedures and standards are defined for all I.T. systems

  Careful screening of personnel during the hiring process

  Separation of duties to ensure that it would take collusion between at least two employees to perpetrate fraud

  Disciplinary procedures in the event of security breaches

- **Operations controls;**

  Backup procedures

  Control of access to data centres by means of smart cards, ID badges, sign-in/sign-out registers

- **Physical protection of data;**

  Controlled access to sensitive areas

  Protection against fire and flood

  Uninterruptible power supplies

- **Access controls to the system and information;**

  Identification and authentication of users

  Password protection

  Different levels of access for different users according to their needs

  Different access rights, e.g. read only, read-write, read-write-update, etc.

  Encryption of sensitive data

  Detection of misuse using, for example, audit control software which detects multiple attempts to get a password correct

- **Disaster recovery plan;**

  (See next chapter.)

Exercises

1. A particular organisation uses a computerised stock control system. On performing the half-yearly stock check it is discovered that the actual stock levels of some of the items are below that shown on the system.

   (a) Describe the functionality which should have been built into the software to minimise the possibility of this happening. (2)

   (b) Explain why this functionality is required. (2)

   NEAB IT04 Qu 5 1997

2. Some software packages can be set up to monitor and record their use. This is often stored in an access log.

   Name **four** items you would expect to be stored in such a log. (4)

   NEAB IT04 Qu 1 Sample Paper

3. Many accounts packages have an audit trail facility. Explain why such a facility is necessary, what data is logged and how this information can be used. (6)

   NEAB IT04 Qu 6 Sample Paper

4. Describe briefly **four** areas you would expect to be covered in a company's security policy. (4)

   New question

Chapter 53 – Disaster recovery

Effects of negligence

The risks to businesses from computer disaster range from spilling a cup of coffee into the computer file server or a workman drilling through a cable to a fire or bomb which completely destroys the building. The results of such an incidence may be catastrophic: a recent survey showed that about 90% of companies which suffered a significant loss of data went out of business within two years. Of these, 43% went out of business almost immediately.

After working for 1 day without essential business data, a company operates at about 96% of its capability. By the tenth day, it is operating at only about 10% of its capability (Figure 53.1).

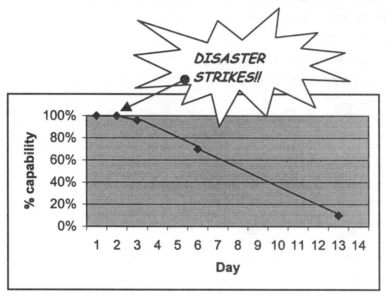

Figure 53.1: Effect of disaster

In the UK, the company and the directors may be prosecuted by the Health and Safety Executive if loss of essential business data or safety data adversely affects the health and safety of the public or the environment. In the case of banking, financial, insurance and related services, loss of essential business data which adversely affects the customer could bring about very costly litigation and fines.

> ➤ **Discussion: Suppose that a supermarket had all its data stored on disks and tapes in a computer room which was destroyed by a small localised fire one night. What sort of data would it have lost? Can you imagine the consequences? How long could it continue to operate?**

Stages in disaster planning

However many precautions are taken, no company can protect themselves completely against a disaster which will wipe out their computer system. What they must do is to ensure that if this happens, they can be up and running again in the shortest possible time. In disaster recovery planning, an essential task is to identify the most critical business functions to be supported by the plan, since covering less vital functions is, in general, too costly.

Contents of a security plan

The first step in solving any problem is understanding and defining it, and then assessing how it may affect the company. A security officer may be appointed who has both the technical and organisational skills to implement a security plan. The key elements of such a plan include:

- A list of the most critical business functions;
- A list of the facilities, hardware, software, data, personnel and other equipment that are necessary to support those functions;
- A method for securing access to all necessary resources;
- A method for getting in touch with all key personnel;
- A step-by-step course of action to follow to implement the plan;
- Education and training of personnel involved in implementing the plan;
- Regular drills to test the effectiveness of the plan.

Disaster recovery plan

Two 'controls of last resort' can be put in place to guard against the failure of a business after a catastrophe – adequate insurance and a disaster recovery plan.

Insurance is not a substitute for loss prevention, and it cannot lessen the likelihood of loss – it can only help to reduce the financial impact of such a loss when it does occur. Insurance premiums will be based in part on the precautions that the company has taken to protect itself against disaster.

A disaster recovery plan has to contain provision for backup facilities which can be used in the event of disaster. Three alternatives are:

- A company-owned backup facility, geographically distant from the main site, known as a 'cold-standby' site.
- A reciprocal agreement with another company that runs a compatible computer system.
- A subscription to a disaster recovery service, such as the one described in the case study below.

Case study: Trust in the Virtual World

Ron Hixon says of his workforce: "I trust them, that's the key." Yet none of those 70 employees has turned up at the office. They will not be in the office tomorrow, either. As he looks round his 6000sq ft of almost deserted premises in Woking, Surrey, he is untroubled.

His staff are computer technicians who work from home. With a modem and a laptop, they are connected to the rest of the company as surely as if they were in the room next door. Mr Hixon's company, Catalyst Technology Solutions, is a service provider to the service sector, providing disaster recovery services for businesses. If a client is hit by fire or flood, or a computer malfunction, they can reload their companies' data onto the Catalyst system and continue to operate as if the crisis had never happened.

The Woking office stands empty, so if a client's premises have been destroyed, they can move in their whole operation. The paradox of running a company with 30,000sq ft of empty office space on three separate sites, and 70-plus employees who work from home appeals to Mr Hixon, who has further plans for revolutionising Catalyst. A new telephone system will soon automatically route calls to workers' home numbers or another location, and divert them to a secretary if the call is unanswered.

"Customers will think they are talking to an office full of people, whereas in fact we could be anywhere."

Meanwhile the offices stay empty, waiting for disaster to strike, while the virtual workforce talk to each other through the ether.

Source: Charlotte Denny, The Guardian 25 August 1997

> ➤ **Discussion: Can you think of some local organisations which would need to make use of a disaster recovery service such as this if they experienced a catastrophe?**

Criteria used to select a contingency plan

The choice of contingency plan will be based upon the costs of the extra provision vs. the potential cost of disaster. Factors which will be taken into account include:

- The scale of the organisation and its I.T. systems;

- The nature of the operation: an on-line system may need to be restored within hours, whereas a customer billing operation may not be unduly harmed by a few day's delay, so long as no data is lost;

- The relative costs of different options: a company with several sites linked by telecommunications may be able to formulate a disaster recovery plan which temporarily moves operations to an alternative site, but need not involve a special 'cold-standby' site, or a 'hot' site provided by a third party;

- The perceived likelihood of disaster occurring: companies in the earthquake zone around San Francisco, for example, are likely to invest more in a disaster recovery service than the average firm in Ipswich.

> ➤ **Discussion: What are the most critical I.T. functions at your school or college? What would be the consequences of a disaster such as fire or theft of computer equipment? What sort of contingency plan would be appropriate?**

Exercises

1. A small company runs a network of 4 PCs on which it keeps records of stock, customer accounts, a mailing list and a multitude of word-processed documents. Draw up a security plan for this company to ensure that it will be able to continue operating normally within a day or so of a disaster such as a fire.

   (20)
   New question

2. Describe **five** facilities that may be provided by a Disaster Recovery Service to which a major bank may subscribe.

   (5)
   New question

3. Describe **two** ways in which a company may raise the awareness of personnel to its security policy.

   (4)
   New question

4. Briefly describe the safeguards a company could use for each of the following threats to its computer system.

   (i) Terrorist bomb;

   (ii) Accidental overwriting of a master file;

   (iii) Hackers outside the organisation;

   (iv) A corrupt employee perpetrating fraud;

   (v) The millennium bug.

   (5)
   New question

Chapter 54 – Implementation of Legislation

Laws relating to I.T.

Legislation governs many aspects of the use of computers within organisations, and it is the responsibility of organisations to ensure that the legislation is implemented. The laws include:

- The Data Protection Act of 1984. (see Chapter 15);
- Copyright Designs and Patents Act of 1988 (see Chapter 12);
- The Health and Safety (Display Screen Equipment) Regulations of 1992 (see Chapter 15).

The Data Protection Act

The Data Protection Act exists to protect the privacy of individuals, its main areas of concern being that:

- Data and information should be *secure;*
- Private, personal or other data should be *accurate;*
- Data stored should not be *misused.*

Organisations should develop their own privacy policies to ensure that the law on Data Protection is upheld. A policy might typically contain two sections, one focussing on the customers and the other on the organisation itself.

A data protection policy

Section 1: Customer Service

1. The policy on data privacy should be publicized, and customers given a copy on request.
2. Customers should be told why their personal information is needed and what use it will be put to. No more data than is necessary should be collected.
3. Data should be obtained directly from the customer, to ensure as far as possible that it is accurate.
4. No data should be used for any purpose other than that which it was collected for, without the customer's consent. This includes selling the data to a third party.
5. Consent should be obtained by providing a clear opt-out check box on any form used to collect data.
6. Customers should be given easy access to files containing their own personal information.
7. Any errors in personal data should be corrected immediately.
8. Customers' concerns should be listened to and acted upon.

Section 2: Organisational culture

1. The company's policy should be clearly communicated to all staff. The policy may form part of a company handbook, form part of a training program, or be posted on notice boards or an Intranet.
2. An awareness of the issue of privacy should be fostered among all employees.
3. Staff should be held accountable for the company's privacy policy. It should be emphasised that if an individual acts contrary to a clause of the Data Protection Act, the individual is personally liable.
4. The effect on privacy of any new proposed system or service should be assessed before it is developed.

5. Reasonable steps should be taken to ensure that all data stored or used is accurate and up-to-date.

6. A schedule should be kept of how long data can be stored before it should be destroyed.

7. A security policy should be developed and enforced to ensure that all data is kept secure from accidental or malicious damage and from unauthorised people looking at it.

8. A senior manager should be designated to be responsible for seeing that the security policy is enforced.

9. All staff should be made aware of their responsibilities to keep data secure by keeping passwords secret, changing them regularly, maintaining physical security of disks, performing scheduled backups etc.

10. Periodic checks should be made to ensure that the policy is being adhered to.

Software copyright

Under the terms of the Copyright Designs and Patents Act of 1988, it is illegal to copy software or run pirated software. The Business Software Alliance (BSA) exists to make organisations and their employees aware of the Law and steps they should take to ensure that it is implemented.

Figure 54.1: The Business Software Alliance provides guidance to companies

The BSA has prepared a step-by-step guide to software management which includes the following advice:

- **Conduct an audit.** Prepare an inventory of your current software situation by conducting an audit using a commercially available audit tool or commissioning an audit service provider. Any illegal software discovered during the audits should be deleted immediately.

- **Purchasing.** Purchase licences for enough copies of each program to meet your current needs. Network operators should consider purchasing a network metering package to restrict the number of users according to the number of licences.

- **Procedures.** Demonstrate your organisation's commitment to using legal software by adopting the following procedures:

    - Appoint a Software Manager to ensure that all appropriate software analysis and management functions are conducted efficiently.

    - Arrange an audit of all machines on a regular basis.

    - Send a memo to all staff reiterating your organisation's concerns about software duplication and advising them of the forthcoming audit. (See Figure 54.2)

- Channel software requirements/purchases through a single point. One of the main entry points for unscrupulous resellers is through a fragmented purchasing system in which various personnel are ordering software.

- Make regular checks on software suppliers and software entering your company.

- Send a memo to staff, and add a note within your company policy and employee handbook, that illegal software copying is a disciplinary offence and that piracy should be reported.

- Request your staff to sign an employee agreement verifying their understanding of the organisation's policy regarding the use of illegal software.

SUGGESTED MEMORANDUM TO EMPLOYEES

To: (Specify distribution)

From: (Senior management official or CEO)

Subject: PC software and the law

Date: (insert)

The purpose of this memorandum is to remind you of (name of organisation)'s policy concerning copying and use of software.

Unlicensed duplication or use of any pirated software program is illegal and can expose you and the company to civil and criminal liability under copyright law.

In order to ensure that you do not intentionally or inadvertently violate copyright, you should not copy any program installed on your computer for any purpose without permission from (insert reference to responsible manager or department). Likewise, you should not install any program onto your computer without such permission, in order to verify that a licence is held to cover such installation.

- The company will not tolerate any employee making unauthorised copies of software.

- Any employee found copying software illegally is subject to termination from the company.

- Any employee copying software to give to any outside third party, including clients and customers, is also subject to termination.

- If you want to use software licensed by the company at home, you must consult with (insert name of manager) in order to make sure such use is permitted by the publisher's licence.

Figure 54.2: A sample memo to staff

Education of employees and a raising of awareness of the problems and consequences of software piracy is a major step in controlling software misuse.

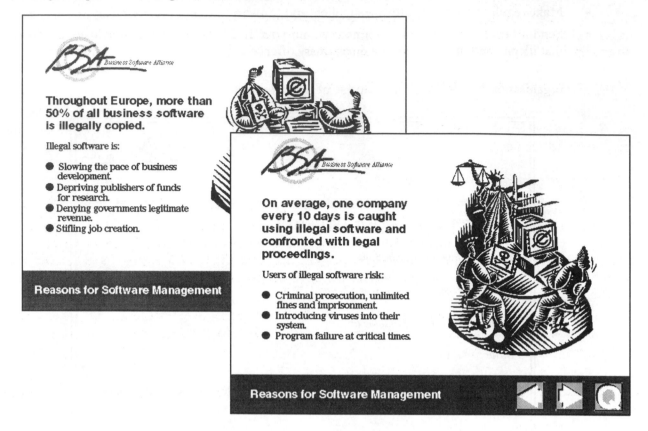

Figure 54.3: Part of a BSA presentation

Health and Safety

Where health is concerned, prevention is always better than cure and the first step is to understand why and how health complaints associated with computer use begin. Measures can then be taken to avoid the bad habits, unsuitable equipment and furniture and poor working environments that are frequently to blame.

Whether people are using computers at home or at the office, the way they interact with their computer affects their physical and mental health. Educating employees and instilling good working practices is one way of preventing problems such as backache, eyestrain and repetitive strain injury (RSI).

Employers should avoid incentive schemes designed to increase the rate of data entry, as applying pressure of this sort has been shown to contribute to the onset of RSI (see case study "Bank staff driven to injury" in Chapter 15).

Encouraging 'ownership' of workspace

Under the Health and Safety at Work Act, employees have a responsibility to use workstations and equipment correctly in accordance with training provided. They are also required to bring any problems to the attention of their employers and cooperate in their correction. One way that employers can help to ensure that employees heed this directive is to involve them in the choice of furniture, hardware and software, as well as in the arrangement of the office space. People generally are better motivated and take a more responsible attitude if they are consulted and allowed to define their own workspace.

Taking regular breaks

Specialists recommend thirty-second 'micropauses' every five to ten minutes, with longer pauses of ten to fifteen minutes every hour or so. Providing regular breaks and coffee-making facilities, as well as varying tasks, can help prevent health problems. Employers who provide this kind of environment are also likely to end up with happier and more productive employees.

Providing the right equipment

There are regulations concerning the type of computer equipment and furniture that must be provided for people who spend a lot of time in front of a VDU. Refer back to Chapter 15 for guidelines on the ergonomic environment.

The employer's responsibility

Employers are responsible for the health and safety of their employees, and they are obliged to demonstrate this responsibility by carrying out a formal evaluation of the working environment and acting on any feedback from the evaluation. This evaluation should either be carried out by an employee whom the Health and Safety Executive recognises as competent, or by an independent professional ergonomist, and it will cover workplace design, including computer hardware, lighting, cooling, humidity and software.

The bottom line is that ignorance of the law is no defence, and sooner or later all organisations will have to invest some money in ergonomics. Companies who disregard their obligations may be successfully sued by injured employees.

> ➤ **Discussion: Does your computer classroom satisfy the ergonomic requirements of the Health and Safety legislation? Does the school or College have an obligation to comply with the terms of the Directive?**

Exercises

1. A Company uses a computer network for storing details of its staff and for managing its finances. The network manager is concerned that some members of staff may install unauthorised software onto the network.

   (a) Give reasons why it is necessary for some software to be designated as unauthorised. (2)

   (b) What guidelines should the network manager issue to prevent the installation of unauthorised software onto the network? (2)

   (c) What procedures might be available to the company to enforce the guidelines? (2)

   NEAB IT04 Qu 6 1997

2. A particular college uses a computer network for storing details of its staff and students and for managing its finances. Network stations are provided for the Principal, Vice-Principal, Finance Officer, clerical staff and teaching staff. Only certain designated staff have authority to change data or to authorise payments.

   (a) What are the legal implications of storing personal data on the computer system? (4)

   (b) What measures should be taken to ensure that the staff understand the legal implications? (3)

   NEAB IT03 Qu 3 Sample paper

Chapter 55 – User Support

The need for support

As computers become more and more powerful, the software that runs on them becomes more and more sophisticated. The 'ease of use' promised by graphical user interfaces like Microsoft Windows has made PCs accessible to more and more non-technical users, so that paradoxically the need for user support is set to continue growing, rather than the reverse. The nature of the support services required by users has also changed since the days of terminals running a single, character-based application: the more features and complexities there are built into the software, the more expertise is required to solve users' problems.

Software companies which create tailor-made I.T. solutions for companies, as well as manufacturers of software packages, all provide user support, though users are normally expected to pay an annual fee for this service, whether or not they use it.

The help desk

User support may be provided in a number of ways, from a simple help desk to a user support centre. The person sitting at the help desk answers telephone queries during office hours and depending on their skill level, attempts to solve the problem or passes it over to an expert. There may be other ways of contacting the help desk such as fax or e-mail, but essentially this is a receive-only service, existing to take queries and resolve them.

The help desk offers a single point of contact for customers, and a good rapport can be built up between the person on the help desk and the customers. All the questions asked by different customers can be stored on a database and this can provide useful information about the usability of the software. The information can then be used to improve future versions of the software or plan training courses.

On the other hand, the work can be demoralising for the person at the help desk, especially if they generally have to pass the problem on to someone else to solve. People typically only call a help desk as a last resort, by which time they are probably quite frustrated and angry and ready to take it out on whoever picks up the phone. Communication can be a problem when the help desk tries to explain the problem to a third party, and quite probably the problem solver will not see the problem as a top priority so that the service may not be very fast or efficient.

The help desk will typically log:

- The user's name and telephone number or postcode;
- Version number of the software;
- Serial number of the software (to ensure that the user has a legitimate copy);
- The nature of the enquiry;
- The time and date of the call.

Using e-mail rather than the telephone is sometimes cheaper and avoids the problem of a telephone line that is constantly busy. Being held in a queue of callers for half an hour or more is not uncommon on the average help line, and it's bad luck if you don't like the music they've chosen to play you while you wait.

Technical support

Technical support exists to solve technical problems and tends to be staffed by specialists who perhaps had some hand in writing the software, but have very little idea of how the software is used in a business context. There may be problems of communication between the expert spouting technical jargon and the business user who wants to know how to get the package to allocate, say, a different level of discount to a particular customer.

Help desk software

Special help desk software such as McAfee's HelpDesk Suite is available for large and small organisations running a help desk.

This software comes with an Expert System database of answers to over 25,000 different hardware and software problems, which enables the staff at the help desk to ask the right questions and let the software diagnose the problem. It also allows the helper to take over the user's computer and screen, calling it up on his own screen and typing in the necessary fix. A 'whiteboard' facility allows all users within an organisation to be notified of a particular problem – say, the printer in a particular area is not functioning, or the network will go down between 5pm and 7pm on Tuesday. Numerous reports are available, for example to track service levels in order to help ensure that service level agreements are being kept.

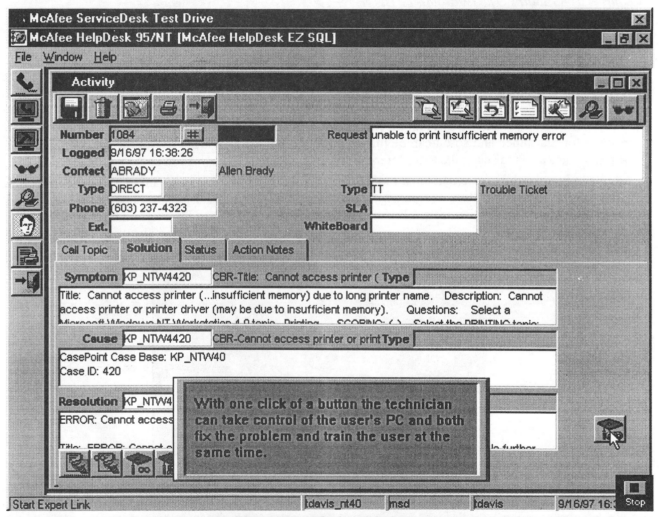

Figure 55.1. Help desk software

> ➢ **Discussion: What other reports would be useful in assessing the efficiency of the help desk service?**

Case study: Call centres

By the year 2001, one in fifty of us will be working in a call centre where hundreds of people take calls on their behalf: the Scottish Highlands, for example, are already dotted with them, including centres for Virgin, the London boroughs and M&G. This 2% of the population will do nothing but answer a telephone all day.

If you have a PC and telephone a number in Watford for technical support, you are quite likely to be rerouted to someone in Dublin, Edinburgh or even Hamburg. The person who answers your call sits in front of a computer, which recommends the questions he asks, and he then searches a database to see if anyone else has ever had the same problem. In other words, your problem is solved by someone who doesn't work for the company you bought your PC from, who wasn't at the number you called, who doesn't even work in the same country, and didn't solve the problem himself!

Source: Tim Phillips, The Guardian 11 December 1997

➢ **Discussion: What are the advantages and disadvantages to an organisation of using a call centre compared with internal help desks using special help desk software?**

Bulletin boards

A bulletin board system (BBS) is an electronic noticeboard to which items of interest, notes, hints and requests for assistance and so on can be pinned. The concept predates wide use of the Internet and some do not require users to subscribe to an Internet Service provider.

A bulletin board can be accessed via a modem in terminal mode, using a program like HyperTerminal in Windows 95. Selecting Start, Programs, Accessories, HyperTerminal brings up a screen which allows you to select New Connection from a File menu. This opens a Connection Description box (Figure 55.2).

Figure 55.2: Connecting to a bulletin board

After selecting OK and on the next screen, typing in the phone number provided in the software user manual, some user identification and password, a menu of options is displayed and the user can access advice on how to solve their problem.

Various other types of bulletin board serviced by software manufacturers can be accessed via the Internet. These often list 'frequently asked questions' (FAQs) and their answers, as well as providing a forum for users to solve each other's problems or refer them to the software manufacturer's experts.

User booklets

Some software support departments issue new users with an introductory guide to things they might need to know about the product they have purchased. The information given might include:

- Instructions to change the password after logging on for the first time;
- The name and address of their local contact;
- The hours that User Support is open;
- How to get printer paper, toner and other consumables;
- Where to go for training.

Newsletters and support articles

Many software companies produce their own regular newsletters. This typically contains tips on how to get the most out of the software, details of forthcoming support meetings and conferences, FAQs, articles and letters sent in by users describing how they have cleverly solved some obscure problem and previews of the inevitable forthcoming upgrade. Computer magazines also regularly have articles on similar topics.

On-lIne help

On-line help can be an invaluable aid to anyone learning a new software package. This typically contains an index of topics and a tutorial for beginners. Microsoft Help has a link to a Web site offering various options (Figure 55.3).

Figure 55.3: On-line help with Internet links

Documentation

Users need different levels of documentation depending on how they are using the software and how expert they are. Clerical workers may need an introductory tutorial, whereas 'knowledge workers' will probably need a reference manual as they use the software for increasingly complex tasks.

> ➤ **Discussion: What are the relative advantages of on-line help and user manuals?**

Exercises

1. (a) Describe **three** items of information a user support line would log when taking a call from a user.
    (3)
    (b) Many user support lines need to share problems and potential solutions between a number of operators who are answering calls. Describe **one** method of achieving this. (3)
    (c) Some user support lines also offer a mailbox facility to enable users to log their problems using e-mail. What advantages does this have for
       (i) the software user;
       (ii) the user support staff. (4)
    NEAB IT04 Qu 8 1997

2. Each day a software house logs a large number of calls from its users to its support desk.
    (a) Describe how the support desk might manage these requests to provide an effective service. (3)
    (b) Describe **three** items of information the support desk would require to assist in resolving a user's problem. (3)
    (c) The software house receives complaints from its users that the support desk is providing a poor service. Describe **three** reports that the software house could produce in order to combat the validity of this claim. (6)
    NEAB IT04 Qu 7 Sample paper

3. "As software becomes increasingly easy to use, the need for user support will decline."
    State whether you agree or disagree, giving **two** reasons to support your answer. (4)
    New question

4. Describe briefly **four** features you would expect to find in help desk software designed to be used by a call centre diagnosing users' problems with various software packages. (4)
    New question

Chapter 56 – Training

The need for training

Companies in industrialised countries spend huge amounts of money, often several million pounds a year, on training their employees. There are numerous different reasons why companies perceive training to be a valuable investment.

- Employees need training to give them the skills, attitude and knowledge required to do their jobs safely and well. This is true at all levels in a company, from the new recruit in a supermarket learning how to use the till and interact with customers, to the manager who needs to learn how to motivate the staff and to make effective decisions.

- New employees often need training before they can be reasonably effective within a company. They may need to be trained in the use of hardware or software they have not used before, or on the operational procedures that have to be followed.

- Existing employees require retraining because companies and jobs are constantly changing, new technologies are installed and new procedures are introduced.

- Well-trained employees are likely to be better motivated and have a better chance of promotion on a well-defined career path.

- Training can lead to increased sales, a better service to customers, better quality products, good safety records, and lower staff turnover.

> ➤ **Discussion: Have you worked in an organisation where you were given training? What were the benefits? Have you been in a situation where training was needed but not given?**

Training in the use of information technology

Training staff in the use of new technology is crucial to the success of any computer system. Unless staff at all levels of an organisation know how to use the new technology effectively, investment in a computer system can be a waste of money.

Training for senior managers

Managers who understand fully the benefits and problems associated with the use of information technology are likely to make better decisions than less well-informed colleagues when:

- establishing a corporate information systems strategy;
- appraising advice from I.T. professionals either within or outside the organisation;
- allocating resources to information systems.

Training for middle managers

Middle management will be responsible for ensuring that computer systems are correctly used, and that accurate, timely and useful information reaches the right people at the right time. They will also be responsible for the organisation's computer security policy. Therefore, they will need training in how to define information requirements, how to integrate systems and how to realise the potential of a new computer system. They will also need training in the use of software such as spreadsheets, communications software, word processing and specialised software needed for their particular job.

Training for users

When a new software package is introduced into a company, users at different levels of the company may require different levels of training. At the lowest level, for example, a clerical worker may need to know how to load a spreadsheet package, enter the daily or weekly sales figures and print a report. A member of the sales staff in an electrical retailer's may need to know how to enter a customer's details to check their credit rating, and put through a sale. A secretary may need to know how to use a word processor to write and print letters and reports, and how to use function keys to activate macros. These activities are **task-based**.

A middle manager or 'knowledge worker', on the other hand, may need **skill-based** rather than task-based knowledge. A marketing manager who has to give a presentation on the expected sales of a new product may need to use a spreadsheet to analyse and graph actual and projected figures and insert the results into a word processed report for the managing director. An office supervisor may design a style for all internal memos and reports, and create a template and macros to automate certain functions, using a word processing package.

> ➤ **Discussion: A company uses a database package to develop a customer invoicing and information system. Identify the different functions that this system could be used for, and different levels of training that would be required by the people using the package.**

Methods of training

There are several different methods by which users can gain expertise in the use of software packages. These include:

* Computer-based training;
* Watching a video training course;
* Interactive video training;
* On-line tutorials supplied with the software;
* Step-through guides;
* Formal, instructor-led training courses.

Computer-based training

Computer-based training has several benefits.

* For an employer, a major benefit is cost. Training courses can easily cost £500 per day per employee, with accommodation costs as an added extra. The investment in a suitable training package can quickly pay for itself if there are large numbers of employees requiring training.
* Staff can do the training at times which fit in with their workload, causing the least amount of disruption. During a slack period a member of staff can be sent to a training room on the premises to do an hour or two of training, or it may take place at the employee's own computer at their desk.
* Employees can study at their own pace and repeat sections which are difficult or which they have forgotten.

- Standardised training. Instructor-led training varies with the trainer and the training centre, whereas computer-aided training offers standardisation. However it cannot guarantee that all employees will gain the same benefit; it is very easy to keep pressing the 'Next' button without taking anything in!

> ➢ **Discussion: Have you ever used an on-line tutorial or other form of computer-based tutorial? What are the disadvantages of this method of learning?**

Instructor-led courses

For some, nothing can replace a good instructor. As one trainer said, "We are not very keen on computer-assisted learning because it is too impersonal. The best training results from the personal inspiration of a good trainer, from his or her ability to communicate with the trainee and whet the appetite for further knowledge and the ways to use that knowledge to good effect." Other advantages of classroom learning include the following:

- Learning is essentially a communal activity and students learn a lot from debate and discussion in the class.

- Peer collaboration in learning can help to develop general problem-solving skills. Learning together has the potential to produce gains superior to learning alone.

- Individuals often have a valuable store of personal knowledge which they can share with a group.

- Many jobs involve working together in teams and rely on successful collaboration with colleagues: formal education in a classroom can help prepare people to work together in groups.

Skills updating

Employees do not need training only when they start a new job, or when new technology is introduced; there is an ongoing need for skills updating and refreshing. An initial training course may be given in the rudiments of the software, which employees need to practice before they can take in new information. Some functions may not be introduced initially; for example year-end procedures may not be taught to everyone, but extra training may be needed for those who need to use these functions. As the new system becomes better understood, managers may want to learn new skills using advanced features. Employees who have been or are about to be promoted may need to learn new aspects of an information system.

Corporate training strategy

Companies with a commitment to training generally have well thought out objectives in their training programmes, and a clear idea of the benefits of training. The primary goal of training in one large company, for example, is stated as "to produce outstanding quality and service, to achieve total customer satisfaction, aggressive sales growth and optimum profits."

Without a training policy, companies can quickly lose their competitive edge. Experience shows that an unable, unwilling unresponsive or unskilled workforce can undermine or negate even the best strategies. On the other hand, companies which are managing the development of their people show enhanced performance because the employees are able, consistent, co-operative, responsible and solvers of problems.

The Department of Trade and Industry has published a booklet entitled 'Partnerships with People' which suggests ideas for a corporate training strategy. (Figure 56.1.)

Ideas worth trying

Develop appraisal systems which focus on individual development. Look at other jobs in the organisation that an individual may aspire to, encourage the development of necessary attributes to take them on.

Seek advice from the TEC/LEC or specialist training adviser to design a development programme for managers.

Provide business training for supervisors, technical managers, union representatives.

Investigate NVQs and encourage staff to take relevant qualifications.

Encourage key staff to develop training skills so they can pass on knowledge.

Make booklets and other self-help learning packages available to staff.

Develop links with local FE colleges – reimburse college fees in full or in part, to encourage people to get into the learning habit.

Encourage relevant people to take HND, degree or professional qualifications.

(Partnerships with People – a DTI booklet)

Figure 56.1: Points to consider in a corporate training strategy

Exercises

1. You are asked to advise an organisation on the introduction of a new software package.
   - (a) With the aid of **three** examples, explain why different users may require different levels of training. (6)
   - (b) Following the initial training you advise subsequent training for users. Give **two** reasons why this may be required, other than financial gain for the agency. (4)

   NEAB IT04 Qu 9 1997

2. Describe briefly **five** facilities you would expect to find in an on-line tutorial for a spreadsheet package. (5)

   New question

3. Describe briefly **three** different methods of training that may be used to train staff in aspects of information technology, explaining **one** relative advantage of each method. (6)

   New question

4. Why should a corporation have a training strategy for staff? (3)

   Give **three** points that could be included in such a strategy. (3)

   New question

Chapter 57 – Project Management

Introduction

A **project** is a short-term activity bringing together people with different skills, equipment and resources to achieve specified objectives. Project management often begins with the selection of a project manager and a project team. The project itself must be broken down into tasks, whose sequence and estimated time for completion is calculated and documented. Projects usually have the following characteristics:

- They have a specific objective – for example, the networking of all the computers in a college, or the introduction of a new computerised enrolment system;

- They must be developed within a specified time period;

- They must be developed within a given budget;

- A team of people is brought together temporarily from different areas to work on the project. When the project is finished, the team will be disbanded.

Selection of a project manager

Once a project has been given the go-ahead by senior management, the first step is the appointment of a project manager. The project manager needs to have the necessary technical skills, but just as important are the managerial skills needed to be able to lead and motivate a group of people from different departments and different levels within the organisation. Good interpersonal skills and business experience are also essential assets.

The tasks of a project manager

The project manager must:
- Plan and staff the project;
- Analyse risk;
- Monitor progress;
- Adjust schedules;
- Report project status;
- Control budgets and salaries;
- Prepare performance appraisals;
- Interact with users, corporate management and project personnel.

Courses in project management are offered by many educational and training establishments.

The project team

One of the first tasks of the project manager may be to pick the project development team. Studies have shown that an ideal team size is between 5 and 7 members, and that as the team size increases, level of job satisfaction drops, absenteeism and turnover rise, and the project may start to miss deadlines. Some projects, of course, are far too large and complex to have such a small team.

> ➤ **Discussion: Adding more people to a team which is behind schedule often has the effect of putting it even further behind schedule. Why?**

Regardless of the size of the project team, it should have a balance of theoreticians and practitioners, idealists and realists, technical and business specialists. Boehm in his book Software Engineering Economics (Prentice Hall 1981) listed five principles of software staffing:

1. **Principle of top talent**. Employ fewer but better people.

2. **Principle of job matching**. Match skills and motivations available to the task at hand.

3. **Principle of team balance**. There needs to be a balance between the technical skills, knowledge and personality characteristics of team members.

4. **Principle of phase out**. There will inevitably be a misfit on the team resulting in "unhealthy results in the long run". Getting the misfit out may not be easy but must be done with adequate thought, time and sympathy.

5. **Principle of career progression**. Bring out the best in people by enabling them to work on tasks that will help them to progress.

Project planning and scheduling

The project manager will divide up the project into phases and the phases into tasks. This may be done by identifying *milestones* which represent significant progress towards completion. Next, the skills that are needed for each of these tasks are identified and the time required for completion of each task calculated, based on the skills and availability of staff. A team leader may be appointed for each of these tasks, and the cost of completion of each task calculated.

Task definition forms the basis of the overall project plan, on which schedules and budgets are based. It is also used to track the progress of a project. Overlooking tasks is a common cause of cost and time overruns in projects, so it is very important to define all the tasks that need to be completed. Tasks that are commonly overlooked include training (or learning new skills), production of reports, project reviews, correction of errors and omissions.

Example: It is proposed to install a new computer network in the 6th form block of a school. What are the tasks involved in completing this project?

Tasks:

1. Carry out initial feasibility study

2. Invite tenders from suppliers

3. Choose a supplier

4. Purchase computers

5. Recable the building

6. Draw up plans for new classroom layout

7. Convert classroom

8. Install computers

9. Purchase network software

10. Install hardware and network software

11. Test network

12. Install end-user software

> **Discussion: Is this list complete? Can any of the tasks be carried out simultaneously?**

Many project managers keep a day-by-day log of the progress and difficulties encountered in a project, which can be an invaluable aid to planning the project schedule of future projects.

Project reviews

Most project schedules need constant updating and revision during the course of the project. It is important to have a formal *review process* to monitor and control the progress of a project. Review sessions every few weeks or so may be held in order to:

- Compare progress against the project schedule;
- Keep management informed and involved in the progress of the project;
- Reconfirm that current task lists and schedules are correct and on target;
- Identify any problems or slippage and come up with solutions;
- Encourage team spirit and communication between team members.

In spite of regular reviews and reports, many projects fail to meet deadlines and cost considerably over budget. Some projects may be so innovative that it is difficult to make accurate estimates. Sometimes excessive pressure on team members to keep to deadlines makes them hesitant to report problems, and sometimes the requirements of the project are changed in midstream. The larger and more complex the project, the more room there is for error. Louis Fried, a project manager, had a number of rules for project management including one which read "Any task that requires more than 10 people can't be done". ("The Rules of Project Management", *Journal of Information Systems Management Summer 1992*)

There are many project management software packages available, and these are discussed in Chapter 70.

Facilities management

Facilities Management (FM) is the use of an independent service organisation to operate and manage the contracting firm's computing and data processing operation. Firms opt to use FM for a variety of reasons:

- They may not have suitably qualified personnel to run their own data processing centre;
- They do not want the responsibility of operating their own computer equipment;
- Their computer centre has been mismanaged in the past and users are dissatisfied;
- They believe it will be better managed externally.

Advantages of FM

FM companies are generally able to attract highly qualified and talented professionals, as they can offer high salaries and challenging, varied work. Experts in various fields such as network management, numerical control or robotics often work for FM companies because they can concentrate full-time on their specialties, whereas they might otherwise have to perform a range of tasks outside their field of interest. They therefore can offer a better range of expertise than might otherwise be available to a client.

FM firms are often able to get better deals for their clients when purchasing new hardware or consumables since they deal in large volumes and get better discounts. They are often able to achieve greater efficiency and reliability from existing computer resources than existing employees. Also, since they are not part of the organisation they can be more flexible in reorganising and redesigning systems without worrying about in-house politics.

FM contracts typically run for between 2 and 6 years, and may include subjects such as availability of personnel, availability of expertise, lines of reporting for personnel, ownership of equipment, ownership of software, security and privacy of data, standards, priorities, limitation and liabilities.

Disadvantages of FM

There are inevitably dangers in handing over I.T. functions to a third party. For example:

- The FM company may fail to deliver, leaving the client with a system that does not work properly or provides an inadequate service. It is crucial to have a legally binding contract giving redress through the courts.

- The FM provider may increase the costs of services as the client becomes 'locked in'.

- Users may find it more difficult to deal with employees from an external organisation whose loyalties lie with the FM company. New boundaries of authority and responsibility have to be drawn between users and data processing personnel.

- Users may worry that they lose control over their data and worry about privacy and security, particularly when the FM company is also servicing a competitor. Can they be sure the FM company is always acting in their best interests?

Outsourcing

The term *outsourcing* can be used to denote any product or service that is purchased from another firm. Car manufacturers, for example, outsource the manufacturing of many components, from door handles to gearboxes. Many firms outsource their cafeteria to food service companies. In general, companies outsource the products and services they either do not want, or are unable, to produce themselves.

Outsourcing of computer hardware, telecommunications services and systems software such as operating systems and DBMSs has long been common, and many organisations purchase software such as stock control, accounting and payroll packages since these products can be bought far more cheaply from companies specialising in these products.

The main difference between facilities management and outsourcing is that FM is concerned primarily with operations of I.T. while outsourcing is primarily concerned with programming and with the use of advanced computer skills like teleprocessing. Where there are economies of scope and scale (i.e. **all** information systems activities are outsourced) then FM and outsourcing are very similar.

Exercises

1. A project team has been appointed by a firm of consultants to write a tailor-made customer billing and accounts system for a medium-sized business. The project team consists of a project leader (the systems analyst) and two programmers and a technician. The project is falling behind schedule and the managing director of the company decides to allocate two more programmers to the team. The project continues to fall further behind.

    Give **three** reasons why this might be so. (6)

    New question

2. The management of a College decides that a college-wide network should be installed to link together all the computers in the College. The estimated cost of the project is £1 million. What factors should the project manager take into account when planning the estimated time to completion of the project? (6)

    New question

3. A project manager has to pick a team of 5 people to work on the design and implementation of a new information system. Give some general guidelines that he should adopt in choosing the team. (5)

4. Explain what is meant by 'facilities management'. (3)

    Describe **two** advantages, and **one** possible disadvantage to a company of adopting this approach.

    (3)

    NEAB IT04 Qu 4 1997

Section 5

Information: Policy, Strategy and Systems

In this section:

Chapter 58 – Policy and Strategy

Chapter 59 – Security and Backup Policies

Chapter 60 – Software Evaluation

Chapter 61 – Communication and Information Systems

Chapter 62 – Types of Network

Chapter 63 – Network Security and Accounting

Chapter 64 – Data Communications and Standards

Chapter 65 – Human-Computer Interaction

Chapter 66 – Music Software

Chapter 67 – Geographical Information Systems

Chapter 68 – CAD/CAM Systems

Chapter 69 – Mathematical and Statistical Software

Chapter 70 – Project Management Software

Chapter 71 – Software Acquisition and Testing

Chapter 58 – Policy and Strategy

The challenge of information management

Within the space of a few decades, businesses have moved from having one mainframe computer to process data for payroll, stock control and customer accounts to having company-wide, often worldwide networks of computers affecting and controlling every aspect of their business. Computers are no longer a centralised resource operated and understood by a few knowledgeable experts: at every level of a company, employees will be interacting with and using computers to perform a huge variety of tasks. Customers may also be interacting with the company's computers through the Internet, cash machines, touch screens in shopping malls and so on.

'Information' is a resource, but one that has completely different properties from other resources such as raw materials or stock. For one thing, it is not depleted when it is used. For another, it is difficult and usually undesirable to keep exclusive ownership of information. It is usually regarded as a shared resource within a company.

The challenge for management is to formulate an information management policy that will help them manage computing resources in an effective and profitable way, and maximise the benefits of information.

We'll look at four different strategic planning issues related to information systems:

- Consistency with business priorities;
- Centralisation vs. decentralisation;
- Different user needs;
- Hardware and software choices.

Consistency with business priorities

A company's information system strategy should be linked to its business plan. This may seem obvious, but in practice, it does not always happen. One method used to try and ensure that it does is to use an approach called the **critical success factors** (CSF) method. This encourages senior executives to identify the company's primary goals and what things must go right for the business to succeed. They then identify measures of performance for each of these CSFs and make sure that the information systems are in place to collect and use this information.

> ➤ **Discussion: Typical example of CSFs include improving customer service, improving supplier relationships, holding the right stock at the right time in the right quantity, and using human resources efficiently.**
>
> ➤ **What performance indicators could be used to measure better customer service?**
>
> ➤ **What are the critical success factors in your school, college or department? How are information systems used to collect information about performance indicators?**

Centralisation vs. decentralisation

Most organisations today retain a department for computing services known for example as the 'Information Systems Department'. This department will have the responsibility for the planning and control of processing, the maintenance of hardware and software and the development of new computerised information systems.

In some organisations, the various tasks connected with managing computer resources are all performed centrally by the Information Systems Department. In other organisations, many tasks are performed by individual departments in a so-called decentralised or 'distributed' system. A centralised system has the advantage of providing a centralised pool of expertise and better control over what hardware and software is purchased. A distributed system, however, allows users in individual departments to develop their own applications and lessens dependence on the central resource.

Different user needs

A typical medium- to large-sized organisation using computers will have a number of different types of users, each with their own different requirements, as shown in Figure 58.1.

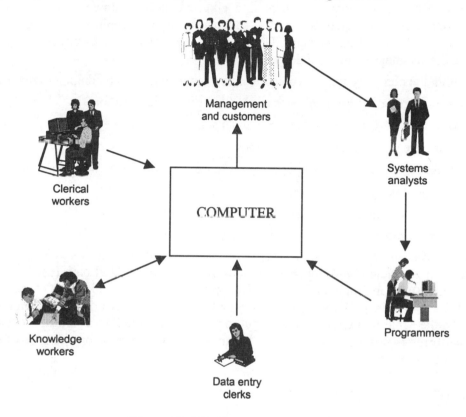

Figure 58.1: Different users in an organisation

Systems analysts, programmers and data entry clerks are computer users who interact with the computer system, but are distinct from 'end-users' who are the ultimate consumers of computer processing and information. Information systems fall into three major categories, each of which has different end-users:

- **Transaction processing systems**. Users: Clerical workers, salespeople, data entry clerks and customers.

- **Knowledge work systems**. Users: Middle managers, professional people such as accountants, engineers and graphic designers.

- **Management support systems**. Users: Senior managers.

End-users require software that is easy to use and which has enough features to help them to get their jobs done as efficiently as possible. They need hardware that is sufficiently powerful to run the software without frustrating delays.

> ➢ **A personnel manager in a large engineering company has asked one of her staff to produce a report showing which Universities they recruited from in the past five years, the proportion of those accepted out of the total interviewed, the proportion of men and women, and various other statistics. What software would be helpful in compiling this report?**

Hardware and software choices

With the trend towards distributed systems, there is a choice between allowing each department to purchase the hardware and software it considers most suitable for its own applications, or controlling all purchases from a central Information Systems Department. Generally the advantages of centralised control outweigh the disadvantages, and include the following:

- All hardware within the company will be compatible and can be linked in a company-wide network;
- Purchasing power is increased if high volumes are ordered by an organisation;
- The organisation is likely to get a better deal on maintenance contracts;
- Employees will not have to learn new systems if they move to another department;
- Training courses can be organised for people using the same software from many departments;
- Site licences can be purchased for software;
- There is better control over the use of unlicensed software;
- Data can be exchanged more easily between similar types of computer.

The term **platform** is used to describe the basic type of computer that an information system uses. A small business might for example choose between a platform based on an Intel chip (used on PCs) or a Motorola Power PC chip (used in Apple computers). The decision would depend on the characteristics of the application and the availability of software that runs on a particular platform. Upgrading to a more powerful computer in the same family costs money but in principle causes few technical difficulties, but moving between platforms is usually more complex because software written for one type of computer will generally not run on another.

Upgrading hardware and software

Many firms face a crucial challenge in the form of **legacy systems**: systems that have been passed down to the current users and IS staff. They are old, often technically obsolete systems that perform essential data processing such as accounting and customer billing. Many of these systems, written in COBOL in the 1960s and 70s, have been upgraded time and time again, using programming methods that are years out of date, and are technically fragile, difficult to maintain and impossible to understand. Because they still work, however, it may be difficult to get the funds to start from scratch with a new system.

Even companies with relatively new information systems face the constant problem of upgrades. Nothing stands still in computing – sometimes it seems as though no sooner have you bought a brand new PC to run your software than a new, better software version comes out that requires an even more powerful processor and twice as much memory to run it. When a company has upwards of a thousand PCs, the problem of upgrading becomes immense. Should everyone upgrade? Should no-one upgrade? Should selected departments upgrade?

Very likely some people would really benefit from the new features of upgraded software. On the other hand, documents created on the latest version of Word, for example, cannot be read in a previous version. This will inevitably cause problems.

> **Discussion: A school has the funds to equip a classroom with a new set of computers running the latest version of Windows. However, the other computers in the school are not powerful enough to run this version. What factors should the computer manager take into account when deciding what to do?**
>
> **What would you do if you were the computer manager?**

Future proofing

Is it possible to make such a shrewd choice of hardware and software that there will be no need to change it for years to come – to 'future proof' your purchases? Experience says a firm No. With processors still doubling in power every 18 months or so, and new versions of software appearing with monotonous regularity every year or two, most individuals and organisations resign themselves to the fact that regular upgrades will be necessary. The best strategy may be to buy hardware that has far more capability than is currently needed in anticipation of future need.

> **Discussion: What are the drawbacks of this strategy?**

Offers from TIME computer systems: Future proof?

Below are some offers from Time Computer Systems advertised over a 25 month period:

Date	Processor	RAM	Disk	Price
January 1996	75MHz Pentium	8Mb	850Mb	£1666
May 1996	100MHz Pentium	16Mb	850Mb	£1291
April 1997	166MHz Pentium	32Mb	2.1Gb	£1291
December 1997	200MHz Pentium	32Mb	4.3Gb	£1099
February 1998	233MHz Pentium	64Mb	6.4Gb	£1099

> **Discussion: Look up the latest offer from TIME Computer Sytems. (Try the back of Thursday's OnLine Section of the Guardian, or Wednesday's Edition of the Interface section of the Times)**

Emulation

One way around the problem of incompatible hardware is to buy 'emulation software' which will enable software written for one machine to run on a different type of machine. This theoretically enables an organisation to buy a different type of hardware and continue to run their existing software. This at least provides a way of keeping an existing system running for another year or two, perhaps while new software is developed or funds acquired to upgrade all the computers and install new software.

Exercises

1. 'If I need an I.T. system I buy whatever hardware and software I want without any regard to anyone.'
    This statement was made by a manager of a department in a company.
    Why is this an inappropriate approach in a large organisation? (6)

    NEAB IT05 Qu 7 Sample paper

2. A teacher in a large college does not like the CAD package available on the college network even though many other staff are quite happy with it. Describe **three** reasons why, in a large organisation, it is inappropriate for the teacher to buy an alternative package regardless of anyone else? (6)

    NEAB IT05 Qu 3 1997

3. A computer user has bought a large number of computer packages for an NEAB PC computer. Due to increasing workload it is necessary to replace this model with a more powerful computer. The user has a choice of

    Either:- buying an NEAB SUPERPC machine which is compatible with the NEAB PC,

    Or   buying a MEGAMACHINE which is a completely different piece of hardware but provides the software emulation of the NEAB PC.

    (a) (i)   Why does the user need to relate the new machine to the NEAB PC? (2)

    (ii) Explain the terms 'compatible' and 'software emulation'. (4)

    (b) Discuss the relative merits of adopting one choice of computer as compared to the other. (4)

    NEAB IT05 Qu 6 Sample paper

Chapter 59 – Security and Backup Policies

Introduction

There are two main ways to ensure that I.T. systems, once up and running, are protected from disaster, misuse or abuse. These are:

- Security measures.

- A personnel policy which covers data security and employee codes of conduct.

Under UK law, the responsibility for the security of the I.T. assets of a company, including its hardware, networks, software, databases and so on lies not with the I.T. department or the security officer, but with the company directors. They are *personally* responsible for the security of these assets. For this reason, they can be expected to give unequivocal support to the formulation and enforcement of an effective security policy.

Security policies were covered in Chapter 52. In this chapter we'll take a closer look at backup strategies.

Backup strategies

Proper backup procedures are the first line of defence against disaster. Both software and data need to be backed up and stored safely, off-site or in a fire-proof safe. Data may need to be backed up at least once a day and taken off-site. Software only needs to be backed up when a change is made or a new version installed.

Many organisations, from hospitals and government departments to banks and manufacturers, are totally dependent on the data held in databases which are continually being updated. A comprehensive backup strategy is required.

Example: A large organisation holds all the data on its database on a 10Gb file server in the office. It uses the following backup strategy:

- The organisation has a service agreement with a local company under which engineers will be at the office in under two hours in the event of any problem.

- The file server contains two disk drives, 'mirrored disks' containing identical data. All transactions are written simultaneously to both disks, so that if one disk crashes, the other disk drive contains all the data. No further transactions are accepted until the disk drive is repaired or replaced by the Service Agency.

- Four backup tapes marked **Monday, Tuesday, Wednesday, Thursday** are stored in a fireproof safe in the office. Each night, the relevant day's tape is loaded, a backup program starts automatically at midnight and backs up the entire contents of the hard disk, which takes several hours. One person in the office (a young Business Studies graduate whose main job is Marketing) is in charge of checking the on-screen messages in the morning to ensure that the backup has completed successfully, and if not, the Service Agency is notified.

- Every Friday, the person responsible for the backup procedures takes the **Friday** tape home, and on Monday, brings back the tape from two Fridays ago to be overwritten the following Friday.

- The Service Agency is responsible for maintaining the hardware and replacing, say, a worn tape drive.

- Occasionally, the tape is tested by restoring it onto a spare machine provided by the agency to check that the data is in fact being correctly backed up and that the hard disk can be correctly restored to its previous state.

Hardware for backups

- For small quantities of data, removable disks are the simplest. Iomega's Zip drive sells for under £100 and takes 100Mb disks similar to floppy disks (£10 each). It can copy 100Mb of data in about 5 minutes.

Figure 59.1: Iomega Zip drive

- For larger backups, tape is the preferred medium. A DAT tape drive with a capacity ranging from 2-24Gb costs about £600 and tape cartridges cost from about £5 to £50 depending on capacity.

- A CD-ROM drive using rewritable optical disks costs about £280. The 650Mb disks cost about £20 each.

Case study: Back up that data

The simplest backup strategy is to copy the contents of your hard disk at the end of each day to a tape or removable disk. Keep Friday's backup for a month, and one backup each month for a year. To prevent mix-ups, give each tape or disk a serial number, and keep a log book. Once done, the backup tape or disk should be stored in a safe place.

You can reduce the volume and time by using 'compression' software, which comes with the tape or disk drive, and by only backing up data files. Software programs do not need to be backed up except when they are changed. If the backup is still unmanageable, you can reduce it by backing up only files which have changed since you last did a backup – an 'incremental' backup. A typical strategy would be to do a full backup on a Monday, and incrementals Tuesday to Friday.

"One small business did backups every day and stored them in a fireproof safe", says Colin Pearson, I.T. adviser at Business Link Staffordshire. "Then some thieves stole the computer and the safe, so they lost the lot."

Once the backup is made, your worries are not entirely over, as self-employed public relations consultant David Bridson discovered. He religiously backs up his data every night onto a removable optical disk. But some months ago he moved his e-mail database to a different directory on his hard disk, and forgot to tell the backup software. Recently, seeing that his hard disk was getting full, he deleted some redundant files.

"Of course, the directories I cleared out were the ones I'd moved all this valuable information to", he says. "I went to each of my five backups and found that none of them contained my up-to-date e-mail list."

Source: Paul Bray, Sunday Times 19 October 1997

Grandfather-father-son backups

Not all organisations use on-line databases. Many companies do their processing in 'batch mode', collecting transactions over a period of time and batching them into sets of say 50 documents. These can then be checked, control totals calculated and entered on a batch header record, and the data entered using a key-to-disk system. (Chapter 26).

> ➤ **Discussion: What sort of organisation might use a batch processing system? Why?**

When batch processing is used, it is not necessary to back up all the data every night. The system uses 'generations' of master files, automatically creating a new 'generation' of master file each time the day's transactions are processed. To understand this process, imagine an equivalent manual system.

A class register for Lower VIa is written out in a register book in alphabetical order of students' names. Halfway through the term, it is decided to combine three classes into two, so a list of 5 extra students is given to the teacher of Lower VIa, who has to write out a brand new register. Unfortunately, three days later, the register disappears. Luckily, however, the teacher still has the old register and the list of names that were to be added, so the new register can be recreated.

In batch processing, transactions are typically processed once a day. A block diagram of the process is shown in Figure 59.2.

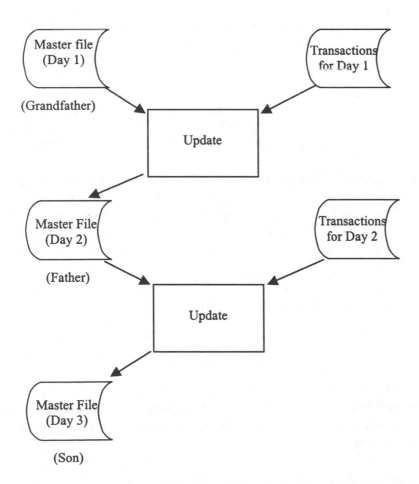

Figure 59.2: Grandfather-Father-Son method of update

When this method of processing is used, it is common to keep at least four generations of the master file along with the transactions that were used to update each generation. On the fifth day, the oldest generation of the master file (the 'grandfather') can be overwritten. Thus, there is always at least one generation of the master file and the corresponding transactions stored off-line in a secure fire-proof safe, with at least one pair off-site.

Personnel policy

A personnel policy covering security must cover:

- **Recruitment**. Most of the deliberate damage done to I.T. assets is by employees, either deliberately or accidentally. Therefore, references must be carefully checked and every care taken to recruit reliable employees.

- **Training**. This can help to prevent costly mistakes, and emphasise the importance of adhering to security procedures.

- **Supervision**.

- **Appraisal**.

- **Separation of duties.** No one person should have the responsibility for and knowledge of the firm's entire computer operation, however small. The first reason for this is that if they left, became ill or went on holiday the system would probably not function smoothly. The second reason is that no one person should know enough about the computer system to be able to destroy them or defraud the company, on their own.

- **Job rotation/Duplication of expertise**. This is a good idea for similar reasons to the above.

- **Termination**. The company must have a clear policy on dismissal or redundancy procedures.

Employee code of conduct

An employee code of conduct can be an effective measure against computer misuse and abuse. Potential employees need to be checked out carefully before they are hired and, once hired, required to sign an employment contract which sets out the types of misconduct, including computer abuse, which will result in dismissal without notice.

Once new employees actually join, they should be given training which includes a general awareness of computer crime and misuse, the company's policy on security, the use of illegal software, the introduction of viruses, reading other people's e-mail and privacy issues including the Data Protection Act. They should be instructed to change their password frequently and to refer to the company's security manual from time to time. Their responsibilities and authorisation for specific duties should be clearly specified.

> ➤ **Discussion: What sort of 'rules' would you expect to find in an employee code of conduct? Draw up a 'code of conduct' for students using school or college computers.**

Exercises

1. A hospital information system holds program files which are rarely changed and large database files which are constantly changing.

   Describe a suitable backup strategy for this system, explaining what is backed up and when, together with the media and hardware involved. (8)

   NEAB IT05 Qu 8 1997

Chapter 60 – Software Evaluation

Introduction

When a decision is made to computerise some aspect of the business, a feasibility study is carried out and then a detailed analysis is made of the user requirements. At some stage a decision has to be made whether to buy a software package 'off the shelf' or have software specially designed and developed either in-house or by outside consultants. In this chapter we'll be looking at methods of evaluating software packages to assess their suitability for the proposed task, and writing an evaluation report.

Choosing software

Suppose that you work for a small business that needs a computerised accounting system. You have been given the task of evaluating accounting packages and making a recommendation. Where do you start? Perhaps you may have heard the names of a few accounting packages, or can find out some names by browsing round PC World or asking a friend. The next thing you might try is to look up a supplier on the Internet – Sage, for example, has a well-known range of accounting packages.

Figure 60.1: Getting information on accounting packages

Exploring a little further in the Sage site will bring up a guide which provides useful advice on finding a suitable package:

- DON'T walk into a shop or dealership and buy the cheapest thing on offer. Remember, it is not the PC that does the real work, it is the software and if you buy a system that is not suited to your business it could cost you a lot of time, money and effort later on. You should make this decision with great care because effectively, you will be running your business on the accounting system.

- DO start to collect some information on accounting software products and PCs and read some of the reviews published in computer magazines.

- DO talk to your accountant, who may be able to advise you about some packages. Information may also be available from professional bodies such as the Institute of Chartered Accountants.

- DO define what it is that you need an accounting software package to do. Do you want to run your whole system on it or just do some sales invoicing? Will you need to automate just the main ledgers or would you like to put sales order processing, purchase order processing and stock control onto the computer? Do you have any special procedures or requirements that you must stick to, whatever the system? Will you want to extract management information for use in decision-making?

When you have answered these questions, you can begin your search in earnest.

(Reproduced with permission from Sagesoft Ltd)

Tailoring the software

Sage emphasises that the first crucial step in selecting a suitable software package is to define exactly what the system must do to fulfil the requirements of the business. Cheaper packages bought off the shelf generally cannot be tailored to individual requirements. More expensive packages can often be configured to match user needs. It is no good buying a standard package that meets 80% of the user's needs but can't cope with the other, crucial, 20%.

Some software houses will be able to tailor an existing package to provide the extra functionality required. However, this is a dangerous option – Tony Collins in his book 'Crash' advises:

"With a standard package there is no such thing as a 'minor' code change. It is like trying to add an appendage to a human being. Imperfect as we are, we are tried and tested and are unlikely to work better with two hearts, or run faster with three legs. If you want to keep the project really simple, buy a package but *don't modify it.*"

Upgradability

A small business trying to keep a tight rein on overheads may be tempted to go for a good, simple and inexpensive package that serves their current needs. As the business expands, the package may no longer be adequate, and the pain of changing to a completely new system can be considerable. Therefore, it is desirable to choose a package that has a clear 'upgrade path' – many companies offer a range of upwardly-compatible packages so that data can easily be transferred to a more powerful package. The upgrades are offered at a special price to existing customers.

Other evaluation criteria

Several other factors need to be considered:

- **Compatibility with existing hardware and software**. Will the package run on existing hardware? Can files be easily transferred from existing systems without re-keying? Can files created in the package be exported to other systems in use in the company?

- **Resource requirements**. Will the system require expenditure on more powerful hardware, or extra staff to key in data?

- **Quality of documentation**. Are manuals supplied? Is there a good on-line help system?

- **Ease of learning**. Are tutorials supplied? Are books on the software available in bookshops? Are training courses available?

- **Ease of use**. Is it easy to use, for example using pull-down menus, icons, helpful error messages when you do something wrong?

- **Technical support**. Is support available? Is it very costly? Often, a technical support contract can add 50% or more to the price of a package, but without it no support at all will be given by the manufacturer.

- **Cost**. This includes the original cost of the package, technical support, and upgrades.

- **Speed**. The speed at which the package carries out critical operations can be measured using benchmark tests (see below).

Benchmark tests

A benchmark test, or performance test, can help determine the efficiency of the product. These tests involve comparing several different software packages by measuring the time that each one takes to perform various tasks. Computer magazines regularly publish the results of benchmark tests on different types of software.

Checking out the manufacturer

An important criterion in selecting a software package is the reputation of the manufacturer and the supplier: the relationship with the supplier can be crucial in getting the right package. It is important that the supplier understands how your business works and what the requirements are, and to provide support when problems arise. Consulting other users, reading magazine articles and visiting suppliers to discuss requirements are all ways of finding out who you can rely on.

Evaluation report

Once a thorough evaluation of possible software options has been made, an evaluation report may be written to document the performance of the software examined, and to make recommendations so that a decision can be made on what software to purchase.

The report will typically contain:

- An introduction stating the purpose of the report;

- The methodology used to evaluate the software options;

- The actual evaluation, including the capabilities of the software, results of benchmark tests, upgrade facilities, compatibility with existing software base etc.

- Recommendations;

- Justifications for the recommended purchase.

Exercises

1. In groups of two or three students, carry out an evaluation of several similar packages e.g. word processing packages, spreadsheets, databases or graphics packages. Write an evaluation report and give a presentation of your recommendations for which package the school/college should invest in.

   New question

2. You are asked to evaluate a software package and produce an evaluation report.
   (a) Describe **four** criteria you would use to evaluate the package. (8)
   (b) What is the function and content of an evaluation report? (4)

   NEAB IT05 Qu 4 Sample paper

3. A system for the production of about one hundred thousand electricity bills per day is required. A number of alternative systems are available for purchase.

    The following features of each alternative system have been given numerical weightings to reflect their relative importance:

Feature	Weighting
A: purchase cost	5
B: maintenance and running costs	10
C: user friendliness of the software	3
D: bill printing speed	12
E: quality of printed output	8

    The required system is selected as follows:

Step 1	Rank each feature of each alternative system in order of merit.	For example, with regard to feature A, purchase cost, the most expensive system would be given a ranking of 1, the second most expensive a ranking of 2, and so on.
Step 2	Multiply each of these rankings by its respective weighting.	For example, with regard to feature E, which has a weighting of 8, the system with the worst printed output would have a computed value of (1 x 8), the system with the second worst printed output a computed value of (2 x 8) and so on.
Step 3	For each alternative system calculate a total of these computer values. The system with the largest total should be selected.	

    (a) Suggest a possible consequence of feature C being given a low weighting. (2)

    (b) Comment on the relative size of the weighting given to feature D in comparison to the other features. (2)

    (c) State **three** advantages of this method of selecting a computer system. (3)

    (d) Identify **four** factors other than those listed which should be taken into account before a system is purchased. Justify your suggestions. (8)

    London Computing Paper 2 Qu 12 1997

Chapter 61 – Communication and Information Systems

Centralised processing systems

Until the 1970s, most organisations using computers were using **centralised** computer systems, with a mainframe computer doing all the processing for the whole company. Sometimes, on-line access to the mainframe computer would be possible from distant 'dumb' terminals – so-called because the terminals consisted of just a screen and a keyboard and no processor of their own. A similar type of centralised processing is still in use for some applications: banks, for example, use ATMs (Automated Teller Machines), a form of terminal containing a microprocessor which dispenses cash and enables customers to query their accounts. The ATMs are connected to a remote central computer which can be accessed from any ATM in the country.

Figure 61.1: An example of centralised processing

Dispersed systems

As the price of hardware dropped, it became more cost-effective to move the processing power to where it was needed, often on individual users' desks. At first, as applications such as spreadsheets and word processors led to an explosion in the popularity of microcomputers, large numbers of standalone computers were to be found throughout an organisation, each running software suitable for a particular application or department but without the ability to communicate with one another. This arrangement could be termed a 'dispersed system'. The shortcomings of this arrangement soon became apparent, however.

> ➤ **Discussion: What were the advantages of having a number of standalone computers instead of having all the processing done on a central mainframe computer with remote terminals connected to it?**
>
> ➤ **What are the drawbacks of this arrangement?**
>
> ➤ **How can these drawbacks be overcome?**

Today, these microcomputers are commonly linked by means of cables and telecommunications into one or more types of **network**, allowing what is known as a 'distributed' system. There is a great variety of different types of network, and they can be categorised broadly into local, wide area and public networks.

Local area networks (LANs)

A local area network consists of a number of computers in the same building or site, connected by cables. No telecommunications lines are needed. Such an arrangement has many advantages over standalone computers:

- It permits the shared use of facilities such as printers, scanners and hard disk space.

- Communication between users becomes possible and, using software such as Lotus Notes, many workers can work on the same document at the same time.

- Software can be loaded on the file server and used by everyone on the network. When it is upgraded, new software has to be loaded only once instead of onto every machine.

- All users can have access to a database.

- Backup of all data held on a central file server can be done automatically every night.

Frequently, one of the facilities of a LAN is a **gateway** – hardware and software which gives all network users access to other networks.

> **Discussion: Is data MORE or LESS secure on a network than on standalone computers? Why?**

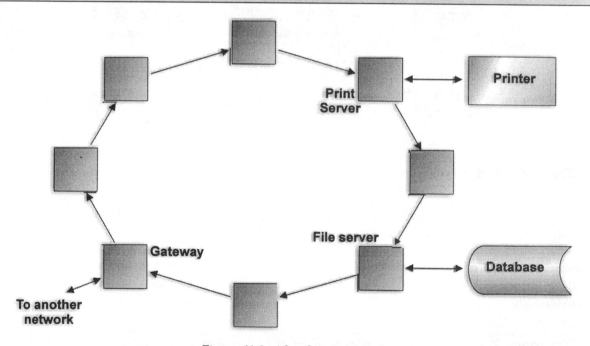

Figure 61.2: A local area network

Wide area networks (WANs)

Large organisations rely on wide area networks for communication and data exchange, not only between branches within the organisation but also between organisations. Booking an airline ticket or paying for goods by credit card are just two examples of transactions that would be impossible without wide area networks.

Distributed processing

With the growth of powerful telecommunications networks, organisations moved away from having a central mainframe to installing minicomputers and microcomputers at remote sites. These distributed processors directly serve local and regional branches and are generally linked together in networks. The dispersion of computers among multiple sites so that local computers can handle local processing needs is called **distributed processing**.

Case study: Pubs get a new round of touch tills

Many pub and restaurant customers can soon expect a slicker service as a new wave of computerised tills reach Britain's busiest bars and cafes.

Touch screen terminals promise to end those minor irritations which can spoil a night out, such as waiting ages for a drink or getting the wrong side order with a meal. Greenalls, a leading leisure company, has begun installing 1,000 InnTouch terminals in its bars and restaurants, which include the Henry's chain, Millers Kitchens and Bygone Inns.

The new tills allow bar staff to simply touch a symbol for each drink ordered and quickly provide the total cost. When a customer orders food, staff will touch a symbol for the main course and then move on to a second screen with all the possible side orders. If a customer orders steak, for example, the screen will show symbols for salads, onion rings, mushrooms and all other accompaniments.

"We expect the tills to speed up customer service by 40 per cent," says Tim Kowalski, Greenalls' financial director. With the new tills and back-up services costing £3 million, Greenalls will be looking for more than improved customer relations from its investment. The tills are linked to a computer in the manager's office at each property and that PC is linked by modem to the 32-bit Windows-based Innmaster system at Head Office.

The system will enable the company to gather immediate information about food and drinks sales, and this will inform decisions on changing menus or launching promotions. "While analysing food sales, for example, we noticed that Wall Street, a busy young persons' pub in Preston, was selling an average of only ten rounds of garlic bread per week," reports Kowalski. "This was at odds with sales in similar houses. We phoned the manager who hadn't realised this shortfall and he was able to brief waiters and waitresses. Consequently, sales increased by 40 to 50 rounds a week which, at a retail price of £1.20 per portion, could add £2,500 to annual sales."

The system also enables managers to monitor staff performance. Gail Pritchard, manager of Off the Wall, Chester, says: "We ran a promotion on Miller Draught with a £10 incentive to the staff member turning in the best performance each shift, and I was able to get an instant printout of everyone's performance.

Touch screens are logical and incredibly fast. They are a huge asset for us, and the staff like them."

Source: Tony Dawe, The Times 18 February 1998

> ➤ **Discussion: Is this a distributed or a centralised system? Where is the processing performed at each stage?**
> ➤ **Describe some of the advantages of the new system.**

Distributed systems may be organised in many different ways. Decisions have to be made on where to locate both the processing power and the databases, and how to connect the nodes (host computers and workstations) of the network. Distributed systems may extend over several levels, with some processing taking place at many different levels. In the case study above, processing is taking place at only two levels: local managers' offices and Head Office. In a large organisation such as for example Ford Motor

Company which has offices and sites all over the world, there may be six or more levels over which processing is distributed, as shown in Figure 61.3.

Figure 61.3: Possible distribution of systems in an organisation

Distributed databases

Although early distributed systems generally worked with a single centralised database, over time the smaller local systems began to store local databases as well. However, local branches frequently still need access to the main company database, which may be held in a different country altogether. Maintaining on-line access to a central database from all over the world can be very expensive – and so the next logical step was to distribute the central database to local processors. A mechanism is then needed to ensure the several versions of the database are properly updated, that the integrity of data is maintained (i.e. that different versions of the data are not held in different places) and that security is maintained.

A **distributed database** is one that is stored in more than one physical location. There are three main ways of distributing a database.

1. The central database can be partitioned so that each remote processor has the data on its own customers, stock, etc.

2. The entire database is duplicated at each remote site.

In both these cases, the two databases have to be reconciled with each other. This is usually done by updating the central database each night to reflect local changes made the previous day.

3. The central database contains only an index to entries which are held on local databases. This system is used for very large databases like the FBI's National Crime Information Centre. A query to the central database identifies the location where the full record is held. The National Westminster Bank uses a similar system to hold details on all its customers.

A variation of this system is not to hold an index, and to simply poll all remote databases until the required record is found. The complete record is then transferred to the local computer that requests it.

> ➢ **Discussion: What sort of organisation could use**
>   (a) **the first type of distributed database?**
>   (b) **the second type of database?**

Advantages and limitations of distributed databases

Distributed systems reduce the dependence on a single, massive central database. They increase responsiveness to local users' and customers' needs. They can provide a better response rate to queries which are handled locally.

Depending on how the distributed database is held, however, it can be highly dependent on powerful and reliable telecommunications systems. Local databases can sometimes depart from central data definitions and standards, and security can be compromised when distribution widens access to sensitive data.

Despite these drawbacks, distributed processing is growing rapidly. For large organisations operating on several sites, the question is not *whether* to distribute but *how* to distribute in order to minimise costs, increase efficiency and provide the best service while not compromising data integrity and security.

Using telecommunications for competitive advantage

The use of telecommunications is increasingly being used to reshape the way that organisations do business, increasing the efficiency and speed of operations, making management more effective and providing better services to customers. For example:

- A large publisher has a telecommunications link to its distributor's warehouse. Under the old system, when an order was received from a bookshop or wholesaler, invoices were printed and sent by post to the warehouse where one copy was sent with the box of books and a second copy retained for reference. Under the new system the invoice is transferred electronically and printed at the warehouse, enabling books to be shipped out at least 24 hours earlier.

- iMVS, the Internet Music and Video stores, takes orders from customers over the Internet. Orders to suppliers are then placed by iMVS electronically in a 'just-in-time' system and the CD or video normally shipped within 48 hours. Confirmation of the order is sent by e-mail to the customer, and in the case of delays, the customer can find out via the Internet where the order has got to.

- Yellow Pages has equipped its sales force with laptop computers from which they can initiate a phone call by clicking a phone number displayed in the database. Instead of faxing sales enquiries and mock-ups for advertisements, mobile staff can now access a fully automated sales system and query the corporate database direct. When an advertisement is approved, it can be sent from the salesperson's home computer to the production department at head office via ISDN.

- SMI, an advertising agency, uses a company-wide internal network (an 'Intranet') to share documents though a single viewing interface, Lotus Notes. Through a password-protected front end, customers can access and inspect prospective campaigns the moment they come off the digital drawing board, and comment on them, sending their text straight into SMI's Notes system. A proposed radio advertisement could be put on the system and a client in Timbuktu could listen to it a minute later.

Public networks

The Internet is the best known example of a public network. Other public networks such as BT's Home Campus educational network, or MSN, the Microsoft network can be accessed on payment of a monthly subscription. Internet subscriptions to magazines such as the Economist are a growing alternative to traditional paper copies. Subscribers can look up any article or topic that has appeared over the past several years.

Look back at Chapter 7, and at the case study below, for some examples of how companies are doing business on the Internet.

Case study: United Parcel Service (UPS)

UPS is a major package delivery and shipping company which does a large part of its business over the Internet. When a manufacturer has products to sell to a customer, they use a service like UPS to deliver the goods.

UPS uses a nationwide cellular system called TotalTrack to provide information at any time, day or night, on the status of a parcel. When the driver picks up a package, it is immediately logged using a portable hand-held computer containing a barcode reader for capturing the barcode identification on the package, and a keyboard for entering additional information such as the destination's area code. On returning to the truck, the driver inserts the hand-held computer into a small computer that transmits the data to the local dispatch centre, where it is recorded on a database. The location data is updated automatically as the package moves through each step on the way to its destination. The combination of telecommunications and computing permits UPS to know the location of every package at any time.

When the package is delivered to the customer, the customer signs for it using a pen-based computer and delivery confirmation is transmitted back to UPS.

Both sender and receiver of the package can track the status of the parcel at any time, day or night, via the Internet using UPS's OnLineTM Office software.

As UPS says: "After placing an order with you most customers have just one question on their minds: When will my shipment arrive? With just one click you can give them the answer! Just go to the UPS OnLineTM Office software and click on Ship Notification. From there, you can send consignees a detailed fax report showing who sent the shipment, where the shipment was sent, and when it's scheduled for delivery. All with no phone calls to make and no calls to answer. There's just no easier way to keep customers satisfied.

> ➤ **Discussion: This is an example of a highly distributed system, with data about each parcel being held at local dispatch centres, accessible from all over the world. What are the advantages of this system to UPS, the consigner of the parcel, and the recipient?**
> ➤ **Apart from knowing where the parcel is, could UPS use this system to provide other services to its customers?**

Exercises

1. (a) What is meant by distributed processing? (2)
   (b) With the aid of an example, describe how distributed processing may be implemented in an organisation which has a Head Office, and several sites each with a number of different departments. (5)
   New question

2. (a) Describe how a distributed database may be implemented. (3)
   (b) Give an example of an organisation that might hold its data in this way. (1)
   (c) What are the advantages and disadvantages of such a distributed database to this organisation? (4)
   New question

3. A supermarket has direct links to some of its major suppliers so that orders can be sent electronically each day for 'just-in-time' delivery of goods that need replenishing. What are the advantages to
   (a) the supermarket
   (b) the suppliers
   of this arrangement (4)
   New question

4. A large national charity holds a central database of donors and recipients. Branch offices equipped with PCs and modems are able to dial in over a telephone line to get lists of members living locally to inform them of local fund-raising events. What would be the advantages to the charity of a distributed system? How would distributed databases be kept in the same state as the central database? (6)
   New question

5.
```
Networks are the future!
```

   Explain why computer networking has developed rapidly over the past 15 years. Your answer should discuss **three** factors which have stimulated this development and **three** implications for society. (6)
   SEB Paper 2 Qu 10 1994

Chapter 62 – Types of Network

Network topologies

The physical arrangement of computers or terminals (commonly referred to as 'nodes') in a network is known as its **topology**. The three most common topologies are star, bus and ring.

Star network

Each node is connected to a central computer known as the **hub**. It is a popular topology for wide area networks, with the central computer often doing most of the processing and being located at the site where the company database is located. All communications between workstations go through the central hub.

Figure 62.1: Star network

The *advantages* of a star topology are:

- Each computer is independent of the rest and is unaffected if one of the other nodes or connections fails.

- The data transmission rate can vary on each link. Some well-used links may be dedicated high-speed lines, whereas other links that are only used occasionally may use a dial-up telephone link. A dedicated leased line gives more reliable and faster transmission but is much more expensive and would only be used when transmission needs to take place throughout most of the day.

- It allows a high degree of security since it is centrally controlled.

It is very suitable for a wide area network where most of the processing is done at Head Office. For example, a fast food chain may have tills connected to a local PC in the manager's office. Every evening, the data on the day's sales are transmitted via a telecommunications link (probably the ordinary telephone network) to the Head Office computer.

The *disadvantages* of a star network are:

- A hub failure affects all users, although local processing can still take place in a distributed system;

- Control of communications at the hub requires expensive hardware, probably a mini or mainframe computer, and complex operating and communications software to control the network.

Bus network

In a bus topology, all the workstations are connected by a single cable which can have a maximum length of about 500 metres. This means that a bus is suitable only for a local area network, and it is a popular configuration widely used in LANs. There is no central computer, but one PC is used as a file server to hold programs and data needed by individual users, and the same or other PCs may be used as print servers and communications servers to allow access to other networks.

Figure 62.2: A bus network

The *advantages* of a bus network are:

- It is easy and inexpensive to install and requires the least amount of cable;
- Additional devices can easily be added without disrupting the network;
- The failure of one workstation or its connection to the main cable (bus) does not affect any other workstations.

The *disadvantages* are:

- If part of the main cable develops a fault, the whole network goes down;
- Cable failure is difficult to isolate;
- Network performance degrades under a heavy load.

Ring network

The ring topology is not suitable for a WAN. There is no host computer in a ring network and none of the nodes need have overall control of access to the network although in practice one node may do so. Messages in a ring flow in one direction only round the ring from node to node. In the 'token ring' system, a message token (a unique character sequence) is passed from node to node and a node can remove the token and either take a message from it or add a message together with the sender's and receiver's addresses.

Repeaters attached to each node are used to regenerate messages as they pass around the ring. The use of repeaters allows a ring network to cover larger distances than other types of local area network, and in fact using optical fibre cable they can span a distance of up to 100 kilometers.

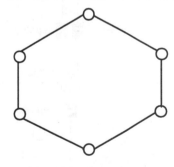

Figure 62.3: A ring network

The *advantages* of a ring topology are:

- There is no dependence on a central computer. Each node can handle data transmission to and from itself;
- Very high transmission rates are possible;

- Transmission of messages around the ring is relatively simple, with transmission being in one direction only.

The *disadvantage* is:

- If one node breaks down, transmission between the other nodes is disrupted.

Connecting LANs on a single site

On a site such as a college, there may be several LANs in different areas of the building. Separate LANs can be connected to provide a college-wide network using **repeaters**, **backbones** and **bridges**.

The standard cabling used in a bus network is **Ethernet**, and this comes in different types:

- Thick Ethernet, which has a solid copper core and can transmit at around 10Mb per second (Mbps);

- Thin Ethernet, which has a core of stranded copper and can transmit at around 2Mbps;

- 10BaseT Standard Ethernet which is the same as most telephone cabling and has a transmission rate of 10Mbps;

Using fibre optic cabling, transmission speeds of 1.24Gbps can be achieved.

A possible strategy, then, is to have a number of LANs connected using 10BaseT Standard Ethernet in various classrooms or departments. Groups of networks are connected via **repeaters** to **bridges**, which in turn connect via a fibre optic cable, which acts as a **backbone**, to the main network controller.

Repeaters allow the effective length of an Ethernet connection to be increased as it reamplifies the signal travelling from one computer to another. Repeaters are also used to enable a signal to travel to another segment of a network.

A bridge is used to connect two LANs of the same type, such as two Ethernet LANs. It can be configured so that only data which needs to cross the bridge actually does, so that most of the traffic will be isolated within a single classroom or department, except when messages are sent to a different part of the network.

A backbone is a very fast section of cable connecting the bridges to the main network server. From here, activity on the network can be monitored.

Figure 62.4: A network configuration joining 5 LANs

Client-server and peer-to-peer networks

Most networks, except very small ones, operate on a client-server system. The 'clients' are normally microcomputers with their own processing power, connected to the file server which holds software and data. When a client wants to use a word processing package or a CAD package, for example, the software is downloaded into the client's RAM. Printing tasks may be handled by a print server, which queues the output from all the machines in the network and passes it to the printer. Both processing power and data may be distributed between the various machines on the network. Backup and security will be handled by the server.

Small networks of no more than 10 computers may use a peer-to-peer configuration, with none of the computers being in control of the network. Software may be held on any of the computers and made available to any other machine on the network. This does have the effect of slowing down the speed at which the software runs, but enables computer users in a small office to share disk space, software and data.

The relative benefits of client-server and peer-to-peer networks are summarised in Table 34.4 in Chapter 34.

Exercises

1. (a) Describe or draw bus and ring network topologies. (4)

    (b) Discuss the factors you would take into account in deciding which topology to use for a local area network. (8)

    NEAB IT05 Qu 10 Sample paper

2. A mail order company has a local area network to process orders and deal with customer accounts. Describe briefly **three** features of a LAN which make it an essential part of the company's operations. (6)

    New question

3. A small manufacturing business currently has 8 staff and 5 computers. The manager feels that the computers should be networked so that staff in the accounts department and manufacturing and dispatch departments can access data on orders and stock levels. You have been asked for advice on whether the business should acquire a peer-to-peer or client-server network. What factors would you take into account when making your recommendation? (5)

    New question

Chapter 63 – Network Security and Accounting

Introduction

Computer networks bring their own particular security problems. One of the great advantages of networks is that data held on databases can be accessed by people from all over the world – but clearly, this poses the threat that the data may be accessed, stolen, altered or deleted by unauthorised people – or even by authorised employees with criminal tendencies. In this chapter we'll look at methods used to help keep data held on networked computers secure, as far as possible. *(No system is completely foolproof!)*

Training users about security

Every employee should be made aware of the company's security policy and of the risks to data held on networks. The importance of following rules and procedures, and of being alert to possible breaches of security, need to be emphasised and understood. Downloading programs from the Internet, for example, can introduce viruses on to a computer network, and so all such files should be virus-checked before use. All employees should be made aware of their responsibilities not to allow strangers access to restricted areas, not to leave machines logged on while they go to lunch and not to write their password down.

Access privileges

The main method of controlling access to data held on a network is by defining **access privileges** for each user. These define for each user exactly which computers and what data he or she is allowed to access, and what they are allowed to do with data they can access. Typical access levels include:

- No access;
- Read only;
- Read and copy;
- Read and update.

Junior nursing staff, for example, might be able to access a patient's medical record in a hospital but not to update it. A doctor from another hospital might be able to read and copy it, and the patient's own doctor would be able to read and update the record.

Access controls can be applied to software as well as data, so that users have access to software needed for their particular tasks, but not to other software.

Access control

Access control may be based on:

- **What you know** – for example a password or PIN number. These suffer from many shortcomings, as users tend to be careless about using obvious words or names, or writing their passwords down. Many computer system break-ins occur because a password has been divulged to someone who appeared to be authorised to know it – for example a repairman. The fraudster can, for example, run a program which appears to be a login procedure but which simply writes a password to a file. The unsuspecting user is then requested to type in their password as part of the 'repair'.

- **What you have** – for example, an ID card perhaps in the form of a smart card or magnetic stripe card.

- **Where you are** – you may be able to gain entry to a computer system only from a specified location or telephone number. Using a **callback system**, the user dials in and enters an ID number and password, and is then automatically disconnected. The computer checks the ID and password and if these are correct, the user is called back at a predetermined telephone number.

- **Who you are** – specialised equipment can check your handprint, retinal image or voice print. These are all forms of **biometric identification**.

All these methods of identifying authorised users can be made less effective if users are careless about leaving terminals unattended when they are logged on. Some systems automatically log off if there is no activity at a terminal for a specified period, say 10 minutes.

Firewalls

Linking to the Internet or transmitting information via Intranets requires special security measures. A **firewall** is software that prevents unauthorised communication into or out of the network, allowing the organisation to enforce a security policy on traffic flowing between its network and the Internet. The firewall is generally placed between internal LANs and WANs and external networks such as the Internet.

Various different types of firewall products are available, such as:

- A router which examines each incoming packet of data, checking its source or destination address. Access rules must identify every type of packet that the organisation does not want to admit;

- Special software that restricts traffic to a particular application such as e-mail or Lotus Notes groupware;

- A 'proxy server' that maintains replicated copies of Web pages for easy access by a designated class of users. Outside visitors to the Web site can be routed to this information while being denied access to more sensitive information.

Audit controls

Audit controls track all activity on a network – for example:

- What programs have been used;
- What files have been opened;
- How many reads and writes have been executed;
- How many times a server has been accessed.

Special monitoring software can also be used to produce statistical profiles and store statistics about the behaviour of each user with respect to objects such as data files or programs. The program can then detect statistically abnormal behaviour of users.

Performance management

Network monitoring software will collect data and statistics on all aspects of network use to help with the management and planning of a network. Data may be collected on:

- Network availability (i.e. switched on and not working);
- Response time (time between making a query and receiving a response);
- Utilisation of hardware resources (CPU, disks, bridges, repeaters, clients and servers);
- Utilisation of software;
- Traffic density in each segment of a network.

These statistics can help to identify bottlenecks and potential problems and aid in planning future developments. By monitoring software usage, it is possible to detect if there are more copies of any particular software package being used than the company has a licence for, and take action.

> ➤ **Discussion: What action should the Computer Centre management take if it detects illegal use of software?**
>
> ➤ **In what other ways could it be useful to monitor software usage?**

Data encryption

Data on a network is vulnerable to wire-tapping when it is being transmitted over a network, and one method of preventing confidential data from being read by unauthorised hackers is to **encrypt** it, making it incomprehensible to anyone who does not hold the 'key' to decode it.

There are many ways of encrypting data, often based on either **transposition** (where characters are switched around) or substitution (where characters are replaced by other characters).

Figure 63.1: Data encryption

In a **transposition** cipher, the message could be written in a grid row by row and transmitted column by column. The sentence 'Here is the exam paper' could be written in a 5 x 5 grid:

```
H E R E *
I S * T H
E * E X A
M * P A P
E R * * *
```

And transmitted as HIEMEES**RR*EP*ETHXA**HAP*

> ➤ **Using the same grid, decode the message ITT*O*E*HRWDNIYA*OS*NITT***

Using a substitution cipher, a 'key' that is known to both sender and receiver is used to code the message. A very simple example is to substitute each letter with the next one in the alphabet.

In practice, since the key must be difficult to break, a much more sophisticated algorithm must be used, with frequent changes of key.

Cryptography serves three purposes:

- It helps to identify authentic users ;
- It prevents alteration of the message;
- It prevents unauthorised users from reading the message.

Exercises

1. A university provides staff and students with access to its computer network.

    (a) Activity on the university's networking system is monitored and an accounting log is automatically produced. Suggest what this log might include and explain why it is useful.   (8)

    (b) Appropriate staff have access to personal and financial data. What steps should be taken to preserve the security of the data in such a system?   (4)

    NEAB IT05 Qu 4 1997

2. One method of encryption used in transmitting data requires data to be placed in a grid with 4 rows and 5 columns. The data enters row by row and is transmitted column by column.

    (a) Show that the data string "THE*EXAM*BEGINS*AT*9" would be sent as

    "TXE*HAGAEMIT**N*EBS9"

    (b) Decode the following received message using the same grid, showing how you obtain your answer.

    "TIS*HSSFI*AOSMGU*EER"   (4)

    London Computing Paper 1 Qu 2 1996

Chapter 64 – Data Communications and Standards

Communications software

Communications software enables computers to communicate with each other, controlling transmission by specifying:

- Speed of transmission;
- Direction of data flow;
- Method of transmission;
- Which computer code is used (e.g. ASCII, EBCDIC);
- Type of parity used (e.g. odd or even).

The rules and procedures for allowing computers to communicate with each other is called the **communications protocol**.

Speed of transmission

Transmission speed is related to the bandwidth of the communications channel. A communications 'channel' is the link between two computers and could be, for example, a telephone line, a fibre-optic or coaxial cable, a microwave or satellite link.

There are two common types of bandwidth called *baseband* and *broadband*.

- **Baseband** carries one signal at a time. A bit value of 0 or 1 is sent by the presence or absence of a voltage in the cable. Baseband signals can travel very fast but can only be sent over short distances. Over about 1000 feet special booster equipment is needed.
- **Broadband** can carry multiple signals on a fixed carrier wave, with the signals for 0 and 1 sent as variations on this wave. Data, audio and video transmission can take place simultaneously.

The speed at which data is sent is expressed as the baud rate, measured in bits per second (bps). The computer code for a single character typically uses 7 or 8 bits, and in addition a start and stop bit and/or a parity bit is added to this, so that each character requires say 10 bits. Thus a speed of 56,000bps means that about 5,600 characters a second can be transmitted.

Modems

Telephone lines were originally designed for speech, which is transmitted in analogue or wave form. In order for digital data to be sent along a telephone line, it must first be converted to analogue form and then converted back at the other end, hence the need for a MOdulator/DEModulator. Modems typically transmit data at rates of between 9,600 and 56,600bps.

Figure 64.1: Modem

Direction of transmission

Communications software sets the transmission protocols that indicate the way that data will flow over the communications channel, which will be one of:

- **Simplex** – data can flow in one direction only. Electronic 'notice-boards' that receive and display information about, for example, train arrival times could use a simplex line, since communication is one-way only;

- **Half-duplex** – data can flow in both directions, but not at the same time, like a CB radio;

- **Full-duplex** – data can flow in both directions at the same time, like a telephone line where two people can both be talking at once.

Serial and parallel transmission

In serial transmission, each bit is transmitted one at a time over a single channel. There are two types of serial mode for sending data – synchronous and asynchronous. In asynchronous transmission, one character at a time is transmitted, with a start and stop bit sent with each character. This is generally used for lower speed transmission, for example on a local area network. Synchronous transmission enables whole blocks of data to be sent in timed sequences, and is much faster.

Figure 64.2: Serial transmission

In parallel transmission, all the bits making up a character, together with a parity bit (if used) are transmitted simultaneously. Parallel transmission is limited to communications over short distances of a few metres, for example between a computer and a printer.

Figure 64.3: Parallel transmission

Telecommunications standards and protocols

In order to allow machines from different manufacturers to communicate with each other over local or wide area networks, standards covering all aspects of communication from the number of pins on connectors to how a particular software package displays a menu at a user's terminal need to be defined.

Although having standards makes it possible to create networks containing hardware from different vendors (such as Apple and IBM), there are tradeoffs. Standards may disallow certain features or capabilities that are valuable in a particular situation but inconsistent with the standard. Standards may also prohibit features which certain vendors have built into their hardware in order to steal a march on the competition – something that is better than other architectures but will not work with other hardware. In spite of this, most people would rather have hardware that has less than the maximum capabilities but is compatible with their other hardware, and welcome the introduction of standards.

Standards can be divided into de facto standards and de jure standards. **De facto standards** are established by the fact that a particular product dominates the market, like Intel microprocessors or Microsoft's products. **De jure standards** are defined by industry groups or by government.

The **OSI** (Open System Interface) was created to guide the development of standards for communications between networked systems, regardless of technology, vendor or country of origin. The standards have been developed by an industry consortium called the International Standards Organisation, and they cover all aspects of network operations and management.

The OSI model divides a network's operation into seven layers (Table 64.4).

Layer	*Function*
1. Physical	Provides access to the telecommunications medium and ensures transmission of the bitstream over it. This includes specifying the type of transmission media, the type of connectors, the speed of transmission, the size and shape of the plug and number of pins on the connector.
2. Data Link	Ensures error-free transmission of blocks of data over a network link, by checking the data flowing in and out of each device on the network. It makes sure that no data loss occurs between two adjacent points in a network and corrects errors in transmission.
3. Network	Routes message (or packets of data) from source to destination and collects data related to billing for network services.
4. Transport	Ensures the integrity of each message from origin to destination. It uses communication software protocols to control the quality of transmissions, and synchronises fast and slow equipment to a rate the system can handle.
5. Session	Establishes, maintains and terminates a connection (session) between two applications running on communicating nodes. A session lasts, for example, from log-on to a specific application to log-off. It is also used for administrative tasks such as security.
6. Presentation	Provides any necessary conversion of characters being sent (encryption/decryption, compression/decompression, or character code conversions, e.g. ASCII to EBCDIC).
7. Application	Provides services to communication application programs; examples include file transfer, running a remote program, allocating a remote peripheral, and ensuring the integrity of remote databases. It defines how the network operating system interfaces with the application software. It also controls sign-on and password checks.

Table 64.4: The OSI seven layer model

As an example, imagine that a user at Node A (a PC) wants to send a file to a user at Node B (an Apple Mac) on a wide area network.

- The **application** layer on both nodes would receive User A's instructions and identify the file;
- The **presentation** layer would ensure that the file, when transferred, was in the appropriate format for the Apple Mac;
- The **session** layer initiates the transfer;
- The **transport** layer breaks up the file into packets (assuming this is a packet-switching network);
- The **network** layer routes the packets to Node B;
- The **data link** layer transmits packets over individual links, checking for errors;
- The **physical** layer makes sure the bits reach Node B.

In a **packet-switching** network, data is split up into separate 'packets' of say 256 bytes, together with identification, sequence and routing information, and each packet may be sent to its destination over a different route, via different computers. If the packets arrive out of sequence, the transport layer will sort them out on arrival.

Other standards and protocols such as IBM's Systems Network Architecture, and standards set up by other manufacturers, exist but there is a strong desire to have just one international standard which will provide a seamless system of communication between any type of network. The OSI model protocol will be the principal means of ensuring this.

Exercises

1. What is the difference between serial and parallel transmission of data? (2)

   NEAB IT05 Qu 1 1997

2. With the growth in computer systems being purchased for use on networks, there is a greater need for manufacturers to conform to standard protocols.

   (a) What are protocols and why are they required? (4)

   (b) The application layer is one of seven layers in the OSI model. Name **three** other layers. (3)

   (c) Briefly describe the role of the application layer in this model. (3)

   NEAB IT05 Qu 6 1997

3. What is the difference between analogue and digital transmission? (2)

   NEAB IT05 Qu 1 Sample paper

Chapter 65 – Human-Computer Interaction

Computers in the workplace

'Ergonomics' – the design and functionality of the environment – was discussed briefly in Chapter 14 (Health and Safety). Applying ergonomics successfully means studying the whole office environment to see how it can be made into a comfortable, safe and productive place in which to work. To begin with, simple measures such as persuading staff to tidy their desks or reorganise the office furniture so that people are not in danger of tripping over telephone and computer cables can achieve a great deal.

Lighting should be carefully chosen so that the office is neither overlit nor underlit, avoiding excessive contrast between lit and unlit areas, or patches of shadow falling on work areas. Computers should not face windows, as the glare will be unbearable, and nor should users be forced to sit facing a window with the sun in their eyes. The optimal position for computer monitors is side on to a window. Windows should have adjustable blinds so that the changing light from the sun can be controlled.

Furniture must be comfortable and adjustable. Poorly designed chairs are responsible for back trouble, and chairs at the wrong height can contribute to the onset of repetitive strain injury (RSI), an affliction which affects people who spend too many hours at a keyboard without breaks and in uncomfortable positions. Short people may need a footrest, and are now legally entitled to ask for one.

Environmental considerations have led to more manufacturers producing energy-efficient computer systems. It is estimated that the electricity used by computers accounts for between 5 and 10% of the USA's annual total commercial electricity bill. Research suggests that computers are used for only a tiny proportion of the time that they are switched on, with over a quarter of the nation's computers running overnight and at weekends. Energy-efficient computers and printers which go into 'sleep' mode, a low-power state, when the unit is inactive, stand to save US businesses $2 billion per year. Apart from the money, the use of energy-efficient products will reduce emission of carbon dioxide by 20 million tonnes, roughly comparable to the emissions of 5 million cars.

Psychological factors

Apart from the physical factors, there are numerous psychological factors which affect our interaction with computers. An understanding of how we receive, process and store information can be used to design effective, user-friendly interactive systems.

Information is received through senses, and a knowledge of human senses and skills is used by interface designers.

- **Vision**. Research has shown, for example, that the eye is less sensitive to blue light than to red or green, and therefore important information should not be displayed in blue text. Also, 8% of males and 1% of females are colour-blind, most commonly being unable to distinguish between red and green. Therefore, no interface should depend on everyone being able to distinguish colours.

- **Hearing**. Sound is commonly used for warning sounds in interfaces, for example to tell the user that they have tried to perform an illegal operation – humans can distinguish between a wide range of sounds and can react faster to auditory stimuli than to visual ones. The SonicFinder for the Macintosh uses auditory icons to represent desktop objects and actions. Copying is indicated by the sound of pouring liquid into a bottle. A file arriving in a mailbox sounds like a large parcel if it is very large, or a light packet if it is small.

- **Touch**. Touch is an important in keyboard and mouse design. The feeling of a button being depressed is an important part of the task of pressing it.
- **Movement**. Speed and accuracy are measures of motor skills and are important considerations in interface design. Users may find it difficult to manipulate small objects and so targets should generally be reasonably large.

Short-term memory

We have two main types of memory: short-term memory and long-term memory. Short-term memory is used for example to remember a telephone number for the length of time it takes to dial it after looking it up. The average person can remember 7 plus or minus 2 digits. Look at the number sequence

472081325

Now write it down. Did you get it right? Now try the sequence

649 723 106

Grouping the digits can increase short-term memory. It is also much easier to remember information that you can find a pattern in. For example, you probably won't be able to remember the sequence of letters

AST NIG HTW EWE NTT OTH ECI NEM AL

However, if you notice that by moving the last character to the first position, you will get a sentence by reblocking the letters into words instead of groups of three, you should have no trouble in being able to reproduce the letters.

Long-term memory

Long-term memory is used for the long-term storage of information – factual information, experiential knowledge and 'rules' about behaviour and procedures are stored here. It differs from short-term memory in a number of respects. Firstly, it has an almost limitless capacity. Secondly, it has a relatively slow access time of approximately a tenth of a second. Thirdly, forgetting occurs much more slowly in long-term memory.

Information can be moved from short-term memory to long-term memory by rehearsal or repetition. In addition, information is easier to remember if it is meaningful. Thus, it is difficult to remember a series of unconnected words such as

Violet hope see gannet builder green yesterday new sadly may

but much easier to memorise a sentence such as

I'll have a crocodile sandwich and make it snappy.

In other words, learning is aided by structure and familiarity.

We all carry around with us a mental picture of how the world works, put together from experiences stored in long-term memory. Consider the sentences:

Richard took his cat to the surgery. After seeing the vet he took the cat home.

You will probably assume from this that Richard consulted the vet, the cat was treated, Richard paid the bill and they left – rather than assuming that Richard took one look at the vet and took the cat home immediately.

Principles and results from research in psychology have been distilled into guidelines for designing user interfaces.

> ➤ **Discussion: One guiding principle for interface design is that you should never use an image which contradicts our mental image of how things are – for example, Red means Stop, Green means Go. Can you think of other examples?**

Designing good software

Interacting with computers can be a daunting, frightening and incomprehensible business to novices, and on occasion an infuriating experience for experts. Repeated failure with a new software package is frustrating and depressing and soon becomes boring. Researchers into human-computer interaction (HCI) study good software design to see what makes it good, and observe people interacting with computers to find out what they find easy, and which parts of the software lead them to make more errors than necessary, or what difficulties they encounter.

Figure 65.1: HCI design cycle

The best user interfaces provide:

- Help for novice users;

- Short cuts for experts;

- 'Metaphors' or images which are meaningful, such as the letter *W* on the icon for Word, or a picture of a printer for a print tool;

- Consistent behaviour which makes use of long-term memory, such as always using the function key F1 for Help, or the Escape key to get out of trouble;

- Clear, helpful error messages;

- Uncluttered screens with effective use of colour, with text that is easy to read.

Text versus graphics

The graphical user interface is appealing and generally far easier to use than a command interface, but sometimes icons cannot express an abstract concept and menus of one kind or another are essential.

Specialist products such as a travel agent's package may use a command interface in preference to a GUI because graphical interfaces generally:

- Occupy more memory;

- Need more space on disk;

- Run more slowly if complex graphics and many windows are open;

- Can be more time-consuming for an experienced operator than simply typing in a command.

Exercises

1. A new shopping centre requires a computerised interactive information system. The system is to have a number of information points distributed throughout the centre. The diagram below shows a plan of the centre.

Key ● computerised information point

▢ Outlets (shops, banks, cafes etc)

The computerised information points have to provide information on each of the following:

Shops; Restaurants; Toilets; Disabled facilities; Advertising; A map of the centre; Banking services.

(a) The system has to have a suitable user interface.

Describe aspects which should be considered when designing the user interface. (4)

(b) Individual outlets will have the facility to use the system to provide up-to-the-minute details of special offers, opening hours, etc.

Describe the hardware and software that would be necessary to implement this facility. (3)

SEB Paper 1 Qu 11 1995

2. (a) Give **six** of the physical and psychological factors which govern how people interact with computer systems. (6)

(b) Give **three** factors which should be considered when providing a sophisticated human-computer interface, explaining the impact of each one on the system's resources. (6)

NEAB IT05 Qu 7 1997

3. (a) What are the factors you need to take into account when designing a screen layout for a database application? (6)

(b) What are the resource implications for providing a sophisticated human/computer interface? (4)

NEAB IT05 Qu 9 Sample Paper

4. The term 'human-computer interface' is used to describe the means of interaction between a computer and its human user. Since microcomputers were first introduced, the design of suitable human-computer interfaces has presented a number of problems.

(a) Name and briefly describe **four** distinct solutions which have been developed by software writers to address these problems. (4)

(b) Discuss an advantage and disadvantage to each of the solutions which you have given in your answer to part (a). (8)

(c) Describe how each solution would detect and deal with an invalid input from the user. (4)

(d) The aim of a human-computer interface is to make interaction with a computer as efficient and effective as possible. Describe **four** criteria which could be used to judge the 'user-friendliness' of any piece of software. (4)

London Computing AS Paper 1 Qu 9 1997

Chapter 66 – Music software

Introduction

In the next few chapters we'll be looking at some specialised applications of computers. Each of these applications has features and functions unique to its purpose and, as we shall see, each package can only be used really effectively by a specialist in the field.

This chapter describes some of the features and facilities available in software packages designed to create, edit and play back all types of sounds, especially music.

Music on the micro

Sound is an important factor in most multimedia packages, from games to encyclopedias playing snippets of Beethoven's 9th Symphony or Madonna's latest hit single. Digital sound technology offers the opportunity to create, modify and hear your own music to the same quality as on top hi-fi equipment.

Sound card

The basic piece of hardware required is a **sound card**, which fits into a vacant slot in the PC. Sound starts off as waves of pressure in the air. Before the computer can store this, it must be digitised – turned into numbers. To hear the sound, the computer must turn the digitised sound back to analogue. The sound card does the conversion from analogue to digital and vice versa.

The sampling rate and the resolution of the sound card determines the quality and accuracy of the sound produced. The **sampling rate** tells you how often the sound card takes a digital snapshot of the sound wave – the higher the sampling rate, the greater the accuracy of the sample (see Figure 66.1). 'CD quality' sound requires a sampling rate of about 44,000 samples per second: a 44kHz frequency.

The **resolution** of the sound card determines how accurately the amplitude of the sound can be measured. An 8-bit sound board uses 8 bits of data to measure sound wave amplitude giving 256 (2^8) sound levels, whereas a 16-bit sound card using 16 bits can represent 65,536 (2^{16}) levels of amplitude.

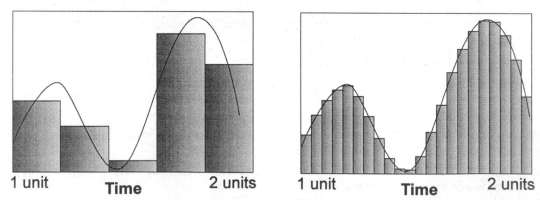

Figure 66.1: Increasing the number of samples in 1 time 'unit' (fraction of a second) means that the sound is more faithfully represented

The sound card also has a built-in **synthesiser** for producing music and sound effects.

MIDI (Musical Instrument Digital Interface)

MIDI is an industry standard applied to electronic musical instruments as well as hardware, cables, connectors and data formats. Adding a MIDI interface to a computer allows it to communicate with, say, a MIDI keyboard, drum pad or guitar.

The MIDI data system stores all the information about each note to be played on the synthesiser, including the pitch, length, dynamics and type of sound. MIDI data in this format is very compact, taking only about 1/20th of the space on disk of even the lowest quality recorded sound samples. For example, a minute's worth of MIDI synthesised music occupies about 30Kb of disk space compared with 600Kb of low quality recorded sound.

Floppy disks and CDs containing MIDI music files can be loaded into a PC's memory and played through a sound card or synthesiser. Because the data is stored as 'instructions' rather than recorded sound, you can speed it up or slow it down, change the pitch, turn a keyboard solo into a voice or guitar solo, or alter the balance between several synthesised instruments.

MIDI Interface   MIDI Synthesiser

Figure 66.2: A MIDI interface connects a keyboard to a computer

Software for creating music

There are two basic types of software for creating music: sequencers and notators. There is some overlap between these categories, with each being able to perform some of the functions of the other.

A **sequencer** is like a multi-track recording studio that allows music to be built up from many separate parts. It can be used by people with relatively little theoretical musical knowledge and, in much the same way as a word processor, it allows complex sound files to be built up from existing files. Facilities are provided to copy, edit, cut, blend and paste sections to create a brand new composition which can then be played back. Magix Music Maker is an example of a package containing over 1000 samples of music and sounds that can be used and arranged in much the same way as clip art.

All the samples on the CD are in 16bit, stereo and 44.1kHz; absolutely top CD quality. If however you want to save memory or use the arrangement for sound mixing, you can convert the music maker samples to 22kHz and/or mono. Use the software to:

- *Create a drumbeat accompaniment*
- *Add music and effects to videos*
- *Make accompanying patterns to go with instrument practice*

Please note that all samples used in an arrangement must be loaded in the computer's RAM. As a general rule,

16Mb holds 100 seconds
8Mb holds 50 seconds

Figure 66.3: A sequencer program to create music

Composing music

Traditionally, composers write music by selecting a key signature, number of beats in the bar, combination of instruments and so on, and then writing each note down on a sheet of manuscript paper. Computers cannot help with most of this – the composer still has to make all the decisions, and decide what notes are going to be used in the tune. But using a computer to write down the music has all of the advantages of a word processor over an old-fashioned typewriter; the music can easily be cut, rearranged and edited.

Using software such as 'Finale', an image resembling a clean sheet of manuscript paper can be displayed on the screen. After inserting the key signature and time signature, the musician then plays each note on the keyboard and presses a key to denote the length of the note – say 5 for a crotchet, 4 for a quaver, 3 for a semi-quaver and so on. The musical notes appear on the screen as they are played. Alternatively, the notes can be 'typed' in without using a musical keyboard.

Once the tune has been recorded, it can be played back, edited and printed out. The musician can, for example:

- Change the key (transpose the music up or down);
- Change the tempo;
- Organise the music on the page, adding slurs, dynamics and other musical signs;
- Add lyrics (words to a tune);
- Extract individual band parts from a complete score, and print them separately;
- Organise several pages of a score before printing it out.

Using technical knowledge

When a musician enters musical notes from a MIDI keyboard or other input device, the computer does not always know what is the 'grammatically correct' note to print on the stave. For example, D sharp and E flat sound the same, but are written one way or the other depending on the key of the music. The line shown in Figure 66.4 was entered by playing the notes on a keyboard:

Figure 66.4: Notes stored by the computer using 'Finale' software

A musician would know that this line should be written as shown in Figure 66.5.

Figure 66.5: The notes corrected manually by a musician

Editing music

The example above shows the level of technical knowledge needed to make effective use of a sophisticated notation package such as Finale. The package assumes a knowledge of music: look at Figure 66.6 which shows a typical dialogue box used in editing the printed music.

Figure 66.6: Musical knowledge is required to use the package

Tidying up the score

A music software package will enable a musician to enter and edit notes, add lyrics and a host of musical symbols. But although it may take only a few minutes to enter the basic composition, it can take many hours of painstaking work to achieve the same quality of printed output as a copyist doing the same thing manually. In Figure 66.7 (a), the musician has entered a simple tune and added words. The computer by default gives the same space to each of the four bars of music, which causes a log-jam of words in the first bar:

Figure 66.7: Editing written music

Work of this nature takes years of training and practice!

Editing sound waves

A third, less common type of software allows the digitised sound wave pattern to be manipulated. Windows 3.1 and Windows 95 Sound Recorder are examples of this. Generally, sound wave editing is used for editing short recorded sounds of a few seconds duration. However, software of this type can also be used to edit digitised audio recordings to remove extraneous noise such as someone coughing in the audience. It can be used in the same way as old-fashioned 'tape-splicing', so that a recording of someone saying "I love Man United and I hate the Spice Girls" can be edited by cutting and pasting to be replayed as "I hate Man United and I love the Spice Girls".

Figure 66.8: A sound wave can be edited

Exercises

1. A recording studio is considering providing a range of specialist software solutions to support its musical recording and composition work.

   List **six** features you would expect such software to include. (6)

   NEAB IT05 Qu 2 1997

2. "Specialist application knowledge is required to make effective use of a software package for composing and writing down music."

   State whether you agree or disagree with this statement, giving **three** examples to back up your point of view. (6)

   New question

Chapter 67 – Geographical Information Systems

An overview of GIS

A Geographical Information System (GIS) is the high-tech equivalent of a map. Maps have been in existence for thousands of years, and are used in numerous applications from finding a route from A to B and locating underground pipes and telephone cables, to displaying population shifts over a period of years and showing economic data.

> ➤ **Discussion: What other data can be shown on geographical maps?**

Maps in their traditional paper form suffer from a number of disadvantages:

- They are difficult and expensive to keep up-to-date;
- They exist on separate sheets of paper and inevitably the area that you are interested in lies at the corner of three or four different sheets;
- They can be very complex and require an expert to interpret;
- It is difficult to overlay different types of information on a single map (e.g. rainfall, plagues of locusts, crops) in order to analyse the data.

A GIS provides the facility to store a multitude of different sets of geographical data and produce a paper map of exactly the right area, showing the information that the user is interested in. It can be defined as an information system that is designed to work with data referenced by spatial or geographic coordinates. It is both a database with specific capabilities for spatially referenced data, as well as a set of operations for working with or analysing the data. For example, by overlaying two maps showing rainfall and population densities, it becomes possible to analyse the relationship between where the most rainfall is and where people settle.

> *"A GIS is a system for capturing, storing, checking, integrating, manipulating, analysing and displaying data which are spatially referenced to Earth."*
> (Chorley, 1987)

Using a GIS in the utilities industry

Many utility companies have implemented a GIS to document their pipelines or cables. British Gas, for example, uses a GIS to document the location, depth, size and maintenance records of their pipes. Other companies, such as the water company described below, are looking into the possibility of installing a GIS to help them to:

- Improve the efficiency of operations by reducing costs;
- Improve levels of service to customers by providing a more fault-free service;
- Improve decision-making in the company by providing access to up-to-date information.

The water company supplying water to about 60,000 properties in the Tendring Peninsula has a network of mains about 1,000Km in length. Details of these mains are recorded on several hundred drawings kept at head office. The plans show pipe diameter, material, class and year laid together with information about abandonments. Copies of the printed plans are made and used to record data on burst pipes. If a pipe bursts, a colour-coded sticker is placed on the plan to mark the location, with the colour denoting the year the burst occurred.

Various other plans exist to show soil corrosiveness, parish boundaries, bulk meter areas and water quality zones.

Information relating to abandoned mains, burst main repairs, relining, water quality and soft cleaning (air scouring, swabbing and flushing) is stored on a database. Pipes are identified by their map reference, but in practice when pipes are cleaned, for example, it is often difficult to record exactly which stretch of pipe has had the work done. A GIS could also be used to generate a set of detailed maps showing the exact location of the underground network in relation to roads and houses, giving details of all the pipes and the position of valves and other fittings. This would help in locating plastic pipes, which once laid, cannot easily be found.

A GIS would enable the information to be stored and displayed geographically, and would also be able to record precisely the location of bursts. Analyses could be performed relating, for example, to soil corrosiveness and frequency of bursts.

GIS in business

The Department of Geography at Edinburgh has a large database relating to the Edinburgh area, containing satellite imagery of Edinburgh and its environs, a street network for the city and detailed locations for individual buildings in the city centre. One of the many uses for the street network involves the modelling of service distribution networks within the capital. The model can be used as a decision-making tool which could save time and money and provide a better service to customers. For example, a system has been developed to look at the implications of the move by a newspaper printing and distribution centre to a different part of the city. Since timing in the delivery of newspapers to newsagents is critical, the aim was to identify the best possible delivery routes.

Marks and Spencer use GIS to help them decide where to open new stores. They can analyse customer profiles, define fuel-efficient delivery routes and use the GIS to generate 'What-if' scenarios to assist in decision-making. These facilities were used to assess the potential for business in Japan, with the result that M & S decided to cancel plans to enter this market.

Sainsbury, Asda, Halfords and Woolworths also use GIS systems to assist strategic planning.

Environmental applications of GIS

GIS are used in many environmental applications, such as, for example:

- Collating, displaying and analysing data about plagues of locusts. The eradication of locusts remains the single most important factor in the prevention of famine in major areas of the world. By analysing the location of plagues, together with historical data for precipitation, temperature and wind, it may be possible to improve pest control methods.

- A computer model of the Greenland Ice Sheet has been developed which simulates how the ice mass responds to changes in global climate or sea level.

- Deforestation over time in the Amazon Basin is monitored by storing and processing data collected from satellite imagery.

Data capture

Capturing the data for a GIS is a time-consuming and painstaking business. The main methods used are:

- Hand-tracing a map with a mouse or 'puck' to collect coordinates of features;

- Using an electronic scanning device to convert map lines and points to digits;

- Keying in the data.

The Colne Valley Water Company, for example, keyed in details of 2,700 Km of pipes together with 'attribute data' showing 12,000 burst locations, all dialysis patients and all sites of special scientific interest. It took 22 temporary staff almost a year to survey, digitise and enter textual data.

Laser mapping equipment operated from an aircraft can give be used to input a quick, accurate reading of the height of land. The laser scanner shoots out beams at the rate of 5,000 to 10,000 per second, scanning the ground at 2-metre intervals, and the time taken for the laser beam to travel to the ground and back again is measured. The height of the aircraft above the ground is simultaneously measured using GPS (Global Positioning System) satellites to give measurements of the lie of the land which are accurate to about 10cm. The computer then converts the data into a 3-D model or map giving a colour-coded representation of height.

This system is being used by an environmental agency to map the flood plains around Christchurch, Dorset, which is prone to flooding when the River Stour and the River Avon burst their banks. Flood risk maps can then be produced, and the system can simulate the effect of a flood so that flood defence schemes can be put in place.

Case study: GIS to the rescue

A new GIS system designed to assist with mountain rescue is undergoing trials in the Lake District. The system uses radio handsets, rugged portable computers and GPS (Global Positioning System). The system is used to help co-ordinate rescues, allowing stranded climbers and walkers to be found quicker. It also ensures that volunteer searchers can be traced if they set off in bad weather.

Each of the digital radio handsets has a built-in GPS unit that transmits its location back to base. This allows the search to be organised from headquarters, ensuring that the areas to be covered are divided efficiently. Each team carries a rugged palmtop PC on which maps of the area are stored. These are constantly updated by the central co-ordinator over the radio network. Once an area has been searched, it is shaded on the map. The computerised maps also allow everyone involved in the rescue to know where the others are.

When a missing person is found, the GPS equipment shows the precise location to all the search parties, and allows the emergency services to get a precise reference point if evacuation by helicopter is required.

Exercises

1. The planning department of a large supermarket chain uses a software package known as
    Geographical Information System (GIS). Give and explain **one** category of data the software would
    need to store to help decision-making concerning:

    (a) the best location for a new supermarket;   (2)

    (b) the most appropriate products the new supermarket should stock.   (2)

    The two categories should be different.

    AEB Computing Paper 1 Qu 7 1997

2. Describe briefly **three** features of GIS software that would be useful to an Electricity Company,
    explaining in each case why the feature you described would be useful.   (6)

    New question

3. Describe **three** ways in which a GIS could be used in the protection of the environment.   (6)

    New question

Chapter 68 – CAD/CAM Systems

CAD systems

CAD (Computer-Aided Design) systems generally consist of a complete hardware and software package, ranging from micro systems available for around £1000 to sophisticated systems used in aircraft and automobile design, costing hundreds of thousands of pounds.

These systems act as tools for designers, not replacing their skills but aiding them in the fast and accurate production of drawings. The benefits of CAD can be summed up as:

- Accuracy;
- Repeatability;
- Speed and flexibility of production.

Ford, for example, use CAD technology and rapid prototyping machines to develop and test early product designs, yielding savings of up to 90% and cost savings of up to 70%. CAD/CAM systems can eliminate backtracking and costly changes and enable Ford to respond quickly to changes in customer demand, reducing the 'time to market' of new products.

Figure 68.1: Ford car design – CAD or hand-drawn?

Specialised hardware for CAD systems

A CAD workstation may be a standalone system, possibly linked to other workstations so that peripherals can be shared, or it may be connected to a mini or mainframe computer. Either way it will have, in addition to its own or a shared processor, input and output hardware chosen from a range of devices available, some of which are described below:

- A high resolution CRT display — typically between 1024 by 1024 and 4096 by 4096 pixels. Most graphics systems use colour screens;
- Sometimes a separate monitor is used for displaying the commands entered by the operator;
- A keyboard for entering commands;

- Programmable function box to allow the operator additional control of functions performed on the screen;

- A joystick;

- A graphics tablet, which contains a grid that corresponds to the resolution of the CRT. Thus, using a hand-held cursor, stylus (similar to a pen) or mouse, any x and y coordinates on the tablet can be mapped directly onto the screen;

- A light pen, an input device which allows the user to interface directly with the CRT display. It allows the user to pick a point or character on the screen and cause some action to be taken;

- A flatbed or drum plotter, which may have up to ten pens of different colours to produce high quality coloured drawings;

- A printer. Ink-jet, laser and thermal printers are among the options for output.

CAD software

CAD systems obviously vary enormously in their capabilities. The more sophisticated systems allow a user to:

- Draw straight lines and polygons, shading them if required;

- Draw mathematically defined curves including circles, arcs, ellipses, parabolas and hyperbolas;

- Move sections of a drawing to different locations;

- Scale or rotate an object;

- Zoom in on a section of a drawing.

Engineering and other drawings can be built up using a 'layer' system, with different features placed on different layers, much like overhead projector transparencies laid on top of each other. Construction lines can be placed on one layer, for example, and a two-dimensional drawing on a second layer. Any combination of layers can then be viewed.

Once a 3-D model has been created, the user can select two-dimensional views or different three-dimensional views.

Figure 68.2: A three-dimensional object created in AutoCAD can be shown from different views

320

Having made a two-dimensional drawing of an object, the software can then show the object in three dimensions, rotate it, shade it, show a view from any angle and shrink or expand it along a given dimension. Properties such as centre of gravity can be calculated. Drawings can be stored in a library on disk for future use. Large aerospace companies, for example, have libraries on disk containing over a million drawings.

Figure 68.3: Different shaded views of the object

Advantages of CAD

Using CAD has many advantages over hand-drawn designs. For example:

- Once the drawing has been created and stored in the computer, it can be used in a CAM system (see below) to manufacture the product or mould.

- The drawing is created by inputting the dimensions and geometry of each line, so that drawings can be held to accuracies of thousandths of a millimetre.

- The CAD system can analyse the properties of a part, and calculate its 'mass properties' such as volume, weight, radii of gyration, bounding box (i.e. how big a box would be required to contain it).

- It saves hours of time, and the drawing can be reproduced and edited, always maintaining top quality, unlike drawings that have been done by hand and rubbed out or altered.

- A wire frame drawing can be rendered to give a realistic image, and one or more 'light sources' introduced to show it lit from different angles. A 3-D model can be shown to a customer who can then readily understand and appreciate the design: in two dimensions, the customer would need to be able to interpret the drawings (e.g. Figure 68.2) and understand the orthographic projection system.

Disadvantages of CAD

Despite the enormous power and versatility of CAD, manual methods still have their place. An industrial designer generally has a high level of freehand drawing skills, and is able to produce realistic perspective drawings. A creative designer may be able to produce drawings that have a high level of impact by exaggerating certain features and introducing an element of personality or 'soul' that cannot be copied by a computer. Manual drawing methods encourage creativity: rather than concentrating on the software, the designer can focus on the creative aspects.

Other disadvantages include:

- Cost – AutoCAD software for a single user costs around £4,000;

- Retraining – many designers need expensive retraining to convert from manual methods to CAD;

- System maintenance – if several CAD terminals are in use, it is generally necessary to have a CAD manager to look after the computers, order new hardware and software as required and generally oversee the running of the system.

Bitmapped versus vector-based graphics

There are two different kinds of graphics; **bitmapped** (also known as pixel-based) and **vector-based** (also known as object-oriented). Paint programs and scanners produce bitmapped images in the form of a collection of pixels, the smallest visual unit that the computer can address. These applications create images by altering the colours or attributes of each individual pixel, and the amount of memory taken up by the image is dependent on the resolution of the display adapter where the image was first created. As a result, finished bitmap images are difficult to edit when you transfer them from one application to another. If you increase the size of a finished bitmap image, you see unsightly white spaces and jagged edges. If you greatly decrease the size of a finished bitmap image, parts of the image may 'smudge' because of the compression involved. Distortion can occur if you transfer bitmapped images to another computer that has a different display resolution.

(i)   (ii)   (iii)

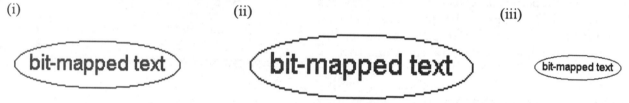

Figure 68.4: Bitmapped graphic image created in a PAINT package: (i) original size (ii) expanded (iii) shrunk

Object-oriented graphics, on the other hand, have none of these limitations. The information used to create and represent a drawing is real geometric data, rather than graphic data. For example, a line is defined by its endpoints, length, width, colour, and so on. A CAD program (and object-oriented graphics software such as CorelDRAW!) then uses this information to create a representation of the line on the computer screen. Since this method of storing information has nothing to do with the resolution of a given display adapter, line-art is considered to be **device-independent**. No matter what computer you use to create an object-oriented graphic, you can stretch, scale and resize it flexibly without distortion. Object-oriented graphics also tend to create smaller files than bitmapped images because the computer does not have to store the attributes of each individual pixel.

(i)   (ii)   (iii)

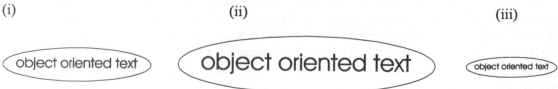

Figure 68.5: An object-oriented graphic created in CorelDRAW!: (i) original size, (ii) expanded, (iii) shrunk.

Another characteristic of CAD programs is the degree of accuracy that can be attained. Since a CAD program works with real geometric data, you can easily draw lines that meet exactly at a point, or move a line to a precise location, or draw an arc of an exact degree. When you zoom in on a portion of a line, no degradation occurs, and you can get an infinite degree of magnification. (The resolution of the laser printer may, as in this case, make the image appear less than perfectly smooth.) Using bitmapped graphics, by contrast, a line degrades when you zoom in and you see the individual pixels.

CAM (Computer-aided manufacturing)

This is the other side of the CAD coin. A complete CAD/CAM system will enable, say, an engineering component to be designed and manufactured using numerically controlled machine tools. The computer performs calculations for defining the tool path and generates the instructions necessary to produce the part. An interactive CAM system will first simulate the machining operation so that the user can make sure the tool does not collide with clamps or fixtures, and make any necessary adjustments before going 'live'.

One of the great benefits of CAD/CAM is 'flexible manufacturing', enabling product changes to be made quickly and inexpensively. Not only is a much wider range of products easily produced but manufacturers are able to respond quickly to current demands, making modifications to their products without the delays that would previously have resulted from a change in setup.

Case study: Rearranging the office furniture

Carleton Furniture is a company who provide furniture for customers such as British Gas, British Telecom, BP and ICL. Services include floorspace planning, full refurbishment and furnishing offices. Typical contracts deal with the refurbishment of large government offices and the furnishing of student residential halls.

When an important customer recently asked for a special order, Carleton Furniture responded within hours. The speed of response – just over a year ago it would have taken a week and a half – won the £150,000 order. The detailed specification of a desk, drawn and fully costed, had taken half a day.

Even more important, the specification put together at such speed actually worked. The people who had to execute the design by cutting the metal and fitting parts, knew their system would not design something that could not be built.

Carleton designers rely on a computer-aided design product, but design is only part of the story. It has also capitalised on its ability to produce quick CAD drawings to launch a specialised service in space planning. A recent £800,000 order was won because the company was able to produce a space-plan within a very tight deadline, partly because it could read in existing measurements from the client's own AutoCAD package.

The company spokesman offered some emphatic do's and don'ts for companies setting out to implement CAD software. "Don't underestimate the culture change that needs to take place within the business", he said. "It's taken us a year longer than we expected. Do make sure you get on with your suppliers. At the end of the day you're investing a great deal: if you can't get on with them, don't do it, however good the software."

> Questions:

a. Outline **six** features of a Computer Aided Design system. (6)

b. Describe briefly **three** advantages to the company of using this system. (3)

c. What sort of 'culture change' do you think would take place in a company as a result of the introduction of such a system? (3)

d. Why is it so important to 'get on with your suppliers'? (3)

e. Describe the difference between bitmapped graphics and vector-based graphics. Why do CAD systems use vector-based graphics? (5)

Exercises

1. A designer in a sector of manufacturing industry is using a workstation with a CAD package. As the designer develops a 2D drawing on the screen, at regular intervals each stage can be added to a hard copy *on the same single sheet of paper* so that at any time this sheet of paper reflects the current state of the designer's drawing as it appears on the screen.

    (a) Outline **two** advantages which CAD offers manufacturing industry. (4)

    (b) Describe, with the aid of examples, the fundamental difference between an object-oriented CAD package and a pixel-based general drawing package. (6)

    (c) Describe, and explain the need for, **three** features of a CAD workstation which distinguish it from a workstation used in a typical business application. (6)

    (d) Compare the operation of a plotter and a dot-matrix printer in producing hard copy of a line drawing. Indicate, giving reasons for your answer, the suitability or otherwise of each for producing the hard copy required by the designer in this case. (8)

    NICCEA Computing Paper 2 1993

2. The management of a local college has decided to buy a computer-aided design (CAD) package to help plan the best use of the available space in the college.

    (a) Describe suitable hardware to support the use of the package. (4)

    (b) Identify **two** features available in a CAD package that are not generally found in a simple drawing package. (2)

    (c) Give, with reasons, **three** advantages of using a CAD package rather than manual methods for this application. (4)

    (d) At various times the management is required to produce statistical reports using a spreadsheet with data currently held in the CAD package. Describe the functionality required by the CAD package to allow this to happen. (2)

    NEAB IT05 Sample Paper

3. Officefurn is a company that provides furniture for large corporate customers. Typical contracts deal with the refurbishment of large offices or hotels.

    The designers use a computer aided design (CAD) package to provide a specialised service demonstrating to clients how best to use their available space.

    (a) State **three** features common to a CAD package and a general purpose graphics package. (3)

    (b) Describe the advantages of using the services offered by Officefurn for each of the following groups of people:

    • The customers

    • The workers who build the furniture

    • The designers. (6)

    (c) State **three** features that distinguish a CAD package from a general purpose graphics package. (3)

    (d) Describe and justify the specialised peripheral equipment required by such a CAD system. (3)

    London Computing Paper 2 Qu 9 1996

Chapter 69 – Mathematical and Statistical Software

Spreadsheets

The most familiar of all mathematical packages is the spreadsheet, used not only in countless business applications but also for statistical analyses. In addition to being able to enter numbers, text and formulae, a spreadsheet package such as Excel offers a range of advanced features for business use.

Sales forecasting tools

Goal Seeker can determine how many items, like houses, you need to sell to generate a total sales figure of, say, £1 million.

	A	B	C	D	E
1	Sales Forecast using Goal Seek				
2					
3	Average Price	75,000			
4	Number to sell				
5	Total Sales	0			
6					

Using Tools, Goal Seek, you can enter…

...and the software calculates the solution:

	A	B	C	D	E	F	G	H
1	Sales Forecast using Goal Seek							
2								
3	Average Price	75,000						
4	Number to sell	13.33333						
5	Total Sales	1000000						
6								
7								
8								
9								
10								

Goal Seek Status

Goal Seeking with Cell B5 found a solution.

Target value: 1000000
Current value: 1000000

OK   Cancel   Step   Pause

Figure 69.1: Using the Goal Seek function in Excel

More sophisticated add-ins like 'Solver' will calculate the optimum sales of several different products to achieve certain targets, subject to constraints specified by the user.

Statistical functions

Excel provides more than 70 different statistical functions from the simple ones like SUM, MAX, MIN to sophisticated analysis tools.

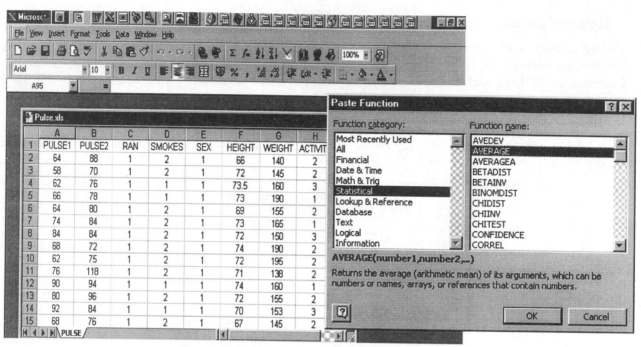

Figure 69.2: Some of the Excel statistical functions

Graphing tools

Spreadsheets offer a wide range of graphing tools such as line graphs, pie charts, bar graphs and scatter diagrams. Excel has a feature called Data Map which has a range of maps of various countries stored in a library, on which can be superimposed, say, dots representing population density. (This is one facility that you could expect to find also in a GIS – see Chapter 67.)

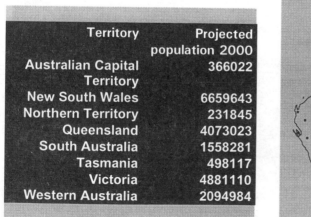

Territory	Projected population 2000
Australian Capital Territory	366022
New South Wales	6659643
Northern Territory	231845
Queensland	4073023
South Australia	1558281
Tasmania	498117
Victoria	4881110
Western Australia	2094984

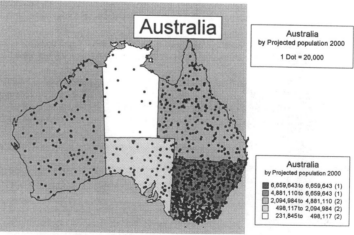

Figure 69.3: Map Data software shows information in a spatial context

Specialised statistical packages

Statistics – the art of collecting and analysing data – has assumed even greater importance in an age where computers can provide us with mountains of data in the twinkle of an eye. We are deluged with consumer data, political, economic, sports, weather and scientific data. Does raising the minimum wage increase unemployment? Does living near a nuclear power station increase the risk of developing leukemia? Has the introduction of tuition fees reduced the number of students applying for Higher Education? Does the current weather pattern suggest that a hurricane may be imminent? Statistical analysis attempts to provide answers to questions such as these.

Statistical analysis software can help to uncover relationships between variables, and test the strength of the relationships. Statisticians may be able to uncover trends by looking at two- and three-dimensional graphs generated by the software. Clearly, however, a knowledge of statistical techniques and mathematics is required to be able to make use of these specialised packages.

The SPSS Professional Statistics packages, for example, provide facilities for:

- Measuring similarities and differences in data;
- Performing different types of statistical analysis;
- Forecasting and time series analysis;
- Producing a variety of presentation-quality tabular reports;
- Producing graphical displays, including displays of multiple response data.

Case study: Using statistics to stop drink drivers

The Cleveland police have used the statistical package SPSS to help them in their fight against drink driving. The software has been used to analyse statistics gathered from breath tests, working out the most likely times, dates and locations for catching offenders. As a result, in 1997 the rate of drink-driving in Cleveland dropped to the point that it has become one of the lowest in the country.

The statistics software has also been used to analyse and improve the public's level of satisfaction with the police. The analysis revealed, for example, that whereas 90% of victims wanted to be told how an investigation was progressing, only 40% were informed. The police are now considering changing the format of their computer files so that feedback is sure to be given.

The police also plan to use the software to look at correlations between crime and its causes so that they can optimise their use of resources in high crime areas.

Mathematical software

Traditionally, computer programs work on the basis of fast, accurate numerical calculations. Nowadays mathematical software is available which can perform algebra as well. This includes:

- Rearranging formulae;
- Solving algebraic equations exactly;
- Calculus techniques such as differentiation and integration;
- Working with vectors and matrices;
- Mathematical function plotting in two and three dimensions.

Commonly used computer algebra packages include Mathematica, Mathcad and Derive. A typical 'session' using Derive is shown below:

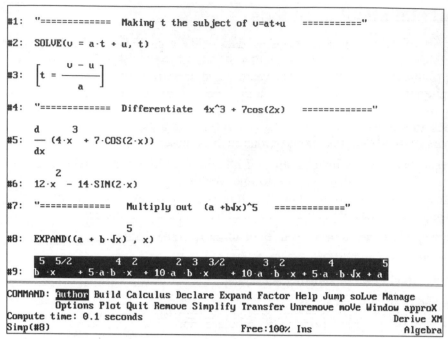

Figure 69.4: Using Derive mathematical software

The advantage of using computer algebra packages is to obtain exact algebraic solutions which are not affected by roundoff error.

Simulation software

Computer simulations are widely used in physical, biological and social sciences as well as in engineering and military applications. They have numerous advantages.

- **Safety**: it is possible, for example, to simulate a nuclear explosion, a car crash or an earthquake and study the effects;

- **Economy**: it is much cheaper to build a computer model of a car and mathematically test the design for strength, wind resistance, fuel efficiency and so on without actually having to build it;

- **Forecasting**: environmentalists, for example, can study the likely effects of deforestation in the Amazon Basin or the lowering of the water table due to increased water usage;

- **Replication**: in the real world it can be difficult or impossible to recreate the conditions under which an experiment was made but, using a computer model, a simulation can be run as many times as needed, changing one or more variables each time.

Exercises

1. Give **three** examples of different facilities you would expect to find in a spreadsheet package that would be useful to each of:
   - (a) a business executive preparing sales forecasts; (3)
   - (b) a statistician employed by the Government to investigate the relationship between poverty and respiratory disease in a particular area of the country. (3)

   New question

2. Describe briefly **three** different types of problem that would require the use of specialist mathematical or statistical software. List **one** (different) feature of the software which would be particularly useful in each case. (9)

   New question

Chapter 70 – Project Management Software

Problems with software projects

Projects of all kinds from bridge- and house-building to computerisation are vulnerable to delay, cost overruns or failure. A catastrophe such as a bridge collapsing or a space shuttle catching fire, however, is likely to be the subject of a massive public enquiry, and the lessons learned often lead to important advances in engineering and construction. When software projects fail, however, silence often follows, although the consequences of failure may have a huge negative impact on an organisation and even lead to bankruptcy. Capers Jones, an expert on software productivity writing in 1989, estimated that for projects involving over 64,000 lines of code:

- Up to 25% of projects were cancelled before completion;

- Up to 60% experienced significant cost and schedule overruns, with many being over a year late and costing twice as much as originally estimated;

- Less than 1% met all the user requirements and were completed on time and within budget;

- As many as 75% of completed projects experienced quality problems resulting in operational difficulties and excessive maintenance costs.

From these statistics it is clear that software projects are particularly difficult to cost and manage. However, any large project such as building the Channel Tunnel or the Millennium Dome has to be very tightly managed and controlled if it is to be completed on time and within budget.

Planning a project

Once a project has been defined and agreed, there are various steps to be followed in the planning process.

Step 1:	Generate a task list.
Step 2:	Clarify roles and responsibilities.
Step 3:	Estimate timing.
Step 4:	Identify task interdependencies and critical path.
Step 5:	Develop a schedule and confirm team assignments.
Step 6:	Analyse risk and devise contingency plans.

Planning a sample project

As an example we'll look at a project which is to analyse, design and implement a new timetabling system in a college. We'll go through the steps that have to be performed, and then see how project management software could be used to help control the project.

For the sample project, all the tasks first have to be written down. They then have to be placed in the correct sequence, and the immediate predecessor of each task identified. One way of doing this is to write each task on a piece of paper or Post-It note and move them around until a satisfactory solution is arrived at. The result may be represented as in Figure 70.1.

Figure 70.1: Identifying tasks and their sequence

Once the team members are known, they can be allocated to particular tasks and the information tabulated as in Figure 70.2.

Task ID	Task	Duration (weeks)	Team Member	Deliverable	Immed-iate pre-decessor
A	**REQUIREMENTS**				
A1	Assess requirements	1.0	James	Requirements document	-
B	**DESIGN**				
B1	Design system	2.5	Barbara	System design document	A1
C	**DEVELOPMENT**				
C1	Modify purchased package	2.0	Gillian	Reprogrammed package	B1
C2	Modify current procedures	1.5	Mark	Procedures manual	B1
C3	Modify manual systems flow	4.0	Barbara	Flowcharts	B1
D	**TEST**				
D1	Test purchased package	1.5	Gillian	Tested package	C1
D2	Test new procedures	1.0	Mark	Tested user procedures	C2
D3	Test manual systems flow	1.0	Barbara	Tested operational procedures	C3
E	**IMPLEMENTATION**				
E1	Implement timetabling system	1.5	James	'Live' system	D1,D2,D3
E2	Train staff	0.5	Mark	Trained staff	D1,D2,D3

Figure 70.2: Task list with immediate predecessors

> ➤ **Discussion: What knowledge does the project manager need to have to draw up these charts and tables?**
>
> ➤ **How much of the above work could be done by project management software?**

Critical path analysis

The longest path through the project is termed the **critical path**. This is the minimum time in which the project can be completed.

Figure 70.3: The critical path network

> ➤ **Discussion: How long will the project take to complete, assuming no hiccups?**

Gantt charts

A Gantt chart shows which tasks can be done in parallel.

Task ID	0	1	2	3	4	5	6	7	8	9	10
Weeks											
A1	▬										
B1		▬▬▬									
C1					▬▬						
C2					▬▬						
C3					▬▬▬▬						
D1							▬▬				
D2						▬▬					
D3									▬		
E1										▬▬	
E2										▬	

Figure 70.4: Gantt chart

Using software tools

Any major project can be broken down into hundreds or even thousands of different activities. As a general rule of thumb, when there are over 100 activities, using project management software is likely to be beneficial. There are literally hundreds of project management software packages available: however, the use of specialised software can only act as an aid to a project manager; it cannot take over the task of project management.

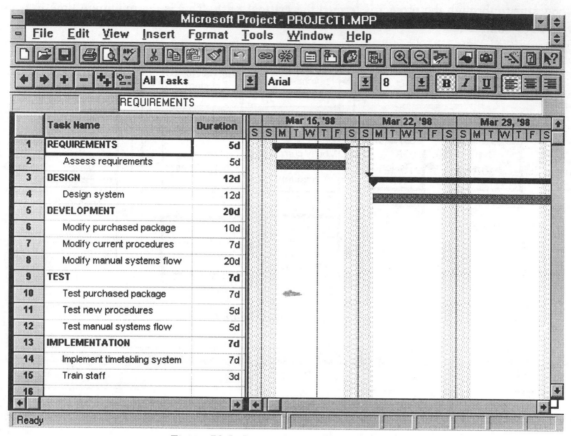

Figure 70.5: Project management software

Typically, project management software will provide the following facilities:

- Allow the user to input the availability of people and other resources such as equipment;
- Generate the critical path;
- Calculate the time required for project completion;
- Identify any 'slack time';
- Find the earliest and latest time of start for each activity;
- Identify 'slippages' as the project progresses;
- Provide information in different sortings and orderings;
- Integrate budget data;
- Allow easy replanning of activities when unexpected events occur;
- Draw different kinds of graphs and charts such as Gantt charts, critical path networks and work breakdown schedules.

> ➤ **Discussion: 'Slack time' may occur in activities which are not on the critical path. What is the latest that activity D2 can start without affecting the time to completion?**
> ➤ **What will happen if Barbara is ill for three weeks at the start of week 3? What could the project manager do to keep the project on track?**
> ➤ **Describe a report, other than the critical path network or Gantt chart, that would be useful for the project manager.**

Ultimately, project management depends not so much on software as on good judgement, experience in project management, skills in estimation and the ability to motivate the project team. But for a large project, software can be an invaluable reporting aid as well as providing alternative solutions for keeping projects on time and within budget when things start to go wrong.

Exercises

1. A range of software packages can be described as 'Project management software'. What is project management software and what does it do? (2)

   NEAB IT05 Qu 3 Sample paper

2. A project manager is using project management software to aid in controlling a large software project. Describe briefly:
   (a) **Three** tasks that the software will be able to perform; (6)
   (b) **Three** tasks that the project manager will have to perform without the aid of software. (3)

   New question

3. Describe briefly **six** facilities that you would expect to find in a project management software package. (6)

   New question

4. In groups of three or four, choose a project such as organising a live event or a group holiday, and draw up a list of tasks. For each task, define duration, person responsible and immediate predecessor. Draw the critical path network and Gantt chart for the project.

   New question

Chapter 71 – Software Acquisition and Testing

Make or buy?

At the start of the systems life cycle, a new computer project is proposed and a feasibility study is carried out to examine the economic, technical and social feasibility of the project. If a decision is made to go ahead, one of the major decisions that will have to be made is how to acquire the software. There are several options:

- The software may be written by the end-user;
- A specialist department within the organisation may design, write, test and document the software;
- External consultants may be called in to write and test the software;
- An off-the-shelf package may be bought, and possibly customised;
- Software may be leased rather than purchased, with the user paying an annual fee for the right to use the product.

End-user-written software

This is normally only an option for a very small project where the end-user is perhaps a computer specialist in their own right. A computer-literate enthusiast in a Recruitment Department, for example, may use a database package such as Access to write an application to input and analyse information about prospective or new recruits to help plan future advertising campaigns.

The advantages of the end-user writing the software is that the requirements are precisely known so no problems of communication arise, and the software is likely to be developed quite quickly in response to a specific need. The disadvantages are that the end-user is very unlikely to provide any technical or user documentation so that when he or she leaves, the software will probably quickly fall into disuse.

This option is only useful for minor projects with a limited life-span.

> ➢ **Discussion: Fifteen or so years ago it was quite common for, say, an enthusiastic doctor at a GP's surgery to buy a PC and develop his own software for an application such as printing out repeat prescriptions. Does this still happen? If not, why not?**

Writing software in-house

Many large organisations have their own department of computer specialists for maintaining existing software and developing new software. It is estimated that as much as 75% of computer specialists' time may be spent on maintenance – keeping existing programs running and making changes to them as required. Any opportunity to participate in a new project is likely to be received enthusiastically. This approach also has the advantage that any confidential information or ideas are kept within the organisation and will not be given to competitors by outside consultants.

However, developing a major new system may require extra staff with specialised skills and such people may be difficult to recruit, especially if they are only needed for a relatively short time. The company may decide it is preferable to bring in outside consultants who have the necessary experience and expertise.

External consultants

For a major project, going to an external software house may be the only solution. The job may be 'put out to tender', with several companies submitting proposals and being invited to give presentations of their proposals before one is chosen. The more complex the project, the greater the pitfalls, and so great care is needed in the choice of consultant. Cost is always a consideration but a consultant who can point to several successful systems already installed may be worth the extra money. The relationship that a consultant builds with the client may be one of the most important factors in implementing a new system successfully.

> ➤ **Discussion: What criteria would you use in deciding between several external consultants who had submitted proposals for delivering a new system?**

Buying a package

If a package is available to do the job, this may be a very safe and relatively inexpensive way to acquire the new software. A package has the following advantages over specially written software:

- It is cheaper than custom-written software – the development costs of the package may be millions of pounds, but the customer may be able to buy it for a few hundred pounds, since sales are made to thousands of other customers;
- It is immediately available and already thoroughly tested so is unlikely to have major bugs in it;
- Documentation is usually available in the form of reference manuals, user guides and tutorials;
- Training courses may be available from third-party trainers;
- Technical support is usually available from the manufacturers via a Web site or telephone line (at a price);
- Other users of the package can be consulted as to its suitability before purchase;
- Upgrades are usually available every year or two.

Disadvantages of a package solution include:

- The package may not do exactly what you want it to do;
- It may not run on the firm's existing hardware;
- It may not interface with other software already in use in the organisation.

Leasing software

Some packages are leased rather than purchased. This means that the user will automatically receive regular upgrades, and the initial expense is less. In the long run, of course, this option may be more expensive.

Modifying existing packages

Sometimes a package is bought and modified. This is in general a very dangerous option as it means that the manufacturer will no longer provide any technical support, and the modifications are likely to cause errors in other parts of the software, which therefore require more modifications, and so on.

Software testing

All software has to undergo a rigorous testing process before it can be released. When a new system is developed, the testing process may typically consist of five stages:

1. **Unit testing**. Each individual component (such as a subroutine or code for a particular function) of the new system is tested.

2. **Module testing**. A module is defined in this context as a collection of dependent components or subroutines.

3. **Subsystem testing**. This phase involves testing collections of modules which have been integrated into subsystems. (For example, the Purchase Order function may be one of the subsystems of an Accounting system.) Subsystems are often independently designed and programmed and problems can arise owing to interface mismatches. Therefore, these interfaces need to be thoroughly tested.

4. **System testing**. The subsystems are integrated to make up the entire system. The testing may reveal errors resulting from the interaction between different subsystems. This stage of testing is also concerned with ensuring that the system meets all the requirements of the original specification.

5. **Acceptance testing**. This is the final stage in the testing process before the system is accepted for operational use. It involves testing the system with data supplied by the system purchaser rather than with simulated data developed specially for testing purposes.

Testing is an iterative process, with each stage in the test process being repeated when modifications have to be made owing to errors coming to light at a subsequent stage.

Figure 71.1: Stages in testing new software

Alpha testing

Acceptance testing is sometimes known as **alpha testing**. For specially commissioned software, this testing continues until agreement is reached between the developer and the system purchaser that the system works correctly and fulfils all the system requirements.

Alpha testing is essential because it often reveals both errors and omissions in the system requirements definition. The user may discover that the system does not in fact have the required functionality because the requirements were not specified carefully enough, or because the developer has overlooked or misunderstood something in the specification.

Beta testing

When a new package is being developed for release as a software package, beta testing is often used. This involves giving the package to a number of potential users who agree to use the system and report any problems to the developers. Microsoft, for example, deliver beta versions of their products to hundreds of sites for testing. This exposes the product to real use and detects problems and errors that may not have been anticipated by the developers. The product can then be modified and sent out for further beta testing until the developer is confident enough in the product to put it on the market.

Software maintenance

It is impossible to produce software which does not need to be maintained. Over the lifetime of any software system or package, maintenance will be required for a number of reasons:

- Errors may be discovered in the software;
- The original requirements are modified to reflect changing needs;
- Hardware developments may give scope for advances in software;
- New legislation may be introduced which impacts upon software systems (e.g. the introduction of a new tax).

Maintenance falls into three categories:

- **Perfective maintenance**. The system can be made better in some way without changing its functionality. For example it could be made to run faster or produce reports in a clearer format.
- **Adaptive maintenance**. Changing needs in a company may mean systems need to be adapted – for example, a single-user system may be adapted to a multi-user system. A new operating system or new hardware may also necessitate adaptive maintenance.
- **Corrective maintenance**. This involves the correction of previously undetected errors. The most costly corrective maintenance currently being undertaken by thousands of companies is the millennium bug – changing the format of dates for a 2-digit year to a 4-digit year.

Source: McKee 1984

Figure 71.2: Maintenance effort distribution

> ➤ **What are some of the possible consequences of the millennium bug to different types of organisation?**

Maintenance releases

The maintenance process is generally triggered by requests for changes from system users or by management. The costs and impacts of these changes is assessed and if the decision is made to go ahead with the proposed changes, a new release of the system is planned. The release will very likely involve elements of adaptive, corrective and perfective maintenance. The changes are implemented and tested and then a new version of the software is released.

Minor changes in software packages are often released with version numbers like Version 3.0, 3.1, etc. Major new releases may be given numbers like version 4.0, 5.0 etc., or a completely new name.

Maintenance is often perceived by software developers as a rather inferior type of activity, requiring less skill than developing new software, and is therefore allocated to less experienced staff. This is probably one reason why such a high proportion of software costs are attributed to maintenance.

A study by Lehman and Belady carried out in 1985 resulted in a set of 'laws' of software maintenance.

---

1. **The law of continuing change**

   A program that is used in a real-world environment necessarily must change or become progressively less useful in that environment.

2. **The law of increasing complexity**

   As an evolving program changes, its structure tends to become more complex. Extra resources must be devoted to preserving and simplifying the structure.

3. **The law of large program evolution**

   Program evolution is a self-regulating process. System attributes such as size, time between releases and the number of reported errors are approximately invariant for each system release.

4. **The law of organisational stability**

   Over a program's lifetime, its rate of development is approximately constant and independent of the resources devoted to system development.

5. **The law of conservation of familiarity**

   Over the lifetime of a system, the incremental change in each release is approximately constant.

The third law above suggests that large systems have a dynamic of their own. Maintenance teams cannot simply make any changes they want to, because of structural and organisational factors. As changes are made to a system, new errors are introduced which then necessitate more changes. Major changes tend to be inhibited because these changes would be expensive and may result in a less reliable system. The number of changes which may be implemented at any one time is limited.

Maintenance is very expensive, being by far the greatest cost incurred in the overall systems life cycle. It is therefore cost-effective to put time and effort into developing systems which are as easy as possible to maintain.

Exercises

1. Before releasing a new package the software company carries out alpha and beta testing.

   (a) What are these two types of testing and why are they both needed? (6)

   (b) Explain why, once the package has been released, there may be a need for maintenance releases and how these might be dealt with. (6)

   NEAB IT05 Qu 8 Sample Paper

2. An examination board is considering developing a system which is to be used for maintaining and processing module test results of candidates.

   - Describe the different ways in which the examination board may be able to provide a software solution.

   - Discuss the issues the examination board should consider before choosing any particular solution.

   (20)

   NEAB IT05 Qu 9 1997

Appendix A

NEAB Syllabus Summary

Information Technology

Scheme of Assessment

In order to accommodate both a modular and linear approach for both A and AS level, a written paper will be set each year on each of CORE 1 (IT01), CORE 2 (ITO2), EXTENSION 1 (ITO4) and EXTENSION 2 (IT05) modules. All papers will have a range of types of question.

Where appropriate, candidates' answers in continuous prose will be assessed for quality of language.

Candidates for Information Technology (AS) will attempt:

CORE 1 (IT01)	Written Paper	30%	2 hours
CORE 2 (IT02)	Written Paper	30%	2 hours
CORE 3 (IT03)	Coursework	40%	

For the Core 3 (IT03) Module candidates will be required to undertake **two minor projects.**

For **each** project the candidate will be expected to tackle a limited problem which is very likely to involve the use of **one** generic application package.

The problem could be set by the candidate's teacher who may then act as the end-user. This can be the same problem for all candidates or may be different if resources permit. Candidates will be expected to demonstrate the advanced facilities within the package to obtain high marks.

The weighting of marks for the assessment of the minor project is approximately one third on Analysis and Design and two thirds on Implementation and Testing and Evaluation.

Candidates for Information Technology (Advanced) will attempt:

CORE 1 (IT01)	Written Paper	15%	2 hours
CORE 2 (IT02)	Written Paper	15%	2 hours
EXTENSION 1 (IT04)	Written Paper	15%	2 hours
EXTENSION 2 (IT05)	Written Paper	15%	2 hours
CORE 3 (IT03)	Coursework	20%	
EXTENSION (IT06)	Coursework	20%	

The Coursework component Core 3 (IT03) will be as outlined for candidates attempting Advanced Supplementary.

For the Extension 3 (IT06) Module candidates will be required to undertake a **major project.**

The project will require candidates to identify and research a realistic problem for a real end-user. It is intended to integrate the relevant skills and concepts developed during the course.

To obtain high marks it is expected that candidates will use a number of advanced tools and techniques to implement the solution.

The marks for the assessment of the major project are equally weighted between Analysis and Design and Implementation and Testing and Evaluation.

CORE 1 (IT01) - Information: Nature, Role and Context

Topic	Amplification	See chapter
1.1 Knowledge, information and data	Understand the distinction between knowledge, information and data. Information has context and its meaning is determined by the context.	8
	Understand that data can be derived from different sources, directly or indirectly.	8,9
	Describe the effect of the quality of the data source on the information produced.	8
	Understand the possible effect of ageing of information; the role of date stamping of information.	8
	Understand the need to encode information as data.	8
	Describe how the encoding of data potentially coarsens precision and/or context. This has implications for the recovery of information where storage, manipulation and retrieval is in terms of the original data.	8,9
	Understand the problems associated with the coding of value judgements.	8,9
1.2 Value and importance of information	Understand that information is a commodity and as such can have a monetary value, the level of which depends on its accuracy, its potential use and its particular intended use.	9
	Describe the overheads involved in ensuring that information is up-to-date.	9
1.3 Control of information	Describe the legal rights and obligations on holders of personal data to permit access. Understand that the sale of entitlement to access to data may mean paying for a more convenient form of access, the right of which already exists. Understand that files on individuals and on organisations that are non-disclosable have commercial value. Describe the access levels required for on-line files.	13,14
1.4 Capabilities and limitations of information technology	Understand that I.T. systems offer fast repetitive processing, vast storage capability, the facility to search and combine data in many different ways which would otherwise be impossible. This can provide quality information	9
1.5 The role of information technology	Make an informed evaluation of the role of information technology in bringing about changes which affect individuals, organisations and society.	1-7
	Discuss individual's, organisations' and society's dependence on information technology systems and the consequences if these systems were to fail.	1

Topic	Amplification	See chapter
1.6 The social impact of information technology	Discuss the potential impact of information technology in business, manufacturing, industry, commerce, medicine, the home and education, including employment issues and benefits to the elderly, disabled and pressure groups.	2 3, 4, 5
	Discuss the benefits and drawbacks of the use of information technology.	8,9
	Discuss the impact of information technology on the location and patterns of work.	1
1.7 Role of communication systems	Discuss the development and use of global communications between single or multiple sources and recipients, including public networks such as the INTERNET.	6
	Explain how information or data held in any part of the world can be accessed from, or despatched to, any other part of the world; access should be independent of location.	6
	Describe the facilities offered and the relative merits of: telephone, fax, e-mail, teleconferencing, viewdata, teletext, remote databases, superdata highways and other important communication systems.	6
	Discuss the development of telematics (informatics).	
1.8 Information and the professional	Discuss the social, moral and ethical issues associated with the introduction and use of information technology systems as they affect a professional working within the industry.	11
	Understand that 'codes of practice' exist separate from any legal requirements with which professionals within the industry are expected to comply.	11
	Discuss the role of professional bodies e.g. the British Computer Society (BCS) in promoting professional development and recall the purpose and operation of an Industry Structure Model.	10
	Describe the personal qualities and general characteristics necessary for a person working within the I.T. industry.	10
1.9 Malpractice & data theft	Discuss the consequences of theft or alteration of data or software for fraudulent purposes.	12
	Recognise the existence of a range of individuals responsible for data theft or malpractice; hackers.	12
	Describe the possible weak points within an information technology system and the issues relating to on-line systems, storage medium, theft or duplication, compromising electronic emanations (TEMPEST), viruses.	12
	Discuss simple processes which protect the integrity of data against malicious or accidental alteration: standard clerical procedures, passwords, levels of permitted access, write protect mechanisms, back-up procedures, restoration and recovery procedures.	13

Topic	Amplification	See chapter
1.10 The legal framework	This section applies to current British legislation and its relationship to the Council of Europe Convention directives.	14
1.10.1 Software and data misuse	Describe the anti-hacking provisions of the Computer Misuse Act.	12
	Describe the principles of software copyright and licensing agreements.	12
1.10.2 Data protection legislation	Recall the nature, purpose and provisions of the current data protection legislation of the Public Register.	14
	Recall the type of information covered and various exemptions from the legislation.	14
	Describe the obligations of data users under the legislation.	14
	Recall the rights of individuals under the legislation. Recall the role of the Registrar in encouraging good practice, acting as Ombudsman and enforcing legislation.	14
	Discuss the implications of the legislation.	14
1.10.3 Health and Safety	Describe the provisions of the current health and safety legislation in relation to the use of information systems.	15
	Discuss the implications of the legislation.	15

CORE 2 (IT02) - Information: Management and Manipulation

Topic	Amplification	See chapter
2.1 Gathering/acquisition/ sampling	Describe the various methods of data capture and identify appropriate contexts for their use. Understand the result of incorrect sampling rates leading to accurate data but inaccurate information.	26,27
2.2 Verification and validation	Understand the distinction between accuracy of information and validity of data.	27
	Explain possible sources and types of error in data capture, transcription, transmission and processing. Describe methods of preventing and reducing such methods.	27
	Describe appropriate validation techniques for various types of data process, from data capture to report generation.	27
2.3 Organisation of data for effective retrieval	Explain, with examples, what is meant by data consistency, data integrity, data redundancy and data independence.	23
	Explain, with examples, the concept of entity relationships and data normalisation.	23, 24
	Understand the importance of appropriate field types and lengths; auto-validation properties of fields which are of a specified data type; single record retrieval by reference to its key.	22
	Describe the importance of record and file structure design in facilitating subsequent retrieval of stored data. Describe the use of primary and secondary keys, indexes and links.	22,25
	Recall the relevant advantages of the use of databases over flat file information storage and retrieval systems.	24
	Describe the nature, purpose and capabilities of a relational database. Explain the use of database files.	24
	Select and justify appropriate file and database structures for particular applications.	24
	Understand various search-query facilities and their use; query by example and query languages.	25
	Explain the purpose of a database management system (DBMS).	23, 25
	Explain the role of the database administrator.	25
	Discuss different approaches to database security in the context of use.	25

Topic	Amplification	See chapter
2.4 Manipulation and/or processing	Describe the different modes of operation; batch, interactive, transaction (pseudo real-time) and identify appropriate contexts for their use.	28
	Describe the characteristics of processing data in the form of text, pictures, numbers and sound.	17
2.5 Effective presentation	Understand the effect that the method and style of presentation has upon the message - design in relation to the intended audience.	30
2.6 Dissemination/distribution	Describe the need for suitable output formats and orderings to communicate the results of data interrogation and undertake report generation.	30
2.7 Hardware; nature, capabilities and limitations	Describe the broad characteristics, capabilities and limitations of current input devices, storage devices, communications devices, processing devices and output devices and identify appropriate contexts for their use and the scope for upgradability.	26, 29, 32
2.8 Software; nature, capabilities and limitations		
2.8.1 Nature and types of software	Describe the distinction between systems software and applications software; the purposes of operating systems.	18, 19
	Describe the nature of package software, generic and specific, and of bespoke software. Describe the general characteristics of generic packages and of integrated packages for processing text, pictures, numbers and sound.	18, 19
2.8.2 Capabilities of software	Describe the desirable features of packages that would be appropriate to particular users and activities such as: links to other packages; search facilities; macro capabilities; application generators; editing capabilities; ability to change or extend data and record structures; short access times; data portability and upgrade paths.	20
2.8.3 Upgradability	Explain the implications of package change/upgrade including file transfer times and problems of incompatibility.	20
2.8.4 Reliability	Explain the difficulties of thoroughly testing complex software and implementations.	20
2.9 Configurability of hardware and software	Describe the need for interfacing with peripherals; storage devices; input and output devices; display devices; describe the need for printer and other peripheral drivers; the inability of printers to display all that is displayed on screen and of screens to show fully the output in final printed form (WYSIWYG); limitations of packages to make full use of all available peripheral facilities.	32,33

Topic	Amplification	See chapter
2.10 Portability of data		
2.10.1 Protocols and standards	Explain the need for portability of information; ease of transferring numerical, graphical and textual data between applications.	21
	Describe the need for standards for interchange of text, numeric data and graphics, for hardware and software, and for common operating systems.	21
2.10.2 Emergence of standards	Recognise the existence of de facto standards based on historic precedent and sales success in comparison to formal standards.	21
2.11 Security of data	Understand the importance of and the mechanisms for maintaining data security. Describe the distinction between security and privacy.	31
2.11.1 Backup systems	Understand the need for regular and systematic backup and procedures for recovery.	31
	Describe the different options available for backup systems.	31
2.12 Network environments	Describe the characteristics and relative advantages of network and stand-alone environments.	34
	Describe network topologies.	34
	Describe Local area, Wide area and other networks.	34
	Describe the characteristics and relative advantages of server-based and peer-to-peer networks.	34
	Describe factors which affect the rate and manner by which data can be transmitted.	35
	Understand the factors affecting compatibility between different systems.	35
	Understand the function of gateways.	35
2.13 User interfaces	Understand the differing capabilities of humans and machines.	36
	Understand the need to facilitate an effective dialogue between humans and machines.	36
	Explain the need to design systems which are appropriate to users at all levels and in different environments; the impact of clarity of structure and layout. Explain the use of command languages, forms dialogue, free format dialogue, menus; text, graphics, icons, colour, sound; keyboard, dedicated keys, soft keys, pointing devices and speech recognition.	36

EXTENSION 1 (ITO4) - Information Systems within organisations

Topic	Amplification	See chapter
1.1 Organisational structure	Understand the basic concepts of organisational structure.	42
1.2 Information systems and organisations	Understand the difference between an information system and a data processing system. Understand the role and relevance of an information system in aiding decision-making.	42, 43
1.2.1 Definition of a management Information System	Recall that an MIS is a system to convert data from internal and external sources into information. This is communicated in an appropriate form to managers at different levels to enable them to make effective decisions for planning, directing and controlling the activities for which they are responsible.	43
1.2.2 The development and life cycle of an information system	Recognise the existence of formal methods, the need for clear time scales, deliverables and approval to proceed.	44
1.2.3 Success or failure of a Management Information System	Understand the factors influencing the success or failure of an information system: inadequate analysis, lack of management involvement in design, emphasis on computer system, concentration on low-level data processing, lack of management knowledge of I.T. systems and their capabilities, inappropriate/excessive management demands, lack of teamwork, lack of professional standards.	45
1.3 Corporate information systems strategy	Describe the factors influencing an information system within an organisation: management organisation and functions, planning and decision-making methods, general organisation structure, responsibility for the information system within an organisation, information flow, hardware and software, standard, behavioural factors e.g. personalities, motivation, ability to adapt to change.	46
1.3.1 Information flow	Describe the methods and mechanisms of information flow within an organisation both formal and informal, and the constraints imposed upon this by organisational structures.	47
1.3.2 Personnel	Understand the levels of task/personnel within an organisation: strategic, implementation, operational, and relate the needs of these three levels to the information system.	47
1.3.3 Developments within MIS	Describe the differences between executive type systems and decision type systems.	47
1.4 Knowledge, information and data		
1.4.1 Knowledge	Discuss the nature of expert systems.	48
	Describe the implications and consequences of the uses of expert systems within organisations.	48

Topic	Amplification	See chapter
1.4.2 Information	Understand management information needs; the concept of relevance and methods of interpretation.	49
	Understand that information has many characteristics and can be classified in many ways. Examples include:	
	Source - internal, external, primary, secondary Nature - quantitative, qualitative, formal, informal Level - strategic, tactical, operational	43,49
	Time - historical, current, future. Frequency - real-time, hourly, daily, monthly. Use - planning, control, decision Form - written, visual, aural, sensory Type - detailed, aggregated, sampled	49
	Discuss the value of information in aiding the decision-making process.	43,47,49
	Understand the difference between internal and external information requirements.	43,47,49
	Describe the characteristics of good information and delivery: relevant, accurate, complete, user confidence, to right person, at right time, in right detail, via correct channel of communication, understandable.	49
	Describe the advantages and characteristics of good information within an applications context.	49
1.4.3 Data (see also Core 1 (IT01))	Understand the nature of data: recorded facts, events or transactions.	50
	Understand the different ways in which data can arise and be captured.	50
	Discuss the ways in which data can arise; direct capture or as a by-product of another operation.	50
	Understand that data may require translation or transcription prior to entry into the system. This can affect the accuracy of the data.	50
	Discuss the impact of quantity and quality of data on the method of data capture and the control mechanisms required to manage the capture.	50
1.5 The management of change	Understand that the introduction or development of an information system will result in change; this must be managed. Factors could include re-skilling, attitude, organisational structure, employment pattern and conditions, internal procedures.	51

Topic	Amplification	See chapter
1.6 Legal aspects	Understand the need for a corporate information technology security policy and its role within an organisation. Factors could include prevention of misuse, detection, investigation, procedures, staff responsibilities, disciplinary procedures.	52
	Describe the content of a corporate information technology security policy.	52
	Describe methods of improving awareness of security policy within an organisation. cross referencing to training and standards.	53
1.6.1 Audit requirements	Understand that many information technology applications are subject to audit.	52
	Describe the need for audit and the role of audit management/software tools software.	52
	Understand the function of audit trails and describe applications of their use; e.g. ordering systems, student tracking, police vehicle enquiries.	52
1.6.2 Disaster recovery management	Describe the various potential threats to information systems. Factors could include; physical security, document security, personnel security, hardware security, communications security, software security.	53
	Understand the concept of risk analysis.	52
	Understand the commercial need to ensure that an information system is protected from threat.	53
	Describe a range of contingency plans to recover from disasters and relate these to identified threats.	53
	Describe the criteria used to select a contingency plan appropriate to the scale of an organisation and installation.	53
1.6.3 Legislation	Understand that the implementation of legislation will impact on the procedures within an organisation.	54
	Describe the methods of enforcing and controlling data protection legislation within an organisation.	54
	Describe the methods of enforcing and controlling software misuse legislation within an organisation.	54
	Describe the methods of enforcing and controlling health and safety legislation within an organisation.	54

Topic	Amplification	See chapter
1.7 User Support	Describe the ways in which software houses provide user support; relate these to cost and package credibility.	55
	Describe the range of user support options available when using industry standard packages. These could include: existing user base, support articles, utilities, specialist bulletin boards.	55
	Select and justify an appropriate user support system for a particular context.	55
	Explain the need for different levels of documentation related to user and task.	55
1.7.1 Training	Explain the need for different levels of training related to user and task.	56
	Understand the difference in approach between skill based and task based training.	56
	Understand the need for continual skill updating and refreshing.	56
	Describe the methods by which users can gain expertise in software use and discuss their relative merits. Methods could include: Computer-Based Training, Interactive Video Instruction, on-line tutorials, step-through guides, formal training courses.	56
	Understand the need to develop training strategies to respond to growing user awareness.	56
1.8 Project management and effective I.T. teams	Understand why projects are often subdivided into tasks and allocated to teams.	57
	Describe what is meant by 'facilities management' and describe the advantages and disadvantages of this approach.	57
	Describe the characteristics of a good team: leadership, appropriate allocation of tasks, adherence to standards, monitoring, costing, controlling.	57

EXTENSION 2 (IT05) - Information management and manipulation - Policy, strategy and systems

Topic	Amplification	See chapter
2.1 Policy and strategy issues	Understand the need for an information management policy.	58
	Understand the strategic implications of software, hardware and configuration choices for an organisation.	58
	Appreciate the range of needs of different users.	58
2.1.1 Methods of enhancing existing capabilities - Future proofing	Discuss the reasons why organisations may wish to upgrade hardware/software provision - factors could include hardware/software development, more powerful PC, organisation ethos, task driven change, software change.	58
	Understand that hardware and software exists which allows packages to run on different platforms.	58
	Understand the advantages and disadvantages of the approach.	58
	Describe strategies for achieving upgrading and emulation	58
2.1.2 Backup procedures	Understand the strategies for backup scheduling and storage of backups (See also ITO1 1.9)	59
2.1.3 Employee Code of Conduct	Understand what is meant by an Employee Code of Conduct; responsibilities, authorisation, security, penalties for misuse.	59
2.2 Software 2.2.1 Evaluation of software	Describe the mechanisms/procedures for software evaluation.	60
	Establish client/user needs, establish software capabilities and match.	60
2.2.2 Evaluation criteria	Understand the need for establishing evaluation criteria; these include Agreed problem specification Functionality Performance - use of benchmarks Usability and human-machine interfaces Compatibility with existing software base Transferability of data Robustness User support Resource requirements including hardware, software and human Upgradability Portability Financial issues - development cost development opportunities.	60

Topic	Amplification	See chapter

2.2.3 Evaluation report	Understand the function of an evaluation report and know that the content will include:
	  methodology used
	  actual evaluation
	  recommendations
	  justifications.
		60

2.3 Communication and information systems	Describe the nature and the significance of communication networks (local, wide area and public).	61
2.3.1 Applications of communication and information systems	Describe the use of networked computers for various applications.	61
2.3.2 Distributed systems	Understand that distribution can apply to both data and control.	61
	Describe the uses of distributed databases and understand the advantages and limitations of such distribution.	61
2.4 Networks	(See also IT02 2.12)	
2.4.1 Types of network	Describe network topologies: bus, ring, star; backbone, repeater, bridge.	34
	Describe and compare network environments: server-based, peer-to-peer.	34
	Select and justify an appropriate network system for a particular application.	34
2.4.2 Network security and accounting	Understand the particular security and accounting problems associated with networks, and recall the steps which can be taken to preserve security.	63
2.4.3 Network environments	Understand how a network environment affects the user interface provided: security, control of software, control of files - access rights.	62 63
2.5 Communication methods	Understand serial and parallel transmission, their advantages and disadvantages.	64
	Understand the difference between digital and analogue transmission.	64
	Recall the use of modems for the transmission of data over analogue communication links, excluding technical details of modems and modulation.	64
2.5.1 Communication standards	Understand why protocols are required and know of the existence, benefits and limitations of standards; the OSI seven layer model.	64

Topic	Amplification	See chapter
2.6 Human/Computer Interaction	Describe the physical factors which affect human/computer interaction; screen is always visible, not facing window, space required by user, colour schemes suited to environment.	65
	Describe the psychological factors which affect human/computer interaction; user friendly, give help to novices, provide short cuts for experts, make use of human long term memory to maximise efficiency.	65
2.7 Human/Computer Interface (see also IT02 2.13)	Recall different approaches to the problem of communication with I.T. systems, including command/menu structures, screen design, nature of error messages, availability of help, user friendliness, ease of learning.	65
	Discuss the resource implications of sophisticated HCI.	65
	Discuss the implications for customising software to develop a specialist HCI.	65
2.8 Software to support specialist applications	Understand the nature, features and purpose of the following types of software: - project management - Geographical Information Systems (GIS) - CAD/CAM systems - Mathematical and statistical - Music.	 70 67 68 69 66
	Understand that specialist application knowledge is required to make effective use of this software.	66-70
	Understand that there are different ways of providing software solutions to specialist applications: - user written, internal development team/department - external software house to specification.	71
	Describe the possible criteria for selection of software solutions to specialist applications and their place within the corporate strategy.	71
2.9 Software reliability	Describe methods of ensuring that software is reliable - α testing, β testing, agreements between software houses and purchaser for testing.	71
	Understand the need for maintenance release(s).	71

Appendix B

NEAB Project Mark Schemes

Criteria for the Assessment of the Minor Projects

The following categories are to be used in the assessment of each minor project. The criteria for marking these categories are listed below. Each minor project is marked out of a total of 45.

Analysis and design (13 marks)

10-13 A detailed requirements' specification has been produced and used as the basis for the derivation of input, processing and output needs. The analysis and design show in detail what is required to carry out the task in a comprehensive manner - this can include layout sheets, record structures, spreadsheet plans, design for data-capture sheets, data modelling, etc as appropriate.

The design indicates an appreciation of the full potential of the appropriate hardware and software facilities and human resources available and also, if appropriate, their limitations. There is an explicit statement of how the named applications package is to be used. The design could be used by a competent person for implementation.

An effective and full testing plan has been devised including the test data and expected outcomes. This plan relates to the requirements' specification and includes appropriate evaluation criteria.

A well-defined schedule of activities has been included.

The analysis and design has been carried out without direct help.

5-9 An outline requirements' specification has been produced but lacks detail and clarity. Input and processing requirements are present but not clear.

The design states which applications package will be used but it may not be explicit about how the software will be used. Design layouts etc are present but show limited appreciation of the needs of the user and the scope of the software. The solution could be implemented with some additional planning and design.

A testing plan is present but is limited in scope or may not relate directly to the specification.

A schedule of activities is present but may be lacking in detail or may be unrealistic. There is only a limited indication of the appropriate facilities to be used.

The candidate may have required some direct help.

1-4 The requirement specification is vague, may be missing or is a restatement of the problem given. There are few, if any, indications of what must be done to carry out the task. Layout sheets etc are simplistic or missing. There is little indication of how the named software will be used.

The testing plan is vague or missing. The solution could not be implemented without major additional planning and design.

The activity schedule is superficial. The candidate required much direct help.

0 The candidate has produced no analysis or design.

Implementation and testing (23 marks)

18-23 The candidate has fully implemented the design unaided and with no obvious defects. The system works and is an effective model.

Many advanced facilities of the software and hardware available were used as appropriate.

The candidate has shown insight in demonstrating effective test data to cover most or all eventualities. Testing is exhaustive and results of testing are fully documented. The candidate has provided detailed user and technical documentation.

12-17 The candidate has implemented the essential elements of the design reasonably effectively and largely unaided. The system works and is effective but has limitations in efficiency.

The fundamental facilities of the software and hardware available were used in an appropriate manner.

The candidate has demonstrated a range of appropriate test data. There is hard copy evidence of testing, cross-referenced to the testing plan. The candidate has provided appropriate detailed user and technical documentation but it is lacking in some necessary detail.

6-11 The candidate has partially implemented the design or has implemented the design but it is only effective in parts. The system is not fully effective and lacks efficiency in the design of the model. The candidate has required some assistance.

Some of the facilities of the software and hardware available were used but not always in an appropriate manner.

The candidate needed assistance in choosing adequate test data, and the system was only tested to a limited extent. The candidate has provided some detailed user and technical documentation but this was limited.

1-5 The candidate has implemented the design in a very limited way that does not meet the design specification. The system does not produce any effective results. The candidate has required considerable assistance.

Few, if any, of the facilities of the software and hardware available have been used.

There is no evidence of testing, or the system has only been tested in a limited way and only with considerable assistance. There is little or no evidence of a user guide and technical documentation.

0 The candidate has not implemented the system.

Evaluation (9 marks)

7-9 The outcomes have been fully evaluated in an intelligent and systematic manner against the evaluation criteria. Appropriate performance indicators have been identified. There is consideration of any limitations and the possibility for enhancement has been discussed.

4-6 The system has been evaluated against some of the evaluation criteria. Some, but not all, performance indicators have been identified. There is some indication of the limitations of the system and, possibly with prompting, a few ideas about enhancement.

1-3 The system has only been partially evaluated against the original specification. This may be because the original specification was poor. Few, if any, performance indicators have been identified. Discussion concerning the limitations or enhancements to the system are largely absent or have required considerable prompting.

0 There is no evidence of evaluation.

Criteria for the Assessment of the Major Project

It is expected that the teacher will be involved in various stages in the development of the candidate's solution. However, in the award of marks, the teacher should attempt to assess solely the candidate's contribution. In applying the criteria account should be taken of the amount of assistance given. The criteria give scope for discriminating between candidates who have tackled more demanding problems as against those who have undertaken less demanding ones.

The following categories are to be used in the assessment of the project. The criteria for marking these categories are listed below. The major project is marked out of a total of 90.

Identification of a valid problem (4 marks)

(i)   Ability to identify a problem in information technology terms (2 marks)

2   The candidate has identified an appropriate problem entirely independently of the teacher.

1   The candidate has required some guidance from the teacher to identify an appropriate problem.

0   The candidate has relied entirely on the teacher to identify the appropriateness of using information technology to solve the problem.

(ii)   Statement of the problem (2 marks)

2   A clear outline statement covering both the context and the nature of the problem was provided.

1   A simple outline statement was provided.

0   No clear statement was given.

Analysis (18 marks)

15-18 The candidate has clearly identified and delimited a substantial and realistic problem, and has recognised the requirements of the intended user(s) and the capabilities and limitations of the resources available. All of the requirements are specified and clearly documented. There is an explicit statement of the applications packages to be used. The candidate has fully identified the information flow and data dynamics of the problem. The analysis indicates an appreciation of the full potential of the appropriate hardware and software facilities available and also, if appropriate, their limitations. The candidate has identified the user's current I.T. skill level and training needs. This stage has been completed without undue assistance.

11-14 The candidate has identified a substantial problem and has recognised many of the requirements of the intended users and many of the capabilities and limitations of the resources available. The documentation is intelligible but is lacking in some respects. The analysis indicates which software will be used but it may not be obvious how the software will be used. The candidate has partly identified the information flow and data dynamics of the problem. Some assistance has been required to reach this stage.

Alternatively, the candidate has identified a relatively straightforward problem and has proceeded unaided, covering most or all of the points required for 15-18 marks.

7-10   The candidate has selected a substantial problem and attempted to identify many of the requirements of the intended users and many of the capabilities and limitations of the resources available but has required assistance in analysing the problem. The candidate has identified only a limited subset of the information flow and data dynamics of the problem. The documentation is available but is incomplete.

Alternatively, the candidate has identified a fairly simple problem and has recognised most of the requirements of the intended users and most of the capabilities and limitations of the resources available. The candidate has required assistance in analysing the problem. The documentation is complete in most respects.

3-6   The candidate has identified a fairly simple problem and has recognised some of the requirements of the intended users and some of the capabilities and limitations of the resources available. Few, if any, indications of what must be done to carry out the task are present. There is little indication of how the software will be used. The candidate has not identified the information flow and data dynamics of the problem. Documentation is weak and incomplete. The candidate has required much assistance in analysing the problem.

1-2   The candidate has identified a simple problem or been given a straightforward problem. There is only minimal recognition of either the requirements of the intended users or the capabilities and limitations of the resources available. The documentation is poor and substantial assistance has been required.

0   No analysis is presented.

Design phase

Generation of possible solutions (6 marks)

The bringing together of the results of the analysis and the gathering and ordering of information related to the background of the problem into the generation of a range of possible solutions which meet them. This may be alternative types of package or alternative solutions within a package.

(i)   Consideration of solutions (4 marks)

3-4   A relevant range of appropriate approaches has been considered. This has been done without assistance.

1-2   A limited range of approaches or only one possible approach has been considered. This may have required some assistance.

0   No consideration has been given to approaches to the solution.

(ii)   Reasons for final choice of solution (2 marks)

2   Compelling reasons are given which have been fully justified and the likely effectiveness has been considered.

1   The reasons given only vaguely support the choice and the likely effectiveness has not been discussed.

0   No reasons or invalid reasons are given.

The detailed design (16 marks)

(i)   The solution design (12 marks)

The solution design should be specified so that a competent person can implement it. There should be a clear specification of how each of the subproblems identified in the analysis is to be solved.

9-12   A completely detailed solution has been specified such that a competent third party could carry it out. The proposed solution is clearly broken down into subproblems with the necessary indications of how these are to be solved. All of the requirements are specified and clearly documented. An effective and full testing plan has been devised. This has been done without assistance.

5-8   Sufficient detail has been given so that the candidate, but not another person, can replicate the solution at a later date. An attempt has been made to break down the problem into subproblems with some indications of how these are to be solved. The documentation is clear but lacking in some respects. A testing plan is present. This has been done without undue assistance.

1-4   A superficial outline of the solution has been chosen so that the candidate is unable to replicate the solution at a later date. Little attempt has been made to break down the problem into subproblems. The testing plan is vague or missing. The documentation is poor and substantial assistance may have been required.

0   No detail of chosen solution given.

(ii)   Planning for implementation (4 marks)

The candidate must give evidence of planning and the use of his/her time, for example, a diagram which indicates (A) estimated time allocation for each phase of the work, (B) sequence of the sections indicating possible times when two sections may run in parallel.

3-4   A well-defined work plan has been included showing in detail how the task is to be carried out. This shows what is required in a comprehensible manner - it can include layout sheets, record structures, spreadsheet plans, design for data-capture sheets, etc as appropriate.

1-2   A work plan is present but may be lacking in detail of how the task is to be carried out. Layouts, etc are present but show limited appreciation of timing and sequencing.

0   No evidence.

Implementation and testing (21 marks)

(i)   Implementation (12 marks)

9-12   The candidate has fully implemented the design unaided, in an efficient manner and with no obvious defects. All or most of the facilities of the software and hardware available were fully exploited. The documentation is clear and thorough.

5-8   The candidate has implemented the essential elements of the design reasonably effectively and largely unaided. The implementation has exploited the relevant features of the software and hardware available to a limited extent only. The documentation contains some weaknesses.

1-4   The design has only been partially implemented. The implementation has exploited few of the relevant features of the software and hardware available. The documentation lacks detail or may be missing completely.

0   There is no implementation.

(ii)   Testing (9 marks)

7-9   The candidate has shown insight in demonstrating effective test data to cover most or all eventualities. There is clear evidence of full end-user involvement in testing. The system works with a full range of test data; the test outputs are annotated fully.

4-6   The candidate has demonstrated a range of appropriate test data perhaps with some assistance. There is some evidence of end-user involvement during testing. The system works with a limited range of test data; the test outputs are annotated to a limited extent.

1-3   There is little evidence of testing. There is only limited involvement of the end-user in testing. It does not meet the design specification.

0   There is no evidence of testing.

Evaluation of the project (15 marks)

12-15   The candidate has identified clearly a full range of relevant criteria for evaluating the solution. The candidate has fully evaluated his/her solution intelligently against the requirements of the user(s).

Appropriate performance indicators have been identified. All possible limitations and enhancements have been identified and relevant modifications clearly specified.

8-11   The candidate has shown some recognition of a range of relevant criteria for evaluating the solution. The candidate has evaluated his/her solution against the requirements of the user(s) in most respects. Some, but not all, performance indicators have been identified. Any modifications to meet possible major limitations and/or enhancements have been specified maybe with assistance.

4-7   The system has only been partially evaluated against the original specification and the requirements of the user(s). This may be because the original specification was poor. Few, if any, performance indicators have been identified. Discussion concerning the limitations or enhancements to the system are largely absent or have required some prompting.

1-3   Little attempt at evaluation has been made. No performance indicators have been identified. Discussion concerning the limitations or enhancements to the system are absent or limited and have required considerable prompting.

0   No attempt at evaluation has been made.

Presentation of the report (10 marks)

8-10   A well-written, fully illustrated and organised report is produced, including a comprehensive user guide. It describes the project accurately and concisely.

5-7   A well-written report is produced but it lacks good organisation. Alternatively a well-organised report is produced but it is of limited quality with a limited user guide.

3-4   The report is of generally poor quality but shows some evidence of organisation. There are a number of deficiencies and omissions.

1-2   The report is poorly organised and presented with few or no diagrams. There are a considerable number of omissions.

0   No report is present.

Appendix C

Book List

Book List

The following books have been invaluable in the preparation of this text and are a useful source of information for staff and students. All prices are approximate, as obviously they tend to increase over time – most were correct in November 1997.

General texts

Alter, Steven **Information Systems: A Management Perspective (2nd Edition)** (1996)
Benjamin Cummings. ISBN 0-8053-2430-5 £25

Good American hardback book, full of useful information, case studies and beautiful colour illustrations. An excellent book for the library.

Heathcote P.M. **Tackling Computer Projects in Access and Visual Basic (2nd Edition)** (1997)
Letts Educational. ISBN 1-84085-001-9 £9.95

Useful advice for project work, with sample projects.

Hussain K.M. and Hussain, Donna **Information Technology Management** (1997)
Butterworth & Heinemann. ISBN 0-7506-2656-9 £35

Awfully expensive but it is a very good resource for second year work. A good book to have in the library.

Laudon, Kenneth et al. **Information Technology and Society** (1994)
International Thomson Publishing. ISBN 0-534-19512-1 £21.95

An excellent American textbook which deserves to be on the library shelf of every school and college offering A Level I.T. Too long and detailed to be used as a student text but a wonderful reference book. Weighing in at 3lbs, too heavy for the average student's schoolbag.

Laudon K. and Laudon J. **Management Information Systems (5th edition)** (1998)
Prentice Hall. ISBN 0-13-906462-1 £25

An even weightier tome (literally), about 800 pages but covers most of the syllabus. A good reference source although it is aimed at undergraduates and would be rather daunting for the average A Level student. Good value for money.

Stern, Nancy and Stern, Robert **Computing in the Information Age** (1996)
John Wiley and Sons Inc. ISBN 0-471-11061-2 £20.95

Another useful American text, beautifully illustrated. A good reference book covering a large part of the syllabus in a rather roundabout way.

Zwass, Vladimir. **Management Information Systems** (1992)
Wm C. Brown. ISBN 0 697 01538 6 £18.25

Good general text, good value for a hardback book.

Books for specific topics

Barrett, Neil **Digital Crime** (1997)
Kogan Page Limited. ISBN 0-7494-2097-9 £12

Written by an ex-hacker with a rather poor grasp of English grammar, but who is nevertheless extremely knowledgeable on all aspects of computer crime and the law. An interesting read.

Bawa, Joanna **The Computer User's Health Handbook** (1994)
Souvenir Press. ISBN 0-285-63207-8 £10.99

Well-written, informative reference book covering all aspects of Health and Safety for computer users. A good chapter on user interfaces.

Bruton, Noel **How to manage the I.T. Helpdesk** (1997)
Butterworth Heinemann. ISBN 07506 3811 7 £19.99

All about helpdesks.

Cavoukian, Ann **Who Knows** (1997)
McGraw Hill. ISBN 0-07-063320-7 £18

A good book on privacy issues in the computer age.

Collins, Tony **Crash – Ten Easy Ways to Avoid a Computer Disaster** (1997)
Simon & Schuster. ISBN 0-684-81688-1 £20

Very entertaining case studies of computer disasters, including many over-ambitious projects which didn't come up to scratch. Good material for 'factors influencing the success or failure of an information system'.

Evans, Alastair **Data Protection Policies and Practice** (1987)
Institute of Personnel Management. ISBN 0 85292 385 6 £10

A very thorough treatment of the Data Protection Act and all its implications, with guidelines for security policies as implemented in various organisations such as B.P. and Kodak.

Gates, Bill **The Road Ahead** (1996)
Penguin Books. ISBN 0-14-024351-8 £7.99

A wonderful account of how to establish a de facto standard by one who knows. Also a generally entertaining account of the current state of technology and (self-fulfilling?) predictions for the future.

Kallman E.A. and Grillo J.P. **Ethical Decision-making and Information Technology** (1993)
McGraw-Hill. ISBN 0-07-033884-1 £14.95

A fascinating book on ethics in computing, with 18 case studies illustrating all manner of ethical dilemmas, excellent for class use. A good book to order for the library.

Sommerville, Ian **Software Engineering (4th Edition)** (1992)
Addison-Wesley. ISBN 0 201 56529 3 £23.95

Good reference book for all aspects of software engineering such as systems development, maintenance and testing. Designed for undergraduates.

Other resources

BSA Guide to Software Management

The Business Software Alliance is an organisation dedicated to stamping out the illegal use of unlicensed software. They produce a FREE folder, CD and presentation floppy disk. Good for a couple of lessons at least! Their address is

BSA Europe, First Floor, Leconfield House, Curzon Street, London W1Y 8AS. Tel: 0171 491 1974

User support/Help desk software

A good resource for this topic is Network Associates, Minton Place, Victoria Street, Windsor, Berks SL4 1EG. Tel 01753 827500. They produce McAfee HelpDesk software and have a good (free) sample CD and information sheets.

Index

1NF, 110
2NF, 112
3NF, 112
Access
    control, 298
    directory, 57
    privileges, 118, 298
    rights, 57
ACM, 44
After-image, 146
Alpha testing, 336
Apple Macintosh, 82
Application
    generators, 94
    packages, 88
Appraisal, 191
ASCII, 75
Audit controls, 299
Audit trail, 250
Authoring packages, 175
Authoring software, 23
Authorisation software, 249
Backbone, 296
Backup, 59
    hardware, 146, 280
    strategy, 146, 279
Bandwidth, 160
Banking, 9
Bar code reader, 123
Bar codes, 237
Baseband, 302
Batch processing, 121, 128, 134
BCS, 44
Before-image, 146
Benchmark tests, 285
Beta testing, 336
Bi-directional, 148
Binary, 75
    arithmetic, 77
    numbers, 77
Biometric security measures, 58
Bit, 75, 101
Bitmapped graphics, 79, 322
Boolean
    values, 78
    variable, 78
Bridge, 160, 296
British Computer Society, 45
Broadband, 302
Buffering, 152
Bulletin boards, 262

Bus
    external, 152
    internal, 152
Bus network, 156, 294
Business Software Alliance, 52, 256
Byte, 75, 101
Cache memory, 72
CAD. *See* Computer-aided design
Call centres, 262
CAM. *See* Computer-aided manufacturing
Careers in I.T., 42
Carrier sense multiple access, 156
CD-ROM, 140
Centralised processing system, 287
Change management, 242
Changeover. *See* Conversion
Channels of communication, 234
Check digit, 129
Checksum, 130
Client-server, 157, 297
Clone, 82
Coaxial cable, 160
Code of conduct, 45, 282
Code of Ethics, 45
Codec, 27
Codes of practice, 47
Command and control system, 167
Command-driven interface, 164
Communications
    links, 159
    satellite, 160
    security, 58
    software, 302
Compiler, 87
CompuServe, 25
Computer
    abuse, 49
    analogue, 75
    crime, 49
    digital, 75
    failure, 5
Computer Misuse Act, 52
Computer-aided design, 12, 319
Computer-aided manufacturing, 13, 323
Computer-based training, 266
Computers
    and health, 63
    and the disabled, 19

in medicine, 16
in schools, 21
Conceptual data model, 107
Control program, 80
Conversion
    direct, 210
    parallel, 210
    phased, 210
    pilot, 211
Copyright Designs and Patents Act, 52, 256
CorelDRAW!, 322
Corporate training strategy, 267
Crime, 49
Critical path analysis, 331
Critical success factor, 274
CSMA-CD, 156
Cylinder, 139
Data, 33
    analysing, 39
    capture, 127
    collecting, 39
    compression, 161
    consistency, 105
    dictionary, 115
    direct collection of, 35
    encryption, 58, 300
    flow, 178
    hierarchy, 101
    indirect collection of, 35
    integrity, 55
    quality, 36
    redundancy, 105
    security, 57
    shareable, 105
    sources, 35
    store, 178
    transmission, 162
    validation, 104, 129
Data flow diagram, 178
Data processing systems, 198
Data Protection Act, 60, 255
Data Protection Registrar, 61
Database, 101
    design, 180
    distributed, 290
    relational, 109
Database administrator, 115
Database Management System, 101, 106, 116
Database security, 118

Database software, 173
Date stamp, 36
DBA, 115
DBMS, 101, 106, 116
De facto standards, 99, 304
De jure standards, 304
Decision
    making, 203
    management, 202
    structured, 202
    unstructured, 202
Decision support system, 224, 225, 231
Denary, 77
Desktop publishing, 174
Device driver, 153
Dialogue boxes, 166
Digitiser, 124
Disaster planning, 58, 145, 252
Disaster recovery plan, 253
Disk
    cylinder, 139
    floppy, 73, 138
    hard, 138
    magneto-optical, 140
    sector, 139
    storage, 72
    track, 139
    write-protecting, 56
Dispersed system, 287
Distributed database, 290
Distributed processing, 289
Documentation, 188, 264
EBCDIC, 75
EDI, 238
Electronic bulletin boards, 25
Electronic data interchange, 238
Electronic emanations, 51
Electronic mail, 25
ELF radiation, 66
E-mail, 25
Embedded objects, 96
Employee code of conduct. *See* Code of conduct
Emulation, 277
Encryption, 58, 300
End-user computing, 221
Entity-relationship diagram, 107
Ergonomic environment, 67
Ethernet, 156, 296
Ethics, 45
Evaluation, 191
Evaluation report, 285
Exception report, 233
Executive information system, 224, 226

Expert system, 34, 228, 231
Expert system shell, 230
External entity, 178
Facilities management, 271
Facsimile transmission, 27
Fax, 27
Feasibility study, 208
Fibre optic cable, 160
Field, 101
Field type, 102
File, 101
File lookup check, 129
File management system, 102
File Transfer Protocol, 96
Firewall, 299
First normal form, 110
Flat file, 102, 113
Foreign key, 109
Format check, 104, 129
Fraud, 50
Ftp, 96
Full-duplex, 303
Future proofing, 277
Gantt chart, 331
Gates, Bill, 72, 81, 83
Gateway, 160
Gb, 72
Geographical Information System. *See* GIS
Gigabyte, 72
GIS, 315
Goal Seeker, 325
Golden Rule, 47
Grandfather-father-son, 281
Graphics, 322
Graphics tablet, 124
Graphing tools, 326
Greatest Good/Least Harm, 47
GUI, 82, 83, 98, 164
Hacking, 49
Half-duplex, 303
Handshaking, 249
Hash total, 128
Health and Safety, 258
    Executive, 66
    Regulations, 66
Help desk, 260
Help desk software, 261
HOLMES, 54
Human-computer interaction, 306
Human-computer interface, 163
Hypertext links, 25
Icon, 167
Impact printer, 148
Implementation, 185, 210, 214, 217

Incremental backup, 146
Indexes, 117
Industry Structure Model, 44
Information, 33
    as a commodity, 40
    characteristics of, 142
    encoding, 35
    external, 200
    flow, 226
    importance of, 39
    internal, 200
    levels of, 233
    management, 274
    operational, 233
    quality of, 233
    sources, 233
    strategic, 233
    tactical, 233
Information system, 198
    executive, 224, 226
    management, 200
    operational, 200
    strategy, 220
Integrated packages, 88
Integrity of data, 55, 247
Interactive processing, 135
Interface
    command-driven, 81
    graphical user, 82
    parallel, 152
    unit, 152
Internet, 9
Interpreter, 87
Interrupt handling, 81
Intranet, 25
ISDN, 27, 160
Joystick, 122
Kant's Categorical Imperative, 47
Kb, 72
Keyboard data entry, 120
Key-to-disk system, 121
Kilobyte, 72
Knowledge, 33
Knowledge work system, 199
Knowledge workers, 34
Knowledge-based system, 34, 228
LAN, 155, 288
Legacy system, 276
Linked objects, 96
Local area network. *See* LAN
Logic bomb, 51
Long-term memory, 307
Magnetic Ink Character Recognition, 122
Magnetic stripe, 122, 238
Magnetic tape, 139

Magneto-optical disk, 140
Mail merge, 91
Mainframe computers, 71
Maintenance
    adaptive, 211
    corrective, 211
    perfective, 211
Maintenance release, 337
Management information system,
    199
    desirable characteristics, 204
Many-to-Many relationship, 112
Master file, 133
Mathematical software, 327
Mb, 72
Megabyte, 72
Memory, 72
Memory management, 80
Menu design, 181
Menu interface, 164
Message token, 157
Methods of conversion, 210
MICR, 122
Microcomputers, 70
Microfiche, 141
Microprocessor, 71
Microsoft, 81, 99
Microwave, 160
MIDI, 78, 311
Millennium bug, 6, 208, 337
Minicomputers, 70
MIS. *See* Management Information
    System
Modem, 161, 302
Mondex, 123
Moore's Law, 71
Mouse, 122
MS-DOS, 82
Multimedia, 22
Multi-tasking, 83
Music software, 310
Musical Instrument Digital
    Interface. *See* MIDI
Natural language, 165
Near letter quality, 148
Netscape, 25
Network
    bus, 294
    public, 291
    ring, 295
    star, 294
    topology, 155, 294
Newsletters, 263
NLQ, 148
Normalisation, 110
Object Linking and Embedding, 95

Object oriented graphic, 322
OCR, 120
OLE, 95
OMR, 123
On-line
    help, 263
    information services, 25
    shopping, 9
Open System Interface, 304
Operational system, 224
Optical Character Recognition, 120
Optical Mark Recognition, 123
Organisations, 194
OSI seven layer model, 304
Outsourcing, 272
Packet-switching network, 305
PAINT package, 322
Parallel conversion, 210
Parity, 76
Parity bit, 130
Partial dependency, 112
Password, 56
Peer-to-peer, 157, 297
Performance management, 299
Periodic backups, 59
Personal privacy, 60
Personnel policy, 282
Personnel safeguards, 250
Phased conversion, 210
Picture check, 129
Picture element, 79
Pilot conversion, 211
Pixel, 79
Pixel-based graphics, 322
Platform, 276
Plotter, 150
Plug and Play, 84
Portability, 96
Post-implementation review, 211
Presence check, 104, 129
Presentation, 144
Presentation packages, 174
Primary key, 103
Primary storage, 137
Printer
    dot matrix, 148
    ink jet, 149
    laser, 149
    thermal transfer, 149
Privacy, 55, 60, 145
Processing, 137
    batch, 134
    interactive, 135
    methods, 133
    mode, 135
    power, 71

    pseudo real-time, 135
    random, 137
Productivity tools, 88, 90
Professional
    bodies, 43
    conduct, 45
    in I.T., 42
Program-data dependence, 105
Project
    management software, 329, 332
    manager, 269
    planning, 270
    reviews, 271
    team, 269
PROLOG, 228
Protocol, 161, 303
Prototyping, 212
Pseudo real-time processing, 135
Public network, 291
Puck, 124
Qualitative objectives, 177
Query by example, 116
Radiation
    ELF, 66
    Van Eck, 51
RAID, 146
RAM, 72, 137
Random processing, 137
Range check, 104, 129
Real-time processing, 135
Record, 101
Recovery procedures, 59
Regulations
    Health and Safety, 66
Relation, 109
Relational database, 109
Relationship, 107
Repeater, 296
Repetitive strain injury, 64, 120
Report generators, 94
Reporting by exception, 142
Requirements analysis, 209
Resolution, 150
Resource allocation, 81
Ring network, 157, 295
Risk analysis, 247
Robot, 14, 16
ROM, 72
RSI. *See* Repetitive Strain Injury
Sampling rate, 310
Satellite, 160
Scanner, 120
Second normal form, 112
Secondary keys, 118
Sector, 139
Security, 145, 298

of data, 57, 247
plan, 253
policy, 250
Sequencer, 311
Sequential processing, 137
Service providers, 24
Seven layer model, 304
Sheep-dip station, 58
Short-term memory, 307
Simplex, 303
Simulation software, 328
Slippery Slope Rule, 47
Smart card, 122, 239
Software
    acquisition, 334
    applications, 87
    bespoke, 87, 88
    copyright, 52, 256
    designing good, 308
    evaluation, 284
    general purpose, 87
    generic, 88
    leasing, 335
    maintenance, 337
    off-the-shelf, 88
    performance monitoring, 87
    reliability, 98
    selecting, 98
    suite, 88
    systems, 86
    tailoring, 284
    testing, 98, 336
    upgradability, 284
Sorting, 118
Sound, 78
Sound card, 310
Sound waves, editing, 314
Speech input, 167
Speech synthesis, 168
Spell checker, 90
Spooling, 153
Spreadsheet, 92, 173, 325
SQL, 117
Stakeholder, 197
Star network, 156, 294
Statistical functions, 326
Statistical package, 327
Storage

primary, 137
    secondary, 137
Stress, 63
Structured Query Language, 117
Supercomputers, 71
Support articles, 263
SWOT analysis, 219
Synthesiser, 310
System
    data processing, 198
    decision support, 224, 225
    design, 210
    failure, 242
    information, 198
    knowledge work, 199
    maintenance, 211
    operational, 224
    transaction
        processing, 198
Systems life cycle, 206
Tb, 72
Technical support, 260
Telecommunications, 24
Teleconferencing, 27
Telephones, 26
Teleworking, 3
Tempest, 51
Template, 91
Terabyte, 72
Test
    plan, 182, 186
    results, 186
Testing, 98, 336
    module, 185
    objectives, 185
    system, 186
Third normal form, 112, 113
Token ring, 157
Topology
    of a network, 155, 294
Touch screen, 122
Training, 265
Training a computer, 167
Transaction, 133
    file, 133
    logging, 118, 146
    processing system, 198
Transcription error, 120, 128

Transmission
    asynchronous, 161, 303
    errors, 130
    parallel, 303
    rate, 162
    serial, 303
    speed, 302
    synchronous, 161, 303
TrueType fonts, 153
Twisted pair, 160
UNIX, 85, 100
Upgradability, 97, 284
Upgrading, 276
User
    booklets, 263
    ID, 56
    manual, 191
Utility programs, 81, 86
Validation, 104
Validation checks, 129
Value judgement, 40
Van Eck radiation, 51
VDU, 150
Vector-based graphics, 322
Verification, 130
Virtual memory, 80
Virus protection, 58
Viruses, 50
Visual display unit, 150
Voice data entry, 120
Voice mail, 27
Voice recognition, 167
WAN, 155, 159, 288
Waterfall model, 207
Web, 9, 25, 29
    creating pages, 175
    setting up a site, 32
Web-browsing software, 25
Wide area network. *See* WAN
WIMP, 82, 167
Windows, 83, 167
Windows 95, 84
Word processing, 90, 172, 188
World Wide Web. *See* Web
WORM disks, 140
Write-protecting disks, 56
WYSIWYG, 92
Zip drive, 146

Have you seen these other titles by P.M.Heathcote?
(Published by Letts Educational)

A Level Computing (3rd edition 1996)

ISBN 1-85805-170-3 Price £11.95

This best-selling book offers comprehensive coverage of A Level Computing topics.
"I have no hesitation in recommending this book to students and staff for its comprehensive coverage and its excellent style." – Dr Kevin Bond, Chief Examiner for A Level Computing

---

Tackling Computer Projects in Access with Visual Basic (2nd edition 1997)

ISBN 1-84085-001-9 Price £9.95

This book provides students with a comprehensive and practical guide on how to tackle a computing project for an A Level, AS Level or Advanced GNVQ course using Access and incorporating modules written in Visual Basic.

"Students following the advice and guidance provided in this book should be able to produce a project report that is worthy of good grades and also develop a real, usable software solution. Any project that satisfies these criteria brings the dual satisfaction of a good academic grade together with a job well done." – Helen Williams, Principal Moderator AEB

A Level Computing Study Guide

By Pat Heathcote and Kevin Bond
ISBN 1-85758-601-8 Price £10.95

Letts Study Guides offer year-round course backup, convenient reference and an approach to revision that really works.

Inspection copies of the above titles can be obtained from:
Letts Educational
Schools and Colleges
9-15 Aldine Street
London W12 8AW
Telephone 0181 740 2268